BRITISH ARM
WHO S
IN THE
AMERICAN REVOLUTION

1775-1783

Steven M. Baule
with Stephen Gilbert

HERITAGE BOOKS
2008

HERITAGE BOOKS

AN IMPRINT OF HERITAGE BOOKS, INC.

Books, CDs, and more—Worldwide

For our listing of thousands of titles see our website
at
www.HeritageBooks.com

Published 2008 by
HERITAGE BOOKS, INC.
Publishing Division
100 Railroad Ave. #104
Westminster, Maryland 21157

International Standard Book Numbers
Paperbound: 978-0-7884-2470-0
Clothbound: 978-0-7884-7061-5

TABLE OF CONTENTS

This compendium is a comprehensive listing of the British Regular Army or "Redcoat" officers who served in North America during the American Revolution from 1775 to 1783. Unfortunately, the scope of this text does not allow for a full articulation of the known service records of each officer. The British Army of the late eighteenth century was one of the most successful armies in the world, and in the earlier nineteenth century; it defeated Napoleon. Much has been written that speaks to the British officers as foppish dandies and generally incompetent. However, more recent scholarship has found that the vast majority of British officers were competent and many were long serving under the severe hardships of overseas assignments. This compendium includes only regular army officers. It does not include provincial officers unless those officers also held regular commissions. Additionally, officers of the British marines and German officers who served in America are not within the scope of this work. Similarly, army officers who only served in the West Indies are not included.

THE BRITISH ARMY OFFICER CORPS

British officers were to be "of the better sort." The purchase system developed in the 1600s was intended to help ensure that the army officers were men of means and therefore, above average social standing. Eighteenth century Britain was a nation of social classes. The upper classes were to lead the lower classes. The soldiers were to come from the meaner sort or society's lowest strata. The upper classes however were born to lead. They would naturally make good officers, as that was the thinking of most British military leaders in the eighteenth century.

Officers came from four sources. The majority of officers received their commissions by purchase. Others, unable to purchase commissions, would serve as volunteers with regiments in the field, hoping to prove themselves to the commanding officer of the regiment and be rewarded with a commission. In times of war, the possibility of raising men for rank was an option. Existing officers striving for quick promotion as well as civilians hoping to obtain a commission sometimes used this method. The fourth, and by far the least common, method of obtaining a commission was through exemplary service as a sergeant.

Purchasing a commission required that the gentleman be a man of means or come from a family of means. A purchased commission was an investment to some extent. The commission could be sold for its face value at a later period. In some cases, commission brokers would add additional charges to obtain a commission in the most desirable regiments. Within a regiment, the seller normally offered his commission to the most senior officer of the rank junior to him. So a lieutenant who was purchasing a captaincy would generally offer his lieutenant's commission to the most senior ensign. If that ensign was unable or unwilling to purchase it, it would be offered to other ensigns in that or other regiments. You were generally unable to purchase more than one rank at a time. The cheapest method of purchase was to obtain an ensigncy in a marching regiment of foot. This cost £400. The cost for purchasing a cornet's commission in the horse guards was £1200. The cavalry officer would also have the added expense of regimental horse furniture and generally more elaborate uniforms. In addition to purchase, most officers could hope to obtain at least one or two "free promotions" due to the death of a senior. When battle or sickness opened a commission, the regimental commander could recommend that officer's replacement without the necessity of purchase. The crown usually confirmed those recommendations and the officer advanced without cost. It was in this method, that volunteers serving with the regiments in active service hoped to further their military careers by obtaining that initial commission. Several volunteers with the regiments in Boston earned preferment to ensigncies after the significant loss of officers at Lexington, Concord, and Bunker Hill.

In many of the regiments raised in late 1778 and 1779, the officers obtained their commissions without purchase. These men, mostly highland Scots, were appointed to their commands through the auspices of the colonel who was raising the regiment. Normally, the captain who raised his company fastest became the senior captain of the regiment and so on until the last company was complete. Normally, the captain would also then be able to have a say in who his subalterns were. He may have assigned them to raise a number of men as well; the first completing his quota, becoming the senior lieutenant, etc. This was a particularly effective method of raising troops in the highlands where the clan ties bound the lower classes to men who would command them.

Non-commissioned officers were normally promoted only after significant service and then most often to the position of quartermaster. Williamson in his 1780 *Elements of Military Arrangements* suggested that subalterns not be allowed to serve as quartermaster; but that a deserving sergeant should be promoted to the rank. William Hamill, the sergeant major of the 10th Foot was promoted to adjutant in that regiment in 1778. He obtained an ensign's commission in 1779 as well. He was promoted to lieutenant in 1784 in addition to still serving as adjutant. Arthur Leversuch, a grenadier sergeant of the 10th Foot, was promoted to quartermaster on June 28, 1775 and held that position at least twenty years.[1] Thomas Holland, the sergeant major of the 18th (Royal Irish) Regiment was promoted to quartermaster in that regiment after many years in the grenadier company. He was promoted to ensign in an invalid company in 1781. William

Musgrave, who had also risen to sergeant major of the 18th Foot replaced Holland on December 17, 1781[2].

Ranks above lieutenant colonel were not open to purchase. George III, like his grandfather and great-grandfather, was conscious that the commissions of colonels and generals should not generally be given as favors from court or allowed to be purchased. Colonelcies were to be merited promotions for distinguished service. He was careful to promote men into the rank of colonel who had long military careers. However, George III was slightly more open to patronage and influence from courtiers in these appointments than his grandfather, George II. After promotion to colonel, further promotion was generally by seniority.[3]

Many of the gentlemen who served as officers in the British Army were aristocrats. Among the twenty-four generals listed in the 1780 British Army List, seventeen were peers. This made nearly 71 percent of the generals peers. Thirty-two of the eighty lieutenant generals, or 40 percent, were peers. Among major generals, only ten of the fifty-one men listed in the 1780 Army List were peers. The numbers continue to dwindle among field grade officers, where 12 percent of colonels, 13 percent of lieutenant colonels and nearly eight percent of majors held peerages.[4]

Odintz's study of 268 officers in line regiments of foot found eighteen aristocrats and twelve from baronetages. Another 155 officers were from the landed gentry while nine came from the families of merchants. Seven were sons of lawyers and the same number were the sons of doctors. Thirty-seven officers came from the colonies and three from Germany. Ten were the sons of army officers and five were sons of bankers. Only five of the officers had come from the enlisted ranks.[5]

These numbers show that more than ten percent of the officers in positions of leadership were peers. However, many officers were also the younger sons of nobles. The extreme number of peers among general officers as compared to field grade officers does not represent a higher level of preferment among peers. The eighteenth century was a dangerous time both in and outside of the service. Many of the general officers listed as peers may have simply inherited their titles since serving in the junior ranks. Sir John Sebright, a lieutenant general in 1780, succeeded to the dignity of Baronet upon the death of his brother in 1765 when he had already been a major general for three years.[6] Others, like Henry Clinton earned his own knighthood through long and faithful service. Sergeant Roger Lamb remarked in his memoirs that a regiment commanded by a peer such as the 33rd Foot, under the command of the Earl of Cornwallis, could look to being more favorably treated by the army administration and the crown than a regiment without such a commander. However, that does not seem always to have been the case. The 38th Foot served a considerable period in the West Indies, where more than half its men perished from disease while under the command of a lord and a baronet.[7]

Among the company officers, captains and below, the number of peers was fairly low outside of the Guards and Horse Regiments. The three regiments of Horse Guards had seven nobles among 80 officers or eight percent. The Foot Guards showed fifteen percent of the officers as nobles in 1780. The First Horse had nobles for 13% of the officers. The Second Horse had 23% noble officers. The 52nd, 54th, and 60th Regiments of Foot showed not a single nobleman among their officers. The 35th Foot had a single lord among their officers in 1780.[8]

Among the troops serving the Board of Ordnance, however, few peers appear among their officers. The 1780 Army List shows no peer listed among the army engineers. In the Royal Artillery, where along with the marines, the purchase of commissions was not allowed, and officers were promoted nearly entirely by seniority, no peers are listed. The

Colonel and Colonel en Second were both peers, but neither had served with the artillery in the junior ranks. In the marines, only four peers were listed among 139 marine officers serving in the rank of captain or above.[9]

By nationality, the officers of the British Army were fairly representative of the British people they were defending. Forty-two percent of the officers were English. Twenty-four percent were Scottish and 31 percent were Irish.[10] The remaining officers were generally of German origin and mainly were serving in the 60th (Royal American) Regiment of Foot that originally had been raised with mostly foreign officers.[11] Within a regiment, the nationality of junior officers tended to be based entirely upon the regiment's current location. When the 18th (Royal Irish) Regiment of Foot was inspected in 1767, at Dublin, twenty-one of the twenty-four company grade officers were Irish.[12] The regiment had served more than ten years in Ireland. When the same regiment was inspected in 1779 at Dover Castle, England, of twenty-three company grade officers, sixteen were English.[13] In 1779, the regiment was still recovering from having been drafted at Boston in late 1775 and had been stationed in southeast England since 1776. The 18th Foot appears to have received its first Scottish officer in more than fifteen years in 1782 when Ensign John Hope joined the regiment. He was still serving as an ensign in 1787 when the regiment was inspected at Gibraltar.[14] The 8th (King's) Regiment of Foot was inspected in 1768 prior to its embarkation for Canada at Dover Castle. Among its junior officers at that inspection were fourteen English officers, three Irish and a single Scot.[15] The 55th Foot was inspected in May 1775 at Charles Fort, Ireland after nearly ten years of service in Ireland. Among nineteen junior officers, fifteen were Irish, two were Scots and two were English.[16] This was true even though the 55th was a regiment raised originally in Stirling, Scotland and was known for having a strong Scottish character well into the 1800s. The exception to this rule tended to be the Highland regiments that were almost entirely officered by Highland officers.

The Highland regiments raised in late 1778 and 1779 also brought a large number of additional highland officers into the British Army. The index to the 1780 Army List shows 114 Campbells, thirty-eight Frazers, and thirty-four McDonnells. Only the English surname of Smith with thirty-seven entries can compete with the huge number of Scottish officers serving during the Revolution.[17]

In terms of age, the British officers were a mixed group as well, although junior officers often appeared to be youthful in the extreme. Gerrit Fisher may be the youngest example found having begun his service between the ages of ten and eleven. In 1775 he was a 29-year-old captain and paymaster for the 55th Foot. James Taylor Trevor purchased his first commission in the 18th (Royal Irish) Regiment of Foot in 1766 at the tender age of twelve. He sold out of the regiment when it was ordered to North America in 1767 and purchased into the 55th Foot that was remaining in Ireland. When the 55th was inspected in May 1775, Trevor was the 55th's Captain-Lieutenant at the age of twenty. He was listed as having been in the service for nine years. Lieutenants Henry O'Hara and Rupert Vallency of the 55th were listed as eighteen years old with two years of service each. Lieutenant Robert Stotsbury was listed as twenty-six with only three years of service.[18] At the other end of the spectrum, Lieutenant Francis Wadman, was forty years old with only eleven years of service when he was inspected with the 18th Foot in 1767.[19] Lieutenant George Buttricke who has served many years as an enlisted man and then as quartermaster in the 46th Foot and then the 18th Foot was listed as forty-four years old and had twenty-seven years of service, although he had only four years of commissioned service. He was older than all but one other officer in the regiment.[20]

The average age of officers tended to be in the upper twenties. Few officers continued in active service beyond their early forties and most subalterns actually serving with their regiments were in their late teens or early twenties. The officers of the 8th (King's) Regiment of Foot averaged 29.4 years of age in 1768; the year they were ordered to Canada. The 18th (Royal Irish) Regiment of Foot averaged 27.7 years of age in 1767 and 29.1 in 1777. The officers of the 55th Regiment of Foot averaged 26.75 years of age when leaving Ireland for North American service in 1775. The 64th Regiment of Foot averaged 26.3 years in 1768. The youngest officer among those samples was a 17-year-old ensign. The oldest was a 55-year-old major.[21]

The length of service for British officers during the period tended to be rather long. Regularly, captains and occasionally lieutenants could be listed as having served for more than a decade. According to Houlding, an average foot officer's career would see him serve four years as an ensign, six more as a lieutenant, and eight as a captain. Majors would on average be promoted to lieutenant colonel after two years of service. This would mean that the average officer could reach lieutenant colonel in twenty years of service. Officers in horse regiments took twenty-one years to reach lieutenant colonel, but only nine years to make major.[22]

When regiments were disbanded at the end of a war, the officers went on the half-pay list. Since the commissions had been purchased, the simple disbanding of the regiment could not revoke their property. The crown continued to pay these men until they entered into another regiment on full pay, or died. The prospect of half pay was the closest thing to a pension system the eighteenth century army had for its officers. In 1780, fifteen officers were still listed as being on half pay since their units were disbanded in 1712 and 1713. However, many officers were eager to trade into a regiment on the establishment. Many half-pay officers from regiments or additional companies disbanded after the Seven Years War were brought back into active service between 1765 and 1775 as replacements for officers who died in service. As an example, two of the six captains in the 18th (Royal Irish) Foot in 1770 had been on half pay at the end of the Seven Years War. In addition, several of the subaltern officers had also been on half pay. Half-pay officers came into the 18th Foot from the 14th, 44th, 60th, 72nd, 79th, 95th, and 113th Regiments of Foot between 1767 and 1774. Most of those from regiments that had been disbanded in 1763 when all regiments of foot above the 70th Foot were reduced. In addition, Lt. Edward Crosby had been a lieutenant in Gorham's North American Rangers.[23]

The costs of commissions were established in 1720 and 1722. They were revised by warrants in 1766, 1772, 1773, and 1783. However, these were established as guidelines and prices sometimes varied depending upon the standing of the regiment and its present station. Lieut. Colonel John Wilkins complained bitterly to General Thomas Gage in 1772 when Gage was trying to get Wilkins to resign that he had paid £4000 for his commission in the 18th (Royal Irish) Foot, but the established price was only £3500. Since Wilkins's regiment was, at that time, stationed in the remote posts of Illinois and western Pennsylvania; he appears to have had little chance to obtain that same amount in selling his commission.[24] Others mention that an ensign's commission in a royal regiment was worth at least £450,[25] but Charles Hoare of the 18th (Royal Irish) Foot bought his for £400, however, the regiment was on American service at the time. Throughout the American War, the prices below appear to have been the standard. They were established January 31, 1766.[26] The purchaser paid the difference in cost between his current commission and the new one he desired.

First and Second Troops of Horse Guards

Commission	Price
First lieutenant colonel	£5500
Second lieutenant colonel	£5100
Cornet & major	£4300
Guidon & major	£4100
Exempt & captain	£2700
Brigadier & lieutenant or Adjutant and lieutenant	£1500
Sub-brigadier & cornet	£1200

First and Second Troops of Horse Grenadier Guards

Commission	Price
First lieutenant colonel	£5400
Major	£4200
Lieutenant & captain	£3100
Guidon & captain	£3000
Sub-lieutenant	£1700
Adjutant	£1400

Dragoon Guards and Dragoons[27]

Commission	Price
Lieutenant colonel	£4700
Major	£3600
Captain	£2500
Captain-lieutenant	£1400

Foot Guards

Commission	Price
Lieutenant colonel	£6700
Major	£6300
Captain	£3500
Captain-lieutenant	£2600
Lieutenant	£1500
Ensign	£900

Regiments of Horse

Commission	Price
Lieutenant colonel	£5200
Major	£4250
Captain	£3100
Captain-lieutenant	£2000
Lieutenant	£1750
Cornet	£1600

Regiments of Foot

Commission	Price
Lieutenant colonel	£3500
Major	£2600
Captain	£1500
Captain-	£800

		lieutenant	
Lieutenant	£1150	Lieutenant	£550
Cornet	£1000	Ensign	£400

In fusilier regiments, including the 21st and 23rd Foot, the ranks of lieutenant and ensign were replaced with first lieutenant and second lieutenant. The costs of such commissions were £550 and £450 respectively. The 7th Foot or Royal Regiment of Fusiliers had twice the number of lieutenants and no ensigns. The 7th Foot did not distinguish between first and second lieutenants as did the other fusiler regiments.

The adjutants' commissions were not sold except in the Horse Guards. A quartermaster's commission was generally not sold nor were those of the surgeon, the surgeon's mate, or chaplain. Some surgeon's commissions do appear to have been sold during this period. However, it appears that less than ten percent of the surgeons purchased their commissions.

DETERMINING SENIORITY

Officers could determine seniority in three ways. All officers held a regimental commission. These were the only types of commissions that could be purchased or sold. The date of that commission established their regimental rank. This determined an officer's seniority within the regiment. In general, most officers also used their regimental rank to determine their seniority in the army on the whole. In some cases, officers may have held seniority in the army above that granted by their regimental commission. In most cases, this was due to the officer exchanging into another regiment at the same rank.

For instance, if Captain John Smith, who was commissioned in the 28th Foot on 23 January 1770, then exchanged into the 14th Foot on 1 February 1772, would maintain his army seniority based upon his 28th Foot commission. His seniority in the army would be based upon the 23 January 1770 date. However, his regimental seniority would be based upon the 1 February 1772 date. If Lt. Adam Jones purchased his first captaincy on 1 May 1771 in the 14th Foot, he would be considered Smith's senior in the regiment.

The second way officers obtained army rank different from their regimental rank was to be granted a higher army rank than their regimental rank. This type of "brevet rank" was not temporary and would be maintained permanently by the officer receiving it. In many cases, senior captains were given the army rank of major to help fill the many field level vacancies the army experienced in America. Captain Charles Edmonstone of the 18th Foot was given the army rank of major in 1772 as post major of Fort Pitt in western Pennsylvania. Many of the senior Royal Artillery officers serving in America were given such advanced army rank as well. Twenty-nine majors were promoted to the army rank of lieutenant colonel on 29 August 1777. Eight of these officers were artillerymen and six were engineers. Seventy-five captains were promoted to army rank of major on the same date. Twenty-six lieutenant colonels were promoted to the army rank of colonel on 19 February 1779. Six of those officers were aides-de-camp to King George III. These officers were addressed by their higher "army rank."

All commissions for general officers granted only army rank since generals inherently commanded multiple regiments. However, most generals also held commissions as the colonel of a regiment as well. For instance, Lieutenant General Benjamin Carpenter was also colonel of the Fourth Regiment of Dragoons. Major General Thomas Gage was also the colonel of the 22nd Foot.

The third method of obtaining an army rank senior to regimental rank was through purchase in the Life Guards or Foot Guards. These officers were the leaders of the King's household troops and were therefore destined to be given preference over the officers in line regiments. The Guards were given dual commissions that provided for an army rank two grades higher than their army rank beginning with their second commissions. Therefore, ensigns in the Foot Guards held seniority as ensigns in the army, but lieutenants in the Foot Guards held army rank as captains. Captains in the Foot Guards held army rank as lieutenant colonels. In fact, Brigadier General Charles O'Hara who fought under Lord Cornwallis was in fact only a captain in the Coldstream Guards, but held army rank as a full colonel. This dual rank system generally assured Guards officers significant seniority over line officers.

The third method for obtaining seniority was through local rank. Local rank was used to ensure that appropriate numbers of senior officers were present within a distant theater. Local rank did not transfer outside of its geographic area. During the American Revolution, local rank was granted primarily in three areas: America (meaning continental North America), the West Indies and the East Indies. In order to ensure that the combined British and German army in North America would be under the control of British officers, Sir Guy Carleton, Sir Henry Clinton, Fredrick Haldimand and Sir William Howe were all given the local rank of general in America in order to outrank the senior German commanders who came to America with their troops. In total, eighteen general officers were promoted to more senior rank in America. Most of these promotions were made on 1 January 1776 including all four of the full generals. Nineteen other officers held local rank in the 1780 Army List including ten in the East Indies, eight in the West Indies and George Bruere, a captain in the 60th (Royal American) Regiment, who held local rank as a lieutenant colonel in Bermuda. In 1774, only five officers had held local rank in America, including three ranking as majors. On 12 and 13 June 1782, twenty officers were granted local rank in India as colonels and lieutenant colonels.

CATEGORIES OF OFFICER RANKS

Officer ranks were generally grouped into five basic categories. From the top down they were: general officers, field officers, company officers, staff officers and warrant officers. General officers were those officers who commanded multiple regiments formed as brigades or larger field organizations. The British Army had several grades of general starting with major general, lieutenant general, general and field marshal. The British Army did not have any active field marshals during the period of the Revolution. The Army Lists include 25 full generals in 1780. However, none of these senior officers served in America during the period. The senior British officers who served in America were lieutenant generals. The British Army had approximately 90 officers of this grade throughout the period. Sir Guy Carleton, Sir Henry Clinton, Fredrick Haldimand and Hon. Sir William Howe who served in America were all lieutenant generals. As noted above, all four were given local rank as full general on 1 January 1776. Major generals were the lowest ranking permanent general officers in the period. The British Army had 73 major generals in 1782. Twenty-six of these had been promoted on 19 October 1781. The rank of brigadier, or brigadier general, was generally used as a temporary rank in this period. The terms appear to have been used interchangeably in the period. In Howe's Orderly Book for 18 October 1775, both terms are used. The Army Lists, a more definitive document uses only the title brigadier. No officers ranked permanently as brigadiers, but two officers held local rank as brigadiers in the East Indies. General Howe promoted several officers to brigadier including Lieutenant Colonel James Grant of the 40th Foot to serve as a brigadier general in the Boston area on 31 July 1775.[28]

Below the general officers were the field officers. The term refers to those officers who commanded a regiment in the field. They were the ranks of major, lieutenant colonel and colonel. These ranks were generally filled with officers who had served more than a dozen years in the army. In reality, many of these officers were often serving as general officers, commanders of brigades or in senior staff positions. In fact, the regimental colonel was rarely, if ever, with the regiment. Those colonels serving in the field with their regiments were all serving as general officers. For instance, Lord Cornwallis was the nominal colonel of the 33rd Foot and Hugh Percy was the colonel of the 5th Foot. Both served as general officers in America. In most cases, the lieutenant colonel was the senior officer present with any regiment on active service. However, either the major or a senior captain often commanded regiments.

Company grade officers were the junior line officers in the army. This group could be further divided between captains and subalterns. Captains commanded companies and this rank was also widely considered to be the lowest rank where a gentleman could live on his army pay. Captains were provided with a number of allowances in order to cover the expenses of running a company. These allowances could often be profitable to an officer who was careful with his men and their equipment. In line regiments, the field officers were also nominal captains and commanded companies as well. So technically those ranks were major and captain, lieutenant colonel and captain, etc. The lieutenant of the colonel's company was known as a captain-lieutenant and was originally the senior lieutenant of the regiment. However, as of

25 May 1772, captain-lieutenants ranked as the junior captain of the regiment. Each infantry or mounted regiment had a single captain-lieutenant. Each artillery company had both a captain and a captain-lieutenant.

The other company officers were collectively referred to as subalterns. These officers included lieutenants and ensigns. Mounted regiments replaced the rank of ensign with cornet. The artillery had first and second lieutenants as did most of the fusilier regiments. These were the 21st Foot or the Royal North British Fusiliers and the 23rd Foot or the Royal Welsh Fusiliers. The Royal Regiment of Fusiliers, the 7th Foot, simply had lieutenants. Regiments of foot generally had 11 lieutenants and eight ensigns. Regiments raised later in the war generally had 100 man companies and had 21 lieutenants and eight ensigns. In battle, two of the ensigns would carry the regimental colors, which was how their title was derived.

Staff officers in the eighteenth century British Army included those officers who performed administrative functions within the regiment. Staff commissions, as mentioned earlier, were generally not available for purchase. Each infantry regiment included four such staff officers, the adjutant, the chaplain, the quartermaster and the surgeon. The adjutant was generally responsible for the administrative duties of the regiment. He was responsible for filing returns and reports and issuing written orders for the regiment's commander. Working with the sergeant major, the adjutant was responsible for forming the regiment for parade and ensuring the regiment's details and guards were all properly filled. Generally, the adjutant also held a separate commission as a lieutenant. Ensigns rarely had enough experience with army life to serve in the role successfully so lieutenants were more commonly placed in this important role. Occasionally the captain-lieutenant or a captain held the position, but that was the exception and not the rule. It was not uncommon for the adjutancy to be filled by a former sergeant promoted from the ranks.

Similarly, the quartermaster was responsible for the regiment's equipment. In addition, he supervised the pioneers, obtained lodging for the regiment or oversaw the layout of its camp. Many eighteenth century authors felt that this job was more suited to a deserving sergeant than to young gentlemen. Often a former sergeant major or other deserving sergeant filled this position. However, most regiments employed a subaltern in this role as well.

The duties of the other two staff officers were of a more professional nature. However, neither chaplains nor surgeons in the eighteenth century British Army were known for their professionalism. The chaplains tended to be absentees and rarely served with their regiments in the field. One who did serve in America, Rev. Newburgh of the 18th (Royal Irish) Foot was court-martialed for immoral behavior and unnatural acts with a soldier. He continued to serve after a six-month suspension. Surgeons similarly were often poorly trained, but did generally serve with their regiments. The poor image of surgeons in the Revolutionary War generally tends to be related to the lack of medical understanding across all medical professionals of the time period than strictly related to the army medical officers, many of whom labored extremely hard to care for their soldiers. In the General Hospital, additional grades of medical officers were necessary. In the hospital, medical officers ranked in the following order: superintendent, inspector, physician, surgeon, apothecary, mate and supernumerary mate. The ranks of purveyor and deputy purveyors also existed, but it is unclear where they fit in the hierarchy.

Engineers were originally staff officers, but the officers of the Corps of Engineers were given regular commissions beginning in 1754. The chief engineer ranked as a colonel. The directors of engineers ranked as lieutenant colonels. The sub-directors ranked as majors and engineers in ordinary ranked as captains. Engineers extraordinary ranked as captain-lieutenants. Sub-engineers and practitioner engineers ranked as lieutenants and ensigns respectively.

In the eighteenth century, warrant officers were more prevalent in the navy than in the army. The primary warrant officer in the British Army of the eighteenth century was surgeon's mate or mate. Unlike the other officers, surgeon's mates were warranted by the colonel as opposed to being commissioned by the King. Surgeon's mates were not listed in the annual Army Lists. Dragoon regiments also had a troop quartermaster who was also a warrant officer. Only two regiments of light dragoons served in America during the Revolution.

USING THE LISTINGS & METHODOLOGY

This work is based upon the earlier work of Worthington Chauncey Ford who compiled a *British Officers Serving in The American Revolution, 1774-1783* in 1897. Two hundred and fifty copies of the book were printed. It is unclear what sources Ford used to compile his text. However, it is probable he used printed *Army Lists*. The authors of this compendium have tried to use the War Office 65 series papers that are based on the printed *Army Lists*, but show changes in status between printings in handwritten notes. In addition, the authors have added those officers of the Royal Engineers and the Foot Guards who served in America. For some reason, those officers were not included by Ford. In addition, due to the fact that some units were assigned to America before or after the printing of the *Army Lists*, Ford appears to have overlooked some units entirely. For instance, the 3rd and 4th Battalions of the 60th (Royal American) Regiment of Foot served in Florida, Georgia and the Carolinas but were not included in Ford's listings. The 83rd Foot was also present, however briefly in New York in 1783, but Ford also omitted its officers. Some other officers also served in America although their regiments were not ever posted to America. In such cases, orderly books and other records have been examined to try to ensure those officers have also been included in this compendium.

The list on the following pages includes each British Army officer who served in the North America colonies and Canada during the American Revolution. For each officer, the listing includes his name, rank and date of commission. In cases where the officer's name is in question, notes to that effect appear in the notes column. Where known, the primary entry is the way the officer used or spelled his own name. The officer's nativity is given where known. In the same manner, his years of birth and death are given where known. In cases where only the birth year is given, it was most likely obtained from regimental inspection returns in the WO27 Series papers. These dates are estimates made from the age of the officers given in those returns. They are most likely correct within a year on either side of the given date. However, in at least one case, an officer listed in inspection returns seventeen years apart but only aged thirteen years. In the same way, the age of the officer at his first commission was determined by the years of service information in the WO27 series returns and is liable to the same range of error.

Information regarding officer casualties was gathered from a wide range of sources, most of which are referenced in a 1999 unpublished manuscript by Steve Gilbert. George Inman's contemporary list of British officer casualties provided much of the core for the casualty data. Additional information was gathered from the WO12 series papers and the WO65 papers already mentioned. The WO12 papers are the regimental muster rolls that were used to pay the soldiers. They were generally completed every six months. Many of them are still extant in Britain for many of the regiments that served in America.

Other information included in the notes came from a wide range of sources. Among primary sources, both published and unpublished orderly books were key sources. Much of the information came from articles in the *Journal of the Society for Army Historical Research*. Rivington's loyalist newspapers printed in New York, provided nearly all of the information regarding the minimal information on marriages in the list. Information on court martials came from orderly books or directly from the WO71 series papers. The WO71 papers are the transcripts of general court martials conducted by the British Army. Some are missing, most notably many from Canada, but they are generally an excellent source of information on the British Army of the period. Information specific to the medical officers who served in America was often found in Johnston's *Roll of Commissioned Officers in the Medical Service of the British Army*.

For example:

Regiment or
Battalion/ Regt.

Name

Rank

Alternative
versions of
the name

Other information

Date of Army
Rank (If different)
always after
regimental date of
rank

Date of
Rank

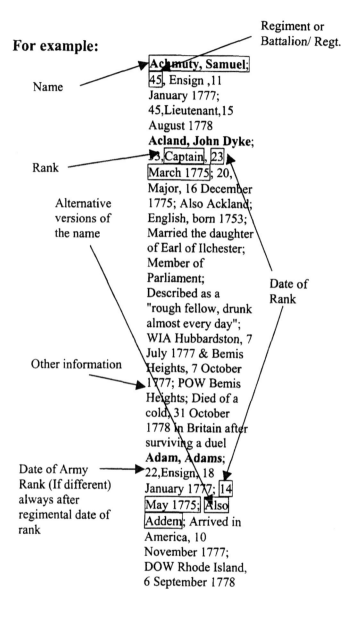

Achmuty, Samuel;
45, Ensign ,11
January 1777;
45,Lieutenant,15
August 1778
Acland, John Dyke;
23,Captain, 23
March 1775; 20,
Major, 16 December
1775; Also Ackland;
English, born 1753;
Married the daughter
of Earl of Ilchester;
Member of
Parliament;
Described as a
"rough fellow, drunk
almost every day";
WIA Hubbardston, 7
July 1777 & Bemis
Heights, 7 October
1777; POW Bemis
Heights; Died of a
cold, 31 October
1778 in Britain after
surviving a duel
Adam, Adams;
22,Ensign, 18
January 1777; 14
May 1775; Also
Addem; Arrived in
America, 10
November 1777;
DOW Rhode Island,
6 September 1778

REGIMENTS THAT SERVED IN AMERICA

During the period of the American Revolution, the British War Office used America to describe the 13 colonies and Canada. East and West Florida, Louisiana and the many West Indian islands were not considered as part of North America by the War Office. Regiments stationed in Louisiana, the Floridas or the West Indies were not included as part of the "American Army." However, this listing does encompass all of the regiments that served in any area that is part of modern Canada or the United States. In addition to the regiments listed below, a number of other officers served in America although their regiments were posted elsewhere.

Regiment	Arrived	Departed
Royal Artillery	1750s	1796
Royal Irish Artillery	1776	1783
Royal Engineers[29]	1750s	1783
16th Light Dragoons	1776	Drafted 1778
17th Light Dragoons	1775	1783
Brigade of Guards in America (1st, 2nd & 3rd Foot Guards)	1776	Interned 1781
3rd Foot	1781	1782
4th (King's Own) Foot		1778
5th Foot	1774	1778
6th Foot	Drafted 1776	
7th (Royal Fusiliers) Foot	1773	1783
8th (King's) Foot	1768	1785
9th Foot	1776	Interned 1777
10th Foot	1767	Drafted 1778
14th Foot	1766	Drafted 1777
15th Foot	1776	1778
16th Foot	1767	Drafted 1782
17th Foot	1775	Interned 1781
18th (Royal Irish) Foot	1767	Drafted 1775/1776
19th Foot	1781	1782
20th Foot	1776	Interned 1777
21st (Royal North British Fusiliers) Foot	1776	Interned 1777
22nd Foot	1775	1783
23rd (Royal Welsh Fusiliers) Foot	1773	Interned 1781

Regiment	Arrived	Departed
24th Foot	1776	Interned 1777
26th Foot	1767	Drafted 1779
27th Foot	1775	1778
28th Foot	1776	1778
29th Foot	1767	1787
30th Foot	1781	1782
31st Foot	1776	1787
33rd Foot	1776	Interned 1781
34th Foot	1776	1786
35th Foot	1775	1778
37th Foot	1776	1783
38th Foot	1774	1783
40th Foot	1775	1778
42nd (Royal Highland) Foot	1776	1783
43rd Foot	1774	Interned 1781
44th Foot	1775	1780
45th Foot	1775	Drafted 1778
46th Foot	1776	1778
47th Foot	1773	Interned 1777
49th Foot	1775	1778
52nd Foot	1774	Drafted 1778
53rd Foot	1776	Interned 1777
54th Foot	1776	1783
55th Foot	1775	1778
57th Foot	1776	1783
59th Foot	1765	Drafted 1775
2/60th Foot	1775	1783
3/60th Foot	1775	1783
4/60th Foot	1775	1783
62nd Foot	1776	Interned 1777
63rd Foot	1775	1782
64th Foot	1768	1782
65th Foot	1768	Drafted 1776
69th Foot	1781	
70th Foot	1778	1783
1/71st (Highland) Foot	1776	1782
2/71st (Highland) Foot	1776	1782
74th (Highland) Foot	1778	1784
76th (Highland) Foot	1779	Interned 1781
80th Foot	1779	Interned 1781
82nd Foot	1778	1782
83rd (Royal Glasgow Volunteers) Foot	1783	
1/84th (Royal Highland Emigrants) Foot	1775	1784
2/84th (Royal Highland Emigrants) Foot	1775	1784

REGIMENTAL DESIGNATIONS FOR REGIMENTS OF FOOT

In addition to the numeric designation for each regiment of foot, regiments were occasionally known by other titles. In 1782, most regiments were given a county designation as well. Some regiments also had nicknames, but the nature of such titles makes it difficult to determine their exact origin at times. Some like the 9th Foot's nickname, The Holy Boys, is most likely from the 19th Century Peninsula Campaigns when their Britannia cap badge reminded the Iberians of the Virgin Mary. The 12th Foot's nickname of The Old Dozen is much more difficult to pinpoint as to its time of origin. These additional titles appear below:

Regiment	Title or County Designation	Nicknames	Modern Designation
1st Foot Guards		The Sand Bags; The Old Eyes; The Bermuda Exiles	The Grenadier Guards
2nd Foot Guards	Coldstream Regt. Of Foot Guards	Coldstreamers; Gen. Monck's Regiment	The Coldstream Guards
3rd Foot Guards		The Jocks; The Kiddies	The Scots Guards
1st Foot	Royal Regiment of Foot	The Royals; Pontius Pilate's Body Guard	The Royal Scots (The Royal Regiment)
2nd Foot	The Queen's Own Regiment	The Tangerines; Kirke's Lambs; The Sleepy Queen's; The Mutton Lancers	The Princess of Wales's Royal Regiment
3rd Foot		The Buffs; The Buff Howards; The Nutcrackers	The Princess of Wales's Royal Regiment
4th Foot	King's Own	Barrell's Blues; The Lions	The King's Own Royal Border Regiment

Regiment	Title or County Designation	Nicknames	Modern Designation
5th Foot	Northumberland	The Shinners	The Royal Regiment of Fusiliers
6th Foot	Warwickshire	The Saucy Sixth	The Royal Regiment of Fusiliers
7th Foot	Royal Fusiliers	City of London Regt.; The Ordnance Regiment	The Royal Regiment of Fusiliers
8th Foot	King's	The Leather Hats	The King's Regiment
9th Foot	East Norfolk	The Holy Boys	Royal Anglian Regiment
10th Foot	Lincolnshire	The Springers; The Poachers	Royal Anglian Regiment
11th Foot	North Devonshire	The Bloody Eleventh	The Devonshire and Dorchester Regiment
12th Foot	East Suffolk	The Old Dozen	Royal Anglian Regiment
13th Foot	1st Sommersetshire	The Bleeders	The Light Infantry
14th Foot	Buckinghamshire	The Old and Bold	The Prince of Wales's Own Regiment of Yorkshire
15th Foot	Yorkshire, East Riding	The Snappers	The Prince of Wales's Own Regiment of Yorkshire
16th Foot	Bedfordshire	The Old Bucks	Royal Anglian Regiment
17th Foot	Leicestershire	The Lilywhites	Royal Anglian Regiment
18th Foot	Royal Irish	The Namurs; Paddy's Blackguards; The Royals	Disbanded, 1922
19th Foot	Yorkshire, North Riding	The Green Howards	The Green Howards

Regiment	Title or County Designation	Nicknames	Modern Designation
20th Foot	East Devonshire	The Two Tens; The Minden Boys; The Double Xs	The Royal Regiment of Fusiliers
21st Foot	Royal North British Fusiliers	Earl of Mar's Grey Beeks	The Royal Highland Fusiliers
22nd Foot	Cheshire	The Two Twos	The Cheshire Regiment
23rd Foot	Royal Welch Fusiliers	The Nanny Goats; The Royal Goats	The Royal Welch Fusiliers
24th Foot	2nd Warwickshire	Howard's Greens	The Royal Regiment of Wales
25th Foot	Sussex		The King's Own Scottish Borderers
26th Foot	Cameronian		Disbanded 1968
27th Foot	Inniskilling Regiment	The Skillingers	The Royal Irish Regiment
28th Foot	North Gloucestershire	The Old Braggs	The Royal Gloucestershire, Wiltshire and Berkshire Regiment
29th Foot	Worcestershire	The Vein Openers	The Worcestershire and Sherwood Foresters Regiment
30th Foot	1st Cambridgeshire	The Triple Xs; The Three Tens	The Queen's Lancashire Regiment
31st Foot	Huntingdonshire	The Young Buffs	The Princess of Wales's Royal Regiment
32nd Foot	Cornwall		The Light Infantry
33rd Foot	Yorkshire, West Riding	The Havercakes	The Duke of Wellington's Regiment (West Riding)
34th Foot	Cumberland	The Cattle Reeves	The King's Own Royal Border Regiment

Regiment	Title or County Designation	Nicknames	Modern Designation
35th Foot	Dorchester (later Sussex)		The Princess of Wales's Royal Regiment
36th Foot	Herefordshire	The Saucy Greens	The Worcestershire and Sherwood Foresters Regiment
37th Foot	North Hampshire		The Princess of Wales's Royal Regiment
38th Foot	1st Staffordshire	The Pump and Tortoise	The Staffordshire Regiment
39th Foot	East Middlesex (later Dorsetshire)	Sankey's Horse; The Green Linnets	The Devonshire and Dorset Regiment
40th Foot	2nd Sommersetshire	The Excellers (XL)	The Queen's Lancashire Regiment
41st Foot	Invalid Regiment (later The Welch)	The Invalids; The Old Fogeys	The Royal Regiment of Wales
42nd Foot	Royal Highland Regiment	The Black Watch; The Forty-Twas	The Black Watch (Royal Highland Regiment)
43rd Foot	Monmouthshire	Wolfe's Own	The Royal Green Jackets
44th Foot	East Essex	The Two Fours	The Royal Anglian Regiment
45th Foot	Nottinghamshire	The Old Stubborns	The Worcestershire and Sherwood Foresters Regiment
46th Foot	South Devonshire	Murray's Bucks	The Light Infantry
47th Foot	Lancashire	Wolfe's Own	The Queen's Lancashire Regiment
48th Foot	Northhamptonshire		The Royal Anglian Regiment

Regiment	Title or County Designation	Nicknames	Modern Designation
49th Foot	Hertfordshire		The Royal Gloucestershire, Wiltshire and Berkshire Regiment
50th Foot	West Kent	The Blind Half-Hundred	The Princess of Wales's Royal Regiment
51st Foot	2nd Yorkshire, West Riding		The Light Infantry
52nd Foot	Oxfordshire		The Royal Green Jackets
53rd Foot	Shropshire	The Brickdusts	The Light Infantry
54th Foot	West Norfolk		The Dosetshire Regiment
55th Foot	Westmoreland	The Two Fives	The King's Own Royal Border Regiment
56th Foot	West Essex	The Pompadours	The Royal Anglian Regiment
57th Foot	West Middlesex	The Diehards	The Princess of Wales's Royal Regiment
58th Foot	Rutlandshire	The Black Cuffs	The Royal Anglian Regiment
59th Foot	2nd Nottinghamshire		The Queen's Lancashire Regiment
60th Foot	Royal American Regiment		The Royal Green Jackets
61st Foot	South Gloucestershire		The Royal Gloucestershire, Wiltshire and Berkshire Regiment
62nd Foot	Wiltshire	The Springers	The Royal Gloucestershire, Wiltshire and Berkshire Regiment
63rd Foot	West Suffolk	The Bloodsuckers	The King's Regiment

Regiment	Title or County Designation	Nicknames	Modern Designation
64th Foot	2nd Staffordshire	The Black Knots	The Staffordshire Regiment
65th Foot	2nd Yorkshire, North Riding		Disbanded, 1968
66th Foot	Berkshire		The Royal Gloucestershire, Wiltshire and Berkshire Regiment
67th Foot	South Hampshire		The Princess of Wales's Royal Regiment
68th Foot	Durham		The Light Infantry
69th Foot	South Lincolnshire	Old Agamemnons	The Royal Regiment of Wales
70th Foot	Surrey (later Glasgow Lowland)	The Glasgow Greys	The Princess of Wales's Royal Regiment
71st Foot	Fraser's Highlanders		Disbanded 1783
72nd Foot	Royal Manchester Volunteers		Disbanded 1783
73rd Foot	MacLeod's Highlanders		The Royal Highland Fusiliers
74th Foot	Argyll Highlanders		Disbanded 1783
75th Foot	Prince of Wales's Regiment		Disbanded 1783
76th Foot	Macdonald Highlanders		Disbanded 1783
77th Foot	Atholl Highlanders		Disbanded 1783
78th Foot	Seaforth Highlanders		The Highlanders
79th Foot	Liverpool Regiment		Disbanded 1783
80th Foot	Royal Edinburgh Volunteers		Disbanded 1783
81st Foot	Aberdeen Highlanders		Disbanded 1783
82nd Foot	Duke of Hamilton's Regiment	Hamilton's	Disbanded 1784
83rd Foot	Royal Glasgow Volunteers		Disbanded 1783

Regiment	Title or County Designation	Nicknames	Modern Designation
84th Foot	Royal Highland Emigrants		Disbanded 1783
85th Foot	Westminster Volunteers		Disbanded 1783
86th Foot	Rutland Volunteers		Disbanded 1784
87th Foot			Disbanded 1783
88th Foot			Disbanded 1784
89th Foot			Disbanded 1784
90th Foot	Yorkshire Volunteers		Disbanded 1784
91st Foot	Shropshire Volunteers		Disbanded 1784
92nd Foot			Disbanded 1783
93rd Foot			Disbanded 1783
94th Foot			Disbanded 1783
95th Foot			Disbanded 1784
96th Foot	British Musketeers		Disbanded 1784
97th Foot			Disbanded 1784
98th Foot			Disbanded 1783
99th Foot	Jamaica Regiment		Disbanded 1783
100th Foot			Disbanded 1783
101st Foot			Disbanded 1785
102nd Foot			Disbanded 1784
103rd Foot	King's Irish Infantry		Disbanded 1784
104th Foot			Disbanded 1784
105th Foot	Volunteers of Ireland		Disbanded 1787

ABRREVIATIONS USED IN THE LIST

ADC	Aide de camp
AG	Adjutant general
Am.	Local Rank in America
Apoth.	Apothecary
BMG	Barracksmaster general
Bn.	Battalion
c.	Circa
Capt. & Lt. Col.	Captain and lieutenant colonel, e.g., a captain in the Foot Guards
CM	Court martialed
Col. Comdt.	Colonel Commandant, used by the Royal Artillery and 60th Foot for commanders of each battalion
Cmd.	Commanded
Coy.	Company
D	Regiment of Dragoons
Depty.	Deputy
Depty. Chap.	Deputy Chaplain, e.g., someone hired to perform the duties of the chaplain in his place, not a military rank
DOR	Date of rank
DOW	Died of wounds
DQMG	Deputy quartermaster general
Drag. Grds.	Regiment of Dragoon Guards
Edin.	University of Edinburgh
Eng. extra. & Cpt.-Lt.	Engineer Extraordinary and Captain-Lieutenant, e.g., a captain-lieutenant in the Royal Engineers
Eng. ord & Capt.	Engineer in Ordinary and Captain, e.g., a captain in the Royal Engineers
F&I	French and Indian War; Also Seven Years War
FG	Regiment of Foot Guards
f.p.	Full pay
Gren.	Grenadiers
H	Regiment of Horse
Hosp.	North American General Hospital

KIA	Killed in action
Knt. Bachelor	Knight Bachelor
Ind. Dept.	Indian Department
Insptr. of Regt. Hosps.	Inspector of Regimental Hospitals, also titled Inspector of Field Hospitals
JSAHR	Journal of the Society for Army Historical Research
Kings Coll. Abd.	King's College, University of Aberdeen
LD	Regiment of Light Dragoons
L.I.	Light infantry
Lieut. & Capt.	Lieutenant and Captain, e.g., a lieutenant in the Foot Guards
Lt. Col. Comdt.	Lieutenant Colonel Commandant, e.g., the commander of a regiment without an established full colonel
Major of Bde	Major of brigade
NAAL	North American Army List
Port.	Portrait
POW	Prisoner of war
Pract. eng. & 2nd. Lt.	Practitioner Engineer and Second Lieutenant, e.g., the junior grade of officer in the Royal Engineers
Prov.	Provincial
Purvyr. & Chief Surg.	Purveyor and Chief Surgeon
QMG	Quartermaster general
RA	Royal Artillery
RAC	Cadet company of the Royal Artillery
RAI	Invalid company of the Royal Artillery
RE	Royal Engineers
Regt.	Regiment
RGB	Royal Garrison Battalion
Riv. Gaz.	Rivington's Loyalist Gazette
Sub-dir. & Maj.	Sub-director and Major, e.g. a major in the Royal Engineers
Sub-eng. & Lt.	Sub-engineer and Lieutenant, e.g., a lieutenant in the Royal Engineers
Supnmy.	Supernumerary
W.I.	West Indies
WIA	Wounded in action
u.	Served under

ACKNOWLEDGEMENTS

As in all fields of endeavor, the authors had a great deal of help in completing this compendium. One of the most rewarding parts about this project was learning what a giving and supportive community of researchers exists with regard to the American Revolution. Linnea Bass provided information about the officers of the Brigade of Guards in America. Todd Braistead provided information about provincial officers as well as other links and leads. Terry Crabb generously provided information from his research on general court martials. John Fredrick provided the core information from which the listings of the 60th (Royal American) Regiment of Foot were built. Paul Pace provided a great deal of information about the officers of the 42nd (Royal Highland) Regiment of Foot. Eric Schnitzer was helpful in providing details about some of the officers who served in Burgoyne's campaign. Don Hagist provided a great deal of assistance and support throughout. Thanks to all. This is a better and more complete piece of scholarship due to their assistance.

In addition, Judy Goveia of the New Trier High School Library constantly searched out and obtained interlibrary loan materials for me. Thanks to Laura Bizar of New Trier High School for her expert proofreading, editing and general support.

[1] Kehoe, (1996) p. 10; Army Lists.
[2] WO 12/3501
[3] Houlding, p. 100 & 115.
[4] Army List 1780.
[5] Odintz, 182.
[6] Cannon, 18th Foot, p. 89.
[7] Army List 1780.
[8] Army List 1780.
[9] Army List 1780.
[10] Peebles, p. 10.
[11] Elting, p. 6.
[12] WO 27/11.
[13] WO 27/42.
[14] WO 27/39.
[15] WO 27/12.
[16] WO 27/35.
[17] Army List 1780.
[18] WO 27/35.
[19] WO 27/11.
[20] WO 27/36.
[21] WO 27/11, 12, 35, & 36.
[22] Houlding, p. 110.
[23] WO 65, Army Lists.
[24] Wilkins to Gage, 10 January 1772, Gage MSS.
[25] Rogers, p. 54.
[26] Simes (1776), p. 347-349.
[27] Light dragoon regiments were included with the other dragoon regiments.
[28] Howe, 57. For a more comprehensive examination of the evolution of the rank of brigadier and brigadier-general see W. B. R. Neave-Hill, The rank titles of brigadier and brigadier-general, JSAHR, XLVIII (190) 96-116
[29] At the beginning of this period, there were no enlisted engineers in the British Army, engineer officers either procured civilians or infantrymen to perform any necessary labor. No enlisted engineers, or sappers as they were called, served in America.

Abbott, Thomas; RA, 2nd Lieut.,1 January 1771; RA,1st Lieut.,7 July 1779; RA, Capt.- Lieut.,1 March 1781

Abercrombie, George; 7, Lieutenant, 29 July 1781

Abercrombie, James; 22, Lt. Colonel, 27 March 1770; English, born 1727; Served in 42nd and 78th Foot; Adjutant General, May 1775; DOW Bunker Hill, 23 June 1775; Most likely accidentally shot by his own men

Abercrombie, William; 22, Quartermaster, 29 May 1776; 22, Ensign,14 August 1778;22, Lieutenant,15 October 1780; From sergeant; Resigned 1 February 1782

Abercromby, James; 44, Colonel, 13 March 1756; Scottish, born 1714 General,25 May 1772 A

Abercromby, James; 3, Captain, 15 May 1765; Major,,29 August 1777

Abercromby, James; 1/71, Lieutenant, 29 August 1776

Abercromby, Robert; 37, Lt. Colonel, 30 November 1775; Am., Brigadier General, date unknown; Cmd. 1st Bn. L.I.; WIA Monmouth, 28 June 1778; Brig. gen. date not listed in NAAL, 1783

Abercromby, Thomas St.Clear; 44, Depty. Chap., 24 December 1774

Abernethie, Stewart; 43, Ensign, 30 November 1775

Abson, George; 1/RA, 2nd Lieut. 1 January 1771; 1/RA, 1st Lieut.,10 April 1778; RA, Capt.- Lieut.,28 June 1780; Assistant Bridge Master

Acheson, Hamilton; 55, Surgeon, 24 February 1775; Also Achinson; Irish, born 1753; First commissioned at age 17; Retired 23 February 1788; Returned to 43rd Foot, February 1792; Apothecary u. Charles Grey, 1794; Died 22 September 1800

Achmuty, Samuel; 45, Ensign, 11 January 1777; 45, Lieutenant,15 August 1778

Acland, John Dyke; 33, Captain, 23 March 1775; 20, Major, 16 December 1775; Also Ackland; English, born 1753; Married the daughter of Earl of Ilchester; Member of Parliament; Described as a "rough fellow, drunk almost every day"; WIA Hubbardton, 7 July 1777 & Bemis Heights, 7 October 1777; POW Bemis Heights; Died of a cold, 31 October 1778 in Britain after surviving a duel

Adam, Andrew; 22, Ensign, 18 January 1777; Also Addem; Arrived in America, 10 November 1777; DOW Rhode Island, 6 September 1778

Adams, Thomas; 70, Ensign, 26 February 1777; Retired 14 October

Addenbroke, John Petter; 57, Ensign, 28 August 1775; 57, Lieutenant, 5 June 1777; 54, Captain, 6 October 1778; ADC to Maj. General Campbell

Adderton, Curwen; 62, Ensign, 9 October 1781

Addison, Henry; 52, Ensign, 25 December 1775

Addison, Nicholas; 52, Captain, 22 April 1762; ADC to Gen. Howe; KIA Bunker Hill, 17 June 1775

1

Addison, Richard; 52, Lieutenant, 19 August 1773; WIA Bunker Hill; DOW Brooklyn, 21 or 28 November 1776

Adey, William Gyde; 35, Ensign 20 October 1780

Adlam, John E.; 40, Lieutenant, 28 September 1762; 40, Capt.- Lieut., 22 November 1775; 40, Captain, 11 December 1775

Adlam, Samuel; 62, Ensign, 18 March 1782

Adye, Stephen Payne; 4/RA, Capt.- Lieut., 1 January 1771; RA, Captain, 14 June 1780, 25 May 1772; Extra Deputy Judge Advocate, 7 August 1775

Affleck, Gilbert; 23, 2nd Lieut., 5 November 1778; 7, Lieutenant, 20 September ; 63, Captain, 30 April 1781

Affleck, James; 43, Ensign, 29 February 1776; WIA Rhode Island; 43, Lieutenant, 9 December 1778; 26, Captain, 15 September 1779

Agnew, James; 44, Lt. Colonel, 12 December 1764; Colonel, 30 September 1775; Scottish, born 1722; First commissioned at age 17; WIA Danbury, CT, 27 April 1777 & Brandywine, 11 September 1777; KIA Germantown, 4 October 1777

Agnew, Peter; 1/,71, Lieutenant, 31 August 1776

Agnew, William; 49, Ensign, 14 January 1775; 49, Lieutenant, 29 October 1776; 24, Captain, 20 May 1767; 24, Major, 14 July 1777; WIA Freeman's Farm, 19 September 1777; Also listed as retired 10 March 1777

Ainslie, Henry; 43, Lieutenant, 15 August 1775, 21 October 1761, Died 8 December 1778

Aked, Joab; 22, Ensign, 23 November 1775; 22, Lieutenant, 14 August 1778; Born Yorkshire, 1757; Not joined until after 17 July 1776; With additional company until arrival in America, 17 October 1781

Akers, John Houston; 55, Ensign, 7 February 1781

Alcock, Jno. Dormer; 47, Captain, 30 April 1771; WIA Bunker Hill, 17 June 1775

Alcock, Wastain; 21, 2nd Lieut., 3 October 1776; 21, 1st Lieut., 28 July 1780

Aldcroft, James; 18, Ensign, 26 July 1775; English, born 1752; First commissioned at age 23

Aldgood, Robert; 46, Ensign, 31 January 1778

Aldgood, Robert; 5, Ensign, 26 August 1780

Aldworth, -; 15, Ensign, 15 August 1775

Aldworth, Boyle; 46, Ensign, 31 January 1778; 55, Lieutenant, 25 September 1780; CM for dueling in September, 1782

Aldworth, Christopher; 34, Ensign, 20 October 1774; 34, Lieutenant, 1 January 1777

Alin, Miles; 57, Quartermaster, 16 August 1778; From sergeant major

Alkins, Thomas; FG, Adjutant, July 1781; From sergeant in 2nd Foot Guards; POW Yorktown

Allan, William; 16, Ensign, 17 September 1776; 16, Lieutenant, 3 May 1780

Allan, William; 16, Ensign, 17 November 1776; 16, Lieutenant, 10 June 1781

Allanson, George; 23,2nd Lieut., 23 April 1776; 23,1st Lieut.,12 May 1778

Allaz, James; 4/60, Captain, 1 September 1775,2 October 1761; Major, 29 August 1777; Joined regt. in 1756; Retired 30 December 1778

Allen, -; 69, Quartermaster, 13 August 1779

Almond, William; RA, Mate, 21 September 1774

Alston, Andrew; 80, Lieutenant, 24 January 1778; DOW Green Springs, 18 July 1781

Alston, James; 1/42, Ensign, 24 August 1779

Amherst, Jeffrey; 1/60, Captain, 27 August 1777; 2/60, Major,1 October 1782; ADC to Gen. Robertson

Amherst, Sir Jeffrey, K.B.; 60, Colonel in Chief, 25 August 1775; Lieutenant General, 19 January 1761

Amiel, Henry; 9, Ensign, 1 January 1781

Amiel, Henry; 22, Ensign, 6 September 1781; Native of New York City

Amiel, Otho; 17, Ensign, 12 November 1778; Native of America; Brother of Robert

Amiel, Robert; 17, Ensign, 7 August 1776; 17, Lieutenant, 7 October 1777; Native of America; Brother of Otho

Amory, -; 69, Lieutenant, 13 September 1780

Anburey, Thomas; Lieutenant, At Stillwater

Ancaster, Robert, Duke of; 15, Captain, 5 November 1777

Ancram, William; 34, Captain, 25 May 1772

Anderson, Alexander; 69, Captain, 31 October 1780

Anderson, Charles Fred.; 35, Ensign, 7 December 1781

Anderson, George; RA, Captain, 25 November 1760

Anderson, George; 28, Ensign, 17 October 1778; 55, Lieutenant, 6 March 1782

Anderson, John; 40, Adjutant, 1 October 1778; 40, Ensign, 6 May 1777; 40, Lieutenant, 1 October 1778; Died 5 March 1780

Anderson, Joseph; 22, Ensign, 26 June 1780; Scottish, born 1756; With additional company until late 1781

Anderson, Peter; 17 LD, Cornet, 29 December 1775

Anderson, Robert; 80, Ensign, 20 January 1778; 80, Lieutenant, 8 March 1781

Anderson, Robert; 82, Lieutenant, 19 January 1778; POW Yorktown, 1781

Andre, John; 54, Captain, 9 September 1779; Major, 8 August 1780; ADC to Sir Henry Clinton, 1779; Depty. Adj. Gen.; Hung as spy, Old Tappen, NJ, 2 October 1780

Andre, John; 7, Lieutenant, 24 September 1771; 26, Captain, 18 January 1777; ADC to Major General Charles Grey, 1775

Andre, Sir William Lewis Bart.; 7 Lieutenant 5 July 1777; 26, Captain, 6 September 1779; 44, Captain, 5 November 1778

Andrew, William; 5, Ensign, 22 November 1775; 5, Lieutenant, 8 November 1777; WIA Brandywine, 11 September 1777; Died 7 September 1780

Andrews, Samuel; 49, Ensign, 17 September 1773; 49, Lieutenant, 23 November 1775; Retired June 1776

Andrews, Thomas; 27, Ensign, 15 June 1778

Ankertel, Matthew; 55, Ensign, 16 July 1774; 17, Lieutenant, 11 May 1776; 57, Captain, 31 January 1778; Irish, born 1757; First commissioned at age 17; WIA Whitemarsh, PA, 7 December 1777; Retired 6 September 1780

Ankertel, Thomas; 30, Lieutenant, 1 June 1778; Also Anketel; WIA Eutaw Springs, 8 September 1781

Anley, Peter Bonamy; 83, Lieutenant, 5 December 1781

Annersley, Charles; 9, Captain, 9 October 1775

Ans, Wrey L'; 28, Captain, 15 August 1775, 3 December 1762; Major, 29 August 1777; Retired 9 June 1778

Anstruther, David; 26, Adjutant, 23 April 1778; 26, Ensign, 15 August 1775; 26, Lieutenant, 2 December 1777; 1/42, Captain, 6 December 1778; WIA English Neighborhood, NJ, 23 March 1780

Anstruther, John; 62, Lt. Colonel, 21 October 1773; Colonel, 17 November 1780; WIA Freeman's Farm, 19 September 1778 & possibly at Stillwater, 7 October 1777

Anstruther, Philip; 7, Lieutenant, 26 January 1770; 7, Captain, 19 February 1777

Anstruther, Philip; 62, Ensign, 8 October 1777

Anstruther, William; 26, Captain, 1 January 1766

Anstruther, William; 1/42, Ensign, 27 July 1783; Scottish, born 1766; First commissioned at age 16

Apthorpe, -; 2/71, Ensign, 20 September 1780

Apthorpe, Charles; 23, 2nd Lieut., 19 April 1774; 23, 1st Lieut., 2 March 1776; 23, Capt.- Lieut., 8 November 1778

Apthorpe, James; 3/60, Lieutenant, 1 March 1782

Arbuthnot, Alexander; 80, Lieutenant, 16 January 1778; 80, Captain, 24 September 1779; 16, Captain,4 December 1779

Arbuthnot, John; 27, Ensign, 15 August 1775

Arbuthnot, John; 4, Lieutenant, 7 August 1776; WIA Germantown, 4 October 1777

Arbuthnot, John; 43, Ensign, 15 September 1776

Arbuthnot, John; 82, Lieutenant, 5 January 1778

Arbuthnot, Robert; 40, Ensign, 14 January 1775; 65, Lieutenant, 24 March 1776

Arbuthnot, Robert; 31, Lieutenant, 10 September 1776

Archdale, Robert; 17 LD, Capt.- Lieut., 15 May 1772; 17 LD, Captain, 25 May 1772

Archer, Edward; 3FG, Lieut. & Capt., 10 June 1771; Retired 1777

Archer, William; 49, Quartermaster, 7 June 1776; 49, Ensign, 15 August 1779

Arcy, John Pomeroy D'; 64, Ensign, 16 February 1780; 64, Lieutenant, 12 February 1783; Irish, born 1761; First commissioned at age 19

Arden, Humphrey; 34, Ensign, 1 March 1776; 34, Lieutenant, 2 August 1780

Armitage, William; 28, Surgeon, 28 May 1779; From mate; Died prior to 15 January 1781

Armourer, Thomas; 46, Surgeon, 25 December 1776; Hosp. Apothecary, 23 March 1780;Hosp. Surgeon, 12 October 1780; Also George A.; From mate; Served in Leeward Isles with Gen. Hosp.; Died prior to 5 August 1792

Armstrong, Andrew; 8, Ensign, 3 November 1779,; 49, Lieutenant, 1 September 1781; Irish, born 1763; Spent time learning "military exercises in London while awaiting his commission"; Ensigncy not purchased; Was "tall for his age"

Armstrong, Archibald; 8, Ensign, 6 November 1778; Ensigncy not purchased

Armstrong, Bigoe; 8, Colonel, 20 October 1772; Lieutenant General, 20 October 1772; Scots-Irish; From Kings and Queens Counties; Originally served in the 18th Foot, commanded by his uncle; Appointed his cousin Edmund Armstrong as regimental agent

Armstrong, C. Nugent; 8, Ensign, 22 March 1780; Ensigncy not purchased; Died 16 January 1781

Armstrong, George; 8, Adjutant, 30 September 1782; 8, Ensign, 23 November 1775; 8, Lieutenant, 1 March 1779; Ensigncy not purchased; Purchased the adjutantcy

Armstrong, John; 27, Ensign, 5 January 1780; 27, Lieutenant, 18 January 1778

Armstrong, John; 35, Ensign, 24 November 1775; Also Thomas; Served 13 years as an enlisted dragoon before commissioning

Armstrong, Marcus; 14, Ensign, 24 November 1775

Armstrong, T. St. George; 8, Ensign, 17 January 1781; Ensigncy not purchased

Armstrong, Thomas; 49, Lieutenant, 28 January 1775

Armstrong, Thomas; 64, Captain, 2 February 1770; 17, Major, 5 October 1778; Irish, born 1745; First commissioned at age 17; Ensigncy not purchased; WIA Brandywine, 11 September 1777; Cmd. light infantry sortie at Yorktown

Armstrong, Thomas; 80, Lieutenant, 27 January 1778

Armstrong, William; 17, Lieutenant, 23 August 1775

Armstrong, William; 64, Capt.- Lieut., 19 February 1781; Asst. Deputy Quartermaster Gen. 12 December 1780; POW Stony Point

Armstrong, William; 8, Ensign, 6 January 1780; Ensigncy not purchased

Arnold , Benedict; 16, Ensign, 30 November 1780

Arnold , John; 10, Lieutenant, 12 May 1760; Lt. date also given 15 August 1775

Arnott, David; 57, Ensign, 20 December 1778; 57, Lieutenant, 9 July 1781

Asgill, Charles; 1FG, Lieut. & Capt., 3 February 1781

Ashe, Lovet; 38, Ensign, 3 July 1772; 38, Lieutenant, 3 May 1776; 63, Captain, 1 March 1782

Ashe, William; 17, Ensign, 2 August 1775; 17, Lieutenant, 7 August 1776

Ashley, Richard; 31, Ensign, 4 April 1776; Died 15 August 1781

Aspinal, John; 21, 2nd Lieut., 25 November 1779,

Astle, Daniel; 46, Captain, 3 July 1772; Retired 13 April 1778 or 19 October 1778

Atkin, Morris; 34, Adjutant, Date unknown; 34, Ensign, 26 April 1776; 34, Lieutenant, 20 October 1781; Also Maurice; Date of adjutancy in Army Lists is blank

Atkinson, Barnabas; 44, Lieutenant, 1 September 1771, 8 September 1756; Irish, born 1727; First commissioned at age 30; Depty. Inspector of Provincial Recruits, 30 October 1777

Atkinson, Charles; 43, Lieutenant, 16 March 1775

Atkinson, John; 28, Ensign, 25 October 1781

Atkinson, Joseph; 46, Captain, 25 May 1772

Aubrey, Thomas; 47, Captain, 30 April 1771; Portrait by N. Hone, 1771

Auchinlech, James; 38, Surgeon, 12 December 1767; Hosp. Surgeon, 5 July 1777; To half pay, 25 December 1783; Died prior to 1808

Aytonne, -; 16, Ensign, 19 October 1780

Babington, Henry; 55, Lieutenant, 20 October 1773; 27, Capt.- Lieut., 6 March 1779; 55, Capt.- Lieut., 3 March 1779; 27, Captain, 6 March 1779; Irish, born 1751; First commissioned at age 19; Died 22 June 1783

Babington, Thomas; 55, Ensign, 20 April 1778; 55, Lieutenant, 6 February 1782,

Bachop, John; 54, Lieutenant, 4 March 1761; 54, Capt.- Lieut., 26 November 1775; 54, Captain, 17 August 1777

Bacon, Dashwood; 28, Ensign, 8 September 1775

Bacon, William; 28, Ensign, 23 August 1775

Badcocke, Thomas; 6, Ensign, 10 December 1771; 6, Lieutenant, 22 November 1775

Baddeley, Thomas; Lieutenant, date unknown; Barrackmaster on Long Island, 1781; Also served in RGB; Died 4 October 1782

Baggs, -; 14, Ensign, 23 November 1775

Bagot, John; 37, Lieutenant, 26 December 1770; Retired 28 December 1776

Bagot, Samuel; 17 LD, Cornet, 4 August 1774; 17 LD, Lieutenant, 10 December 1777; 17 LD, Captain, 15 April 1779

Bailey, George Mathias; 33, Ensign, 14 November 1775; 33, Lieutenant, 12 July 1777; Also George Matthew

Bailey, James; 57, Ensign, 17 February 1781

Bailey, Mackay Hugh; 20, Adjutant, 2 August 1775; 20, Lieutenant, 4 August 1774

Bailey, Richard; 23, Quartermaster, 22 July 1758; 23, 1st Lieut., 25 December 1770, 7 October 1762; 62, Captain, 1 March 1776; Asst. Deputy Quartermaster General, 1777

Bailey, Thomas; FG, Mate, 24 April 1776; FG, Surgeon, 5 December 1780

Baillie, Alexander; 21, 1st Lieut., 29 November 1771, 27 July 1758; 9, Capt.- Lieut., 23 September 1776; 9, Captain, 10 August 1777

Baillie, George; 19, Lieutenant, 25 July 1778;

Baillie, James William; 7, Lieutenant, 29 May 1765, 19 April 1772; 7, Captain, 3 June 1774; Extra Major of Bde, 1781

Bain, James; 1/60, Capt.- Lieut., 14 May 1778; 1/60, Captain, 25 December 1778, 14 May 1778; Original company was an additional company in London. He was sent to Charleston to recruit among Continental prisoners on 27 September 1780 but his mission was scratched. He was taken prisoner himself and paroled on 27 February 1781. He returned to duty on 9 August 1781

Bain, William; 2/71, Ensign, 5 December 1775; 2/71, Lieutenant, 14 October 1778

Baird, John; 53, Captain, 1 December 1775

Baird, Robert; 82, Captain, 4 January 1778

Baird, Sir James, Bart.; 17, Lieutenant, 24 May 1775; 1/71, Capt.-Lieut., 8 December 1775; 2/71, Captain, 23 August 1776; WIA Germantown, 4 October 1777; Accused of atrocities in 1778

Baker, Aaron; 27, Chaplain, 30 May 1777

Baker, Aaron Abraham; 20, Chaplain, 11 October 1777; From clerk

Baker, Benjamin; 5, Adjutant, 14 March 1772; 5, Lieutenant, 7 November 1759; 5, Capt.- Lieut., 25 June 1775; 5, Captain, 22 November 1775; Night rider at Lexington; Extra Major of Bde., 1777

Baker, Benjamin; 35, Ensign, 6 July 1779; Son of Thomas Baker, 5th Foot

Baker, Hugh Cossart; 27, Ensign, 24 December 1776; 27, Lieutenant, 17 September 1778;

Baker, Thomas; 5, Quartermaster, 20 July 1774; 5, Lieutenant, 1 September 1771 5, Capt.- Lieut., 20 November 1775; 5, Captain, 7 October 1777; Father of Benj. Baker, 35th Foot; WIA Lexington and Concord, 19 April 1775; Resigned 2 May 1778

Baker, William; RAI, 1st Lieut., 1 January 1771; Died Newfoundland, 9 February 1778

Balaguier, John; 5, Ensign, 20 February 1773; 5, Lieutenant, 23 November 1775; WIA Bunker Hill, 17 June 1775; Retired 13 January 1776

Balcarras, Alexander, Earl of ; 1/42, Captain, 28 January 1771; 53, Major, 9 December 1775; 24, Lt. Colonel, 8 October 1777; 2/71, Colonel, 13 February 1782, 29 August 1777; Surname Lindsey; Scottish, born 1752; First commissioned at age 15; WIA Hubbardton, 7 July 1777; POW Saratoga; Cmd. L.I.; WIA Bemis Heights, 7 October 1777; Port. Avery 6 (1907)

Baldwin, Henry; 47, Ensign, 30 April 1771; 47, Lieutenant, 18 June 1775; WIA Lexington and Concord, 19 April 1775

Balfour, James; 6, Captain, 22 February 1768; 6, Major, 16 April 1777

Balfour, Nesbitt; 4, Captain, 26 January 1770; 4, Major, 4 June 1777, 6 November 1776; 23, Lt. Colonel, 31 January 1778; WIA Bunker Hill, 17 June 1775; ADC to Maj. Gen. Howe, 1777

Balfour, Thomas; 9, Adjutant, 1 January 1781; 9, Ensign, 2 March 1776; 9, Lieutenant, 30 August 1779

Balfour, William; 57, Adjutant, 16 May 1779; 57, Ensign, 9 October 1775; 57, Lieutenant, 5 December 1777; 57, Captain, 6 September 1780

Ball, -; 21, 2nd Lieut., 25 April 1777; 21, 1st Lieut., 1 September 1780

Ball, Abraham; 80, Ensign, 24 September 1780

Ball, Bent; 63, Lieutenant, 6 November 1772; 63, Capt.- Lieut., 14 October 1777; 63, Captain, 13 June 1778; WIA Brandywine, 11 September 1777; Accused of atrocities in 1778

Ball, Edward; 22, Mate, 1 October 1782

Ball, George; 59, Lieutenant, 14 December 1759

Ball, Henry; 15, Ensign, 19 January 1776; 15, Lieutenant, 18 January 1778; WIA Germantown, 4 October 1777

Ball, Isaac; Hosp., Mate, Prior to 1783; Stationed at New York, 1783

Ball, John; 80, Ensign, 24 September 1779; , 6

Ballmer, James; 16, Lieutenant, 12 February 1781, 11 February 1763

Balneaves, Archibald; 2/71, Lieutenant, 13 December 1775; POW Boston, 17 June 1776

Balneaves, John; 74, Captain, 22 January 1780, 29 December 1777, Also Archibald; Exchanged from 77th Foot with Peter Murdoch

Balvaird, Peter; 80, Ensign, 19 January 1778; 80, Lieutenant, 124 September 1779; Also Belvair or Balneaves; KIA Green Springs, VA, 6 July 1781

Bamford, William; 40, Captain, 25 March 1775, 25 May 1772; Also Bomford; Acting Town major, New York, 11 October 1776; Retired 18 October 1778

Banks, Joseph; 35, Quartermaster, 25 July 1775; 35, Lieutenant, 17 July 1775; DOW White Plains, 27 or 28 December 1776

Banks, Paul; 62, Lieutenant, 9 December 1767, 20 October 1761; 20, Capt.- Lieut., 11 November 1776; 20, Captain, 11 November 1776

Banks, Thomas; 70, Lieutenant, 27 July 1775; 70, Captain, 2 September 1779

Barber, Richard; 40, Ensign, 5 March 1775; 40, Lieutenant, 16 January 1777; KIA Brandywine, 11 September 1777

Barbutt, Burton Gage; 15, Lieutenant, 7 August 1776; 15, Capt.- Lieut., 12 November 1779; 15, Captain, 12 November 1779

Barclay, David; 76, Quartermaster, 25 December 1777; 76, Lieutenant, 2 January 1778; 76, Captain, 6 September 1780; Paymaster in Riv. Gaz.

Barcroft, Ambrose William; 63, Ensign, 20 April 1778; 63, Lieutenant, 22 November 1780; WIA & POW Eutaw Springs, 8 September 178

Bard, William; 35, Lieutenant, 12 July 1773; "KIA Bunker Hill, 17 June 1775

Barde, Lewis; 4/60, Lieutenant, 2 September 1779

Barker, Emanuel; 16, Captain, 23 April 1774; Also Immanuel; Son of the chaplain to the Duke of Devonshire, later the Dean of Raphoe in Ireland; Attended Manchester School, class of 1759; From 35th Foot; Retired 13 April 1778

Barker, John; 4, Lieutenant, 3 December 1771; 10, Captain, 13 January 1776; At Lexington and Concord; ADC to Maj. Gen. Smith; Still captain in 10th in 1787; Extant diary; Retired as colonel 27th Foot

Barker, William; 16, Lieutenant, 17 June 1761; 16, Capt.- Lieut., 6 May 1774; 16, Captain, 22 November 1775, 6 May 1774, Died New York City, 2 July 1782

Barlow, Edward; 6, Ensign, 2 May 1776

Barlyor, Richard; FG, Mate, 24 April 1776; Also Bailey; Temporary assignment as acting surgeon for Guards

Barnard, John; 54, Ensign, 22 March 1779, 25 September 1761

Barnes, John; RA, 1st Lieut., 8 September 1774

Barnes, Joseph; 55, Chaplain, 24 February 1775; Irish, born 1745; First commissioned at age 30

Barnes, Richard Tyrrel; 2/60, Ensign, 21 April 1779; 27, Lieutenant, 13 October 1780; Also Tyrell; On duty in New York in early 1779; On duty with German recruits in England in late 1779; On command in New York, 24 December 1780

Barnewall, Robert; Hosp. Apothecary, 21 September 1782; From mate; Stationed Leeward Isles

Baron, Edward; 4, Capt.- Lieut., 16 December 1775; 4, Captain, 6 November 1776; Major in Volunteer Regiment, Nova Scotia Militia, 16 July 1776; Colonel in Cumberland County, Nova Scotia Militia, 29 August 1780

Barr, George Wm.; 64, Ensign, 26 May 1780; Foreigner, born 1761; First commissioned at age 15

Barr, William; Hosp. Purveyor & Chief Surg., 1 January 1776; Also Barre; Served in F&I at Gen. Hosp.; Retired to half pay, 17 Sept. 1784; Died c1805

Barrett, Joseph; RAI, Captain, 15 November 1765; Died St. Johns, Newfoundland, 23 August 1777

Barrett, Sam. Tuffnell; 64, Ensign, 29 November 1779; 64, Lieutenant, 4 April 1782

Barrett, Thomas; 23, 1st Lieut., 23 August 1779

Barrett, William; 40, Quartermaster, 17 May 1779

Barriedale, John Lord; 76, Major, 29 December 1777; ADC to Sir Henry Clinton; WIA Ft. Clinton, 7 October 1777 & Charleston, 30 March 1780

Barrington, William; 7, Lieutenant, 22 February 1775; 70, Captain, 26 December 1778; ADC to Gen. Prescott; POW 14 July 1777; Married in Spring 1778

Barron, Edward; 4, Lieutenant, 25 October 1770, 18 October 1762, WIA Bunker Hill, 17 June 1775; Mapmaker

Barrow, Thomas; 16, Ensign, 13 April 1772; 16, Lieutenant, 20 November 1775; 3/60, Captain, 27 April 1778; Deputy Paymaster General, 1778; Died prior to 20 November 1779; Aged 56

Barry, David; 16 LD, Surgeon, 13 November 1775, 19 October 1764, From 70th Foot; Retired 20 December 1777

Barry, Henry; 52, Lieutenant, 23 September 1772; 52, Captain, 4 January 1777; Also Berry; Captain Nova Scotia Volunteers, 26 December 1775; Acting Town major at Newport R.I., 1778; Depty. Adjutant-General, 13 July 1780; POW Eutaw Springs, possibly WIA as well; Exchanged prior to 17 April 1782

Bartlet, Benjamin; 31, Ensign, 29 December 1779

Bartlet, Fredrick; 70, Ensign, 2 March 1778; 70, Lieutenant, 5 March 1779; Also Barrett

Barton, -; 52, Quartermaster, 12 August 1778

Barwell, William; 16, Ensign, 3 November 1774; 16, Lieutenant, 13 April 1778

Basset, Henry; 10, Major, 11 September 1765

Basset, Thomas; RE, Eng. ord. & Capt., 25 May 1772; In America from ?-1783; Served at Pittsburg, Newfoundland

Bassett, James; 29, Captain, 16 March 1774; 10, Ensign, 28 June 1771, 7 December 1764

Bassett, Richard; 10, Lieutenant, 28 November 1775; 10, Captain, 31 January 1778

Bassett, Thomas; 5, Ensign, 23 June 1775; 5, Lieutenant, 31 March 1777

Bateman, Richard; 20, Ensign, 1 March 1776; 20, Lieutenant, 20 September 1777

Bathe, John; 15, Adjutant, 6 January 1776; 15, Ensign, 3 March 1779, 19 February 1779; 15, Lieutenant, 30 July 1778

Bathurst, Samuel; 46, Lieutenant, 15 August 1775, 6 November 1761; 46, Capt.- Lieut., 20 November 1780

Batt, Thomas; Adjutant, 5 May 1775; Had retired as captain in 1773; Replaced within two days of his appointed as adj. of the Lt. Inf. Bn.; Later served as captain and major of the Royal Fencible Americans

Battersby, James; 29, Lieutenant, 16 December 1773; 29, Captain, 16 February 1778; WIA Bemis Heights, 7 October 1777; According to Inman, committed suicide in London, after 1781, but exchanged to half-pay in 1784

Battersby, Robert; 29, Ensign, 29 December 1775; 34, Lieutenant, 1 November 1780

Battier, John Gaspard; 5, Captain, 28 November 1771; Served at Lexington and Concord as cmdr. of the 5th L.I. Coy.

Battier, William; 5, Captain, 16 March 1774

11

Batut, John; 14, Lieutenant, 25 December 1770, 17 March 1761; 14, Captain, 10 December 1775; WIA Great Bridge, VA, 9 December 1775

Batwell, Lullum; 46, Lieutenant, 1 May 1775; 46, Capt.- Lieut., 7 June 1777; 46, Captain, 7 June 1777

Bayard, John, 2/60, Lieutenant, 20 October 1772; Son of William Bayard of New York; On leave in 1776 & 1777; Lieutenant Colonel, King's Orange Rangers, 25 December 1776; Returned to 2/60th in 1783

Bayer, John Otto; 38, Captain, 25 July 1771; Retired 3 May 1776

Bayley, Nicholas; 1FG, Lieut. & Capt., 4 October 1770; 1FG, Capt. & Lt. Col., 3 July 1777; Retired 18 July 1780

Bayley, Zachary; 65, Ensign, 11 January 1774; 65, Lieutenant, 12 December 1775

Baylie, John; 65, Ensign, 16 August 1768; 65, Lieutenant, 15 June 1775

Baylis, John; 63, Ensign, 23 October 1776; 63, Lieutenant, 13 April 1778

Baynes, George; 5, Ensign, 29 October 1778

Baynes, Robert; 65, Ensign, 3 June 1774

Bayntun, Geo. Worden; 23, 2nd Lieut., 22 November 1775; 23, 1st Lieut., 10 March 1777;

Beacroft, Richard; 24, Lieutenant, 13 February 1766; 24, Capt.- Lieut., 8 October 1777; 24, Captain, 8 October 1777; Acting asst. engineer during the Saratoga Campaign; Served with Fraser's Advanced Corps

Beatson, Thomas; 46, Lieutenant, 11 July 1781, 31 August 1780

Beauclerk, George; 3FG, Ensign, 3 May 1775; 3FG, Lieut. & Capt., 9 February 1778;Later Lord, 4th Duke of Albans

Beaumont, Hammond; 26, Surgeon, 18 March 1761; Hosp. Surgeon, 21 May 1777

Beaver, Arthur; 52, Ensign, 24 November 1775; 33, Lieutenant, 11 June 1778; Also Beevor; WIA Charleston, May 1780 & Guilford CH, 15 March 1781; With recruits at Halifax, 11 March 1783

Beckwith, -; 27, Ensign, 3 September 1775; Died 23 December 1776

Beckwith, Ferdinand A. F.; 33, Ensign, 25 October 1779; 37, Lieutenant, 18 September 1780

Beckwith, George; 37, Adjutant, 29 January 1776; 37, Lieutenant, 7 July 1775; 37, Capt.- Lieut., 2 July 1777; 37, Captain, 20 May 1778; Major; 30 November 1781, ADC to Gen. Knuphausen 2 April 1778

Beckwith, John; 27, Lt. Colonel, 1 May 1775, 19 January 1762, Retired 25 October 1775

Beckwith, Malby; 3, Lieutenant, 1 June 1778; KIA Eutaw Springs, 8 September 1781

Beckwith, Onslow; 23, 1st Lieut., 25 January 1771; 45, Captain, 10 February 1776; WIA Bunker Hill, 17 June 1775

Beckwith, Wm. Henry; 28, Ensign, 19 October 1778; 28, Lieutenant, 25 January 1782

Bedingfield, Bacon; 19, Chaplain, 4 October 1770

Beecher, George; FG, Quartermaster, 6 November 1777; Acting QM from 20 October 1776; Resigned 12 August 1778

Beecher, John Gainsford; 16, Ensign, 10 December 1771, 23 December 1767; 16, Lieutenant, 26 May 1775; Died 17 September 1780

Beevor, John; 17 LD, Chaplain, 12 July 1780

Beil, James; Hosp., Mate, Prior to 1783; At New York as POW, 1783

Belchier, John; 64, Captain, 2 February 1776

Bell, Bryan; 44, Ensign, 3 July 1772; 4, Lieutenant, 13 January 1776; 46, Captain, 18 August 1778; ADC to Major-General Vaughan, 1777

Bell, Charles; 57, Captain, 31 August 1770

Bell, David John; 19, Captain, 12 August 1779

Bell, Richard; RGB, Surgeon, 25 September 1778; To half pay, 1783; Died c. 24 June 102

Bell, Robert; 64, Chaplain, 5 August 1759; Scottish, born 1736; First commissioned at age 33; Commission date also listed at 1 August 1758

Bellaers, John; 46, Ensign, 10 February 1777; 46, Lieutenant, 22 March 1780

Bellett, William; 22, Ensign, 11 February 1779; English, born 1762; Transferred to additional company, 1782; Never served in America

Bellew, Patrick; 1FG, Lieut. & Capt., 22 February 1773; WIA & POW, Monmouth, 28 June 1778

Bellingham, William; 45, Ensign, 9 August 1778

Benard, Arthur; 3, Lieutenant, 26 January 1781; Stayed in Ireland according to WO 8/6, 273-279

Bendyshe, Richard; RE, Pract. eng. & 2nd Lt., 13 March 1772; In America from 1776-1778

Bennett, Richard; 2/60, Ensign, 6 February 1776; On duty in New York

Bennett, Thomas; 8, Adjutant, 22 December 1778; 8, Lieutenant, 1 August 1770; English, born 1746; First commissioned at age 15; Served on expeditions with Indian allies; Beat a Pvt. Burgess without cause for missing a drill movement

Bennett, Wm. Pearce; 5, Quartermaster, 7 October 1777; 5, Ensign, 15 April 1776; Sold out, 2 May 1778

Benson, George; 44, Quartermaster, 28 November 1771; 44, Lieutenant, 5 June 1771; 44, Captain, 4 October 1776; Irish, born 1751; First commissioned at age 17; Extra Major of Bde, 1781

Benson, Henry; 49, Ensign, 23 November 1775; 49, Lieutenant, 27 April 1777

Berclay, George; 22, Captain, 25 December 1770, 28 October 1760; 35, Major, 30 October 1776; Also Barclay; English, born 1741; Transferred to 35th Foot, 30 October 1778

Bernard, Andrew; 27, Lieutenant, 14 April 1781

Bernard, Benjamin; 23, Lt. Colonel, 28 August 1771; WIA Lexington and Concord, 19 April 1775; Died 20 August 1776; Also listed as retired 30 January 1778

Bernard, Peter; 27, Ensign, 4 June 1777; Retired 15 June 1778

Bernard, Peter; Hosp. Apothecary, 9 April 1778; From 10th Dragoons; For the garrison at Halifax

Berriedale, John, Lord; 17, Lieutenant, 7 July 1775; 57, Captain, 25 November 1775; Also Earl of Caithness; WIA Fts. Clinton & Montgomery, 6 October 1777

Berry, George; 26, Ensign, 25 September 1781

Bertie, Robert, Lord; 7, Colonel, 20 August 1754; Lieutenant General; 18 December 1760;

Bertie, Robert, Lord; 15, Captain, 5 November 1777; Died of drinking and rioting in England, 8 July 1779

Best, Elias; 30, Lieutenant, 1 June 1778; 22, Ensign, 6 June 1776; Served in additional company until 6 June 1777; Resigned 13 April 1779

Best, James; 49, Ensign, 6 August 1778

Bethune, John; 1/84, Chaplain, 14 June 1775

Bethune, Benj. Faneuil; 70, Ensign, 14 October 1778; 70, Lieutenant, 11 November 1780; Native of Boston, MA; born 1761; First commissioned at age 17; Transferred to 64th Foot

Bethune, James; 21, Captain, 25 May 1772; Died 7 June 1777 possibly at Quebec

Bevan, John; 35, Ensign, 23 November 1775

Bevill, St. Leger; 62, Ensign, 30 September 1777; Absconded from Cambridge in violation of his parole in 1778. Described as "low in stature, has been bred to the Sea, talks like a Seaman"

Bewes, George; 18, Lieutenant, 27 February 1772; English, born 1747; First commissioned at age 22

Bibby, Thomas; 24, Lieutenant, 8 January 1775; 7, Capt.- Lieut., 19 January 1781

Bibby, Thomas; 80, Capt.- Lieut., 18 September 1780; 80, Captain, 18 September 1780; Asst. Deputy Adjutant General, 1781

Biddulph, Edward; 3, Lieutenant, 1 May 1772; 3, Captain, 17 December 1780

Billinghurst, George; 3, Lieutenant, 20 April 1776; WIA & POW Eutaw Springs, 8 September 1781; Appointed to Emm. Chaussers, 7 May 1778

Binbino, Stephen; 54, Lieutenant, 29 September 1780; Promotion published on 10 October 1780

Bingham, Charles; 35, Ensign, 25 December 1776

Bingley, John; 65, Ensign, 7 November 1774; 65, Lieutenant, 5 February 1777

Birch, John; 27, Lieutenant, 23 August 1775; 27, Captain, 2 December 1777; WIA Brandywine; Retired 10 September 1778

Birch, Samuel; 17 LD, Lt. Colonel, 24 April 1773, 25 May 1772; Colonel, 17 November 1780; Am., Brigadier General, 14 September 1780; Commandant of New York

Birch, Zephaniah; 26, Ensign, 12 December 1781

Bird, Henry; 8, Lieutenant, 22 February 1768, 3 October 1764; 8, Capt.-Lieut., 11 May 1778; 8, Captain, 11 May 1778; Welsh; Listed as English in WO 27, born 1748; First commissioned at age 15; Heir to Goytree Estate in Monmouth; Served on expeditions with Indian allies; Died in Egypt in 1800

Bird, John; 15, Lt. Colonel, 13 January 1776; KIA Germantown, 4 October 1777

Bird, John Taylor; 16, Lieutenant, 23 September 1773; ADC Gen. Tryon, 20 April 1777

Birmingham, John; 63, Ensign, 15 August 1775; 63, Lieutenant, 7 October 1777;

Bishop, Robert; 64, Surgeon, 11 April 1766; Hosp. Apothecary, 31 August 1779; Irish, born 1732; First commissioned at age 34; Died 27 September 1809

Bishopp, Harry; 17 LD, Major, 24 April 1773

Black, Harmon; RA, 2nd Lieut., 8 December 1779; Transferred to Loyal Irish Volunteers in 1778; Returned to RA in 1779; Died 1782

Black, John; 17 LD, Cornet, 13 April 1779

Blackader, Stephen; 53, Ensign, 6 June 1778

Blackall, Arthur; 62, Adjutant, 6 April 1782; 62, Lieutenant, 20 October 1774; 62, Capt.- Lieut., 18 March 1782

Blacker, Henry; 62, Ensign, 21 December 1775; Lieutenant, 8 October 1777; Also Blake; WIA Bemis Heights, 7 October 1777

Blacker, Henry; 65, Ensign, 15 May 1771; 65, Lieutenant, 22 November 1775

Blacker, William; 54, Lieutenant, 7 July 1775; Possibly WIA December 1777

Blackett, William; 14, Captain, 29 May 1761; Died Portsmouth, VA, 15 October 1775, possibly "of drink"

Blackmore, Robert; 10, Lieutenant, 11 September 1765; 10, Capt.- Lieut., 18 November 1776

Blackwood, John; 21, 2nd Lieut., 21 February 1776; 21, 1st Lieut., 8 June 1777;

Blackwood, William; 18, Lieutenant, 26 December 1770; 18, Captain, 25 July 1775; Irish, born 1749; First commissioned at age 18

Blagden, Sir Charles; Hosp. Physician, 19 October 1775; Born 17 April 1748; M.D. Edin. 1768; Fellow Royal Society, 1772; To half pay 1785; Knight Bachelor, 1792; Died near Paris, 26 March 1820

Blair, -; 3, Ensign, 8 November 1781; From volunteer

Blair, Hugh; 1/71, Chaplain, 23 November 1775

Blair, John; 10, Ensign, 15 July 1776, 13 May 1776; 10, Lieutenant, 3 March 1778

Blake, Charles; 34, Surgeon, 15 May 1772, 2 June 1770, From 54th Foot; Retired 11 October 1779; Possibly appointed surgeon for Montreal 25 December 1783; If so, died c. 1818

Blake, John; 24, Captain, 7 July 1775; WIA Freeman's Farm, 19 September 1777

Blakeney, William; 23, Captain, 6 October 1762; 23, Major, 24 November 1775; Lt. Colonel, 30 January 1778; WIA Bunker Hill;, 17 June 1775; Exchanged to major 65th Foot; Retired by 1780

Bland, James; 46, Adjutant, 31May 1773; 46, Ensign, 16 March 1775; Lieutenant, 13 April 1778;

Bland, Thomas; 28, Ensign, 26 October 1775; 28, Lieutenant, 19 August 1778;

Blankley, H. Stanford; 31, Ensign, 23 February 1776;

Blathwayt, James; 6, Lieutenant, 5 March 1774;

Blayney, Cadwallader Lord; 38, Colonel, 24 November 1766; Died 10 December 1775, not in America

Bleamish, William; 19, Lieutenant, 29 June 1780

Blenman, Joseph; 4, Ensign, 26 February 1776; 4, Lieutenant, 18 December 1777; WIA Germantown, 4 October 1777

Blennerhassett, Conway; 19, Lieutenant, 1 Junc 1778

Blennerhassett, John; 10, Ensign, 6 February 1772; DOW Staten Island, 14 or 15 July 1776

Blewett, Edward; 49, Ensign, 16 December 1780

Blick, Abraham; 44, Ensign, 15 October 1778; 44, Lieutenant, 2 November 1779

Bliss, Daniel; 8, Ensign, 13 September 1783; From volunteer

Bliss, Samuel; 2/84, Lieutenant, 14 June 1775; From volunteer

Blomfield, John; 19, Ensign, 20 March 1779; 19, Lieutenant, 9 September 1781

Blomfield, Robert; 19, Ensign, 30 June 1780

Blond, Nathaniel; 47, Ensign, 24 November 1775; 47, Lieutenant, 3 August 1781

Blood, Edward; 57, Ensign, 18 August 1778

Blood, Neptune; 62, Ensign, 29 May 1777; 62, Lieutenant, 27 July 1781

Blood, Thomas; 64, Ensign, 12 January 1770; 64, Lieutenant, 17 August 1774

Bloomfield, Thomas; RA, Capt.- Lieut., 29 January 1773; RA Major of Bde; WIA Freeman's Farm, 7 October 1777

Blount, Charles; 38, Ensign, 26 November 1775

Blucke, John; 23, Adjutant, 6 October 1776; 2nd Lieut., 20 January 1774; 23, 1st Lieut., 10 February 1776; 23, Capt.- Lieut., 9 August 1780; Resigned as adjutant, 25 October 1778; Asst. Judge-Advocate, 1782

Blundell, Bryan; 46, Ensign, 1 May 1775; 35, Lieutenant,.10 February 1777; From Liverpool; Helped raise the 79th or Liverpool Regiment; Promoted captain in 79th, 10 January 1778

Blunt, Charles; 54, Lieutenant, 2 February 1780

Blunt, Henry; 4, Lt. Colonel, 24 November 1775, 20 September 1775

Bodens, George; 4, Ensign, 22 November 1775; 4, Lieutenant, 5 July 1777; WIA Germantown, 4 October 1777 & while serving on HMS Magnificent, 6 July 1779

Boggs, James; Hosp. Mate, Prior to 1783; Stationed at New York, 1783

Boiswell, David; 44, Ensign, 10 February 1776

Boland, Edward; 40, Ensign, 18 August 1778; 40, Lieutenant, 7 March 1780

Bolton, George; 20, Ensign, 27 June 1777

Bolton, Mason; 9, Major, 31 May 1773; 8, Lt. Colonel, 11 November 1776; Drowned Lake Ontario, 31 October 1780

Bolton, Thomas; 26, Ensign, 19 June 1775; 26, Lieutenant, 30 October 1777; Killed in a duel in either 1777 or 1787 with an Ensign Forster at Montreal; If not killed in 1777, he is listed as retired 30 August 1779

Bomford, Thomas; 64, Lieutenant, 12 July 1770; 35, Captain, 6 June 1776

Bonamy, John; 83, Lieutenant, 15 January 1783

Bond, Joseph; Hosp., Sprnmy. Mate, Prior to 1783; At Lancaster, PA as POW, 1783

Boniface, Francis; 3/60, Ensign, 28 July 1778; 4/60, Lieutenant, 4 September 1779; From Emmerick's Chasseurs

Bonnell, Isaac; Barrack Master, Staten Island, 1782

Bontine, James; 40, Ensign, 31 August 1774; 40, Lieutenant, 23 November 1775

Booker, Thomas; 53, Lieutenant, 3 March 1776

Boorback, Barnet; 55, Mate, April 1774; English, born 1748; First joined the service at age 26; Promoted to captain, 24 October 1776 in 1st Bn. Delancey's Regt. Still serving 1783

Boothby, Sir William; 6, Colonel, 18 November 1773; Lieutenant General; 25 May 1772

Bordmore, Scrope; 23, Chaplain, 22 October 1778

Borland, John Lindall; 22, Ensign, 24 November 1775; 22, Lieutenant, 14 August 1778; Born near Boston, 18 August 1754; Served as a private in the Loyal American Association, 1775; WIA Rhode Island, 29 August 1778; To additional company late 1778

Borough, Randall; 15, Lieutenant, 15 August 1775, 28 July 1762

Borough, William Blackney; 26, Lieutenant, 1 April 1767, 25 December 1762; 26, Capt.- Lieut., 19 October 1778; 26, Captain, 19 October 1778

Boscawen, Florentius; 3FG, Ensign, 22 February 1775; 3FG, Lieut. & Capt., 24 December 1777; WIA Young's House, NY, 3 February 1780; Died at sea, 18 April 1782

Boscawen, George Evelyn; 4, Ensign, 9 May 1774; 63, Lieutenant, 1 December 1775; 5 D, Captain, 4 November 1777;Born, 1745; MP Truro, 1774-1780

Boscawen, Hon. George; 23, Colonel, 16 January 1761; Lieutenant General; 22 February 1760, From Charlton Forest, Oxford; MP Truro, 1761-1774; Died 11 May 1775

Boscawen, Nicholas; 2FG, Ensign, 6 June 1773; 2FG, Lieut. & Capt., 20 January 1777; Retired 1790

Bosville, William; 2FG, Lieut. & Capt., 11 January 1769; Retired June 1777

Boswell, David; 64, Lieutenant, 21 March 1778; Also Boiswell; Scottish

Botet, Anthony; 10, Lieutenant, 15 May 1765; 10, Capt.- Lieut., 22 November 1775; 10, Captain, 18 November 1776;

Bourke, Charles; 40, Lieutenant, 15 August 1775, 20 October 1761;

Bourne, Geo. Stuart; 2FG, Lieut. & Capt., 15 July 1768; Died in New York, 14 October 1776

Bourne, Robert; 52, Adjutant, 25 October 1777; 10, Ensign, 29 March 1773; 52, Lieutenant, 26 August 1776; Appointed to Emmerick's Chaussers, 7 May 1778

Bowater, George; RA, 1st Lieut., 11 November 1779

Bowe, George; 4/60, Chaplain, 5 February 1776; Also Bowes

Bowen, Henry; 16, Ensign, 2 August 1779;

Bowen, James; Lieutenant; Fourier to the army, August 1776; From half-pay

Bower, William; 83, Ensign, 13 March 1783

Bowes, Fredrick; 64, Lieutenant, 1 January 1766; 64, Capt.- Lieut., 17 August 1774; 64, Captain, 22 November 1775; Scottish, born 1745; First commissioned at age 17; Extra Major of Bde, 31 October 1780

Bowie, James; 22, Ensign, 18 September 1781; To 57th Foot, 20 July 1783

Bowland, John; 40, Ensign, 10 September 1781

Bowler, Elias; 15, Quartermaster, 25 November 1775; 15, Ensign, 4 June 1777; 15, Lieutenant, 10 October 1778

Bown, James; 30, Surgeon, 18 November 1775; Also Brown; Retired 20 March 1783

Bowne, Essex; 9, Ensign, 1 June 1780

Bowyer, John; 54, Captain, 7 September 1771

Boyce, William; 16 LD, Adjutant, 10 February 1775; 16 LD, Cornet, 22 July 1775

Boyd, Alexander; 65, Ensign, 26 September 1777

Boyd, Charles; 82, Captain, 6 January 1778; Major of Bde, Halifax

Boyd, George Fredrick; 2/84, Surgeon, 8 May 1776; Served in Gen. Hosp. in Germany during 7 Yrs War; Died Basingstoke, 6 May 1801

Boyd, James; 54, Ensign, 7 September 1781

Boyd, John; Hosp., Mate, Prior to 1783; Possibly from mate 49th Foot; Stationed at New York, 1783

Boyd, Joseph; 28, Lieutenant, 15 August 1775, 20 May 1761

Boyd, St. Lawrence; 38, Captain, 3 July 1772; Also given name as Lawrence; WIA Bunker Hill, 17 June 1775

Boyd, Thomas Moore; 16, Ensign, 10 June 1781

Boyde, Thomas; 16, Captain, 4 February 1769; Major; 17 November 1780

Boyes, James; 14, Ensign, 16 December 1773; 14, Lieutenant, 15 October 1775

Boyes, Robert; 71, Mate, date unknown; 15, Surgeon, 18 March 1777; From mate 71st Foot; By purchase; KIA Brimstone Hill, W.I., January 1782

Boyle, Moore; 27, Ensign, 23 August 1775; 27, Lieutenant, 22 December 1778; Died 30 March 1783

Braban, William; 37, Ensign, 29 July 1779; 37, Lieutenant, 29 April 1781

Brabazon, Edward; 22, Captain, 7 December 1772; Extra Major of Bde, 26 December 1779; POW Yorktown, 1781

Brabazon, George; 44, Ensign, 5 October 1776; 44, Lieutenant, 19 January 1779;

Brabazon, Malby; 65, Captain, 19 March 1774; Major; 25 July 1772; Retired 12 December 1775

Brackenbury, Carr. Thomas; 33, Ensign, 12 July 1777; 54, Lieutenant, 28 April 1779; 54, Captain, 1 April 1871

Brackenbury, Richard; 70, Lieutenant, 10 October 1778

Bradshaw, Alexander David; 46, Capt.-Lieut., 12 October 1780, 10 June 1780; Died 21 November 1780

Bradshaw, John Smith; 33, Lieutenant, 13 September 1779

Bradshaw, John Smith; 17 LD, Cornet, 1 June 1777; 17 LD, Lieutenant, 30 May 1780; 17 LD, Capt.- Lieut., 7 August 1780; 17 LD, Captain, 7 August 1780

Bradshaw, Lawrence; 46, Ensign, 25 September 1780; Also Branshaw

Bradstreet, Samuel; 40, Captain, 10 November 1761; 40, Major, 11 December 1775

Bradstreet, Simon; 3/60, Ensign, 24 April 1779

Brandwood, Oliver; 49, Ensign, 1 September 1871

Branthwayt, John; 26, Ensign, 28 April 1870

Branwood, Thomas; 49, Quartermaster, 20 January 1779

Bray, William; 6, Ensign, 22 July 1773; 6, Lieutenant, 2 May 1776

Breary, Christopher; 4, Ensign, 3 December 1771; 4, Lieutenant, 23 November 1775; 4, Capt.- Lieut., 29 September 1780

Breley, Alexander; 54, Lieutenant, 5 October 1770; 3/60, Capt.- Lieut., 3 February 1780; Also Brely; Retired 9 June 1781; Served in Florida,

Brereton, Robert; 45, Chaplain, 11 January 1741;

Brereton, Thomas; 30, Capt.- Lieut., 9 October 1778

Brereton, William; 17, Adjutant, 24 February 1775; 17, Captain, 24 May 1775

Brereton, William; 64, Major, 29 April 1781; WIA Monmouth, 28 June 1778 with 1st Gren. Bn.; A notorious duelist and gamester; Majority also listed as 20 April 1781

Bresse, John; 54, Captain, 16 May 1764, 11 May 1763; Major; 29 August 1777

Brett, Patrick; 1/84, Ensign, 23 August 1783

Breyton, John; 65, Ensign, 6 June 1776

Brice, Arthur Hill; 7, Captain, 28 November 1766, 13 February 1762, Retired 9 June 1778

Brick, Daniel; 22, Lieutenant, 15 August 1775, 20 December 1760, From 20th Foot; Never served in America; To 85th Foot, 29 March 1783

Brickenden, George; 31, Ensign, 21 March 1776; Died 18 September 1776, possibly in Canada

Brietendack, -, Baron; 4/60, Lieutenant, 21 November 1777; First name not listed

Brindle, Francis; Hosp. Mate, Prior to 1783; With Kings American Dragoons, 1783

Brindley, George; Deputy Commissary, 1778; KIA Elizabethtown, NJ, 1780

Brindley, Henry; 28, Chaplain, 18 August 1769

Brisbane, Stuart; 54, Ensign, 18 August 1778; 54, Lieutenant, 29 September 1780

Briscoe, Musgrave; 47, Captain, 22 March 1782

Briscoe, Robert; 65, Captain, 22 February 1771

Briscoe, Wastel; 16 LD, Lieutenant, 31March 1775; Also Bristow; WIA New York, 16 October 1776

Brissett, John; 63, Ensign, 19 September 1779

Bristow, Skeff. Gore; 46, Ensign, 26 October 1775; 46, Lieutenant, 6 January 1779; WIA Brandywine, 11 September 1777

Brock, Fredrick; 3/60, Ensign, 8 February 1776; KIA Baton Rouge, LA, 21 September 177

Brock, John; 8, Ensign, 24 November 1775; 8, Lieutenant, 3 November 1779; Also Brooke; Killed in a duel

Broderick, Hon. Henry; 33, Ensign, 23 March 1775; 33, Lieutenant, 8 August 1776; 55, Captain, 12 June 1777; Major; 4 July 1781, English, born 1759; First commissioned age 15; ADC to Gen. Cornwallis, 28 January 1777

Brodie, Alexander; 10, Ensign, 13 September 1776; 4, Lieutenant, 20 September 1778; From volunteer, 42nd Foot

Brodie, George; 21, Captain, 1 April 1776

Bromfield, Stephen; 54, Captain, 7 March 1758; 40, Major, 7 September 1781, 10 November 1780; Also Broomfield; WIA Groton, CT, 6 September 1781

Bromhead, Edward; 27, Chaplain, 22 September 1769

Bromhead, Edward; 31, Chaplain, 9 January 1763

Bromhead, Gonville; 62, Quartermaster, 18 January 1770; 62, Lieutenant, 3 March 1776; Born 1760; First commissioned at age 10; Lieutenant General, June 1813

Bromhead, Jonathan; 54, Ensign, 28 July 1778

Bromwick, John Hyde; 38, Ensign, 22 June 1781

Bronwin, St. John; 35, Ensign, 21 July 1779; From Suffolk; Commissioned under Lord Cornwallis's patronage

Brooke, -; 16, Ensign, 23 November 1775; 16, Lieutenant, 18 September 1780;

Brooke, Arthur; 52, Ensign, 18 June 1775; 52, Lieutenant, 8 May 1777; Also Brooks; From volunteer; WIA Bunker Hill, 17 June 1775, "shot through the body" after obtaining the top of the entrenchment

Brooke, Robert Bounds; 8, Ensign, 6 November 1772; 8, Lieutenant, 8 May 1777

Brooks, John; 46, Lieutenant, 22 November 1780, 13 August 1780

Brown, David; Hosp. Mate, Prior to 1783; In Virginia as POW, 1783

Brown, George; 10, Ensign, 24 November 1775; 10, Lieutenant, 30 October 1777

Brown, George; 28, Ensign, 16 June 1780

Brown, Gore; 35, Ensign, 5 July 1780; Also Browne; Grandfather had been an RA officer; From Dublin merchant family

Brown, John; 2/60, Major, 28 September 1775; Cmd. St. Augustine, 1775-1777; To Scotland, 1777; Retired 22 October 1780

Brown, John Fred.; 28, Ensign, 15 September 1781

Brown, Peter; 2/RA, 1st Lieut., 4 January 1771

Brown, Peter; Hosp. Mate, Prior to 1783; Stationed at New York, 1783

Brown, Richard; 46, Ensign, 8 April 1781

Brown, William; 35, Captain, 3 February 1769; Died Boston, 16 July 1775

Browne, -; 21, 2nd Lieut., 14 December 1774; Shot by sentry as POW in Boston when his carriage did not stop at a sentry post

Browne, -; 80, Ensign, 7 July 1781

Browne, Andrew; 21, Chaplain, 25 March 1777; Also Brown; From clerk

Browne, Andrew; 44, Capt.- Lieut., 15 May 1772; 44, Captain, 22 November 1775, 25 May 1772; Scottish, born 1744; First commissioned at age 13; DOW Brooklyn, 3 October 1776

Browne, Birnie; 21, 2nd Lieut., 9 February 1780

Browne, Charles; 15, Ensign, 30 September 1775; 15, Lieutenant, 20 December 1776

Browne, Francis; 27, Captain, 16 March 1775; Died 13 August 1779

Browne, George; 1/60, Capt.- Lieut., 4 October 1780; In Nicaragua by April 1780; To captain in 88th Foot, 11 August 1781

Browne, George; 14, Ensign, 22 December 1772; 14, Lieutenant, 18 June 1775

Browne, George; 1/60, Lieutenant, 29 September 1775

Browne, George; 40, Ensign, 8 February 1776

Browne, George; Hosp. Apothecary, 25 June 1775; Also Brown; To half pay, 1783; Died prior to 14 June 1795

Browne, George Gav.; Hosp., Sprmmy. Mate, Prior to 1783; Stationed at New York, 1783

Browne, Henry Bowen; 52, Ensign, 20 August 1773; 52, Lieutenant, 22 November 1775

Browne, Herb. Gwyn; 6, Captain, 22 February 1771

Browne, John; 3/60, Major, 22 September 1775; Also Browne; Joined regt. in 1756

Browne, John; 23, 1st Lieut., 20 May 1776;

Browne, John; 69, Lieutenant, 25 December 1778; WIA St. Kitts, 28 January 1782

Browne, John; 23, 2nd Lieut., 1 March 1775
Browne, John Ham.; 53, Lieutenant, 1 December 1775
Browne, John Hamilton; 44, Ensign, 4 March 1777; 7, Lieutenant, 9 June 1778
Browne, Leonard; 4, Lieutenant, 26 December 1770; WIA Bunker
Hill,17 June 1775; Retired 29 May 1776
Browne, Richard; 31, Lieutenant, 29 March 1774; 31, Captain, 2 September 1781
Browne, Richard; 63, Lieutenant, 14 December 1774
Browne, Richard; 38, Ensign, 19 June 1776; Also Broone
Browne, T. Mitchell; 30, Ensign, 24 December 1779
Browne, Thomas; 26, Captain, 3 March 1772; DOW Brooklyn, 4 October 1776
Browne, Thomas Gunter; 37, Lieutenant, 28 July 1779
Browne, William; 14, Lieutenant, 10 June 1766, 24 October 1760; 14, Capt.- Lieut., 22 November 1775; 14, Captain, 15 October 1775; 49, Major, 12 October 1778
Browne, William; 52, Captain, 24 June 1771; "Spy at Lexington and Concord; Asst. Engineer at Boston, 1775; Extra Major of Bde, 1777
Brownlow, Charles; 57, Captain, 14 December 1774; 57, Major, 18 September 1779; 57, Lt. Colonel, 31 May 1782; WIA Fts. Clinton and Montgomery, 6 October 1777; Cmd. Gren. Bn ., 1783
Brownrigg, -; 14, Ensign, 22 November 1775;
Brownrigg, J. Studh; 38, Ensign, 28 January 1771, 26 December 1770; 38, Lieutenant, 22 November 1775; Barrack Master, New York 1781
Bruce, Andrew; 38, Major, 25 July 1771; 54, Lt. Colonel, 10 March 1777; Am., Brigadier General, date unknown; WIA Bunker Hill, 17 June 1775; ADC to Sir Henry Clinton 1781; Brig. gen. date not listed in NAAL, 1783
Bruce, Hon. Thomas; 65, Lt. Colonel, 19 March 1770;
Bruce, James; 70, Lt. Colonel, 9 February 1775; ADC to Sir Henry Clinton, 1781
Bruce, James; 76, Ensign, 31 December 1777; 70, Lieutenant, 10 November 1780
Bruce, John; 76, Captain, 27 December 1777;
Bruce, William; Hosp. Phys. Extra., 25 December 1776; Hosp. Physician, 1778; May have been surgeon prior to appointment at phys. extra.; Died prior to 27 March 1780
Bruch, Cudsworth; 15, Ensign, 7 December 1781
Brudenell, Rev. Mr.; Chaplain, 1 September 1780; Staff chaplain at New York
Brudnell, Thomas; 24, Ensign, 1 December 1778; 62, Lieutenant, 1 January 1781

Bruen, Henry; 63, Captain, 29 October 1763; 15, Major, 12 July 1777; Lt. Colonel, 20 November 1780; Extra Depty. Quartermaster Gen., 1777

Bruere, George; 18, Lieutenant, 4 February 1769, 16 March 1761

Bruere, George; 3/60, Captain, 15 November 1776; Son of Royal Governor of the Bahamas; Brother of John; Petitioned Gage for a company in the 14th Foot after his brother's death

Bruere, John; 14, Lieutenant, 17 April 1773; Commission date also possibly 1763; DOW Bunker Hill; Listed as Adjutant in Howe OB; Son of Royal Governor of the Bahamas; Brother of George

Buchan, Hugh; 31, Lieutenant, 6 March 1776;

Buchanan, Alexander; 26, Ensign, 2 December 1777; RA, Captain, 1 January 1759

Buchanan, Francis Jr.; Major; 23 July 1772

Buchanan, Peter; 74, Ensign, 1 September 1781

Buchanan, Rob. Ham.; 21, 2nd Lieut., 24 July 1776; 21, 1st Lieut., 13 March 1779

Buchanan, William; 47, Ensign, 20 February 1773; ADC to Gen. Howe, 19 June 1775

Buchanan, William; 35, Lieutenant, 20 March 1772; Died 6 February 1777; 35, Capt.- Lieut., 4 January 1777

Buckeridge, Charles Allen; 37, Ensign, 9 May 1774; 37, Lieutenant, 20 December 1776; WIA Germantown, 4 October 1777; Lost at sea, 12 August 1778

Buckeridge, R'd Henry; 17, Captain, 29 April 1782

Buckley, William; 29, Ensign, 9 July 1776

Bulkeley, James; 22, Ensign, 27 May 1776; 7, Lieutenant, 10 January 1777; 43, Captain, 21 May 1778

Bulkeley, John; 14, Ensign, 17 June 1777

Bulkeley, Richard; 59, Ensign, 30 October 1772

Bull, John; 6, Captain, 30 September 1772

Bullock, Richard; 4, Ensign, 14 September 1775; 4, Lieutenant, 24 January 1777; 4, Captain, 3 December 1779

Bunbury, Abraham; 62, Captain, 21 December 1775; WIA Stillwater, 7 October 1777

Bunbury, Benjamin; 17 LD, Lieutenant, 30 June 1766; Retired 10 May 1776 or 31 October 1776

Bunbury, Joseph; 49, Lieutenant, 14 January 1775

Bunbury, Thomas; 47, Ensign, 18 June 1775; 47, Lieutenant, 6 June 1777; Died 9 March 1780

Bunbury, Thomas; 16, Ensign, 9 May 1782; From volunteer

Bunbury, William; 54, Lieutenant, 27 March 1765, 8 December 1762; 54, Capt.- Lieut., 17 August 1777; 54, Captain, 16 November 1777, 17 August 1777

Bunbury, William; 17, Ensign, 23 August 1775; 49, Lieutenant, 28 August 1776; Faced a court of inquiry in 1787 for drinking tea with the QM Sgt. and eating with the Sgt. Major

Burbutt, Burton Gage; 5, Ensign, 20 July 1774

Burch, James; 4, Chaplain, 2 December 1768; Leave of Absence from 15 July 1778 until 15 July 1779

Burchoft, Samuel; 16 LD, Mate, 1 June 1778; Listed as Commander in Chief's promotion

Burgoyne, John; 16 LD, Colonel, 18 March 1763; Major General; 25 May 1772; Am., Lieutenant General, 1 September 1775; Resigned 1779; MP Prestons, 1768-1792

Burke, -; 62, Ensign, 18 August 1778

Burke, John; 46, Ensign, 12 January 1781

Burnett, George; 33, Captain, 16 April 1768; Scottish, born 1744; First commissioned at age 16

Burnett, John; 8, Lieutenant, 21 April 1768, 8 March 1764; 8, Capt.- Lieut., 12 December 1781; Son of a navy captain; Served briefly in the navy before entering the army

Burnett, Peter; 14, Quartermaster, 10 June 1768; 14, Ensign, 24 July 1772; 14, Lieutenant, 25 March 1774

Burnett, Robert; 21, 1st Lieut., 1 April 1776

Burnett, William; 26, Ensign, 13 February 1781

Burns, John; 46, Ensign, 8 September 1775; 46, Lieutenant, 12 August 1778

Burrand, Henry; 4/60, Lieutenant, 6 February 1776; 4/60, Captain, 18 September 1777; From RA; Served in America 1778-1783; Acting artillery and engineer officer at St. Augustine, 1779; MP Lymington, 1780-1788

Burroes, James; 7, Lieutenant, 24 July 1775; 7, Capt.- Lieut., 18 September 1780; 7, Captain, 18 September 1780

Burroughs, -; 47, Lieutenant, 1 January 1780

Burton, Richard; 4, Ensign, 18 August 1780

Bush, George; 34, Quartermaster, 22 October 1779; Died 26 December 1779

Butler, James Goddard; 4, Lieutenant, 22 April 1775; Retired 5 July 1777

Butler, John; 83, Ensign, 2 April 1783

Butler, William; 65, Major, 16 May 1766; 38, Lt. Colonel, 1 August 1775; WIA Bunker Hill, 17 June 1775; Assistant Commissary 1777; Retired October 1778

Butler, William; 49, Ensign, 26 May 1781

Butler, William; 8, Ensign, 22 November 1775; Also Walter; American; Also held a lieutenant's commission in Butler's Rangers; Served on expeditions with Indian allies; KIA Canada Creek, NY, 30 October 1781

Butter, James; 83, Adjutant, date unknown; 83, Lieutenant, 18 January 1778

Butterwick, Robert; 15, Captain, 7 July 1775

Buttricke, George; 18, Quartermaster, 11 July 1767; 18, Ensign, 21 January 1773; 18, Lieutenant, 15 November 1776; English, born 1733; First commission at age 31; From quartermaster 46th Foot; Previously sergeant-major of 1st Bn. 60th Foot; To Western Essex Militia as Captain-Lieutenant 24 February 1780; Letters from his service in Illinois in Pennsylvania Hist. Magazine

Bygrave, Wm. Aug.; 16 LD, Cornet, 25 December 1775; 26, Captain, 16 January 1782

Byng, George; 30, Lieutenant, 17 November 1780

Byrd, Thomas Talyor; 3/60, Captain, 14 July 1776; At Pensacola, 1779; ADC to Gen. Robertson, 29 January 1778; Returned to America and died in Virginia in 1802

Byron, John; 2FG, Lieut. & Capt., 1 May 1777; From ensign in the 68th Foot

Cadogan, Edward; 7, Lieutenant, 24 November 1775; 49, Captain, 7 August 1778; Died St. Lucia, 5 January 1779

Cahill, Matthew; 20, Surgeon, 13 September 1769; Retired 7 April 1784; Died 27 June 1800

Cairn, Edward; 43, Captain, 8 April 1762; 43, Major, 10 July 1775; Also Cane or Cone; Appointed Town Major at Boston, 21 November 1774; Retired 7 October 1775

Cairns, David; 1/84, Lieutenant, 16 July 1776

Calcroft, Hen. Fox; 21, 2nd Lieut., 18 December 1776

Calder, Patrick; 64, Capt.- Lieut., 2 July 1770; Irish, born 1739; First commissioned at age 17; WIA Danbury, 28 April 1777; Retired 13 April 1778

Calder, Sir Henry Bt.; 49, Lt. Colonel, 12 July 1773, 6 November 1769; Colonel, 25 November 1778;

Calderwood, William; 16, Ensign, 10 June 1772; 16, Lieutenant, 22 November 1775; KIA Roupel's Ferry, SC, 3 February 1779

Caldwell, David; Hosp. Apothecary, 1 January 1776; From surgeon, 9th Foot; To half pay; Died Dublin, 19 May 1787

Caldwell, Fitzmaurice; 46, Lieutenant, 23 August 1775; WIA aboard HMS Sultan serving as marine, 6 July 1779

Caldwell, Henry; Am., Major, 2 September 1772; Am., Lt. Colonel, 10 June 1776

Caldwell, John; 8, Lt. Colonel, 27 October 1772; Irish; Died at Ft. Niagara, 31 October 1776

Caldwell, John; 8, Ensign, 26 December 1774; 8, Lieutenant, 11 May 1778; Son of an Irish Baronet; Nephew of Lt. Col. John Cadwell; Irish; "Learned the military arts in Dublin" prior to commissioning; His uncle suggested to his father that he be given a eighty pound allowance annually while on the Great Lakes and 100 pounds at any other posting

Caley, Cornelius; 20, Lieutenant, 14 July 1781, 29 March 1781

Callaghan, James; 63, Ensign, 14 March 1772; 63, Lieutenant, 22 November 1775; Also O'Callaghan; ADC to Gen. Howe, 19 June 1775; Port. extant in JSAHR

Callander, Kenneth; 1/42, Ensign, 3 August 1778; 1/42, Lieutenant, 31 December 1780; From volunteer; Had a reputation as an excellent swordsman; Fought a duel with Ens. Eld, January 1780"

Callander, William; 80, Ensign, 10 March 1781; 80, Lieutenant, 8 September 1781; From ensign, Queen's American Rangers, 11 June 1780

Calvert, Harry; 23, 2nd Lieut., 24 April 1778; 23, 1st Lieut., 2 October 1779;

Cambel, John; RE, Eng. extra. & Cpt.-Lt., 4 March 1776; In America from 1766-1780; Served at West Florida, New York

Cameron, -; 1/71, Ensign, 25 April 1780; From volunteer; Possibly WIA Charleston, 26 April 1780

Cameron, Alexander; 46, Lieutenant, 31 December 1769; 37, Captain, 12 August 1778; Married 3 April 1781

Cameron, Alexander; 1/71, Ensign, 4 November 1780

Cameron, Angus; 2/71, Lieutenant, 17 October 1781; Died Yorktown, 20 October 1781

Cameron, Angus; 1/71, Ensign, 20 September 1779; Died Charleston, 5 May 1780

Cameron, Angus; 2/71, Ensign, 30 September 1779; Died 3 November 1780

Cameron, Charles; Captain, 1782; Extra Major of Bde

Cameron, Charles; 1/71, Capt.- Lieut., 10 March 1777; 1/71, Captain, 3 August 1778; KIA Savannah, 29 December 1779

Cameron, Charles; 76, Captain, 1 January 1778

Cameron, Charles; 1/71, Lieutenant, 23 November 1775, 28 October 1761

Cameron, Donald; 1/71, Adjutant, 23 November 1775; 2/71, Ensign, 2 December 1775

Cameron, Donald; 2/71, Lieutenant, 3 August 1778; Never joined; Died 2 November 1780

Cameron, Duncan; 43, Captain, 17 August 1773; POW, Redoubt No. 10, 14 October 1781

Cameron, Evan; 76, Lieutenant, 10 January 1778;

Cameron, James; 1/42, Lieutenant, 28 August 1775, 8 September 1761

Cameron, John; 74, Lieutenant, 24 December 1777

Campbell, Alexander; 74, Major, 26 December 1777

Campbell, Alexander; 62, Captain, 6 November 1772, 26 September 1772

Campbell, Alexander; 63, Captain, 12 October 1781; ADC, 1782 or 1783

Campbell, Alexander; 74, Captain, 25 December 1777

Campbell, Alexander; 2/84, Captain, 14 June 1775; From half pay 106th Foot; WIA Bunker Hill, 17 June 1775 & Kennett Square, PA, 9 September 1777; Accused of spying at Philadelphia, 11 March 1778; Acquitted

Campbell, Alexander; 55, Ensign, 8 September 1775; 55, Lieutenant, 5 November 1777; WIA Princeton, 3 January 1777

Campbell, Alexander; 22, Ensign, 19 September 1780; Scottish, born 1761

Campbell, Alexander; 52, Ensign, 27 January 1777

Campbell, Alexander; 1/71, Ensign, 6 November 1780

Campbell, Alexander; 74, Ensign, 26 December 1777

Campbell, Alexander; Lieutenant; Prior to 1763, Serving as a volunteer with RA while on half pay most likely from the 42nd Foot; WIA Bunker Hill, 17 June 1775

Campbell, Archibald; 2/71, Lt. Colonel, 23 November 1775; Colonel, 7 December 1770; From Inverness, Argyll, 1739-1791; Served in India until 1773; POW Boston, 17 June 1776; Exchanged for Ethan Allen; MP Stirling Bughs, 1774-1780; Buried Westminster Abbey

Campbell, Archibald; 29, Captain, 2 August 1769; 29, Major, 17 November 1780;

Campbell, Archibald; 69, Captain, 10 May 1780;

Campbell, Archibald; 74, Captain, 20 December 1777

Campbell, Archibald; 74, Captain, 22 December 1777

Campbell, Archibald; 26, Lieutenant, 25 December 1770, 26 July 1760, KIA Ward's House, NY 16 or 17 March 1777

Campbell, Archibald; 1/71, Lieutenant, 8 January 1778

Campbell, Archibald; 1/71, Lieutenant, 23 December 1775; KIA 7 January 1778

Campbell, Archibald; 2/71, Lieutenant, 28 November 1775

Campbell, Archibald; 2/71, Adjutant, 24 November 1775; 2/71, Lieutenant, 29 November 1775; POW Boston, 17 June 1776; Probably died 9 September 1780

Campbell, Archibald; 2/71, Lieutenant, 29 December 1778

Campbell, Archibald; 74, Lieutenant, 25 December 1777

Campbell, Archibald; 1/71, Ensign, 25 November 1775

Campbell, Archibald; 2/71, Ensign, 28 November 1775

Campbell, Archibald; 2/71, Ensign, 11 March 1777

Campbell, Archibald; 2/84, Ensign, 11 December 1779; From volunteer

Campbell, Charles; 1/71, Captain, 29 December 1778; POW Boston, 17 June 1776; KIA Fishing Creek, SC, either 18 August 1780 or 18 September 1780

Campbell, Charles; 1/71, Capt.- Lieut., 11 November 1778

Campbell, Charles; 1/71, Lieutenant, 25 November 1775

Campbell, Colin; 19, Captain, 30 June 1780

Campbell, Colin; 35, Captain, 28 June 1775; Scottish; Attended St. Andrews University; WIA Bunker Hill, 17 June 1775

Campbell, Colin; 35, Lieutenant, 27 July 1759; 35, Capt.- Lieut., 17 July 1775, 11 March 1762; 35, Captain, 22 November 1775; WIA Bunker Hill, 17 June 1775

Campbell, Colin; 2/42, Captain, 24 March 1780; From 36th Foot

Campbell, Colin; 55, Lieutenant, 26 September 1772; 44, Capt.- Lieut., 4 October 1776; 44, Captain, 4 October 1776; Scottish, born 1754; First commissioned at age 17; WIA Princeton, 3 January 1777; Retired 28 November 1777?

Campbell, Colin; 1/71, Captain, 14 October 1778; WIA Stono Ferry, SC, 20 June 1779

Campbell, Colin; 1/84, Captain, 14 June 1775, 25 May 1772, From half pay 7th Foot

Campbell, Colin; 7, Lieutenant, 3 June 1774

Campbell, Colin; 74, Lieutenant, 27 December 1777; Died about 18 May 1782

Campbell, Colin; 74, Lieutenant, 28 December 1777; A Colin Campbell died prior to May 1782; Also one a native of America

Campbell, Colin; 74, Lieutenant, 31 December 1777; A Colin Campbell died prior to May 1782; Also one a native of America

Campbell, Colin; 74, Lieutenant, 2 January 1778; A Colin Campbell died prior to May 1782; Also one a native of America

Campbell, Colin; 1/71, Quartermaster, 17 October 1778; 1/71, Lieutenant, 7 October 1777

Campbell, David; 4, Ensign, 11 November 1773; 35, Lieutenant, 29 December 1775

Campbell, David; 63, Lieutenant, 13 June 1778; WIA Eutaw Springs, 8 September 1781

Campbell, David; 26, Ensign, 14 November 1777

Campbell, David; 1/71, Quartermaster, 23 November 1775; Never joined

Campbell, Donald; 74, Ensign, 22 December 1777; 74, Lieutenant, 13 October 1781; Died 1782

Campbell, Donald; 74, Captain, 19 December 1777; KIA Virginia, prior to 22 June 1781

Campbell, Dougal; 1/42, Lieutenant, 30 August 1775, 1 November 1761, Retired 27 October 1777

Campbell, Dougal; 1/71, Lieutenant, 22 December 1775; Removed to S. Carolina Loyalists and Cpt. Lt. and Adj. 26 May 1778

Campbell, Dougal; 2/71, Lieutenant, 14 December 1775

Campbell, Dugald; 74, Capt.- Lieut., 20 January 1779; 74, Captain, 22 June 1781; Replaced KIA namesake

Campbell, Dugald; 1/42, Ensign, 31 May 1777; 1/42, Lieutenant, 26 August 1778

Campbell, Dugald; 2/42, Lieutenant, 26 August 1778; POW Boston, 17 June 1776 as volunteer with 2/71st, Newfoundland, 1778

Campbell, Dugald; 74, Lieutenant, 19 December 1777

Campbell, Dugald; 1/42, Ensign, 18 October 1778; 1/42, Lieutenant, 1 January 1781

Campbell, Duncan; 2/84, Captain, 14 June 1775; From half pay 42nd Foot

Campbell, Duncan; 15, Lieutenant, 15 August 1775

Campbell, Duncan; 26, Quartermaster, 13 July 1767; 26, Ensign, 1 March 1770; 26, Lieutenant, 25 September 1781; POW, Ft. Ticonderoga, 10 May 1775

Campbell, Duncan; 1/71, Ensign, 14 October 1778; 1/71, Lieutenant, 18 September 1780; Probably a POW Boston, 17 June 1776 as volunteer

Campbell, Duncan; 74, Lieutenant, 3 January 1778

Campbell, Duncan; 26, Ensign, 19 October 1778; Probably a POW Boston, 17 June 1776 as volunteer

Campbell, Duncan; 2/84, Ensign, 6 November 1780; From volunteer

Campbell, George; 1/42, Ensign, 27 September 1777; 1/42, Lieutenant, 18 October 1778; Scottish, born 1761; First commissioned at age 15; Probably a POW Boston, 17 June 1776 as volunteer; Married in Spring 1780

Campbell, Henry Fletcher; 35, Colonel, 10 August 1764; Major General; 25 May 1775; Lieutenant General; 29 August 1777, Scottish; Son of Andrew Lord Milton, head of the Fletchers of Saltoun; Owned extensive estates in East Lothian; Attended Dalkeith School

Campbell, Hugh; 35, Ensign, 15 August 1775; 35, Lieutenant, 18 October 1778; CM for killing another officer in a duel over the clumsy paddling of a canoe, April 1783

Campbell, Hugh; 1/71, Lieutenant, 21 December 1775; POW Boston, 17 June 1776 ; WIA Camden, 16 August 1780; Promoted to captaincy in 94th Foot

Campbell, James; 2/71, Major, 24 April 1781

Campbell, James; 33, Captain, 25 May 1772; Scottish, born 1742; First commissioned at age 18

Campbell, James; 69, Captain, 15 March 1776

Campbell, James; 40, Ensign, 1 May 1775; 40, Lieutenant, 14 March 1777

Campbell, James; 1/42, Ensign, 24 April 1774; 1/42, Lieutenant, 20 March 1776;1/42, Captain, 18 August 1778; Scottish, born 1753; First commissioned at age 20; Promoted to captain 77th Foot, 27 December 1777 or from lieut. 57th Foot; Returned to regiment 1778

Campbell, James; 54, Quartermaster, 18 July 1779; 54, Ensign, 2 September 1778; 54, Lieutenant, 18 February 1781

Campbell, James; 57, Lieutenant, 13 May 1769

Campbell, James; 1/71, Lieutenant, 20 October 1778; Died 8 September 1780

Campbell, James; 55, Ensign, 10 December 1779

Campbell, James; 2/71, Ensign, 26 August 1776

Campbell, John; 57, Lt. Colonel, 1 May 1773, 1 February 1762; 57, Colonel, 17 November 1780, 1 May 1777; Am., Major General; 2 July 1773; 19 February 1779, POW Pensacola; ADC to the King

Campbell, John; 74, Lt. Col. Comdt., 25 December 1777, 25 May 1772; 74, Colonel; 17 November 1780; Am., Brigadier General, 1780?; From Ballimore; Served in the F&I War with 78th Foot; Died 10 September 1794; Brig. gen. date not listed in NAAL, 1783

Campbell, John; 22, Lt. Colonel, 24 June 1775; English, born 1732; Resigned 11 October 1778

Campbell, John; 74, Major, 30 December 1777; Exchanged to 100th Foot, 7 February 1781; Appears to have exchanged into the 2/42nd Foot in 1783; His army date of rank is also given as 23 October 1779, that is probably inaccurate

Campbell, John; 1/42, Ensign, 10 August 1775; 1/42, Lieutenant, 31 May 1777

Campbell, John; 40, Ensign, 14 March 1777; 40, Lieutenant, 27 October 1777; 55, Captain, 12 May 1778; WIA Germantown, 4 October 1777

Campbell, John; 1/71, Captain, 2 December 1775; Possibly also held a provincial majority dated 20 June 1779; KIA Savannah, 8 April 1779

Campbell, John; 74, Captain, 23 December 1777

Campbell, John; 74, Captain, 24 December 1777

Campbell, John; 74, Capt.- Lieut., 23 December 1777

Campbell, John; 23, 2nd Lieut., 24 November 1775; 23, 1st Lieut., 16 October 1776; Died prior to 15 December 1781

Campbell, John; 44, Lieutenant, 5 July 1772; Irish, born, 1751; First commissioned at age 19; Adjutant to Light Infantry battalion, 16 December 1775

Campbell, John; 4/60, Ensign, 10 February 1776; 4/60, Lieutenant, 3 October 1781; From 3/60th; Died at Spanish Town, 3 September 1781

Campbell, John; 7, Lieutenant, 9 May 1774

Campbell, John; 2/71, Lieutenant, 24 December 1775

Campbell, John; 74, Lieutenant, 30 December 1777; KIA Yorktown, 1781

Campbell, John; 82, Lieutenant, 1 September 1781

Campbell, John; 1/71, Ensign, 19 October 1781

Campbell, John; 74, Ensign, 20 December 1777

Campbell, John; 74, Ensign, 23 December 1777

Campbell, Kenneth; 74, Lieutenant, 4 January 1778

Campbell, Lawrence Robert; 2/71, Captain, 6 December 1775; POW Boston, 19 June 1776; WIA Stony Point, NY, 16 July 1779

Campbell, Mungo; 55, Major, 31 August 1770; 52, Lt. Colonel, 16 June 1776; Scottish, born 1732; First commissioned at age 17; KIA Fort Clinton, 6 October 1777

Campbell, Neil; 74, Quartermaster, 19 December 1777; 74, Lieutenant, 21 December 1777; 2/84, Captain, 7 July 1780

Campbell, Patrick; 44, Captain, 10 December 1768; Major; 23 July 1772, Scottish, born 1741; First commissioned at age 18

Campbell, Patrick; 2/71, Captain, 25 November 1775; 1/71, Major, 26 October 1779; POW on Warship, c. 1779; POW Yorktown Redoubt No. 10, 14 October 1781

Campbell, Patrick; 2/71, Captain, 30 December 1775

Campbell, Patrick; 45, Lieutenant, 3 August 1778

Campbell, Robert; 2/84, Lieutenant, 14 June 1775; 2/84, Captain, 20 September 1780; In Boston, 1775; WIA Eutaw Springs, 8 September 1781

Campbell, Robert; 38, Lieutenant, 15 August 1775, 21 April 1760

Campbell, Robert; 2/71, Lieutenant, 30 November 1780

Campbell, Robert; 35, Ensign, 22 November 1775

Campbell, Robert; 1/71, Ensign, 29 November 1775

Campbell, Robert; 2/71, Ensign, 19 October 1778

Campbell, Smollett; 2/71, Ensign, 1 December 1775; 2/71, Lieutenant, 3 August 1778; WIA Savannah, 9 October 1779 while serving with mounted troops; Died near Camden, SC, August 1780

Campbell, Thomas; 30, Captain, 9 October 1778

Campbell, Thomas B.; Hosp., Mate, Prior to 1783; Stationed at New York, 1783

Campbell, Touchet; 38, Ensign, 22 November 1775; 38, Lieutenant, 7 February 1779

Campbell, William; 24, Lieutenant, 26 September 1772; 24, Capt.- Lieut., 1 December 1778; Asst. Deputy QMG, 1781

Campbell, William; 6, Lieutenant, 15 August 1775, 14 February 1759

Campbell, William; 83, Captain, 17 January 1778

Campbell, William; FG, Adjutant, 7 June 1777; Adjutant 2 Bn.; KIA New Haven, CT, 5 July 1779; Commissioned as ensign posthumously in 3rd Foot Guards. The earliest known commission from the ranks in the 3rd Guards

Cancannon, James; RA, 2nd Lieut., 14 February 1782

Cane, Maurice; 6, Lt. Colonel, 7 June 1775, 25 May 1772

Cannon, John; 57, Captain, 9 October 1775; Retired 28 April 1778

Cannon, Patrick; 16 LD, Adjutant, 11 March 1777; 16 LD, Cornet, 14 December 1776

Carden, Hans; 3/60, Captain, 1 February 1780; Died 30 September 1781

Carden, John; 19, Lieutenant, 20 March 1779; From volunteer?

Carleton, Christopher; 31, Captain, 25 May 1772; 29, Major, 13 September 1777

Carleton, Sir Guy K.B.; 47, Colonel, 2 April 1772; 84, Colonel, 15 June 1782; Major General ; 25 May 1772; Lieutenant General; 29 August 1772; Am., General, 1 January 1776; 1724-1808; Gov. of Quebec, 1768-1778 & 1785 -1795; Later Baron Dorchester

Carleton, Thomas; 29, Lt. Colonel, 2 August 1776, 31 July 1776

Carlisle, Robert; RA, 1st Lieut., 1 January 1771

Carmichael, And.; 16 LD, Cornet, 26 December 1775

Carmichael, James; 40, Quartermaster, 13 November 1775; 40, Ensign, 17 May 1779

Carmichael, Robert; 10, Lieutenant, 25 December 1770, 1 April 1761; 10, Captain, 2 June 1777; Retired 13 April 1778

Carncross, Hugh; 47, Major, 29 September 1770

Carnie, Thomas; 83, Lieutenant, 25 October 1781

Carr, Robert; 35, Lt. Colonel, 5 March 1775; Attended the Royal Military Academy in Caen, France; DOW White Plains, 28 October 1776

Carrique, Richard; 16, Lieutenant, 4 February 1769

Carrol, Edward; 16, Lieutenant, 20 May 1771

Carroll, Dwyer; 49, Ensign, 1 April 1773; 49, Lieutenant, 22 November 1775; Retired 31 May 1778

Carroll, Fredrick; 16, Lieutenant, 4 February 1769; KIA Pensacola, 7 July 1781

Carruthers, John; 47, Ensign, 16 May 1780

Carter, Christopher; Hosp., Mate, Prior to 1783; Stationed at New York, 1783

Carter, John; RA, Captain, 7 December 1763; POW Saratoga; Died Virginia, 17 March 1779

Carter, William; 40, Ensign, 20 February 1773, 5 June 1771; 40, Lieutenant, 22 November 1775; Retired 27 October 1777

Carthrae, John; 82, Quartermaster, 3 January 1778; 82, Lieutenant, 3 January 1778, 4 October 1766, At Siege of Penobscott

Cartwright, Edward; 4/60, Ensign, 4 September 1779

Cary, Hon. George; 43, Colonel, 26 September 1766; Major General; 30 April 1770; Lieutenant General; 30 April 1770

Cary, Isaac; 17, Ensign, 7 July 1775; 17, Lieutenant, 7 August 1776; Also Carey; Arrested for marauding in 1778, released after a lengthy pre-trial confinement

Casement, William; 3, Lieutenant, 20 December 1770; Died 7 November 1781

Castell, John; 55, Ensign, 11 November 1777; 55, Lieutenant, 22 December 1780

Castleman, John; 69, Adjutant, 9 October 1781; 69, Lieutenant, 3 March 1780

Castleman, Paul Colville; 69, Captain, 14 May 1781

Cathcart, Andrew; 15, Captain, 21 August 1765; 10, Major, 29 June 1778; WIA Brandywine, 11 September 1777 & Monmouth, 28 June 1778 with 1st. Gren. Bn.

Cathcart, Hon. Charles Allan; 23, 2nd Lieut., 10 March 1777; From Clackmanan, 1759-1788; From volunteer

Cathcart, John; 28, Captain, 14 March 1772

Cathcart, William, Lord; 17 LD, Lieutenant, 14 November 1777; 17 LD, Captain, 10 December 1777; 38, Major, 13 April 1779; Born 1755; Brother-in-law of Sir Thomas Graham; Read for the bar in Edinburgh before joining the army; ADC to Sir Henry Clinton, 25 May 1778

Cather, John; 40, Ensign, 12 May 1775;40, Lieutenant, 26 January 1780; Also Cates; Died 7 April 1781

Caulfield, William; 19, Ensign, 29 June 1780

Cavan, Richard, Earl of; 15, Colonel, 7 September 1775; 55, Colonel, 3 August 1774; Major General ; 25 May 1772; Lieutenant General; 29 August 1777, Irish, born 1732; First commissioned at age 13; Died 2 November 1778 in Ireland

Cavanagh, Arthur; 19, Ensign, 17 November 1780

Cavendish, Fredrick Lord; 34, Colonel, 30 October 1760; Lieutenant General, 30 April 1770; 1729-1803; MP Derby, 1754-1780

Cawthorne, William; 44, Captain, 15 August 1775, 16 December 1761; Major; 29 August 1777

Chadwicke, -; 27, Ensign, 1 September 1775

Chadwicke, James; 16, Captain, 4 February 1769; Retired 24 May 1776

Chaloner, Walter; Depty. Commissary Gen., December 1779

Chambault, F. de; 24, Ensign, 5 October 1777; 44, Lieutenant, 3 November 1779

Chambers, Ab. Annex; 69, Ensign, 18 May 1780; WIA St. Kitts, 28 January 1782

Chambers, Brett; 5, Lieutenant, 20 July 1774; Died 30 or 31 March 1777

Chamier, Daniel; Commissary General, 1777; Auditor of Accounts, 1778

Champagne, Forbes; 4, Ensign, 29 May 1773; 4, Lieutenant, 26 January 1776; 23, Captain, 24 April 1779; Irish; Son of the Dean of Clanmacnoise; WIA Germantown, 4 October 1777; Adj. 1st L.I., 19 March 1778; Ast. AG, 10 June 1778

Champagne, Josias; 31, Adjutant, 1 June 1777; 31, Ensign, 28 January 1775, 24 May 1776; 31, Lieutenant, 1 June 1777

Chandler, Edward; 46, Lieutenant, 1 September 1771; 49, Capt.- Lieut., 6 January 1779; 27, Captain, 4 December 1779

Chapman, Benjamin; 18, Captain, 2 June 1771; Irish, born 1744; First commissioned at age 16

Chapman, Ligonier; 37, Adjutant, 11 August 1778; 37, Lieutenant, 3 March 1772; WIA Brandywine, 11 September 1777

Chapman, Thomas; 23, 2nd Lieut., 20 May 1776; 23, 1st Lieut., 3 May 1778

Charleton, Thomas; RA, 2nd Lieut., 14 February 1782

Charleton, Thomas R.; RA, 1st Lieut., 7 July 1779; RA, Capt.- Lieut., 1 January 1782; WIA Savannah, 1779

Charleton, William; RA, 1st Lieut., 7 July 1779

Charlton, Edward; 5, Ensign, 4 July 1777; 5, Lieutenant, 21 January 1779; WIA Bunker Hill, 17 June 1775

Charlton, John; Hosp., Surgeon, February 1775; Surgeon to the hospitals in North America

Charlton, John; 2/60, Lieutenant, 6 March 1777; On command in New York in 1776; Possibly WIA 25 September 1780; Returned to Ireland to recover health, 25 September 1780

Charlton, William; 20, Lieutenant, 2 March 1776

Charlton, William; 5, Ensign, 14 March 1772; 5, Lieutenant, 23 June 1775; DOW Germantown, 7 November 1777; Listed as a captain on Inman's List

Cheap, James; 74, Lieutenant, 7 January 1778

Cheshire, Edward; 40, Ensign, 20 October 1774; Retired 6 May 1777

Chester, William; 15, Chaplain, 9 July 1779

Chester, William; 35, Major, 1 February 1781, 17 November 1780

Chetwynd, Hon. William; 52, Ensign, 21 February 1772; 52, Lieutenant, 18 June 1775; 46, Captain, 23 December 1776; WIA Bunker Hill, 17 June 1775; WIA Boston Neck, 30 July 1775; ADC to Maj. Gen. Valentine Jones, 14 May 1776; Died St. Lucia, prior to 14 January 1779

Chewton, George, Viscount; 2FG, Lieut. & Capt., 12 August 1773; 2FG, Capt. & Lt. Col., 16 May 1778; 87, Lt. Col. Comdt., 4 October 1779, 16 May 1778, 1751-1789; Later 4th Earl Waldgrave; MP Newcastle under Lyme, 1774-1780; ADC to Gen. Cornwallis, February 1776-January 1778 & 1779 to 1781; ADC to Gen. Clinton, 1781

Chilton, Robert; 69, Lieutenant, 24 December 1778

Chisholm, Alexander; Hosp., Mate, Prior to 1783; Stationed at New York, 1783

Chisholme, Colin; 1/71, Ensign, 3 August 1778; 2/71, Lieutenant, 18 September 1780; Died 17 January 1781

Chisholme, Colin; 2/71, Surgeon, 24 November 1775; To half pay, 1783; M.D. Kings Coll. Abd, 1793; Fellow Royal Society, 1808; Author of Manual of Diseases of Tropical Climates... 8 vol. London, 1795; Practiced Grenada & Bristol; Died London, 1825

Chisholme, Duncan; 1/71, Captain, 26 November 1775

Chisholme, Valentine; 1/42, Lieutenant, 10 December 1768, 23 July 1762, Scottish, born 1731; First commissioned at age 29; Retired 31 May 1777

Christie, Gabriel; 1/60, Lt. Colonel, 18 September 1775, 27 January 1762; 2/60, Col. Comdt., 14 May 1778; Quartermaster general in Canada, 1776

Christie, John; 6, Lieutenant, 30 September 1772; 4/60, Captain, 26 September 1775; Died June 1782

Christie, Napier; 22, Ensign, 15 August 1775; 3FG, Ensign, 27 May 1776; 3FG, Lieut. & Capt., 18 September 1779; In additional company, 22nd Foot; To Foot Guards, 27 May 1776; POW Yorktown

Christie, Robert; 38, Lieutenant, 27 October 1763; 38, Capt.- Lieut., 21 July 1775; 38, Captain, 22 November 1775; WIA Bunker Hill, 17 June 1775

Chrystie, James; 2/71, Lieutenant, 7 December 1775; Asst. Commissary, 1778

Church, John; 49, Ensign, 26 May 1779

Church, T. Toweron; 24, Chaplain, 21 December 1775

Churchill, George; 34, Captain, 6 January 1776

Churchill, Horace; 18, Ensign, 24 June 1773; 40, Captain, 1 August 1780, 4 October 1779

Clark, James; 83, Captain, 8 December 1780

Clarke, Alured; 54, Lt. Colonel, 26 October 1775, 20 September 1775, Port in Strachan, plate 7

Clarke, Alured; 7, Lt. Colonel, 10 March 1777; Am., Brigadier General, date unknown ; Possibly a POW, Cowpens; Brig. gen. date not listed in NAAL, 1783

Clarke, Francis Rush; Inspector & Superintendent of His Majesty's Provision Train, 1781

Clarke, George; 43, Ensign, 7 July 1780; Died 17 February 1783

Clarke, J.G.; 55, Ensign, 3 December 1781

Clarke, John; 59, Lieutenant, 23 July 1759

Clarke, John; 4/60, Quartermaster, 5 February 1776

Clarke, John Montague; 43, Ensign, 10 July 1775; From volunteer; Ensigncy also 12 July 1775; Retired 1 December 1779

Clarke, Robert; RA, 1st Lieut., 9 April 1782

Clarke, Robert; 80, Lieutenant, 4 February 1778

Clarke, Thomas; 31, Colonel, 3 May 1780; Am., Major General, 1 January 1776, 29 August 1777

Clarke, Thomas; 4/60, Ensign, 5 September 1779; From ensign, Georgia Loyalists

Clarke, William; 15, Ensign, 14 November 1775

Clarke, William; 15, Lieutenant, 14 November 1775; 15, Captain, 4 June 1777

Clarke, William; 35, Lieutenant, 28 June 1775

Clarke, William; 45, Lieutenant, 27 February 1782, 8 December 1781

Clarkson, -; 46, Adjutant, 2 October 1777; From sergeant; Depty. Barracks Master, Philadelphia, 1777

Clavering, Robert; 33, Ensign, 18 March 1782

Clavering, Sir John K. B.; 52, Colonel, 1 April 1762; Lieutenant General; 30 April 1770; Died British Isles, 13 May 1778

Clay, Wald. Pelh.; 40, Ensign, 27 May 1777; 40, Lieutenant, 17 May 1779

Clayton, Robert; 17, Captain, 1 May 1775; Attended Manchester School, class of 1762; Allowed to return to England, 1 January 1781

Cleghorn, George; 22, Ensign, 24 July 1775; 22, Lieutenant, 13 January 1777; From volunteer; WIA Rhode Island, 29 August 1778; To 38th Foot, June 1780; Captain, 26 June 1780

Cleland, W. Charles; 49, Ensign, 9 October 1778

Cleland, William; 33, Mate, date unknown ; 33, Surgeon, 5 November 1778; Exchanged to half pay, 82nd Foot, 8 February 1786; died c. 1817

Clements, Robert; 8, Lieutenant, 24 December 1770, 4 September 1756; 8, Captain, 29 March 1776; Served as a "private gentleman" in the First Troop of Horse Guards; Promoted lieutenant in 31st Foot, but reduced with all other former rankers in 1763; His protest obtained him a commission in the 8th Foot

Clephane, -; 65, Ensign, 5 February 1777

Clerges, George; 34, Ensign, 1 January 1777, 10 July 1776, Died 6 February 1783

Clerk, George; 43, Lt. Colonel, 8 February 1775; LI Bn. Commander, 1775-1776; Barrack Master General, 4 June 1776; Retired August 1780

Clerk, Thomas; 65, Surgeon, 13 January 1777; Hosp., Physician, 22 May 1781; M.D. Edin, 1776; Stationed at New York, 1783; To half pay 6 February 1784; Died 29 September 1794

Clerke, Francis Carr; 3FG, Lieut. & Capt., 26 July 1775; ADC to Gen. Burgoyne, DOW Bemis Heights, 13 October 1777

Cleveland, Samuel; RA, Lt. Colonel, 1 January 1771, 2 January 1762

Cleveland, Samuel; 7, Lieutenant, 26 March 1773;16, Captain, 24 May 1776; Granted six month leave of absence from 15 July 1778

Clewlow, George; 15, Ensign, 2 August 1775; 15, Lieutenant, 1 December 1775

Clieland, Molesworth; RA, 2nd Lieut., 15 March 1771; Also Cleland or Cleyland; KIA Skenesboro, NY, 6 July 1777

Cliffe, Loftus; 46, Lieutenant, 1 September 1771, 13 February 1762; 52, Capt.- Lieut., 13 April 1778; 52, Captain, 13 April 1778

Cliffe, Walter; 28, Ensign, 22 December 1776; 7, Lieutenant, 9 June 1778; From volunteer; Extant letters; Died 2 December 1781

Cliffe, Wastel; 63, Ensign, 31 August 1781

Clinton, Sir Henry K.B.; 84, Colonel, 16 December 1778; Am., Lieutenant General, 1 September 1775, 29 August 1777; Am., General, 1 January 1776; 1730-1795; MP Newark, 1774-1784

Close, Farmen; 65, Ensign, 23 November 1775

Clinton, Lord Thos. Pelham; 1FG, Capt. & Lt. Col., 5 April 1775; 1759-1797; MP Lewes, 1780-1796; ADC to Gen. Clinton; not at Yorktown.; Lord - Later Earl of Lincoln.; Promoted colonel 75th Foot in 1782

Clowes, George; 8, Ensign, 14 September 1770; 8, Lieutenant, 10 March 1776; Served at Fort Michilimackinac; Was known for shady financial dealings while serving on the Great Lakes; Served on expeditions with Indian allies

Clunes, John; 26, Ensign, 2 January 1782

Clunes, John; 28, Ensign, 20 September 1780

Coane, Conolly; 62, Lieutenant, 21 December 1775; Also Crane; served with Company of Marksmen, 23 August 1777

Coare, R. Thatcher; 17, Ensign, 6 September 1780

Coates, James; 19, Lt. Colonel, 26 October 1775, 11 September 1775

Coates, John; 29, Ensign, 26 July 1781

Cochrane, Hon. Charles; 7, Lieutenant, 1 April 1768; 4, Captain, 6 May 1774; Lexington Night Rider; Major British Legion, 1778; 1FG, Lieut. & Capt., 21 November 1778; 1FG, Capt. & Lt. Col., 25 January 1781; ADC to Gen.Cornwallis; KIA Yorktown

Cochrane, James; 82, Chaplain, 3 July 1778

Cochrane, Thomas; 23, 1st Lieut., 26 December 1770; 23, Capt.- Lieut., 22 November 1777; 23, Captain, 30 May 1778, 22 November 1777, WIA Bunker Hill, 17 June 1775

Cochrane, Thomas; 2/71, Ensign, 4 November 1780

Cockburn, John; RA, 1st Lieut., 7 July 1779; RA, 2nd Lieutenant, 7 August 1771; In South in July 1780; Also acting quartermaster

Cockburn, Peter; 35, Ensign, 1 February 1781; Scottish; Son of an ordinance officer, grandson of a clergyman; nephew of James Cockburne

Cockburn, Sir. W. J. Bt.; 26, Ensign, 26 May 1780

Cockburne, James; 35, Captain, 13 April 1767; 35, Major, 13 January 1776; 35, Lt. Colonel, 30 October 1776; Son of John Cockburne, a Kilkenny physician; Served in West Florida in the 1760s; Promoted ahead of seniors to lt. colonel for gallantry in action; Involved in a duel; CM and dismissed, June 1783

Cockburne, William; 35, Lieutenant, 12 April 1780; Son of James Cockburne; Served as a "volunteer" from age 10 until obtaining an ensigncy

Cockle, Teasdale; 37, Lieutenant, 15 August 1775, 27 November 1760, Also Taylor Croker; From Marines

Codd, Robert; 59, Ensign, 18 December 1770

Coffin, -; 33, Ensign, 12 October 1781

Coghlan, John; 23, 2nd Lieut., 9 February 1776; 7, Lieutenant, 18 January 1777

Coglan, Roger; 1/60, Ensign, 10 December 1780; 1/60, Lieutenant, 24 September 1781; With additional companies in England

Coker, William Lawrence; 38, Capt.- Lieut., 31 December 1769; DOW, Bunker Hill, 20 July 1775

Colden, Jonathon Massey; 44, Ensign, 31 January 1778; 44, Lieutenant, 8 September 1779; From 2nd Bn. New Jersey Loyalists; Drowned at sea, probably 28 October 1779

Cole, Pennel; Hosp., Surgeon, 1 January 1776; From mate in Gds., 1774; To half pay, 25 December 1783; Died Worcester, 25 June 1833

Cole, Thomas; 53, Adjutant, 6 April 1778; From sergeant major

Colhoun, Walter; 83, Lieutenant, 28 January 1778

Colins, Thomas; 1FG, Lieut. & Capt., 16 July 1773; 1FG, Capt. & Lt. Col., 22 February 1781; Major of Bde, March 1778; Died 1 June 1781

Colleton, Charles S.; RA, 2nd Lieut., 15 March 1771; Drowned on HMS Ontario or on Lake Ontario, 1 October 1780

Colley, Cha. Pleydell; 19, Lieutenant, 1 June 1778

Collier, Edward; 52, Lieutenant, 19 August 1774, 3 May 1770; 52, Capt.-Lieut., 8 May 1777; 52, Captain, 13 April 1778; WIA Fort Washington, 16 November 1776

Collier, William; RA, 2nd Lieutenant, 15 March 1771; Secretary to Major Gen. Wm. Phillips,

Collington, John Wheeler; 33, Ensign, 21 September 1777; 33, Lieutenant, 17 August 1780; Also Collingham; WIA Camden, 17 August 1780

Collins, Edward; 15, Ensign, 12 September 1777; 46, Lieutenant, 3 March 1779

Collins, Robert; RA, 1st Lieut., 1 January 1771; Killed in Charleston, SC magazine explosion, 15 May 1780

Collins, Thomas; 1FG, Lieut. & Capt., 6 July 1773; Major of Brigade

Colochoun, Ludovick; 2/71, Lieutenant, 15 December 1775; 74, Captain, 21 December 1777; 4/60, Major, 15 September 1783; Also Colquhoun; From Luss; POW Boston, 19 June 1776; Cmd. gren. co. in 1779; To half-pay 25 April 1784

Colquhoun, James; 3FG, Quartermaster, 1 June 1779; From quartermaster sergeant; in 3rd Foot Guards; WIA Guilford CH, 15 March 1781; At Charleston in 1782; Also listed possibly incorrectly as adjutant; Commission date also 16 June 1779

Colquhoun, William; 1FG, Lieut. & Capt., 4 July 1776

Colridge, James; 6, Ensign, 24 November 1775

Colt, Adam; 14, Ensign, 14 July 1777; Scottish; To lieutenant 72nd Foot, 14 May 1778; Capt. 73rd Foot, 1 October 1778; To major, 100th Foot January 1783; Died 1785

Colville, Hon. Charles; 28, Ensign, 6 March 1782

Colville, Hugh; 54, Adjutant, 25 November 1776; 54, Ensign, 29 September 1772; 54, Lieutenant, 21 December 1775

Combe, Boyce; 5, Ensign, 7 May 1776; 55, Lieutenant, 27 December 1778

Combe, King; 5, Ensign, 3 March 1779

Combie, William; 3/60, Lt. Colonel, December 1779

Comerford, John; 3, Ensign, 12 August 1779; 3, Lieutenant, 9 September 1781

Compton, William; 65, Captain, 16 May 1766; Retired 24 April 1776

Congreve, William; RA, Capt.- Lieut., 28 May 1766, 25 May 1772, WIA Long Island, 27 August 1776

Connel, Morgan; 20, Ensign, 6 April 1776; 20, Lieutenant, 25 April 1782; KIA Freeman's Farm, 19 September 1777 or Stillwater, 7 October 1777

Connelly, John; 44, Ensign, 2 November 1779

Conner, Fitz Maurice; 16, Capt.- Lieut., 4 February 1769; 16, Captain, 25 May 1772; From half pay, 96th Foot

Conner, Henry Eglington; 16, Captain, 15 August 1775, 18 February 1761; Major; 29 August 1777

Connor, George; 63, Ensign, 10 June 1778

Connor, John; Hosp., Apothecary, Prior to 1781; Hosp., Surgeon, 3 May 1781; To staff Leeward Isles, 3 May 1781; Died prior to 20 March 1787

Connor, Patrick; Hosp., Apothecary, Prior to 1781; To Leeward Isles, 24 May 1781; To half pay, 1783

Conolly, William; 18, Lieutenant, 2 June 1771; Irish, born 1747; First commissioned at age 20

Conran, Henry; 27, Major, 1 September 1775; WIA Danbury, CT, April 1777

Conran, Henry; 49, Ensign, 4 October 1780

Conway, Hon. Robert Seymour; 1FG, Capt. & Lt. Col., 18 October 1775; 1748-1831; First commission at age 16; MP Oxford, 1771-1784; ADC to Gen. Clinton; Hon.; Retired 1782

Conway, William; 83, Captain, 20 March 1783; From 3rd Foot Guards

Cook, George; 28, Ensign, 9 June 1778; 28, Lieutenant, 9 June 1780

Cooke, Henry; 20, Ensign, 2 March 1776

Cooke, Edward; 1/84, Ensign, 1 August 1782; Also Cook

Cooke, John; 38, Ensign, 8 September 1775; 20, Lieutenant, 3 March 1776; KIA Freeman's Farm, 19 September 1777

Cooke, John; 38, Lieutenant, 6 July 1778

Cooke, John; FG, Chaplain, May 1776; Also Samuel; Resident of Monmouth, New Jersey; Not at Yorktown

Cooke, John Wilbar; 37, Quartermaster, 11 April 1763; 37, Lieutenant, 15 August 1775; WIA Brandywine, 11 September 1777

Cooke, Stephen; 37, Lieutenant, 9 February 1779, 11 September 1762; 37, Capt.- Lieut., 20 May 1778; 37, Captain, 20 May 1778; WIA Brandywine, 11 September 1777; Deputy Barrack Master General R.I. 1778; Drowned New York City, 6 May 1783

Cooke, Thomas Ivy; 17 LD, Lieutenant, 7 August 1780; Served with Queens Rangers

Cooke, William; 27, Captain, 25 May 1772; Retired 5 July 1777

Cooper, -; 20, Ensign, 27 November 1776

Cooper, David; 14, Adjutant, 24 July 1772; 14, Lieutenant, 1 June 1773, 1 May 1762; 14, Captain, 24 March 1774

Coore, Thomas; 54, Captain, 16 August 1770; 28, Major, 6 October 1778; At Rhode Island in command of L.I., 29 August 1778

Coote, Eyre; 37, Adjutant, 20 May 1778; 37, Ensign, 15 April 1774; 27, Lieutenant, 6 November 1772; 37, Lieutenant, 27 January 1776; 37, Captain, 10 August 1778

Coote, George; 24, Capt.- Lieut., 2 March 1776; 24, Captain, 14 July 1777

Coote, Sir Eyre K.B.; 37, Colonel, 19 February 1773; Major General ; 29 September 1775; Lieutenant General; 29 August 1777, English, 1726-1783; MP Poole, 1774-1780; Died of the effects of a stroke in Madras, India, 27 April 1783

Coote, Thomas; 8, Lieutenant, 15 August 1775, 18 January 1760; 34, Capt.- Lieut., 1 November 1780; Lieutenancy not purchased; Neighbor of Bigoe Armstrong

Cope, James; 40, Lieutenant, 14 January 1775

Cope, Joseph; 63, Ensign, 7 October 1777; 63, Lieutenant, 3 May 1780; DOW Blackstocks, 22 November 1780

Cope, William; 63, Ensign, 15 May 1776; 63, Lieutenant, 5 November 1777; Also Caope; KIA Blackstocks, 17 September 1780

Copley, John; 34, Quartermaster, 27 December 1779

Cormick, John; Hosp., Mate, Prior to 1783; POW in 1783

Cornfield, William; 47, Ensign, 22 November 1775; 47, Lieutenant, 22 October 1779; Also Caulfield

Cornwallis, Charles Earl; 33, Colonel, 21 March 1766; Major General ; 29 September 1775; Am., Lieutenant General, 1 January 1776, 29 August 1777, English, 1738-1805; First commissioned at age 17; Attended Eton and Clare College

Cornwallis, Fredrick; 33, Lieutenant, 15 January 1772; 33, Captain, 2 February 1776, 13 February 1762, English, born 1753; First commissioned at age 15

Corrance, John; 8, Major, 23 November 1762; English, born 1717; First commissioned at age 24

Corser, Thomas; 17, Ensign, 24 September 1778

Cosby, William; 45, Ensign, 26 May 1780

Cotter, -; 24, Ensign, 1 January 1781

Cotter, Edward; 5, Ensign, 4 January 1777; 5, Lieutenant, 29 October 1778; At Little Egg Harbor, 1778

Cotter, George; 24, Lieutenant, 7 July 1775

Cotton, -; 27, Ensign, 29 June 1778

Cotton, Richard; 33, Lieutenant, 27 January 1774; 33, Captain, 25 December 1776; English, born 1751; First commissioned at age 17; WIA Long Island, 27 August 1776; DOW Camden, 30 September 1780

Cotton, William; 27, Major, 4 December 1779

Cotton, William; 27, Captain, 3 May 1770; 31, Captain, 1 June 1773; 31, Major, 2 September 1781

Courtney, Conway; 15, Lieutenant, 29 August 1775; 15, Capt.- Lieut., 30 July 1778; Died 29 May 1779, possibly on St. Kitts

Cousseau, James; 37, Major, 7 July 1775; Lt. Colonel, 17 November 1780

Couture, Peter; RE, Pract. eng. & 2nd Lt., 15 March 1780; In America from 1780-1782; Served at New York

Cowell, John Holden; 64, Ensign, 17 July 1777; 64, Lieutenant, 28 May 1779; Also Coswell; WIA Eutaw Springs, 8 September 1781

Cowley, William; 22, Captain, 15 August 1775, 13 February 1762; Major; 29 August 1777, Irish, born 1741; With additional company 1775 to October 1779; Returned to additional company, December 1781

Cowper, Christopher; 5, Lieutenant, 5 August 1758

Cox, James Hadley; 30, Chaplain, 12 September 1780

Cox, John; Hosp., Sprnmy. Mate, Prior to 1783; With Grenadiers, 1783

Cox, John; 17, Ensign, 3 May 1776; Died 8 or 9 September 1777

Cox, Nicholas; 16, Captain, 25 October 1774; Major; 23 July 1772

Cox, Thomas; 1FG, Capt. & Lt. Col., 5 February 1772; 3rd Major 1FG in England, February 1781

Cox, William; 5, Lieutenant, 28 November 1771; 21, 1st Lieut., 20 September 1777; 5, Captain, 7 October 1777; WIA Lexington and Concord, 19 April 1775; At Little Egg Harbor

Coxon, Michael; 3, Captain, 1 May 1779; Possibly Major of Bde

Cracroft, Charles; 30, Captain, 4 January 1781

Craig, James Henry; 47, Captain, 14 March 1771; 82, Major, 25 December 1777; 82, Lt. Colonel, 31 December 1781; WIA Bunker Hill, 17 June 1775; WIA Hubbardton, 7 July 1777; Majority also given as 22 December 1777

Craig, Peter; 57, Major, 14 December 1774; Cmd. 1st L.I. Bn. 31 January 1777 to 5 March 1778; Promoted to lieutenant colonel of 56th Foot, 9 January 1779

Craigie, George; 40, Ensign, 24 May 1776; 40, Lieutenant, 12 May 1778; 40, Captain, 26 January 1780; DOW Groton, CT, 7 September 1781

Cramond, James; 1/42, Lieutenant, 5 September 1775; WIA Brooklyn, 27 August, 1776; ADC to Gen. Knyphausen; Died 30 August 178 of yellow fever

Cramond, John; 4, Lieutenant, 5 May 1769; 4, Captain, 22 November 1775

Crane, Robert; 33, Quartermaster, 14 March 1774; 33, Captain, 9 April 1774; English, born 1746; First commissioned at age 16

Crane, William; 15, Ensign, 10 October 1778

Crauford, Robert; 26, Ensign, 28 April 1780, 20 April 1780; 26, Lieutenant, 7 March 1781, 2 June 1780

Crause, Charles; 65, Lieutenant, 26 May 1769, 26 April 1762; 65, Capt.-Lieut., 5 February 1777

Craven, Benjamin; 22, Ensign, 13 July 1777; 63, Lieutenant, 18 September 1780; WIA Springfield, NJ, 7 or 8 June 1780; Transferred to 63rd Foot, 18 September 1780; Barracks Master Staten Island, 1782

Crawford, Chr.; 47, Ensign, 24 August 1781

Crawford, David; 1/42, Ensign, 20 March 1776; 1/42, Lieutenant, 18 March 1778; 83, Capt.- Lieut., 24 January 1778

Crawford, George; RA, 2nd Lieut., 14 July 1782

Crawford, John; Assistant Commissary, 1778

Crawford, Robert; 17, Ensign, 28 November 1778

Crawfurd, Henry; 52, Lieutenant, 6 November 1765; 52, Captain, 18 June 1775; WIA Bunker Hill, 17 June 1775, leg amputated; Transferred to invalids, 18 February 1777

Crawfurd, John; 26, Capt.- Lieut., 27 January 1772; 26, Captain, 25 May 1772;

Creed, Henry; 33, Major, 9 April 1774; Irish, born 1735; First commissioned at age 17

Creswell, John; 70, Ensign, 20 May 1779

Crewe, Richard; 17 LD, Captain, 11 July 1769; 17 LD, Major, 25 February 1776; Retired 1 June 1778

Crichton, Patrick; 43, Ensign, 6 October 1778; 43, Lieutenant, 30 May 1780

Crockatt, James; 17, Ensign, 31 January 1778; Sold out 10 September 1778

Crofton, Hyacinth; 69, Ensign, 2 June 1779; 69, Lieutenant, 28 January 1782

Crofton, Marcus Lowther; 19, Lieutenant, 1 June 1778

Crofts, Richard; 20, Lieutenant, 26 September 1775

Crofts, Willes; 34, Quartermaster, 6 February 1779

Crofts, Willes; 34, Lieutenant, 14 March 1772

Croker, Henry; 49, Lieutenant, 31 August 1774; 49, Capt.- Lieut., 4 December 1779

Croker, John; 63, Lieutenant, 11 July 1775; 63, Captain, 20 April 1778; Also Crocker; Paid L2000 for captaincy; Died 27 August 1780

Croker, Michael; Hosp., Apothecary, 5 September 1775; Stationed at New York, 1783; To half pay 25 December 1783; Died 16 June 1800

Croker, Richard; 28, Lieutenant, 2 March 1776, 15 October 1761; 5, Lieutenant, 2 March 1776; WIA Bunker Hill, 17 June 1775

Croker, Taylor; 37, Lieutenant, 15 August 1775, 27 November 1760; 37, Capt.- Lieut., 24 September 1779; 4/60, Capt.- Lieut., 24 April 1779; From 37th Foot, returned to same in 1779

Croker, Taylor; 28, Lieutenant, 6 January 1776; Also Crocker; Also listed as in 37th Foot

Croker, Thomas; 38, Ensign, 19 February 1777; 38, Lieutenant, 2 August 1780

Crosbie, William; 38, Captain, 9 May 1769; 35, Major, 20 September 1778; 7, Major, 29 October 1778; 22, Lt. Colonel, 24 April 1781, 6 May 1780; English, born 1752; ADC to Sir Henry Clinton, 25 May 1778; Barracks Master General, 1 July 1780; From 3/60th Foot

Crosby, Edward; 18, Lieutenant, 8 September 1774, 15 September 1762, English, born 1750; First commissioned at age 12; From half pay, Gorham's Rangers

Crozier, John; 29, Captain, 25 December 1770, 21 October 1761; Major; 29 August 1777

Cuffe, Michael; 27, Captain, 19 August 1770; 27, Major, 18 January 1778; Cmd. 2nd L.I. Bn, from 24 April 1778; Retired 13 October 1778

Cullen, -; Hosp., Sprnmy. Mate, Prior to 1783; Stationed at Halifax, 1783

Cullen, William; 53, Lieutenant, 2 March 1776; 53, Captain, 13 September 1781; WIA Hubbardtown, 7 July 1777

Culliford, William; 20, Captain, 2 March 1776

Cumine, Archibald; 26, Ensign, 2 December 1777; 26, Lieutenant, 28 April 1780

Cumine, George; 59, Ensign, 30 December 1774

Cuming, Alexander; 52, Ensign, 22 November 1775; 1/42, Lieutenant, 18 August 1778; Also Cumine; Scottish, born 1757

Cuming, George; 80, Captain, 23 January 1778; WIA Green Springs, VA, 6 July 1781

Cuming, Patrick; 1/71, Lieutenant, 28 December 1775; WIA & POW Stony Point, NY, 16 July 1779; Died 3 November 1780

Cumins, James; 26, Ensign, 30 October 1777; 26, Lieutenant, 17 October 1779

Cumins, James; 33, Ensign, 1 October 1777; Also Cummings; From volunteer; WIA Brandywine

Cummins, John; 20, Ensign, 30 April 1782

Cummis, James; 27, Ensign, 3 May 1780

Cunningham, John; 69, Captain, 31 July 1781

Cunninghame, A. Mont.; 76, Captain, 31 December 1777

Cunninghame, Adam; 21, 2nd Lieut., 7 August 1780

Cunninghame, Alexander; 82, Lieutenant, 13 January 1778

Cunninghame, Geo. Aug.; 22, Ensign, 12 March 1773; 22, Lieutenant, 29 May 1776; Irish; KIA Drake's Farm, NJ, 2 February 1777

Cunninghame, George; 80, Ensign, 24 January 1778; 80, Lieutenant, 7 July 1781; Possibly WIA Virginia, 1781

Cunninghame, John; 52, Ensign, 30 May 1778

Cunninghame, John; 80, Lieutenant, 31 January 1778; From volunteer; Possibly WIA Virginia, 1781 POW Yorktown; Died Lancaster, PA, March 1782

Cunninghame, John; 55, Ensign, 24 October 1781

Cunninghame, Peter; 40, Ensign, 5 July 1780

Cunninghame, Robert; 14, Colonel, 30 December 1777; Major General; 25 May 1772

Cunninghame, William; 76, Captain, 30 December 1777; Provost Marshal, July 1776

Cuppaidge, George; 26, Lieutenant, 26 December 1770; 17, Capt.- Lieut., 16 July 1779

Currey, Hunter; 5, Ensign, 7 October 1777; From volunteer; WIA Brandywine; DOW while serving as a marine in the West Indies, 7 September 1780

Currie, Andrew; 22, Ensign, 7 June 1775; 22, Lieutenant, 28 November 1776; Also Curry; Died due to a fall from his horse, 5 September 1781

Currie, George; 53, Surgeon, 3 March 1760

Curry, Samuel; 21, 1st Lieut., 21 February 1772; Also Currie; KIA Freeman's Farm, 19 September 1777

Curzon, Hon. Charles Wm.; 33, Ensign, 8 August 1776; 33, Lieutenant, 9 December 1777; 33, Capt.- Lieut., 11 October 1781; 4/60, Capt.- Lieut., 4 October 1782?; Son of Lord Howe; WIA Guilford CH, 15 March 1781; KIA Yorktown, 10 October 1781

Cushman, Thomas; 15, Ensign, 5 October 1777; Also Cashman, from volunteer

Cuyler, Cornelius; 46, Captain, 9 May 1764; 55, Major, 15 January 1776; 55, Lt. Colonel, 16 November 1777; ADC to Sir William Howe; Carried dispatches to England in the winter of 1777-1778

D'Arcy, Constantine; RA, 2nd Lieut., 1 June 1778; RA, 1st Lieut., 12 July 1780; Also D'Arc; From Provincial establishment as "gentleman cadet"

D'aubant, Abraham; RE, Eng. extra. & Cpt.-Lt., 25 May 1772; In America from 1776-1782; Served at Rhode Is., Halifax, New York

D'Oyly, Francis; 1FG, Lieut. & Capt., 4 April 1775; KIA Brooklyn, 27 August 1776 while attached to 52nd Foot

Da Costa, Thomas; 3, Captain, 25 May 1772

Dacres, William; 26, Ensign, 23 February 1777; 26, Lieutenant, 24 April 1779, 8 December 1769

Dade, Thomas; 20, Chaplain, 2 August 1760

Dalgleish, Charles; 80, Ensign, 21 January 1778; 80, Lieutenant, 10 March 1781

Dalgleish, John; 21, 2nd Lieut., 7 May 1776; 21, 1st Lieut., 20 September 1777; From the Dutch service

Daliston, Thomas; 15, Chaplain, 19 October 1762; 18, Chaplain, 4 May 1776; English, born 1736; First commissioned at age 24

Dalley, Alex. Adolphus; 31, Ensign, 21 July 1779

Dalling, John; 3/60, Col. Comdt., 16 January 1776; Major General; 29 August 1777; Lieutenant General; 20 November 1782, Governor of Jamaica, 1782; To colonel of 37th Foot, 1783

Dalling, John William; 3/60, Ensign, 12 February 1779; 3/60, Lieutenant, 8 January 1781

Dalrymple, Charles; 22, Lieutenant, 24 July 1775

Dalrymple, George; 1/42, Ensign, 12 July 1773; 1/42, Lieutenant, 24 February 1776; 1/42, Captain, 20 August 1778; Scottish, born 1754; CM but acquitted, 7 September 1778 for stealing rum from his landlord; First commissioned at age 15; Promoted to captain, 1/73rd Foot, 23 December 1777. He appears to have continued to serve with the 42nd for nearly a year after his promotion in the 1/73rd

Dalrymple, James; 43, Lieutenant, 8 February 1775; 57, Captain, 31 December 1777; WIA Bunker Hill, 17 June 1775

Dalrymple, John; 14, Lieutenant, 6 January 1772; 14, Captain, 27 February 1775; Listed as KIA in 1777 but true facts are unclear; Was listed as AWOL on 1 August 1775

Dalrymple, John; 63, Lieutenant, 3 July 1765; KIA Bunker Hill, 17 June 1775

Dalrymple, Stair Park, Lord; 2/73, Captain, 29 September 1778; ADC to Gen. Henry Clinton, 12

Dalrymple, William; 14, Lt. Colonel, 27 March 1765; Quartermaster General, 29 August 1777

Dalton, Anthony; 37, Lieutenant, 2 August 1771; 37, Capt.- Lieut., 4 December 1778; 37, Captain, 4 December 1778

Dalton, David; 55, Ensign, 16 July 1774; 55, Lieutenant, 25 January 1777; Irish, born 1755; First commissioned at age 19

Dalton, Don. Foster; 28, Ensign, 14 May 1774; 28, Lieutenant, 29 October 1776

Dalton, Joseph; 63, Quartermaster, 13 November 1775

Dalway, Robert; 10, Captain, 24 July 1766

Daly, John; 54, Ensign, 21 December 1775; 54, Lieutenant, 28 April 1779

Daly, Peter; 28, Captain, 22 September 1775; Also Daley; WIA La Vigie, 18 December 1778

Dalyell, Thomas; 2/42, Captain, 24 March 1780; From 32nd Foot

Dambourgess, Francis; 1/84, Lieutenant, 27 February 1776; Commission also dated 25 December 1775

Dame, George; 8, Lieutenant, 26 December 1770; American; Listed as English in WO 27, born 1750; First commissioned at age 13; Also held a provincial commission

Dame, George; 1/84, Ensign, 12 June 1775; Commissioned ensign, 8th Foot

Damer, Hon. George; 87, Major, 5 October 1779; Son of Lord Milton; Served with 2nd Bn. Gren, 1780; Adjutant to Major Gen. Wm. Phillips's command, 1781

Dance, Thomas; 46, Ensign, 5 April 1778

Dancey, William; 33, Captain, 27 January 1774; 33, Major, 14 October 1778; Also Dansey; English, born 1745; First commissioned at age 15; WIA Brandywine, 11 September 1777; Letters extant in H. Soc.

Danterroche, H.; 62, Ensign, 21 November 1775; Also D'Antroch; WIA & POW Stillwater, 19 September 1777

Darby, Christopher; 54, Capt.- Lieut., 13 September 1779; 54, Captain, 13 September 1779; Also Darbey

Darby, Christopher; 33, Ensign, 26 November 1776; 33, Lieutenant, 21 September 1777

Darby, Edw. Hawke; 15, Ensign, 20 June 1777

Darby, William; 4/60, Ensign, 25 June 1780

Darby, William John; 17, Captain, 12 December 1774; 7, Major, 10 August 1780; Son and grandson of army officers who held positions at court; Attended public school; When promoted to lieutenant over the heads of more senior ensigns, the promotion was protested to the Secretary of War

Darcus, James; 38, Ensign, 18 June 1775; Also Dorcus; From volunteer with 4th Foot; to RGB as Lieutenant, 30 September 1778

Darling, Christopher; 45, Adjutant, 10 September 1778; 45, Ensign, 21 July 1779; Also Darkins; From sergeant major

Darragh, Charles; 21, 2nd Lieut., 20 September 1777

Daunt, Thomas; 54, Ensign, 6 October 1776; 54, Lieutenant, 1 July 1779; From volunteer with 2nd Gren. Bn.; WIA Groton, CT, 6 September 1781

Davenport, -; 23, 2nd Lieut., 24 November 1775

Davenport, Edward; 6, Ensign, 25 October 1773

Davids, Daniel; RA, 1st Lieut., 7 July 1779

Davidson, Alexander; 1/84, Surgeon, 14 June 1775; Resigned 25 December 1780

Davidson, Robert; 83, Captain, 29 June 1783

Davies, -; Adjutant, 1779; Town Adjutant of New York

Davies, David; RA, Chaplain, 1 January 1771

Davies, George; 54, Chaplain, 12 March 1774

Davies, James; 31, Lieutenant, 21 November 1777

Davies, James; 31, Ensign, 22 February 1776

Davies, James; 53, Ensign, 29 March 1776; Also Davis; Died 16 June 1777

Davies, Richard; 53, Capt.- Lieut., 2 March 1776; 53, Captain, 2 March 1776

Davies, Thomas; RA, Captain, 1 January 1771; Extant watercolors

Davies, William; 52, Captain, 3 May 1765, 14 January 1760, Also Davidson; KIA Bunker Hill, 17 June 1775

Davies, Williams; 38, Ensign, 15 August 1775; 38, Lieutenant, 19 February 1777; 38, Captain, 11 September 1779

Davies, Williams; 57, Lieutenant, 25 November 1775, 23 July 1762, Died 4 June 1777; Possibly WIA Bound Brook, NJ

Davies, Wm. Conninges; 15, Ensign, 24 August 1780

Davy, Thomas; 57, Surgeon, 12 December 1770; Hosp. Surgeon, 1 March 1781; Also Davye; To half pay 25 December 1783; Died 11 January 1826

Dawson, Charles; 62, Captain, 29 February 1776

Dawson, George; 38, Lieutenant, 31 July 1769; 57, Capt.- Lieut., 6 October 1778; 16, Captain, 17 February 1781, 30 May 1778, Extra Asst. Deputy QMG, 1779

Dawson, Henry; 31, Ensign, 6 March 1781; 43, Lieutenant, 29 June 1775; DOW Bunker Hill, 2 September 1775

Dawson, Henry; 43, Ensign, 23 January 1771

Dawson, Thomas; 3, Major, 20 April 1776

Dawson, William; 57, Captain, 13 May 1769

Day, John; 14, Ensign, 14 April 1776

Dayrell, Paul; 52, Captain, 19 August 1773

De Birniere, Henry; 10, Ensign, 14 September 1770, 22 August 1770; 10, Lieutenant, 30 June 1775; Spy and Guide at Lexington and Concord

De Birniere, John; 18, Lieutenant, 4 February 1769, 9 August 1760, Irish, born 1745; First commissioned at age 12; Spoke French, Interpreter at Kaskaskia, IL, 1772 to 1776

De Courcy, Hon. James; 40, Lieutenant, 14 January 1775; WIA Brandywine, 11 September 1777, with 2nd Bn. L.I.; Given leave of absence to recover, 1778; Lt. Governor of Gravesend and Tilbury, 1778

De Crousax, Louis; 3/60, Ensign, 21 May 1778

De Crousax, Henry; 3/60, Lieutenant, 21 September 1779; Also Cransaux

De Diemar, Charles; 3/60, Lieutenant, 15 December 1782

De Diemer, Fredrick; 3/60, Captain, 20 June 1778; From Hanoverian Army; Raised Black Hussars in New York

De Gentzkow, Fred.; 3/60, Lieutenant, 1 November 1776

De Lancey, John Peter; 18, Ensign, 19 November 1771; 18, Lieutenant, 26 July 1775; 18, Capt.- Lieut., 3 March 1780; Native of NewYork born 1753; First commissioned at age 18; Lt. & adj., Ferguson's Riflemen, 1777; Major, PA Loyalists 14 October 1777; Served with United Corps of PA and MD Loyalists in Florida

De Lancey, Oliver; 17 LD, Captain, 15 May 1775; 17 LD, Major, 3 June 1778; 17 LD, Lt. Colonel, 3 October 1781; ADC to Cmd. in Chief, 1778; Depty. Adj.. General, 10 October 1780

De Lancey, Warren; 17 LD, Cornet, 1 August 1780

De Laplace, William; 26, Captain, 18 April 1766; Also de la Place; POW Ft. Ticonderoga, 10 May 1775; Retired 9 April 1777

De Montrond, Fred. ; 4/60, Lieutenant, 20 March 1776; 4/60, Capt.-Lieut., 24 May 1779; 4/60, Captain, 1 March 1782, 24 May 1779

De Peister, Arent Schuyler; 8, Captain, 23 November 1768; 8, Major, 6 May 1777; A native New Yorker; Listed as English in WO 27, born 1736; First commissioned at age 19; Served as quartermaster in the 1760s; Also DePeyster

De Traytorrens, Imbert; 3/60, Ensign, 7 February 1776

De Visme, Samuel; 3/60, Lieutenant, 1 April 1779; 3/60, Captain, 15 December 1782; Also Devisine; Paymaster to 60th Foot in New York, 1782

Dean, Richard; 31, Surgeon, 21 August 1765; Also Deane; Died prior to 13 August 1794

Dean, Thomas; 9, Ensign, 14 July 1777; 9, Lieutenant, 28 September 1781

Deburgh, Hon. John Thomas; 1FG, Lieut. & Capt., 6 June 1770; 1FG, Capt. & Lt. Col., 15 June 1776; To 68th Foot in 1783

Deerhurst, George Viscount; 64, Ensign, 2 May 1776; 17 LD, Lieutenant, 28 November 1776

Deighton, Robert; 55, Ensign, 11 May 1776; 55, Lieutenant, 20 April 1778

Dela Douespe, Henry; 2FG, Capt. & Lt. Col., 1 May 1777; Retired February 1779

Delacherois, Nicholas; 9, Captain, 1 September 1771; 1736-1829; First commission at age 20; Resigned 5 January 1776; Self-portrait in JSAHR, v.51 (205), p. 5

Delamain, Tho. Maple; 35, Ensign, 12 March 1774; 35, Lieutenant, 23 November 1775;

Delap, Robert; 10, Ensign, 4 December 1769; Resigned 30 March 1775

Delaval, Francis; 23, 2nd Lieut., 21 August 1776; 4, Lieutenant, 10 March 1777

Delgarno, John; 8, Ensign, 19 December 1768; 8, Lieutenant, 22 November 1775

Delholme, John; 19, Surgeon, 2 August 1769; Also Denholme; From mate; To staff Grenada, 28 March 1787; Died prior to 9 May 1789

Delhuntry, Lawrence; 26, Lieutenant, 28 February 1766; 5, Capt.- Lieut., 29 June 1778; Promoted to captain in RGB, 30 October 1778

Denis, Bernard; 40, Ensign, 15 August 1775; 40, Lieutenant, 12 September 1777

Dennis, George; 43, Ensign, 18 August 1778; 43, Lieutenant, 24 October 1781

Dennistoune, William; 55, Ensign, 5 November 1777; 55, Lieutenant, 10 December 1779; Died Antigua, 5 February 1782

Dering, Charles; 28, Captain, 23 August 1775; Also Deering; KIA White Plains, 28 October 1776

Desaguliers, Fredrick; RA, 2nd Lieut., 11 November 1773; KIA Princeton, 3 January 1777

Desbrisay, Jasper; 17, Ensign, 28 September 1775; 43, Lieutenant, 10 September 1780

Desbrisay, Thomas; RA, 1st Lieut., 7 July 1779

Despard, Andrew; 59, Lieutenant, 26 December 1770; 79, Captain, 13 January 1778; Deputy Adjutant Gen., 1781; Listed as major in NAAL, 1783 without first name

Despard, John; 7, Lieutenant, 1 September 1768, 12 May 1762; 23, Capt.- Lieut., 5 October 1777; 7, Captain, 7 October 1777; Major, Volunteers of Ireland, 25 May 1778

Destalieur, James; RA, Surgeon, 1773

Dewar, David; 2/71, Ensign, 2 November 1778

Dick, Robert; 80, Chaplain, 17 January 1778; Died 30 October 1782

51

Dickenson, Richard; RA, 2nd Lieut., 29 June 1781

Dickins, Richard; 43, Ensign, 17 October 1778

Dickson, Alexander; 16, Major, 20 May 1771; 16, Lt. Colonel, 11 January 1776

Dickson, Hugh; 29, Capt.- Lieut., 26 December 1776

Dickson, James; 80, Lieutenant, 1 February 1778

Dickson, William; 1/42, Ensign, 6 March 1779; 1/42, Lieutenant, 28 April 1781; 1/42, Captain, 2 February 1782

Dickson, William; 4, Ensign, 23 January 1777; 4, Lieutenant, 6 March 1779; WIA Germantown, 4 October 1777

Digby, Thomas; 46, Ensign, 15 August 1775; 37, Lieutenant, 13 April 1778

Digby, William; 55, Lieutenant, 1 April 1773

Dilkes, Thomas; 49, Major, 20 February 1773; Retired 12 July 1777

Dilkes, William Thomas; 49, Ensign, 4 December 1779; 49, Lieutenant, 1 September 1781

Dillon, James; 54, Ensign, 11 February 1777; 54, Lieutenant, 10 October 1779; Died New York, 28 September 1780; Death notice listed him in 59th Foot erroneously

Disney, Daniel; 44, Captain, 22 September 1767, 4 October 1760; 2/71, Major, 7 August 1776; 38, Major, 10 March 1777; English, born 1730; First commissioned at age 18

Disney, Fredrick; 21, Captain, 19 February 1766; Major; 10 November 1780

Ditmas, Harry; 15, Lieutenant, 7 July 1775; 15, Captain, 25 November 1776; WIA York Island, 1776, Danbury, CT, 27 April 1777, Germantown, 4 October 1777 & Monmouth, 28 June 1778

Dixon, Charles; 1/60, Capt.- Lieut., 13 November 1776; 1/60, Captain, 12 November 1776; With 1/60 Gren. Coy. in Nicaragua, 1780

Dixon, Fletcher; 34, Chaplain, 17 September 1773

Dixon, George; RA, 1st Lieut., 28 February 1782

Dixon, Mathew; RE, Sub-dir. & Maj.,4 December 1770; Lt. Colonel; 29 August 1777; In America from 1776-1778; Served at New York

Dobbin, Leonard; 47, Surgeon, 28 January 1771; Died prior to 23 May 1796

Dobbyn, John; 9, Captain, 7 October 1775

Dobbyn, Michael; 33, Ensign, 27 November 1775

Dobson, Henry; 16, Captain, 28 February 1766

Dobson, Robert; 20, Ensign, 2 August 1775; 20, Lieutenant, 28 March 1777

Dod, Toby; 55, Ensign, 10 December 1779

Dodd, James; 49, Ensign, 22 March 1780

Dodd, Thomas; 16 LD, Cornet, 2 August 1775
Dodge, William; 45, Ensign, 27 October 1779
Dodgson, Richard; 82, Ensign, 10 September 1779; Probably died
Penobscot, ME, July 1779
Dods, James; 49, Chaplain, 1 September 1775; From clerk
Dodworth, George; 34, Ensign, 4 October 1780
Don, John; 21,1st Lieut., 23 February 1776; KIA Freeman's Farm, 19
September 1777 while serving with Fraser's Marksmen
Donaghy, John; 3, Ensign, 26 January 1781
Donaldson, Alexander; 1/42, Captain, 31 March 1770; 76, Major, 19
December 1777; Scottish, born 1738; First commissioned at age 20
Donaldson, Thomas; 31, Lieutenant, 21 February 1776; 31, Captain, 4
November 1777
Dondon, Patrick; 52, Surgeon, 23 May 1776; Also Dordon or Dundon;
From surgeon, Royal Fencible Americans; To half pay by 1785; Died
prior to 28 March 1795
Donkin, Robert; 23, Captain, 25 December 1770; 44, Major, 5 October
1777, 23 July 1772; Lt. Colonel; 29 August 1777, Wrote a book, with
subscriptions going to the relief of widows and orphans; Cmd. Royal
Garrison Regiment from 1 November 1779
Donkin, Rufane Shawe; 44, Ensign, 21 March 1778; 44, Lieutenant, 9
September 1779
Dore, Brewster; 28, Ensign, 23 August 1775; Died 27 January 1777
Dorrington, Thomas; 43, Ensign, 22 November 1775; 57, Lieutenant, 6
October 1778
Dougharty, Richard; 69, Ensign, 14 April 1781
Douglas, Boleyn; 37, Captain, 15 August 1775
Douglas, David; 49, Ensign, 27 April 1777
Douglas, Dun. Hamilton; 21, 2nd Lieut., 6 January 1779
Douglas, James; 15, Lieutenant, 6 May 1762; 15, Capt.- Lieut., 13 May
1776; 15, Captain, 13 May 1776; WIA Brandywine, 11 September 1777 &
La Vigie, 18 December 1778
Douglas, James; 29, Lieutenant, 27 February 1776; KIA Hubbardtown, 7
July 1777
Douglas, Robert; 47, Captain, 31 March 1775; Major; 29 August 1778
Douglas, Robert; RA, 1st Lieut., 25 April 1777; RA, Capt.- Lieut., 21 July
1779; Married in December 1777; Died Charleston, 1780
Douglas, William; 21, 1st Lieut., 10 March 1775
Douglas, William; Hosp., Surgeon, 11 December 1775; Surgeon to the
Garrison of South Carolina until 1782
Dougleston, Roderick; 82, Lieutenant, 13 July 1783

Dowdeswell, Thomas; 1FG, Lieut. & Capt., 26 April 1776; Retired June 1778

Dowling, James; 47, Ensign, 18 June 1775; 29, Lieutenant, 14 July 1777; From volunteer; Served with 20th Foot on Saratoga campaign; WIA Freeman's Farm, 19 September 1777; Bemis Heights, 7 October 1777; Died 26 March 1781

Dowling, Oliver; 43, Ensign, 16 October 1775; 22, Lieutenant, 18 August 1778; Irish, born 1758; From 43rd Regiment; POW French Navy, 1780; Exchanged 1781

Dowling, Richard; 20, Captain, 7 July 1775; WIA Freeman's Farm, 19 September 1777; Died 31 March 1780

Dowling, Richard; 22, Ensign, 15 October 1780; Death "occasioned by leaping" 6 April 1783 in New York

Downes, Edward; 46, Captain, 12 November 1767; Retired 2 July 1777

Downes, Patrick; 5, Captain, 20 February 1773; DOW Bunker Hill, 24 June 1775

Downing, Henry; 55, Captain, 17 September 1773; Irish, born 1741; First commissioned at age 21; WIA Brandywine, 11 September 1777; POW at La Vigie, 18 December 1778

Downing, John; RA, Capt.- Lieut., 1 July 1779;

Doyle, John; 40, Adjutant, 24 May 1776; 40, Lieutenant, 1 March 1775, 17 September 1773, WIA Germantown, 4 October 1777; Replaced as adjutant, 6 April 1777

Doyle, Welborne Ellis; 55, Lieutenant, 17 September 1773; 55, Capt.-Lieut., 5 November 1777; Irish, born 1754; First commissioned at age 16; Lieutenant colonel, Volunteers of Ireland, 25 May 1778

Doyle, William; 24, Ensign, 16 July 1774; 24, Lieutenant, 27 November 1776; WIA Stillwater, 7 October 1777

Doyley, Hadley; 52, Lieutenant, 22 November 1776; Also D'Oyley; KIA Brandywine, 11 September 1777

Drakeford, Richard; 26, Captain, 15 August 1775, 25 May 1772

Drewe, Edward; 35, Captain, 12 March 1774; 35, Major, 29 October 1778, 28 October 1779; Also Drew; Son of an Exter landowner and MP; Attended Exter; WIA Bunker Hill, 17 June 1775; Majority cost 4000 guineas, an "uncommon great sum"; CM in June 1780 for being unable to "drill the regiment" and cashiered

Drummond, -; 44, Ensign, 8 September 1779;

Drummond, Adam; 33, Ensign, 13 December 1773; 33, Lieutenant, 27 November 1775; Scottish, born 1757; First commissioned at age 16; DOW Brandywine, 21 September 1777

Drummond, Andrew Jn.; 1FG, Ensign, 12 August 1773; 1FG, Lieut. & Capt., 22 January 1777

Drummond, Duncan; RA, Captain, 24 October 1761; RA, Major, 16 May 1781, 29 August 1778; 13 1178; Lt. Colonel; 29 August 1777, ADC to Sir Henry Clinton, 1777

Drummond, Gavin; 1/42, Ensign, 31 January 1776; 1/42, Lieutenant, 5 October 1777; Scottish, born 1755; First commissioned at age 19

Drummond, George; Hosp., Mate, Prior to 1783; Stationed at New York, 1783

Drummond, Hon. James; 2/42, Captain, 23 March 1780; From lieutenant, 66th Foot

Drummond, James; 40, Ensign, 10 October 1776; 43, Lieutenant, 10 August 1778

Drummond, John; 26, Ensign, 22 February 1776; 26, Lieutenant, 19 October 1778; 26, Captain, 28 April 1780

Drury, Edward; 63, Lieutenant, 29 October 1768; 63, Captain,16 May 1776; KIA Brandywine, 11 September 1777

Drury, James; 63, Ensign, 18 June 1775; 57, Lieutenant, 12 September 1777; 23, Captain, 5 September 1779; From volunteer; WIA Camden, 16 August 1780

Drury, Richard Vere; 59, Ensign, 14 August 1775

Dryden, John; Hosp., Sprnmy. Mate, Prior to 1783; At New York as POW, 1783

Duffe, Alexander; 46, Captain, 15 August 1772, 3 May 1762

Duffe, Hon. Lewis; 8, Captain, 17 December 1761; 8, Major, 4 March 1776; Scottish, born 1736; Son of Earl of Fife; Family represented Elginshire in Parliament; Attended St. Andrews University; First commissioned at age 20; Sold out after a disagreement over promotion

Duffe, James; 40, Captain, 28 February 1766, 19 October 1762; Major; 29 August 1777

Duffe, William; 7, Lieutenant, 14 December 1770; 26, Captain, 9 April 1777

Duffield, -; 49, Ensign, 15 August 1775; Died 28 March 1776

Duffield, Francis; 1/60, Lieutenant, 13 November 1772; 3/60, Captain, 3 August 1777; In Prevost's Force from St. Augustine; Transferred to cmd. a company of the 1/60th by 1783

Dugan, Pat.; 15, Ensign, 6 November 1778

Duke, Charles; 26, Ensign, 18 September 1779

Duke, George; 33, Ensign, 28 April 1773; 33, Lieutenant, 26 November 1775; 26, Captain, 10 September 1779; English, born 1757; First commissioned at age 15

Dumaresque, John; 22, Adjutant, 4 December 1779; 22, Ensign, 22 November 1775; 22, Lieutenant, 12 July 1777; 22, Captain, 31 December 1781; English, born 1760; Arrived in America June 1777

Dumas, James; 30, Lieutenant, 9 October 1778

Dumas, Peter; 82, Ensign, 6 January 1778; 82, Lieutenant, 18 September 1780;Dep. Commissary General, Prior to 1783

Dunbar, Alexander; 2/42, Lieutenant, 28 March 1780; From Sutherland Fencilbles

Dunbar, James; RA, Captain, 3 December 1781

Dunbar, James; RA, Captain, 21 December 1777; Served with Burgoyne; Died New York, 11 August 1783

Dunbar, Thomas; 43, Lieutenant, 7 August 1775; 70, Captain, 1 February 1781

Dunbar, William; 1/84, Captain, 13 June 1775

Dunbar, William; Major, 1775; From half pay, 44th Foot; Town Major Quebec, 1775 - 1782

Duncan, Alexander; RA, Capt.- Lieut., 7 July 1779; Died Charleston, 24 February 1782

Duncan, William; 2/84, Chaplain, 1 August 1782

Duncanson, Robertson; 2/71, Lieutenant, 1 December 1775; 1/71, Captain, 12 November 1778; POW Boston, 19 June 1776; POW Stony Point, 16 July 1779

Duncanson, William; 82, Ensign, 3 January 1778; 82, Lieutenant, 18 September 1780

Dundas, Alexander; 34, Major, 6 January 1776; 8, Lt. Colonel, 1 November 1780; Scottish; Served with the Scotch Brigade in Holland prior to British service

Dundas, Francis; 1FG, Ensign, 4 April 1775; 1FG, Lieut. & Capt., 23 January 1778; 1FG, Capt. & Lt. Col., 11 April 1783; POW; Parole to May 1783; To 45th Foot, June 1783

Dundas, Thomas; 80, Lt. Colonel, 27 December 1777; Scottish; MP Orkney and Shetland, 1771-1780; Peace commissioner at Yorktown

Dundas, Thomas; 63, Captain, 20 May 1769; 65, Major, 20 January 1776; Supnmy. ADC to Gen. Clinton, 5 January 1776

Dundee, Peter; 7, Captain, 25 December 1770; Retired 19 February 1777

Dunglass, William, Lord; 2FG, Ensign, 20 July 1774; 2FG, Lieut. & Capt., 25 March 1778; DOW Guilford CH, 12 December 1781

Dunlap, Andrew; 2/71, Lieutenant, 30 August 1776; 82, Captain, 8 January 1778; At Penobscot, 1779

Dunlap, George; 74, Lieutenant, 1 January 1778; Also Dunlop; Cmd. 54th L.I. Co. in 1781; POW, Yorktown

Dunlap, Hutchinson; 53, Captain, 25 May 1772

Dunlap, James; 82, Lieutenant, 11 January 1778; POW since March 1779; Recommended to Alex. Campbell's captaincy

Dunlap, St. John; 80, Ensign, 30 January 1782; From lieutenant in Queen's American Rangers, 25 September 1780

Dunn, Thomas; 15, Lieutenant, 3 February 1764, 13 September 1762

Dunn, Thomas; 22, Ensign, 14 August 1778; 63, Lieutenant, 18 September 1780; Served in additional company 22nd Regt. until 14 August 1779; DOW Yorktown, 21 October 1781

Dunne, Edward; 76, Ensign, 10 November 1780

Duport, Robert; 47, Lieutenant, 1 September 1771; 47, Capt.- Lieut., 3 August 1781

Durnford, Andrew; RE, Sub-eng. & Lt., 6 March 1775; In America from 1775-1783; Served at West Florida, New York; Extra Asst. DQMG; Stole a servant woman

Durnford, Desmaretz; RE, Sub-eng. & Lt., 10 January 1776; In America from 1777-1779; WIA, Bennington, 16 August 1777

Durnford, Elias; RE, Eng. ord. & Capt., 25 May 1772; In America from 1762-1780; Served at West Florida, Havana

Dusseaux, Joseph; 6, Quartermaster, 12 January 1770; 6, Lieutenant, 12 January 1770; 6, Capt.- Lieut., 22 November 1775; 6, Captain, 2 May 1776;

Dusseaux, William; 6, Lieutenant, 6 January 1771; 6, Quartermaster, 16 March 1776; 6, Capt.- Lieut., 16 April 1777

Dutton, John; 38, Lieutenant, 21 March 1765, 4 January 1763, KIA Bunker Hill, 17 June 1775

Duvernet, Henry; RA, 2nd Lieut., 17 June 1772

Dyer, James; 49, Chaplain, 7 October 1746; Died 1 September 1775

Dyer, John Swinerton; 1FG, Lieut. & Capt., 4 October 1765; 1FG, Capt. & Lt. Col., 21 November 1777; To 1st Foot Gds., 14 May 1778; Later baronet

Eagle, A. Solomon; 35, Ensign, 7 October 1775; KIA White Plains, 28 October 1776

Eagle, Solomon; 43, Ensign, 3 September 1775;

Earl, Joseph; 44, Ensign, 1 November 1779; Died of consumption, New York City, late September 17816

East, William; 43, Ensign, 15 September 1775

Eberhard, George; 3/60, Adjutant, 1 September 1775; 3/60, Ensign, 22 May 1779

Eccles, Joseph; 10, Ensign, 2 June 1777; Retired 9 February 1778

Eccles, Joseph; 20, Ensign, 3 June 1781

Eccleston, John Dan.; 47, Ensign, 16 April 1773; 47, Lieutenant, 23 November 1775; Died 31 December 1779

Ecuyler, Simeon; 4/60, Captain, 2 September 1775, 22 April 1762, Joined regt. in 1756; To half-pay in 1763; Died 17 September 1777

Edge, Fane; 53, Adjutant, 24 May 1775; 53, Lieutenant, 13 April 1768; 53, Captain, 6 April 1778

Edmondstone, Charles; 18, Captain, 27 May 1758; Major; 23 July 1772, Irish, born 1731; First commissioned at age 16; Cmd. at Fort Pitt from 1768 to 1772

Edmondstone, Will.; 1/42, Ensign, 31 December 1780; 1/42, Lieutenant, 2 February 1781

Edmonstone, Arch.; 1FG, Lieut. & Capt., 19 February 1776; ADC to Gen. von Reidesel, September 1776 until October 1777; POW with convention army; Died in 1780 after returning to England

Edwards, Alexander; 53, Lieutenant, 1 March 1776, 18 October 1761

Edwards, Arthur; 10, Surgeon, 14 August 1765; Hosp., Apothecary, 8 October 1778; From 10th Foot; Listed as Master Apothecary in 1778; Resigned 3 May 1782

Edwards, Hamilton; 53, Ensign, 6 March 1780

Edwards, James; 28, Lieutenant, 23 August 1775; 4/60, Lieutenant, 4 September 1775, 23 June 1762, WIA Brandywine; To 4/60th 22 September 1775

Edwards, John; 45, Ensign, 15 August 1778

Edwards, John; 45, Lieutenant, 15 August 1775, 22 October 1761

Edwards, John; 16, Chaplain, 14 January 1767

Edwards, Tennison; 30, Adjutant, 12 November 1778; 30, Lieutenant, 1 June 1778

Edwards, Thomas; 6, Capt.- Lieut., 5 March 1774; 6, Captain, 22 November 1775

Edwards, William; 37, Ensign, 10 February 1778; 37, Lieutenant, 29 April 1781;

Edwards, William; 16, Chaplain, 6 March 1780

Effingham, T. Earl of; 22, Captain, 6 February 1772, 1 August 1766, Thomas Howard; English, born 1746; Resigned 6 June 1775; Never served in America

Eiston, George; 35, Ensign, 18 October 1778; Son of a "fashionable" Edinburgh solicitor; perhaps Catholic; Attended Catholic St. Gregories School at Douay, France

Eld, George; 2FG, Ensign, 30 March 1776; 2FG, Lieut. & Capt., 5 May 1780; Came to America, 1779; Served with grenadiers while an ensign; Attacked by Lt. Callendar of the 42nd in NYC, January, 1780; POW Yorktown

Elige, John Peter; 15, Surgeon, 6 November 1772; From mate 33rd Foot; Retired 18 March 1777

Elliot, Edward; 9, Ensign, 28 September 1781

Elliott, Fra. Percival; 14, Ensign, 15 December 1773; 14, Lieutenant, 23 November 1775; Sent home with invalids, 4 July 1777

Elliott, James; 37, Capt.- Lieut., 15 August 1775

Elliott, John; 7, Lieutenant, 20 September 1780; 28, Captain, 3 September 1781, 1 June 1781, KIA Frigate Bay, St. Kitts, between 25 and 28 January 1782

Elliott, William; 21, 2nd Lieut., 31 October 1781

Ellis, John Joiner; 18, Lieutenant, 21 January 1775; English, born 1748; First commissioned at age 22

Ellis, Samuel; 21, 1st Lieut., 10 September 1776, 5 October 1775

Ellis, Samuel; 15, Lieutenant, 24 May 1781

Ellis, Samuel; 65, Lieutenant, 6 May 1776

Ellison, Peter Hedn.; 64, Lieutenant, 1 January 1766; Also H. Peter; English, born 1746; First commissioned at age 16

Elliston, Peter Hedman; 35, Captain, 8 October 1775; 17 LD, Captain, 6 June 1776

Elphinstone, John; 4/60, Ensign, 6 September 1779; 1/71, Lieutenant, 5 June 1780

Elphinstone, Rt. Dal. Horn; 53, Colonel, 5 February 1770; Major General; 30 April 1770; Lieutenant General; 29 August 1777

Elsdren, Wm. Rolfe; 26, Ensign, 9 August 1779

Elwes, Henry; 22, Captain, 25 May 1772; English, born 1740

Elwin, Peter; 33, Ensign, 9 April 1774; 33, Lieutenant, 2 February 1776; English, born 1753; First commissioned at age 20; Retired 11 June 1778

Emerson, William; 46, Ensign, 8 September 1775

Emmerson, Cornelius; 52, Lieutenant, 31 January 1778

Engel, James Samuel; 45, Quartermaster, 17 September 1773; 45, Lieutenant, 8 September 1768; 45, Capt.- Lieut., 22 November 1775; 45, Captain, 22 November 1775

England, Patrick; 5, Ensign, 25 June 1775; 5, Lieutenant, 4 July 1777; From volunteer; Quartermaster for L.I. Bn. from 9 June 1775 until 25 June 1775

England, Poole; 47, Lieutenant, 16 April 1773; 47, Captain, 17 May 1782; WIA Bunker Hill, 17 June 1775

England, Richard; 47, Captain, 29 September 1770; 47, Major, 3 August 1781, 17 November 1780, WIA Bunker Hill, 17 June 1775; Deputy Quarter Master Gen., 1781

Enys, John; 29, Ensign, 22 April 1775; 29, Lieutenant, 16 February 1778; Extant diary

Erle, Charles; 24, Lieutenant, 28 March 1775

Erle, Thomas; 28, Colonel, 15 July 1773; Major General; 30 April 1770, Died 4 March 1777

Erskine, Archibald; 1/42, Captain, 7 September 1771; 22, Major, 6 December 1778; Scottish, born 1749; First commissioned at age 15; Extra Major of Bde., 1777; Retired 30 April 1781

Erskine, Francis; 23, 2nd Lieut., 23 November 1775; 23, 1st Lieut., 22 April 1777; 4/60, Captain, 30 December 1778; Aboard HMS Isis, August 1778

Erskine, Sir James; 35, Lieutenant, 24 September 1778

Erskine, Sir William Kt.; 1/71, Lieutenant, 23 November 1775, 25 January 1762; 80, Colonel, 16 December 1777, 4 March 1777; Am., Colonel, 23 April 1775; Am., Brigadier General, 7 October 1776; Major General; 19 February 1779

Estrange, Richard L.; 47, Capt.- Lieut., 6 November 1769; 47, Captain, 22 November 1775, 25 May 1772, Also L'Estrange; Drowned Canada, 5 April 1778

Estrange, Thomas L.; 54, Ensign, 26 October 1775; 7, Lieutenant, 18 August 1778;

Etherington, Thomas; 2/60, Lt. Colonel, 19 September 1775; Court martialed but exonerated for the fall of St. Vincent to the French

Eustace, Charles; 33, Captain, 25 November 1775; Major; 29 August 1777; Lt. Colonel, 18 March 1779; ADC to Gen. Cornwallis, 1777

Eustace, Charles; 33, Ensign, 24 March 1777; Resigned 1 September 1777

Evans, Edward; 23, Captain, 28 August 1771; Retired 21 March 1778

Evans, John; 38, Ensign, 12 September 1777

Evans, John; 45, Ensign, 23 December 1777; From volunteer; WIA Brandywine with 1st L. I. Bn.; Served with L.I. as ensign

Evans, John; 54, Lieutenant, 7 September 1771

Evans, William; 45, Lieutenant, 17 September 1773; 28, Captain, 25 May 1772; Appointed adjutant, 2nd. L.I. Bn. 27 May 1776

Evatt, Henry; 16 LD, Cornet, 28 December 1775

Evatt, John; 70, Captain, 9 April 1777

Evelyn, William; 29, Colonel, 3 November 1775; Major General ; 30 April 1770; Lieutenant General; 29 August 1777

Evelyn, William Glanville; 4, Captain, 16 October 1772; DOW Pell's Point Landing, 6 November 1776; Left most of his money to an American mistress; Extant letters

Everard, Thos. Potter; 22, Ensign, 27 January 1773; 22, Lieutenant, 22 November 1775; English, born 1752; Retired 24 June 1779

Everest, John C.; 64, Lieutenant, 16 May 1766; 64, Capt.- Lieut., 22 November 1775; English, born 1745; First commissioned at age 17; Appointed Acting Asst. Engineer 26 May 1776; Retired 3 May 1776

Exon, Thomas; 54, Chaplain, 29 December 1781

Eyre, Edmund; 54, Major, 26 October 1775; 64, Lt. Colonel, 5 March 1782, 17 November 1780, WIA Groton, CT, 6 September 1781
Eyre, Edward; 40, Captain, 15 August 1775, 18 October 1761; Major; 29 August 1777
Eyre, Thomas; 9, Ensign, 21 December 1781, 26 September 1781
Eyre, William; 47, Ensign, 15 August 1775; 47, Lieutenant, 6 June 1777
Eyres, Thomas; 23, 2nd Lieut., 11 March 1777; 35, Lieutenant, 28 October 1778; Irish, born 1759; Attended Ballitore School; Apprenticed to an apothecary for several years; From volunteer; POW at Long Island; Had a very aggressive temper, often on the verge of being dismissed from the service; CM and suspended for six months for beating the surgeon's mate, July 1779; Fought at least two duels; CM and cashiered July 1779 for provoking a fight with his major
Faesch, George; 4/60, Captain, 22 September 1775; Joined regt. in 1756; Died 1779
Fage, Edward; RA, Capt.- Lieut., 7 July 1779
Fairie, James; 82, Lieutenant, 16 January 1778 **Fairlamb, John;** RA, 1st Lieut., 1 January 1771; RA, Capt.- Lieut., 18 December 1777; WIA Stono Ferry, SC, 20 June 1779; Promoted to Captain in 1782; Transferred to an Invalid Company, October 1782 **Fairlough, Samuel;** 3, Ensign, 29 November 1780; Also Fairtlough
Falconer, Hon. William; 15, Ensign, 15 August 1775; 15, Lieutenant, 25 November 1776; KIA Brandywine, 11 September 1777
Fanshawe, Henry; 83, Lt. Colonel, 4 June 1781, 9 May 1781, Retired 16 April 1783; Probably did not serve in America
Farley, Henry; 44, Ensign, 9 June 1778; 44, Lieutenant, 1 November 1779
Farmer, Jasper; 21, Capt.- Lieut., 21 February 1776; 21, Captain, 21 February 1776; Native of New Jersey
Farmer, Robert A.; 3/60, Ensign, 8 January 1781;
Farquhar, Fra. Wm.; 29, Ensign, 25 December 1775, 9 October 1775; 29, Lieutenant, 17 February 1778;
Farquhar, William; 20, Capt.- Lieut., 13 May 1776; 20, Captain, 13 May 1776; WIA Freeman's Farm, 19 September 1777
Farquharson, Murray; 83, Lieutenant, 8 December 1778
Farquharson, Thomas; 2/42, Surgeon, 21 March 1781; Resigned 7 September 1784
Farren, George; 65, Chaplain, 4 May 1761
Farrier, John; 4, Capt.- Lieut., 14 November 1771; 4, Captain, 22 November 1775, 25 May 1772
Farrington, Anthony; RA, Captain, 23 May 1764; RA, Major, 11 March 1782, 17 November 1780, Extra Major of Brigade, 1777; ADC to Sir Henry Clinton; Commissary of Accounts, 1783

Farrington, Charles; RA, Major, 1 January 1771; Served at Germantown; Died Woolwich, England, 23 February 1782

Fatio, Francis P.; 4/60, Ensign, 2 September 1779; 4/60, Lieutenant, 1 December 1782; From lieutenant of South Carolina Loyalists, 25 April 1779

Faucitt, Walker Dawson; 3FG, Ensign, 30 October 1772; 3FG, Lieut. & Capt., 16 January 1777; 44, Captain, 10 May 1777, 16 January 1777, Retired 12 May 1778

Faucitt, William; 15, Colonel, 12 November 1778; Major General; 29 August 1777; Lieutenant General; 20 November 1782

Faucitt, William; 3FG, Lieut. & Capt., 18 May 1773; 3FG, Capt. & Lt. Col., 18 September 1779; ADC to Gen. de Heister; ADC to Gen. Knyphausen; Retired 1787

Fearon, George; 22, Ensign, 24 November 1775; Also Fearn; Never served in America; Resigned 21 November 1776

Fearon, George; 31, Ensign, 21 February 1776; 31, Lieutenant, 20 November 1777

Featherstone, William; 21, 1st Lieut., 18 November 1768; 21, Capt.- Lieut., - September 1777; 47, Captain, 25 December 1777; Also Fisher; WIA Bemis Heights, 7 October 1777

Feltham, Jocelyn; 26, Lieutenant, 1 January 1766; 26, Capt.- Lieut., 7 October 1777; 26, Captain, 2 December 1777; POW Ft. Ticonderoga, 10 May 1775

Fenner, H. Christian; 3/60, Lieutenant, 7 February 1776

Fenner, Samuel; 22, Capt.- Lieut., 24 June 1775; 22, Captain, 22 November 1775; Irish, born 1735; To additional company 21 November 1775; Did not return to America

Fenningan, Patrick; 16, Ensign, 27 January 1778

Fenton, -; 44, Ensign, 15 August 1775; Replaced 1 March 1778

Fenton, James; 43, Ensign, 9 December 1778

Fenwick, R. George; 16, Ensign, 24 April 1779; Son of Robert,

Fenwick, Robert; RA, Capt.- Lieut., 1 January 1771; RA, Captain, 25 May 1772; Bridgemaster to the Army; Died in New York, 23 May 1779; Left a widow and seven children

Fenwick, William; 33, Ensign, 13 April 1778; 33, Lieutenant, 1 October 1780

Ferguson, David; 43, Major, 26 October 1777; 1/71, Lt. Colonel, 31 December 1781

Ferguson, David; 23, Captain, 21 August 1765;

Ferguson, John; 24, Quartermaster, 6 April 1776; 24, Ensign, 31 August 1774; 24, Lieutenant, 14 July 1777

Ferguson, Joseph; 23, Captain, 27 January 1764; 46, Major, 10 October 1776;

Ferguson, Joseph; 27, Lt. Colonel, 12 October 1780

Ferguson, Patrick; 70, Captain, 1 September 1768; 2/71, Major, 25 October 1779; Cmd. Ferguson's Riflemen; WIA Brandywine 11 September 1777; KIA King's Mountain, 6 October 1780

Ferguson, William; 24, Captain, 3 February 1776

Fermor, Henry; 18, Lieutenant, 3 June 1771; 18, Captain, 26 July 1775; English, born 1750; First commissioned at age 16

Festing, Maurice Greene; 28, Ensign, 27 May 1776; 28, Lieutenant, 8 January 1778

Field, James; 44, Captain, 30 June 1766, 20 October 1761; Major; 29 August 1777, English, born 1743; First commissioned at age 12

Field, John; Hosp., Surgeon, 19 October 1775; Retired 27 March 1781

Field, John Ventris; 15, Ensign, 20 October 1779

Fielde, William; 4/60, Ensign, 20 May 1779; 4/60, Lieutenant, 3 April 1782; Also Field

Fielding, Isaac; 9, Adjutant, 17 August 1777; 9, Lieutenant, 17 August 1777; WIA Ft. Ann, 9 July 1777; Died 31 December 1780

Fielding, Viscount; 7, Lieutenant, 4 March 1777

Fife, Archibald; 9, Lieutenant, 7 October 1775

Figge, James; 59, Capt.- Lieut., 28 May 1770; 59, Captain, 29 March 1775, 25 May 1772

Finch, John; 1FG, Adjutant, 28 April 1776; 1FG, Lieut. & Capt., 22 April 1776; Bde. Adj.; DOW Short Hills, NJ, 29 June 1777

Finch, William; 27, Lieutenant, 3 May 1775;

Finlay, James; 3/60, Ensign, 10 February 1776; Cmd. troops serving as marines aboard the HMS Rebecca, 25 June 1777; KIA Roupel's Ferry, SC., 3 February 1779

Finley, John; 44, Ensign, 19 January 1779; 83, Lieutenant, 30 January 1778

Finucane, -; 82, Ensign, 18 September 1780;

Fish, Benjamin; 4, Quartermaster, 18 June 1775; 4, Lieutenant, 7 January 1771, 31 July 1760; 44, Captain, 4 October 1776; WIA Brandywine, 11 September 1777

Fish, Joseph; 9, Ensign, 7 October 1775; 9, Lieutenant, 14 July 1777

Fisher, Garret; 55, Captain, 23 January 1773; English, born 1746; First commissioned at age 11; WIA Germantown, 4 October 1777

Fisher, James; 62, Ensign, 20 October 1779

Fisher, James; Hosp., Mate, 25 October 1778; Hosp., Surgeon, 1 October 1783; Stationed at Quebec; Died Edinburgh, 26 June 1822

Fitch, William; 65, Ensign, 16 August 1775

Fitz Gerald, Hunt; 35, Captain, 20 March 1772; WIA White Plains, 28 October 1776

Fitzgerald, -; 37, Ensign, 6 June 1778

Fitzgerald, -; 63, Ensign, 19 October 1781

Fitzgerald, Edward; 10, Captain, 27 March 1767; 57, Major, 30 May 1778; WIA Bunker Hill, 17 June 1775

Fitzgerald, George; 2/42, Lieutenant, 14 June 1775

Fitzgerald, George Tobias; 62, Adjutant, 26 October 1775; KIA or DOW Stillwater, 11 October 1777

Fitzgerald, Gerald; 2/84, Lieutenant, 14 June 1775

Fitzgerald, Henry; 23, 2nd Lieut., 26 February 1772; 23, 1st Lieut., 23 November 1775

Fitzgerald, Hugh; 57, Ensign, 29 June 1778; 57, Lieutenant, 14 July 1780;

Fitzgerald, James; 26, Ensign, 7 October 1777; 26, Lieutenant, 28 April 1780

Fitzgerald, Lord Edward; 19, Lieutenant, 20 September 1780, 14 April 1780; 19, Captain, 1 August 1782; WIA Eutaw Springs, 8 September 1781; First attempt to obtain a captaincy was refused by George III

Fitzgerald, Richard; 30, Ensign, 8 March 1780

Fitzgerald, Samuel; 35, Quartermaster, 28 December 1776; 35, Ensign, 28 June 1775; 35, Lieutenant, 18 August 1778; From volunteer; Ensigncy also given as 12 July 1775

Fitzpatrick, Hon. Richard; 1FG, Lieut. & Capt., 13 September 1772; 1FG, Capt. & Lt. Col., 23 January 1778; 1748-1813; MP Tavistock, 1774-1807; Irish MP; Retired April 1783

Fitzroy, Charles; 11 D, Cornet, 27 August 1779; ADC to Lord Cornwallis,1780

Fitzroy, George Ferdinand; 3D, Lieutenant, 24 June 1778; WIA Charleston, 10 April 1780

Fiva, Anthony; Deputy Provost Marshall, 1781

Fleming, Arthur; 34, Ensign, 3 March 1776; 19, Lieutenant, 1 June 1778;

Fleming, John; 62, Lieutenant, 28 April 1774; Died 24 March 1777

Fleming, Michael; 64, Captain, 25 December 1770; Major; 23 July 1772

Fleming, William; 64, Major, 12 December 1767; English, born 1744; First commissioned at age 15

Fletcher, Alexander; 1/84, Ensign, 16 July 1776; Listed as captain-lieutenant in 1781, but not in 1780 Army List; CM for repeated misconduct and dismissed, 1781

Fletcher, Andrew; 21, 2nd Lieut., 28 July 1780

Fletcher, Henry; 1/84, Lieutenant, 12 May 1778

Fletcher, Richard; 37, Ensign, 18 November 1775; 37, Lieutenant, 6 June 1778

Fletcher, William; 65, Surgeon, 20 June 1770; Retired 9 January 1777
Flint, James; 1/71, Ensign, 3 August 1778; 2/71, Lieutenant, 17 October 1779; From volunteer; POW Boston, 19 June 1776; WIA & POW Cowpens, 17 January 1781
Flood, Charles; 46, Lieutenant, 23 August 1775
Floyer, William; 3/60, Ensign, 24 February 1776; 3/60, Lieutenant, 17 March 1779
Flyn, Charles; RA, 1st Lieut., 7 July 1779; Died Canada, 7 November 1781
Foillet, Thomas; 63, Captain, 25 July 1771; Also Foilliot; WIA Bunker Hill, 17 June 1775; Sold out 11 July 1775
Fonblanque, John Thomas; 17 LD, Cornet, 3 June 1778
Foord, B. Bowes; 26, Ensign, 25 October 1781
Forbes, Alexander; 46, Ensign, 7 July 1779
Forbes, Alexander Philip; 40, Lieutenant, 1 May 1775; WIA La Vigie, 18 December 1778
Forbes, Arthur; 57, Ensign, 12 December 1777
Forbes, Arthur; 2/71, Lieutenant, 29 December 1775
Forbes, Charles; 14, Ensign, 26 September 1775
Forbes, David; 34, Adjutant, 14 November 1775; 34, Lieutenant, 5 October 1770; 34, Capt.- Lieut., 1 January 1777; 34, Captain, 1 January 1777; Possibly WIA Freeman's Farm, 19 September 1777
Forbes, Gordon; 34, Captain, 12 April 1764, 7 October 1762; 9, Major, 11 November 1776; WIA Freeman's Farm, 19 September 1777
Forbes, John; 29, Captain, 25 December 1775, 20 October 1761; Major; 29 August 1777
Forbes, John; 40, Adjutant, 6 April 1777; 40, Ensign, 14 January 1775; 40, Lieutenant, 28 December 1775; 40, Captain, 1 October 1778; WIA Germantown, 4 October 1777
Forbes, John; 1/71, Ensign, 22 September 1779; 1/71, Lieutenant, 19 October 1781;
Forbes, John; 16, Ensign, 8 November 1780
Ford, James; 7, Lieutenant, 24 July 1775
Ford, Samuel; 47, Lieutenant, 6 April 1778
Ford, William; RA, Quartermaster, 1 January 1771; RA, 1st Lieut., 28 April 1773; Died Bath, England, 3 February 1782; Sick since 1780; Died as captain-lieutenant?
Fordyce, Charles; 14, Captain, 9 September 1763, 8 October 1761, KIA Great Bridge, VA, 9 December 1775

Forest, James; 38, Ensign, date unknown; From volunteer; WIA Germantown, 4 October 1777; Commission date between 10 October 1778 and 6 February 1779

Forester, Anthony; 16, Captain, 20 May 1771; 54, Captain, 5 March 1782; WIA Pensacola, 7 July 1781

Forester, Matthew; 45, Ensign, 20 August 1778

Forrest, James; 17, Lieutenant, 19 February 1781; Native of Boston, MA; To Captain in Loyal Irish Volunteers, 7 December 1775

Forrester, David; 80, Lieutenant, 22 January 1778;

Forster, Christian; 55, Lieutenant, 16 July 1774; 55, Capt.- Lieut., 10 December 1779; 55, Captain, 10 December 1779; Irish, born 1754; First commissioned at age 18; POW June 1777

Forster, George; 21, Major, 5 November 1776

Forster, George; 8, Captain, 25 December 1776; English, born, 1726; First commissioned at age 19; Served as adjutant in the 1760s; At the Cedars

Forster, M. Fredrick; 64, Ensign, 28 May 1779; English, born 1765; First commissioned at age 14

Forster, Richard; 28, Ensign, 18 August 1780; Died 2 December 1781

Forster, Thompson; Hosp., Surgeon, 19 October 1775; Also Thomson Foster; Stationed at New York, 1783; To half pay 25 December 1783; Died Southwell, Notts. 19 December 1830; Kept journal 1775-1777

Forster, William; 24, Ensign, 3 February 1776; 24, Lieutenant, 1 December 1778

Forsyth, William; 83, Ensign, 12 March 1782

Fosbrook, William; Hosp., Cutler, Prior to 1783; Stationed at New York, 1783

Foster, Nicholas; 24, Ensign, 3 March 1776

Fothergill, John; 52, Ensign, 18 August 1778

Fowke, William; 8, Ensign, 10 June 1771

Fowler, Alexander; 18, Lieutenant, 12 August 1768, 4 March 1763, CM for bearing false witness against Cpt. Payne of 18th Foot; Sold out 1775

Fowler, George; 38, Quartermaster, 21 July 1775; 38, Ensign, 7 February 1779; Appointed adjutant 1st Gren. Bn. 17 May 1776

Fowler, John; 47, Ensign, 23 February 1781

Fownes, Thomas; 16, Captain, 6 January 1772, 31 January 1772

Fox, Hon. Henry Edward; 38, Captain, 14 February 1774; 49, Major, 12 July 1777; 38, Lt. Colonel, 12 October 1778; Am., Brigadier General, date unknown; Sprnmy. ADC to Sir Wm. Howe, 7 October 1776; Cmd. 2nd Bn. Gren, May 1780; Brig. gen. date not listed in NAAL, 1783

Fox, Hopkins; 35, Chaplain, 24 February 1775

Fox, John; 33, Adjutant, 22 October 1778; 33, Ensign, 18 August 1780; From sergeant major; WIA Guilford CH, 15 March 1781

Foxlow, William; 62, Ensign, 29 March 1776

Foxon, James; 10, Ensign, date unknown; Cashiered 16 April 1776; Not mentioned in WO 65 papers

Foy, Edward; RA, Captain, 2 February 1764; Sec. to Gen. Carleton; Died 27 April 1779

Foy, Louis; 29, Ensign, 29 October 1779

Foy, Louis; 44, Ensign, 7 September 1779; May be the same man as above

Framingham, Haylet; RA, 2nd Lieut., 29 April 1780

Francquefort, Peter; 15, Lieutenant, 30 September 1775

Franklin, Robert; 1/42, Lieutenant, 6 September 1775; 1/42, Capt.- Lieut., 27 July 1783; Irish, born 1752; First commissioned at age 19; POW Boston, 19 June 1776

Fraser, Aeneas; 2/42, Lieutenant, 23 March 1780

Fraser, Alexander; 34, Captain, 11 November 1776; Scottish; From 20th Foot; Served in F&I War 78th Foot; Led Fraser's Marksmen; Assistant Superintendent of Indian Affairs, Canada, 1776-1777

Fraser, Alexander; 1/84, Captain, 14 June 1775; Scottish, c1729-1799; Served in F&I War 78th Foot

Fraser, Alexander; 1/84, Capt.- Lieut., 14 June 1775; 1/84, Captain, 10 May 1780

Fraser, Alexander; 1/84, Ensign, 17 October 1782

Fraser, Alexander; 9, Capt.- Lieut., 13 May 1776

Fraser, Alexander; 1/71, Lieutenant, 12 December 1775; Possibly POW Boston, 19 June 1776; One Alex. Fraser was a POW, not both however; Died 24 May, 17 September or 15 October 1780

Fraser, Alexander; 1/71, Adjutant, 17 October 1778; 1/71, Lieutenant, 19 December 1775; Possibly POW Boston, 19 June 1776; One Alex. Fraser was a POW, not both however; Died 15 October 1780

Fraser, Alexander; 1/42, Ensign, 8 August 1783; Scottish, born 1762; First commissioned at age 20

Fraser, Alexander; 69, Ensign, 28 January 1782;

Fraser, Charles; 23, 2nd Lieut., 3 August 1778; 23, 1st Lieut., 10 August 1780; From ensign Queen's American Rangers, 19 September 1777. Originally a volunteer

Fraser, Edward; 1/71, Lieutenant, 3 August 1780; Possibly 2nd Bn. not 1st Bn.

Fraser, Edward S.; 2/71, Captain, 20 June 1781

Fraser, Erskine; 2/71, Ensign, 14 October 1780; 1/71, Lieutenant, 21 July 1781

Fraser, Henry David; 64, Ensign, 20 September 1776; 1/42, Lieutenant, 23 November 1778; Scottish, born 1762; First commissioned at age 16

Fraser, Hon. George; 44, Ensign, 27 January 1779; 1/42, Lieutenant, 31 May 1780, 16 October 1779

Fraser, Hugh; 1/42, Adjutant, 20 March 1776; 1/42, Ensign, 17 December 1777; 1/42, Lieutenant, 19 October 1778; Scottish, born 1752; First commissioned at age 14

Fraser, Hugh; 1/71, Lieutenant, 9 December 1775; POW Boston, 19 June 1776; Possibly WIA Ft. Clinton, 6 October 1777

Fraser, Hugh; 2/84, Lieutenant, 27 February 1776; POW Carolina, 1776

Fraser, James; 2/71, Lieutenant, 10 December 1775; POW Boston, 19 June 1776

Fraser, James; 1/71, Captain, 8 April 1779, 20 December 1760, Possibly WIA Bonumtown, NJ, 10 May 1777

Fraser, James; Major; 29 August 1777

Fraser, James; RA, 2nd Lieut., 11 July 1782

Fraser, John; 76, Captain, 28 December 1777

Fraser, John; 82, Lieutenant, 17 January 1778

Fraser, John Daniel; 17, Ensign, 18 November 1775, 26 October 1775; 17, Lieutenant, 31 January 1778; Scots-Irish; Father retired as a colonel

Fraser, John G.; RA, 2nd Lieut., 10 February 1780; RA, 1st Lieut.,10 February 1780; Acting Paymaster 30 July 1782

Fraser, Malcom; 1/84, Captain, 14 June 1775; 1733-1815; Served in F&I War 78th Foot; Raised 130 Irishmen for the 84th Foot; To 60th Foot after American War

Fraser, Peter; 1/71, Ensign, 7 December 1775; 1/71, Lieutenant, 14 October 1778; POW Boston, 19 June 1776; Died 4 November 1780,

Fraser, Simon; 71, Colonel, 25 October 1775; Major General; 25 May 1772; Lieutenant General; 29 August 1777; Scottish, 1726- 12 February 1782; 12th Lord Lovat; Raised 78th in F&I War; MP Inverness-shire, 1761-1782

Fraser, Simon; 24, Lt. Colonel, 14 July 1768; Brigadier General; 8 June 1776, DOW Bemis Heights, 8 October 1777

Fraser, Simon; 1/71, Captain, 23 November 1775; 1/71, Major, 14 October 1778; Scottish, c1738-1813; Served in F&I War, 78th Foot; WIA Danbury, CT, between 25 & 27 April 1777; Depty. Quartermaster Gen., 1781; Raised 133rd Foot in 1794; 2nd in cmd. Scotland, c1800

Fraser, Simon; 1/84, Ensign, 15 August 1783

Fraser, Thomas; 1/71, Adjutant, 25 May 1780; 1/71, Lieutenant, 20 December 1775; 2/71, Captain, 18 February 1781; Possibly WIA Ft. Clinton, 6 October 1777

Fraser, Thomas; 2/71, Lieutenant, 11 December 1775

Fraser, Thomas; 2/71, Lieutenant, 4 January 1776; WIA Stono Ferry, SC, 20 June 1779; KIA Yorktown, 16 or 19 October 1781

Fraser, William; 1/42, Ensign, 3 August 1778; Scottish, born 1767; Entered service at age 12; From volunteer; With 1st L.I. Bn. as ensign, 17 August 1778; Ensigncy also listed as 13 September 1778

Fraser, William; 1/42, Lieutenant, 25 August 1779

Fraser, William; 1/42, Ensign, 25 August 1779; Resigned 26 July 1783

Fraser, William; 1/42, Ensign, 13 September 1780

Fraser, William; 1/71, Surgeon, 23 November 1775; 16 LD, Surgeon, 20 December 1777; Purchased into 16th L.D.; Retired 8 November 178

Frazer, Edw. Satchwell; 1FG, Ensign, 24 November 1773; 1FG, Lieut. & Capt., 3 July 1777; To 4th Foot

Frederick, Anthony; 15, Ensign, 18 November 1775; KIA Germantown, 4 October 1777; He may have been promoted to lieutenant posthumously

Frederick, Mariscoe; 54, Colonel, 30 April 1770; Major General; 30 April 1770; Lieutenant General; 29 August 1777

Frederick, Thomas; 54, Ensign, 26 January 1779; 54, Lieutenant, 1 April 1781; 54, Captain, 14 October 1781; Possibly WIA Charleston, 1781

Freeman, Anthony; 9, Chaplain, 25 July 1771

Freeman, James; 59, Ensign, 13 February 1765, 21 October 1762; 59, Lieutenant, 1 November 1774; To captain, Royal Fencible Americans, 26 July 1775

Freeman, John; 28, Lieutenant, 28 November 1771; 28, Capt.- Lieut., 14 January 1779; Died and immediately buried, 27 June 1780

Freeman, John; 7, Lieutenant, 8 January 1768;

Freeman, Quin John; 24, Ensign, 7 July 1775; 24, Lieutenant, 8 October 1777

Freeman, Thomas; 64, Ensign, 15 February 1776; 64, Lieutenant, 26 February 1778; Also Freemantle; WIA Brandywine, 11 September 1777; WIA Charleston, 23 April 1780; DOW Camden or Charleston 21 August 1780

Freer, Robert; 80, Surgeon, 17 January 1778; To half pay, 1784; M.A. Kings Coll. Abd. 1765; M.D. 1779; Professor of medicine, U. of Glasgow, 1796; Died Glasgow, 9 April 1727

French, Arthur; 22, Lieutenant, 14 July 1769, 15 November 1762, Irish, born 1752; WIA 8 December 1777; Served in rifle coy. 1st L.I. Bn, 1777; Resigned January 1779; To 88th Regiment October 1779. Son of Christopher French

French, Arthur; 47, Ensign, 16 December 1771; 47, Lieutenant, 25 July 1775; Appointed Fraser's Marksmen, 1777

French, Christopher; 22, Captain, 23 July 1772, 25 October 1756; 22, Major, 24 June 1775; Lt. Colonel; 29 August 1777; POW, 1775; Cmd. 1st L.I. Bn., 20 January 1777; Cmd Queen's Rangers, 30 January 1777; To 52nd Regiment, 3 November 1777

French, Eyre Power; 54, Captain, 1 December 1775; 38, Major, 8 September 1781; 52, Lt. Colonel, 3 November 1777; Also Trench; Retired 5 October 1778

French, George; 63, Lieutenant, 2 October 1773, 12 December 1770, Retired 13 April 1778

French, Jeremiah; 29, Major, 26 July 1773; 31, Lt. Colonel, 13 September 1777

French, Joseph; 35, Ensign, 23 December 1776; 35, Lieutenant, 28 October 1778

French, Robert; 31, Ensign, 16 August 1781

Frith, John; 37, Ensign, 11 March 1774; 37, Lieutenant, 18 November 1775; Retired 23 March 1778

Frost, James; RA, 1st Lieut., 1 November 1776; WIA Germantown, 4 October 1777

Fry, Philip; 8, Ensign, 11 May 1778

Fuge, John; 52, Ensign, 23 September 1772; 52, Lieutenant, 18 June 1775

Fuller, Bartholomew; 49, Surgeon, 7 September 1776; By purchase; Resigned 26 August 1786

Fuller, George; 19, Ensign, 9 September 1781

Furlong, Jonathan; 14, Major, 27 March 1765

Furnival, Thomas; FG, Quartermaster, 12 August 1778; From quartermaster sergeant; 2nd Bn. QM; Promoted to Bde QM 17 April 1779; Subject of a Board of Enquiry, 3 January 1781; POW and paroled, Yorktown

Fuser, Lewis Valentine; 4/60, Lt. Colonel, 20 September 1775; From 1/60th Foot; Joined regt. in 1756; Died at St. Augustine, 17 February 1780

Fyers, William; RE, Sub-eng. & Lt., 7 May 1779; In America from 1775-1783; Served at Boston, New York and Charleston

Fyffe, James; 80, Ensign, 13 September 1780

Gabbett, Joseph; 15, Lt. Colonel, 17 August 1768; Colonel, 25 May 1772;

Gabbett, Joseph; 55, Ensign, 27 October 1775;

Gabbett, Joseph; 15, Ensign, 25 November 1775

Gage, Henry; 7, Lieutenant, 25 March 1777; 26, Captain, 24 April 1779

Gage, Hon. Thomas; 22, Colonel, 29 March 1762; 17 LD, Colonel, 18 April 1782; Lieutenant General; 30 April 1770, Resigned 18 April 1782

Gage, James; 45, Ensign, 23 March 1775; 45, Lieutenant, 11 January 1777

Gair, Edward; 5, Surgeon, 7 September 1776; From mate; Died 21 November 1780

Gair, William; 28, Ensign, 19 August 1778; 28, Lieutenant, 25 October 1781

Galbraith, James; 64, Lieutenant, 12 November 1767; Scottish, born 1738; First commissioned at age 25

Gale, Samuel; Cashier at Charleston, 1782

Gallaway, John; 35, Ensign, 25 March 1778; Involved in a duel

Galpine, Thomas; 6, Ensign, 20 May 1777

Gamble, George Aug.; 4, Ensign, 23 October 1778

Gamble, John; Hosp., Mate, Prior to 1783; With Queen's Rangers, 1783

Gamble, John Henry; 30, Lieutenant, 17 November 1780

Gamble, Thomas; 16, Lieutenant, 28 September 1770, 26 September 1762; Am., Captain, 14 November 1771; 47, Captain, 1 August 1775; Am., Major, 26 November 1778; POW Princeton; Exchanged 7 March 1777; Majority also dated 6 November 1778

Garden, Alexander; 23, Quartermaster, 23 September 1781

Gardiner, Charles; 43, Ensign, 22 July 1781

Gardiner, James; 4, Ensign, 18 August 1778; 4, Lieutenant, 15 November 1780

Gardiner, John; 40, Lieutenant, 1 April 1773, 24 May 1762, Retired 1 May 1775

Gardiner, Robert; 59, Ensign, 17 July 1770, 20 October 1761

Gardiner, Valentine; 55, Captain, 25 December 1765, 15 June 1765; 16, Major, 11 January 1776; English, born 1730; First commissioned at age 14; ADC to Gen. Howe, 12 May 1776

Gardiner, William; 45, Captain, 31 March 1770; 10, Major, 30 October 1777, 4 March 1777; 45, Lt. Colonel, 29 June 1778; ADC to Sir Wm. Howe, 1777; WIA Monmouth, 28 June 1778 with 2nd. Gren. Bn.

Gardner, H. Farrington; 16 LD, Capt.- Lieut., 6 November 1772

Garforth, Francis; 63, Ensign, 2 December 1777; 7, Lieutenant, 19 September 1779; 22, Captain, 1 May 1782

Garnett, Wm. Augustus; 34, Lieutenant, 20 October 1774; 1/84, Captain, 20 October 1781

Garnock, James; 5, Quartermaster, 19 June 1779; From sergeant-major; Died 29 August 1780

Garstin, John; 35, Ensign, 11 August 1779; Irish; Son of a RA officer who held estates in Bedford; Attended Ballitore School

Garth, George; 1FG, Capt. & Lt. Col., 6 February 1772; Colonel; 19 February 1779; Am., Brigadier General, 17 June 1779; ADC to the King, 19 February 1779; 3rd Major in England, March 1782

Gartside, Thomas; 16 LD, Cornet, 23 November 1775

Gary, -; 38, Surgeon, 5 July 1777; Also Garce; From mate; Died 24 August 1780

Gascoyne, Isaac; 20, Ensign, 8 February 1779

Gaskill, John; 20, Lieutenant, 14 December 1770; 20, Capt.- Lieut., 1 June 1778

Gason, John; 40, Ensign, 12 December 1774; 40, Lieutenant, 11 December 1775; 40, Capt.- Lieut., 15 October 1778; 40, Captain, 15 October 1778;

Gaul, William; 35, Major, 12 March 1774

Gaylard, Thomas; 34, Captain, 1 September 1771, 17 January 1760, Died 31 December 1776

Geary, Francis; 16 LD, Cornet, 4 March 1773; KIA Flemington, NJ, 14 December 1776

Gedstanes, George; 30, Ensign, 31 January 1780

Gem, Richard; 19, Lieutenant, 10 July 1776;

Gemmill, John; Hosp., Mate, Prior to 1783; Stationed at New York, 1783

Geneway, Lewis; 3/60, Quartermaster, 1 September 1775

Gerald, Hunt Fitz; 35, Captain, 20 March 1772

Gethin, Wm. St. Lawrence; 45, Ensign, 5 July 1780

Gew, James; Hosp., Sprnmy. Mate, Prior to 1783; Stationed at New York, 1783

Gibbons, Thomas; 23, 1st Lieut., 27 January 1764; 23, Capt.- Lieut., 6 October 1776; 23, Captain, 5 October 1777

Gibbons, Thomas; 44, Ensign, 15 May 1772; 44, Lieutenant, 22 November 1775

Gibson, Edward; 30, Ensign, 29 June 1780

Gibson, Edward; 4, Ensign, 21 February 1780

Gibson, James; 80, Ensign, 22 March 1779; 80, Lieutenant, 20 July 1781

Gibson, Patrick; 8, Quartermaster, 7 April 1779

Gibson, Thomas; 63, Ensign, 14 December 1774; Gibson, Thomas; 63, Lieutenant, 16 May 1776; KIA Blackstocks, 20 November 1780

Gibson, Thomas; 63, Ensign, 16 May 1776; 63, Lieutenant, 21 January 1778

Giddes, Alexander; 31, Ensign, 9 August 1780

Gifford, James; 14, Captain, 21 August 1765, 31 March 1763

Gilbert, Roger Pomeroy; 3, Adjutant, 12 August 1779; 3, Lieutenant, 7 March 1768

Gilbert, Walter Raleigh; 20, Lieutenant, 7 July 1775

Gilchrist, Harry; 1/42, Lieutenant, 6 March 1776; DOW Monmouth, 26 August 1778 with 2nd. Gren. Bn.

Giles, William; 19, Adjutant, 2 August 1769; 34, Lieutenant, 1 March 1776, 26 October 1761; 19, Capt.- Lieut., 12 November 1778

Gilfillan, Thomas; 55, Adjutant, 2 January 1774; 64, Lieutenant, 10 March 1777; 1/71, Captain, 19 February 1781; Scottish, born 1738; First commissioned at age 36; Most likely promoted from the ranks; Extra Asst. Depty. Quartermaster Gen., 1779

Gilfillan, John; 83, Lieutenant, 13 December 1782

Gillan, John; 55, Captain, 28 May 1768; Major; 17 November 1780, Scottish, born 1740; First commissioned at age 16

Gillaspie, -; 4, Surgeon, 5 July 1777; Also Gillespie; From mate 45th Foot; Died prior to 9 July 1789

Gillaspie, James; 15, Ensign, 20 April 1778; 15, Lieutenant, 7 November 1781; Lieutenancy also dated, 26 June 1781

Gillaspie, Rollo; 45, Ensign, 1 April 1776; 45, Lieutenant, 21 July 1779

Gillaspy, Lawrence; 65, Ensign, 2 August 1775

Gillies, James; Hosp., Sprnmy. Mate, Prior to 1783; Stationed at New York, 1783

Gilman, George; 27, Adjutant, 6 September 1765; 27, Capt.- Lieut., 8 September 1775; 27, Captain, 8 September 1775

Gilman, George Massey; 27, Adjutant, 9 April 1777; 27, Ensign, 21 September 1777; 27, Lieutenant, 20 September 1781

Gisborne, James; 16, Colonel, 4 March 1766; Major General; 30 April 1770; Lieutenant General; 29 August 1777, Died 13 May 1778, probably in Britain

Gladwin, Henry; Lt. Colonel, 17 September 1763; Colonel; 29 August 1777, Originally served with 80th Foot in F&I War; Deputy Adj. Gen. in America, 1774

Glazier, Beamsley; 4/60, Major, 23 September 1775; 4/60, Lt. Colonel, 6 June 1780; Also Glasier; Cmd. grenadiers on 2/60, 3/60 & 4/60 during southern campaign, 1779-1780; Given land grant on St. John's River, New Brunswick

Gledstanes, Ralph; 28, Lieutenant, 24 May 1775; 55, Capt.- Lieut., 25 October 1781

Glenie, James; RE, Pract. eng. & 2nd Lt., 23 February 1779; In America from 1777-1779

Glyn, Thomas; 1FG, Ensign, 7 June 1773; 1FG, Lieut. & Capt., 15 June 1776

Gloster, John; 65, Surgeon, 30 May 1781; From mate; Exchanged to half pay 75th Foot, 17 April 1784; Died prior to 22 July 1789

Goakman, Richard; 2/71, Lieutenant, 22 June 1781, 17 March 1780

73

Godwin, William; RA, Capt.- Lieut., 1 January 1771; RA, Captain, 25 May 1772

Gold, Richard; 47, Lieutenant, 23 August 1758; KIA Bunker Hill, 17 June 1775; May have DOW 18 June 1775

Goldfrapp, John George; 15, Adjutant, 22 February 1771; 15, Lieutenant, 13 April 1772; 15, Captain, 26 October 1775; WIA Germantown, 4 October 1777

Goldsmith, Henry; 54, Ensign, 12 July 1773; 54, Lieutenant, 27 November 1775; WIA Fall River, MA, 31 May 1778

Goldsworthy, William; 27, Ensign, 18 January 1779; 49, Lieutenant, 3 May 1780

Goll, John Daniel; RA, 1st Lieut., 1 August 1767

Gomm, William; 46, Lieutenant, 8 September 1775; 55, Captain, 25 September 1780; WIA La Vigie, 18 December 1778; Lost an eye

Goodenough, Edward; 17, Major, 15 June 1773, 23 July 1772;

Goodere, John; 38, Ensign, 18 August 1778

Goodricke, John; 1FG, Ensign, 14 June 1776; 1FG, Lieut. & Capt., 26 December 1779; Also Goodrich; DOW Guilford CH, 15 March 1781

Gordon, -; 83, Ensign, 15 January 1783

Gordon, Abraham Cyrus; 21, 2nd Lieut., 8 October 1777; From volunteer; Formerly ensign, 24th Foot; WIA Germantown, 4 October 1777

Gordon, Alexander; 49, Ensign, 4 October 1776; Died 22 May 1778

Gordon, Alexander; 2, Lieutenant, 6 November 1778; Native of Boston

Gordon, Alexander; FG, Mate, 4 March 1776; Assigned 2nd Guards Bn. 1 August 1776; POW Yorktown

Gordon, Andrew; 26, Captain, 7 September 1768; 26, Major, 18 January 1777

Gordon, Archibald; 53, Lieutenant, 2 August 1775

Gordon, Archibald Kinloch; 65, Lieutenant, 26 August 1767; 65, Captain, 3 June 1774

Gordon, Charles; 1/71, Lieutenant, 2 December 1775; 26, Captain, 8 January 1778

Gordon, Charles; 83, Lt. Colonel, 17 April 1783; Lt. Colonelcy also listed as 2 April 1782

Gordon, Cosmo; 3FG, Capt. & Lt. Col., 18 May 1773; WIA Springfield, NJ, 23 June 1780; Not POW after Yorktown; Wounded in a duel with Lt. Col. Thomas over Gordon's conduct in New Jersey. Thomas was killed; Retired 1784

Gordon, David; 59, Quartermaster, 29 June 1775

Gordon, G. Henry; 9, Lieutenant, 31 May 1780, 12 April 1780

Gordon, George; 65, Quartermaster, 12 October 1776; 65, Ensign, 12 January 1770; 65, Lieutenant, 2 August 1775; Native of Boston, MA; Promoted to lieutenant colonel 29th Light Dragoons, 16 March 1798

Gordon, Harry; RE, Eng. ord. & Capt., 4 January 1758; Lt. Colonel; 29 August 1777, In America from 1755-1778; Served at Niagara, West Indies, Canada

Gordon, Hon. John; 52, Captain, 15 August 1775; Major; 23 July 1772; Lt. Colonel, 29 August 1777

Gordon, Hon. Lockhart; 35, Captain, 16 August 1776; Major; 23 July 1772; Lt. Colonel, 29 August 1777; Second son of the Earl of Aboyne; Attended University of Glasgow

Gordon, Hugh Mackay; 2/71, Ensign, 10 March 1777; 16, Lieutenant, 27 April 1778; Native of Boston, MA; From private, Loyal American Associators, 1775; Deputy Inspector General of Provincial Forces, 1779; ADC to General Campbell, 1782; Eventually promoted Major General in 1811

Gordon, James; 80, Major, 16 December 1777, 29 August 1777, POW Yorktown; Died New York, summer 1783

Gordon, James; 26, Ensign, 25 January 1771; 26, Lieutenant, 17 March 1777; DOW Ft. Clinton, 29 October 1777

Gordon, James; 55, Ensign, 11 May 1776; 55, Lieutenant, 18 August 1778

Gordon, James; 3/60, Ensign, 2 September 1775; 3/60, Lieutenant, 21 May 1778; KIA Mobile, AL, 7 January 1781

Gordon, James; 21, Chaplain, 12 January 1757

Gordon, John; 54, Captain, 7 July 1775

Gordon, John; 27, Ensign, 7 August 1776

Gordon, John William; RA, 2nd Lieut., 23 February 1779; Killed in Charleston powder magazine explosion, 15 May 1780

Gordon, Lord Adam; 26, Colonel, 27 December 1775; Major General; 25 May 1772; Lieutenant General; 29 August 1777, 1726-1801; MP Kincardineshire, 1774-1788

Gordon, Patrick; 29, Lt. Colonel, date unknown; DOW near St. John's, 1 August 1776

Gordon, Paulus AE; 47, Ensign, 1 April 1780

Gordon, Robert; 44, Ensign, 3 July 1772; 35, Lieutenant, 27 December 1775; Died 16 April 1779

Gordon, Robert; 54, Mate, 1775; 54, Surgeon, 30 July 1779; By purchase; Retired by sale of commission, 13 September 1781; Served as mate at Gen. Hosp. Jamaica and Home after sale; Died 27 May 1822

Gordon, Thomas; 1FG, Lieut. & Capt., 23 May 1764; 1FG, Capt. & Lt. Col., 4 July 1776; Retired April 1780

Gordon, William; 54, Captain, 15 October 1781

Gordon, William; 1/71, Lieutenant, 10 March 1777

Gordon, William; 2/71, Ensign, 23 November 1775

Gordon, William; 2/71, Lieutenant, 18 September 1779

Gordon, William; 76, Ensign, 6 September 1780

Gordon, William Brau; 52, Lieutenant, 12 January 1773; 52, Captain, 15 August 1775; Died Banff, Scotland, 8 December 1776

Gore, John; 5, Captain, 14 March 1772; KIA Monmouth 28 June 1778, with 1st Gren. Bn.

Gore, Paul; 27, Captain, 16 August 1774, 13 February 1762

Gore, Ralph; 33, Ensign, 16 April 1778; 33, Lieutenant, 24 April 1781; WIA Guilford CH, 15 March 1781

Gore, Ralph; 34, Ensign, 21 February 1776l 34, Lieutenant, 22 October 1779

Gore, William; 33, Lieutenant, 26 December 1770; 33, Capt.- Lieut., 6 January 1776; 33, Captain, 6 January 1776; Irish, born 1751; First commissioned at age 15

Gore, William; 49, Adjutant, 16 July 1774; 49, Lieutenant, 30 March 1770, 31 January 1760; 49, Capt.- Lieut., 22 November 1775; KIA White Plains, 28 October 1776

Goreham, John W.; RA, 2nd Lieut., 29 April 1780

Gorges, Thomas; 33, Ensign, 17 February 1774; 33, Lieutenant, 26 January 1776

Gorges, Thomas; 10, Captain, 9 December 1777; Also Georges; English, born 1758; First commissioned at age 15

Gough, Thomas; 44, Ensign, 3 July 1772; 44, Lieutenant, 7 December 1775

Gould, Augustus; 3/60, Ensign, 21 May 1779

Gould, Buckley; 59, Ensign, 26 December 1770

Gould, Edward Thoroton; 4, Lieutenant, 14 November 1771; WIA & POW, Concord, MA, 19 April 1775

Gould, Hubort; 65, Lieutenant, 15 August 1775, 27 October 1761

Gould, John; Hosp., Mate, Prior to 1783; Stationed at Halifax, 1783

Gould, Paston; 30, Lt. Colonel, 28 March 1764; Colonel, 29 August 1777

Gould, Sir Charles; 2FG, Lieut. & Capt., 22 March 1781; POW, later Sir Charles Morgan, Bt.;Depty. Judge Advocate General

Gouldnay, Adam; 22, Lieutenant, 30 May 1773; 4, Captain, 4 June 1777; English, born 1745; Adjutant, 1st. Gren. Bn., 23 September 1776; To 4th Foot, 4 June 1777

Gowan, Thomas; 30, Lieutenant, 1 June 1778

Gowdy, James; 27, Surgeon, 22 December 1776; From mate; By purchase; Died 10 November 1778

Grafton, J. Marmaduke; 4, Ensign, 20 March 1778

Graham, Alexander; 55, Lieutenant, 20 January 1779, 27 December 1778

Graham, Charles; 1/42, Captain, 7 September 1771; 1/42, Major, 25 August 1778; Scottish, born 1750; First commissioned at age 10

Graham, Colin; 16, Captain, 17 April 1769, 28 October 1760; Major, 29 August 1777, WIA Roupel's Ferry, SC, 3 February 1779 and Saltketcher River, SC, 18 March 1780

Graham, Francis; 37, Adjutant, 10 April 1769; 37, Lieutenant, 20 May 1761; 37, Capt.- Lieut., 27 January 1776; 37, Captain, 27 January 1776; Died from a fit of apoplexy in New York, 3 December 1778

Graham, Gorges; 34, Ensign, 29 March 1776; 1/84, Lieutenant, 17 January 1782; Also George; CM for "three days of riotous, disorderly and abusive behaviour," apologized at head of regt. August 1781

Graham, Henry; 1/42, Ensign, 11 November 1777; 1/42, Lieutenant, 2 February 1779

Graham, James; 57, Captain, 8 May 1777; 37, Major, 30 December 1781;

Graham, James; 1/42, Lieutenant, 1 March 1773; Scottish, born 1744; First commissioned at age 15

Graham, James; 57, Ensign, 9 January 1776; 1/42, Lieutenant, 18 August 1778

Graham, James; 64, Lieutenant, 23 November 1778, 18 August 1778, WIA Eutaw Springs 8 September 1781

Graham, John; 1/42, Lieutenant, 20 February 1767, 31 July 1760

Graham, John; 1/71, Capt.- Lieut., 23 August 1776; 1/71, Captain, 23 August 1776; Scottish, born 1740; First commissioned at age 18; Died 7 April 1779

Graham, John; 35, Ensign, 20 October 1774; 35, Lieutenant, 28 December 1776;

Graham, John; 82, Lieutenant, 12 January 1778; WIA Penobscot, ME, 31 July 1779

Graham, John James; 4/60, Lieutenant, 21 November 1776

Graham, Patrick; 1/42, Lieutenant, 8 September 1775; 1/42, Captain, 5 June 1778; 2/42, Major, 31 March 1780; Scottish, born 1755; First commissioned at age 17; WIA White Plains, 28 October 1776; Listed as KIA in the Peter Force Papers; Died 1784

Graham, Samuel; 76, Capt.- Lieut., 9 April 1779

Graham, Samuel; 31, Ensign, 20 November 1777

Graham, William; 1/42, Quartermaster, 18 January 1760; 1/42, Lieutenant, 23 November 1772; 45, Captain, 1 March 1773; Scottish, born 1753; First commissioned at age 16

Gramme, David; 19, Colonel, 25 May 1768; Lieutenant General; 25 May 1772

Gramme, David; 52, Ensign, 12 January 1773; 52, Lieutenant, 25 June 1775; DOW Bunker Hill, 4 July 1775

Gramme, John; 54, Lieutenant, 21 June 1772; 54, Capt.- Lieut., 7 September 1781

Grant, -; Lieutenant, 1779; Acting Barrack Master for New York

Grant, Alexander; 1/42, Ensign, 1 March 1773; 1/42, Lieutenant, 23 May 1776; Scottish, born 1752; First commissioned at age 20; Possibly WIA White Plains, 28 October 1776 (either Alexander or one of Johns is listed as WIA); Possibly WIA Charleston, 5 April 1780

Grant, Alexander, 1/42, Ensign, 18 March 1778; 1/42, Lieutenant, 24 August 1779; Nicknamed "Saunders?"; Possibly WIA Charleston, 5 April 1780; Left service by 1782

Grant, Alexander; 55, Ensign, 10 December 1779; 55, Lieutenant, 3 December 1781

Grant, Alexander; 1/71, Lieutenant, 25 August 1776, 7 November 1759; Probably WIA Camden, 16 August 1780

Grant, Alexander; 64, Ensign, 30 October 1776; DOW Brandywine, 3 October 1777

Grant, Alexander; Hosp., Surgeon, 11 February 1775; Later Inspector of Regt. Hosp.; To half pay 25 December 1783; Died 29 September 1817

Grant, Andrew; 22, Lieutenant, 18 October 1762, 10 October 1762; 22, Capt.- Lieut., 22 November 1775; 22, Captain, 30 October 1776; Scottish, born 1734; Retired 23 May 1779

Grant, Archibald; 1/84, Ensign, 12 June 1775; 1/84, Lieutenant, 21 June 1777; Lieutenancy also given as 25 December 1776

Grant, Charles; 1/42, Lieutenant, 9 August 1762; 1/42, Captain, 20 March 1776; Scottish, born 1743; First commissioned at age 16

Grant, David Alexander; 1/84, Captain, 14 June 1775; From lieutenant 60th Foot

Grant, Francis; 63, Colonel, 6 November 1768; Major General; 30 April 1770; Lieutenant General; 29 August 1777, Died 1 January 1782

Grant, Francis; 55, Ensign, 5 July 1780

Grant, James; 40, Lt. Colonel, 26 July 1760; 55, Colonel, 11 December 1775, 25 May 1772; Am., Major General, 1 January 1776, 29 August 1777; Scottish, 1720-1806; MP Tainsburghs, 1773-1780

Grant, James; 40, Major, 12 December 1770; 40, Lt. Colonel, 11 December 1775; KIA Brooklyn Heights, 27 August 1776

Grant, James; 49, Captain, 25 May 1772

Grant, James; 14, Ensign, 18 June 1775; 14, Lieutenant, 24 October 1776

Grant, James; 16 LD, Cornet, 27 December 1775; 16LD, Lieutenant, 15 August 1775, 20 October 1760

Grant, James; 27, Ensign, 7 July 1779

Grant, James; 57, Ensign, 5 June 1777, 1 September 1776
Grant, James; 1/84, Ensign, 1782; From sergeant
Grant, James Murray; 2/71, Ensign, 21 June 1781
Grant, John; 2/42, Captain, 25 December 1781; Retired 20 April 1782
Grant, John; 2/42, Captain, 27 March 1780; From 2/1st Foot
Grant, John; 40, Lieutenant, 8 September 1781; 1/42, Lieutenant, 1
September 1775, 11 November 1761, Possibly WIA White Plains, 28
October 1776 (either Alexander or one of Johns is listed as WIA)
Grant, John; 1/42, Lieutenant, 14 January 1775; 2/42, Lieutenant, 14
January 1775; Scottish, born 1739; First commissioned at age 22; Possibly
WIA White Plains, 28 October 1776 (either Alexander or one of Johns is
listed as WIA); In Newfoundland, 1778
Grant, John; 57, Lieutenant, 18 October 1778
Grant, John; 1/71, Ensign, 27 November 1775; 1/71, Lieutenant, 14
October 1778
Grant, John; 2/71, Ensign, 8 December 1775; 2/71, Lieutenant, 3 August
1778
Grant, John; 76, Lieutenant, 31 December 1781
Grant, John; 4, Ensign, 6 March 1779
Grant, John; 40, Ensign, 15 January 1779
Grant, John; 2/71, Ensign, 20 October 1779; KIA Yorktown, 19 October
1781
Grant, John; 1779; Commissary and Paymaster of Artillery
Grant, John Burgoyne; 7, Lieutenant, 16 October 1778
Grant, Malcolm; 2/71, Ensign, 19 October 1779; KIA Guilford CH, 15
March 1781
Grant, Michael; Hosp., Mate, Prior to 1783; Stationed at New York,
1783; To surgeon, Bahamas, 1 January 1784
Grant, Patrick; 6, Surgeon, 18 November 1769; From mate; Commission
by purchase; Died prior to 25 February 1780
Grant, Richard; Chaplain, 1775; Chaplain to the garrison at St. Johns
Grant, Robert; 24, Major, 5 March 1775; KIA Hubbardtown, 6 July 1777
Grant, Robert; 2/71, Lieutenant, 2 January 1776
Grant, Robert; 21, 2nd Lieut., 1 September 1780
Grant, William; 1/42, Major, 5 October 1777, 23 July 1772; Lt. Colonel,
29 August 1777; Scottish, born 1734; First commissioned at age 11;
Retired 25 August 1778
Grant, William; 1/42, Quartermaster, 18 January 1770; 1/42, Captain, 23
July 1758
Grant, William; 55, Quartermaster, 24 November 1777; 55, Adjutant, 27
December 1778; 55, Ensign, 31 January 1779; 55, Lieutenant, 7 February
1781

Grant, William; RA, 2nd Lieut., 1 January 1771

Grant, William; 46, Ensign, 6 January 1779

Gration, John; 1/84, Adjutant, 17 January 1782; From sergeant major, 34th Foot

Gratton, William; 64, Quartermaster, 10 April 1769; 64, Ensign, 7 October 1775; 64, Lieutenant, 24 May 1776; 64, Captain, 24 June 1782; Irish, born 1746; First entered service as surgeon's mate, 1767; WIA, Danbury, between 25 and 27 April 1777; WIA Charleston, prior to 12 May 1780

Gray, Charles; 31, Lieutenant, 9 Match 1776

Gray, George; 59, Captain, 6 May 1767

Gray, Henry George; 26, Ensign, 17 October 1779

Gray, John; 38, Ensign, 17 September 1773

Gray, John; 3, Lieutenant, 9 December 1780; Stayed in Ireland according to WO 8/6, 273-279

Gray, Robert; 55, Captain, 18 September 1760; Major; 23 July 1772, Scottish, born 1732; First commissioned at age 13; Died 14 May 1776

Gray, Warner Wall; 9, Captain, 26 September 1772

Graydon, Alexander; 44, Lieutenant, 10 March 1764, 14 September 1760; 44, Capt.- Lieut., 22 November 1775; 44, Captain, 8 August 1776; Irish, born 1740; First commissioned at age 18

Graydon, Hamilton; 27, Ensign, 22 February 1782, 17 September 1761

Grayton, John; 53, Ensign, 2 March 1776

Green, -; 26, Adjutant, 7 December 1779; 26, Lieutenant, 1 September 1779

Green, -; 62, Ensign, 20 September 1777

Green, -; 5, Quartermaster, 30 August 1780; From sergeant major

Green, Charles; 31, Adjutant, 20 July 1773; 31, Captain, 3 November 1774; ADC Gen. Philips; WIA Freeman's Farm, 19 September 1777

Green, Edward; 28, Ensign, 13 January 1779

Green, Justly Watson; RA, 2nd Lieut., 28 April 1773

Green, Michael; 49, Ensign, 26 May 1781; 10, Lieutenant, 14 September 1770

Green, William; 30, Lieutenant, 12 November 1778; Died Charleston, SC, 27 July 1781 at age 19

Greene, Joseph; 40, Captain, 14 January 1775

Greene, Robert; 63, Ensign, 1 March 1779; 63, Lieutenant, 19 October 1781

Greening, Thomas; 33, Lieutenant, 2 December 1768; 33, Capt.- Lieut., 26 November 1775; 33, Captain, 25 January 1776; English, born 1744; First commissioned at age 19

Greet, Thomas; 23, Chaplain, 30 October 1760

Gregor, John; 1/42, Lieutenant, 27 August 1775, 28 July 1760
Gregory, Arthur Chapl.; 7, Lieutenant, 6 January 1771; Died 23 July 1775
Grenville, Richard; 2FG, Capt. & Lt. Col., 4 April 1772; 1742-1823; MP Buckingham, 1774 -1780; From captain in 24th Foot
Gresley, Walsingham; 34, Ensign, 1 July 1780
Greville, Henry; 2FG, Lieut. & Capt., 12 February 1781; POW, paroled September 1782
Grey, Alexander; 40, Ensign, 24 October 1778; 40, Lieutenant, 8 September 1781
Grey, Charles; 28, Colonel, 4 March 1777; Am., Major General, 4 March 1777, 29 August 1777
Grey, John; 28, Ensign, 11 June 1778; 28, Lieutenant, 20 September 1780
Grier, Robert; 20, Ensign, 4 March 1776; 20, Lieutenant, 1 October 1778
Grierson, -; 44, Ensign, 1 March 1779; Drowned at sea, probably 28 October 1779
Griffin, George; 54, Ensign, 7 July 1775; 54, Lieutenant, 16 November 1777
Griffith, Richard; 17 LD, Chaplain, 31 December 1772
Grimsfert, -; 4/60, Ensign, 21 September 1782
Grimston, John; 3FG, Lieut. & Capt., 8 January 1781; POW, paroled August 1782
Grinfield, William; 3FG, Lieut. & Capt., 9 December 1767; 3FG, Capt. & Lt. Col., 3 February 1776; Brought drafts from England; POW; Paroled December 1782; Retired 1795
Grisdale, Benjamin; 33, Chaplain, 22 February 1768; English, born 1747; First commissioned at age 21
Grogan, William; 16, Quartermaster, 24 February 1776; 16, Ensign, 22 February 1771; 16, Lieutenant, 6 May 1774
Grose, Francis; 52, Ensign, 27 January 1775; 52, Lieutenant, 23 November 1775; WIA Fort Clinton, 6 October 1777; WIA Monmouth, 28 June 1778; Promoted to captain in 85th Foot 1 September 1779
Grove, Grey; 23, Captain, 14 July 1762; DOW Brooklyn, 5 October 1776
Guarlay, -; 62, Ensign, 2 April 1781
Gubbins, William; 43, Lieutenant, 28 January 1771
Gumbleton, Henry; 4, Ensign, 22 June 1780
Gunning, John; 43, Captain, 30 September 1768
Gunning, John; 82, Lt. Colonel, 25 December 1777, 23 January 1775; 82, Colonel, 15 June 1781; Dpty. Adjt. Gen. In North America
Guydickens, Gustavus; 3FG, Capt. & Lt. Col., 22 February 1775; Retired 1793

Guyon, Stephen; 23, 2nd Lieut., 28 October 1778; KIA Yorktown, 12 October 1781

Gwynn, Daniel; 9, Ensign, 20 December 1776; 9, Lieutenant, 5 April 1781

Gwynne, Fran. Edw.; 16 LD, Major, 2 August 1775

Gylby, John; 20, Ensign, 29 August 1780

Hadden, Edward; 20, Ensign, 1 October 1778

Hadden, Robert; 4, Ensign, 6 January 1776; 4, Lieutenant, 3 November 1777; DOW Germantown, December 1777

Hadfield, John; 27, Surgeon, 11 November 1778; From mate; Died prior to 7 December 1785

Hailes, Harris Wm.; 38, Ensign, 25 May 1777; 38, Lieutenant, 11 September 1779

Halcott, Mathew; 4, Lieutenant, 18 June 1775; To invalid co. at Jersey, c1776-7

Haldane, Henry; RE, Sub-eng. & Lt., 2 March 1777; In America from 1777-1782; Served at NY & w/ Cornwallis; ADC to Lord Cornwallis 1781

Haldimand, Fredrick; 1/60, Col. Comdt., 11 January 1776; Am., Major General; 25 May 1772; Am., General; 1 January 1776

Haldimand, Louis; 45, Lieutenant, 14 December 1775; 29, Capt.- Lieut., 1 August 1779

Haldimand, Peter; 3/60, Lieutenant, 9 September 1777

Hale, William John; 45, Ensign, 22 November 1775; 45, Lieutenant, 2 March 1776; WIA Princeton, 3 January 1777

Hales, John; 65, Lieutenant, 12 December 1770; 65, Captain, 12 December 1775; Probably DOW Bunker Hill, 2 August 1775; If so, was never captain

Hall, -; 54, Adjutant, 7 January 1775; Probably John

Hall, Charles; 14, Surgeon, 20 December 1758

Hall, Francis; 3FG, Capt. & Lt. Col., 3 May 1775; KIA Catawba, 1 February 1781

Hall, George; 30, Ensign, 7 June 1778

Hall, John; 54, Ensign, 10 October 1779; 54, Lieutenant, 30 September 1781

Hall, John; 46, Captain, 13 April 1767; ADC to Gen. Massey, 7 July 1777

Hall, Thomas Moore; 52, Ensign, 23 November 1775; DOW, Woodbridge, NJ, 10 March 1777

Hall, William; 62, Lieutenant, 1 January 1774; 62, Captain, 21 November 1776

Hall, Wm. Cornwallis; 28, Ensign, 5 August 1775, 1 May 1773; 28, Lieutenant, 14 July 1777

Hall, Zachariah; 70, Lieutenant, 13 August 1776
Hallwood, Henry; 14, Lieutenant, 3 March 1773
Hamar, Ibbetson; 7, Lieutenant, 27 October 1772; WIA English
Neighborhood, NJ, September 1777; Leg amputated below the knee; Later
served in 72nd Foot; Transferred to Plymouth Invalid Coy. by 1784
Hamerton, Michael; 55, Lieutenant, 26 September 1772; 55, Captain, 11
May 1776; Also Hammerton; Irish, born 1752; First commissioned at age
17; ADC to Gen. James Grant, 1777
Hamilton, -; 53, Ensign, 17 June 1777
Hamilton, Alex. James; 45, Lieutenant, 1 May 1775
Hamilton, Alexander; 22, Ensign, 12 March 1773; 22, Lieutenant, 7
August 1776; Scottish; WIA Kickamuet River, RI, 26 May 1778; Resigned
14 August 1778; Remained in America
Hamilton, Alexander; 31, Lieutenant, 29 January 1773, 14 May 1768,
Died 19 November 1777
Hamilton, Claud; 74, Lieutenant, 6 January 1778; 54, Captain, 14
October 1781
Hamilton, David; 19, Lieutenant, 12 August 1779
Hamilton, David; 35, Capt.- Lieut., 6 March 1779
Hamilton, David; 4, Lieutenant, 29 May 1773
Hamilton, Douglas; 3, Lieutenant, 2 June 1778; WIA & POW Eutaw
Springs, 8 September 1781
Hamilton, George; 52, Lieutenant, 26 December 1770; 52, Captain, 22
November 1775
Hamilton, Gustavus; 15, Ensign, 18 November 1775; 15, Lieutenant, 20
June 1777
Hamilton, Gustavus; 47, Ensign, 10 July 1776; 47, Lieutenant, 1 April
1780
Hamilton, Gustavus; 17, Ensign, 26 October 1775
Hamilton, Harry; 64, Ensign, 2 February 1770
Hamilton, Henry; 17, Adjutant, 9 April 1777; 17, Ensign, 9 September
1777; 17, Lieutenant, 18 September 1780; May have also been
commissioned in 2/84th Foot
Hamilton, Isaac; 18, Major, 16 December 1767; Irish, born 1726; First
commissioned at age 21; Retired July 1775
Hamilton, James; 2FG, Lieut. & Capt., 27 April 1770; 2FG, Capt. & Lt.
Col., 28 October 1779; Colonel, 17 November 1780; Retired 1 February
1781
Hamilton, James; 21, Lt. Colonel, 11 March 1774, 25 May 1772
Hamilton, James; 10, Lieutenant, 6 February 1772; WIA Bunker Hill, 17
June 1775
Hamilton, John; 37, Captain, 7 July 1775; Died 19 May 1778

Hamilton, John; 16, Adjutant, 13 April 1778; 16, Ensign, 22 November 1775; 16, Lieutenant, 3 May 1780

Hamilton, John; 18, Lieutenant, 26 November 1772, 26 October 1761

Hamilton, John; 3, Lieutenant, 1 June 1778

Hamilton, John; 5, Ensign, 31 August 1776; 5, Lieutenant, 8 September 1780

Hamilton, John; 17 LD, Cornet, 30 December 1775

Hamilton, Otho; 59, Lt. Colonel, 15 December 1770

Hamilton, Robert; 18, Captain, 21 January 1773; Irish, born 1744; First commissioned at age 21

Hamilton, Robert; 82, Lieutenant, 15 January 1778

Hamilton, Sir Rob. Bt.; 40, Colonel, 20 March 1770; Major General; 29 September 1775; Lieutenant General; 29 August 1777

Hamilton, Thomas; 1/71, Lieutenant, 3 January 1776

Hamilton, W. Osborne; 34, Lieutenant, 6 January 1776

Hamilton, William; 40, Lieutenant, 28 April 1774; 40, Capt.- Lieut., 6 March 1780; 40, Captain, 6 March 1780

Hamilton, William; 44, Ensign, 11 February 1777; 44, Lieutenant, 7 September 1779

Hamilton, William; 5, Ensign, 31 August 1776; 5, Lieutenant, 26 May 1779; Alternative commission date 21 January 1779; Drowned 1780

Hamilton, William; 63, Lieutenant, 14 March 1772; Cashiered 1 December 1775

Hamilton, William; 14, Ensign, 16 March 1776

Hamilton, William; 49, Ensign, 22 May 1778

Hamilton, Wm. Henry; 37, Ensign, 7 July 1775; 37, Lieutenant, 2 July 1777; 37, Captain, 29 August 1780

Hammel, -; 24, Ensign, 10 August 1777

Hand, -; 38, Ensign, 10 October 1778; From volunteer

Hand, Edward; 18, Ensign, 27 February 1772; Irish, born 1743; First commissioned as mate, 1766; Retired 1774; Served in Continental Forces

Handasyde, Talbot Blayney; 38, Ensign, 30 April 1771

Handcock, John; 15, Ensign, 16 November 1777; 15, Lieutenant, 8 October 1779

Handfield, Charles; 22, Adjutant, 22 January 1776; 22, Lieutenant, 30 September 1772; 22, Capt.- Lieut., 15 October 1780; English, born 1753; Brother of Edward Handfield; Resigned adjutancy, 4 December 1779

Handfield, Edward; 22, Captain, 7 June 1775; English, born 1742; Brother of Charles Handfield

Handfield, John; 65, Captain, 18 October 1762

Handfield, William; 38, Captain, 15 August 1775, 5 May 1762; Major; 29 August 1775, Asst. DQMG., April 1776

Hanger, George; 1FG, Ensign, 31 January 1771; ADC to Sir Henry Clinton

Hankey, Richard; 10, Ensign, 10 May 1776; 10, Lieutenant, 7 October 1778

Hanson, Ralph; 19, Captain, 12 November 1778

Hanway, Hanway; 4, Ensign, 24 November 1775

Harcourt, Hon. William; 16 LD, Lt. Colonel, 24 June 1768, 28 November 1764, ADC to the King, 1777

Harding, Benjamin Haughton; 17, Ensign, 23 May 1776; 17, Lieutenant, 14 August 1780

Harding, Henry; 46, Lieutenant, 28 September 1775

Harding, Joseph; 65, Ensign, 18 June 1775; From volunteer

Harding, Thomas; 15, Capt.- Lieut., 24 May 1781

Harding, Thomas; 44, Ensign, 23 November 1775

Hare, Thomas; RA, Capt.- Lieut., 1 July 1779

Harling, William; 38, Ensign, 25 November 1775; 7, Lieutenant, 18 August 1778

Harnage, Henry; 62, Major, 21 December 1775; Lt. Colonel, 17 November 1780; WIA Freeman's Farm, 19 September 1777

Harrington, Henry; 62, Capt.- Lieut., 28 March 1777; Commission date also listed as 18 August 1778

Harris, George; 5, Captain, 15 July 1771; 5, Major, 7 October 1777; Born, 1748; Eldest son of a curate; Fought a duel in 1766; WIA Bunker Hill, 17 June 1775; Iron Hill, PA, 3 September 1777; WIA La Vigie, 18 December 1778

Harris, John Adolphus; 34, Captain, 28 November 1771; 1/84, Major, 22 October 1779; WIA Hubbardton, 7 July 1777

Harris, John Hill; 33, Lieutenant, 9 April 1774; English, born 1752; First commissioned at age 17; DOW Brandywine, 30 September 1777

Harris, Samuel; 29, Ensign, 10 September 1781

Harris, Thomas; 28, Captain, 12 December 1774

Harris, Thomas; 45, Ensign, 25 March 1775; 45, Lieutenant, 30 October 1777

Harris, Thomas; 5, Ensign, 24 November 1775; 5, Lieutenant, 4 December 1777; DOW La Vigie, 18 December 1778; Brother of Major George Harris

Harris, Thomas; 27, Surgeon, 28 September 1769; Retired 22 December 1776 by selling his commission

Harris, William; 40, Adjutant, 1 April 1773; 40, Lieutenant, 15 March 1768; 40, Capt.- Lieut., 28 December 1775; 40, Captain, 21 September 1777

Harrison, George; 54, Ensign, 4 October 1780

Harrison, John; 7, Lieutenant, 4 February 1767, 31 March 1763; 7, Captain, 25 March 1777; Died 14 October 1780

Harrison, John; 59, Lieutenant, 28 August 1771, 15 October 1761

Harrison, Martin; 28, Ensign, 3 November 1777; 28, Lieutenant, 22 February 1779

Harrison, Robert John; 52, Ensign, 22 September 1772 or 18 June 1775; 52, Lieutenant, 29 May 1776; From volunteer; WIA Bunker Hill, 17 June 1775; Ensigncy also given as 25 June 1775

Hart, George; 46, Ensign, 23 August 1775; 46, Lieutenant, 7 June 1777; 55, Capt.- Lieut., 3 March 1779; 55, Captain, 3 March 1779

Hart, Henry; 54, Lieutenant, 25 November 1775, 10 November 1762, Died New York, 9 October 1779

Hartcup, Thomas; RE, Eng. extra. & Cpt.-Lt., 4 March 1776; In America from 1776-1783; Served at New York and Halifax

Hartley, Henry; 47, Adjutant, 11 March 1782

Hartley, William; 44, Ensign, 9 September 1779

Harvey, George; 62, Ensign, 6 April 1776; 62, Lieutenant, 18 August 1778

Harvey, James Leigh; 33, Ensign, 9 December 1777; 33, Lieutenant, 10 September 1779; Also James Lee; WIA Guilford CH, 15 March 1781

Harvey, Pierce; 63, Quartermaster, 18 January 1770; 63, Capt.- Lieut., 5 March 1775; 63, Captain, 22 November 1775

Harvey, Stanhope; 14, Captain, 6 April 1772, 9 April 1760

Harvey, Stephen; 62, Lieutenant, 29 February 1776; Also Hervey; DOW Freeman's Farm, 19 September 1777; Age 16 at his death

Harvey, Stephen; 7, Lieutenant, 15 August 1775; Also Hervey

Haslam, Anthony; 5, Captain, 15 August 1775; Major; 23 July 1772; Lt. Colonel, 29 August 1777

Haslewood, William; 63, Captain, 25 May 1772; Also Hazelwood

Hassard, William; 44, Ensign, 3 July 1772; 74, Lieutenant, 24 November 1775; 44, Captain, 31 January 1778

Hastings, Charles; 12, Lieutenant, 26 January 1776; Illegitimate son of the Earl of Huntingdon; WIA Danbury, 25 or 27 April 1777 while serving with 15th Foot

Hastings, George; 45, Ensign, 13 September 1780

Hastings, Robert; 26, Ensign, 8 December 1766; 26, Lieutenant, 11 May 1774

Hatchel, Phillip; 44, Mate, date unknown; To surgeon Maryland Loyalists, 31 August 1779; Transferred to Loyal American Regiment, 12 August 1780 or 25 October 1780

Hatfield, John; 43, Captain, 25 May 1772

Hatton, Henry; 8, Captain, 12 October 1771; English, born 1748; First commissioned at age 19

Haughton, Charles; 53, Lieutenant, 3 July 1772; Died from a fall, Quebec, 9 May 1776

Haughton, Richard; 53, Lieutenant, 30 April 1771; Served with Fraser's Marksmen; WIA Ft. Ticonderoga, 2 July 1777

Haughton, William; 45, Lieutenant, 25 March 1775

Haughton, William; 53, Lieutenant, 17 September 1775; Also Houghton; Assaulted and beaten by Lt. Magrath, December, 1775; Resigned due to the incident, 13 December 1775

Haverkam, James; 10, Ensign, 31 May 1776; 10, Lieutenant, 31 January 1778

Haverkam, James; 55, Lieutenant, 15 January 1779; Also Haversham

Haviland, -; 14, Ensign, 3 March 1773; 14, Lieutenant, 22 February 1775

Haviland, William; 45, Colonel, 1 June 1767; Lieutenant General; 25 May 1772

Hawker, Earle; 62, Captain, 7 March 1772; 62, Major, 18 March 1782

Hawkins, Charles; 46, Ensign, 11 July 1780

Hawkins, Joseph; 2/84, Ensign, 25 December 1775; 2/84, Lieutenant, 11 December 1779; From sergeant 22nd Foot

Hawkins, Richard; 57, Ensign, 5 July 1777

Hawkshaw, Hugh; 49, Ensign, 28 January 1775; 49, Lieutenant, 10 March 1777

Hawkshaw, John; 69, Captain, 26 June 1777

Hawkshaw, Thomas; 5, Lieutenant, 28 November 1771; 5, Capt.- Lieut., 8 November 1777; 5, Captain, 29 June 1778; WIA Lexington and Concord, 19 April 1775

Hawley, Henry; 45, Ensign, 15 August 1775

Hawthorn, William; 80, Lieutenant, 26 January 1778; 80, Captain, 24 September 1779

Hay, Adam; 35, Lieutenant, 5 July 1780

Hay, Adam; 31, Captain, 8 March 1776

Hay, Alexander; 62, Ensign, 26 October 1775; 62, Lieutenant, 20 September 1777; WIA Freeman's Farm, 19 September 1777

Hay, Alexander; 7, Lieutenant, 25 December 1765, 28 October 1760; 7, Capt.- Lieut., 22 November 1775; 7, Captain, 22 November 1775; Retired 4 March 1777

Hay, David; 57, Quartermaster, 18 January 1770; 57, Lieutenant, 5 July 1768; 23, Capt.- Lieut., 29 August 1778

Hay, Edward; 65, Ensign, 15 August 1775

Hay, George; 80, Captain, 17 January 1778; Major; 29 August 1777

Hay, J; 64, Ensign, 24 September 1773

Hay, James; 83, Lieutenant, 1 February 1778

Hay, John; 1/84, Capt.- Lieut., 27 February 1776; 28, Captain, 9 April 1777; From 28th Foot adjutant to 84th Foot; DOW La Vigie, 18 December 1778

Hay, John; 4, Lieutenant, 24 November 1775

Hay, John; 26, Ensign, 31 October 1770

Hay, William; 22, Lieutenant, 22 January 1776; To additional company, March 1777; Retired 14 August 1778

Hay, William; 35, Ensign, 18 January 1778

Hayes, Edward; 16, Ensign, 7 June 1775; 16, Lieutenant, 13 April 1778; Also Heyes

Hayes, John; Hosp., Surgeon, 1776; Retired after 1782; Probably same as Jon. McNamara

Hayes, John McNamara; Hosp., Surgeon, 1 January 1776; Hosp. Physician, 26 November 1779; Stationed at New York, 1783; To half pay 25 December 1783; M.D. Rheims, 1784; Died London, 19 July 1809

Hayman, John; 17, Ensign, 4 January 1777; 17, Lieutenant, 12 November 1778

Haynes, Walter; 59, Ensign, 5 May 1769; 59, Lieutenant, 5 December 1774; WIA Bunker Hill, 17 June 1775

Hayter, Thomas; 14, Ensign, 19 April 1773;14, Lieutenant, 27 February 1775

Hazelton, George; 7, Surgeon, 29 April 1776; Also Hazelton; Commission also 29 April 1780; Staff, Lower Canada, 1784; M.D. St. Andrew, 1785; Died c. 1821

Hazelton, Rowland; 17, Ensign, 5 October 1777; 4/60, Lieutenant, 30 May 1778; 16, Lieutenant, 4 February 1779; From volunteer; WIA Roupel's Ferry, SC, 3 February 1779

Heaphy, George Blen.; 53, Ensign, 11 April 1782

Hearst, Fr. Seymour; 65, Lieutenant, 26 December 1770

Heatley, Wm. Campbell; 44, Ensign, 22 November 1775; 44, Lieutenant, 29 June 1778

Hecht, Fred. William; Asst. Commissary, 1778

Heig, James; 35, Ensign, 25 May 1780

Heighington, John; 23, 2nd Lieut., 25 September 1771; 23, 1st Lieut., 22 November 1775

Hely, -; 35, Ensign, 18 August 1778

Hely, Fredrick; 28, Lieutenant, 29 October 1778

Hely, Pierce; 10, Lieutenant, 24 July 1766; 4, Captain, 6 November 1776

Helyar, Charles; 7, Lieutenant, 8 May 1776; 7, Captain, 1 February 1780; KIA Cowpens, 17 January 1781

Helyar, John; 7, Lieutenant, 26 February 1780

Henderson, James; 4/60, Surgeon, 10 November 1775; Died Haddington, 15 April 1813

Henderson, James; RA, Surgeon, date unknown; Died of fever, New York, 19 July 1780; Possibly attached to the RA from the General Hospital

Hennis, Wm. Howe; 23, 2nd Lieut., 22 November 1777; 23, 1st Lieut., 13 September 1779

Hepburn, James; 49, Captain, 26 November 1771; Died 8 August 1775

Hepburne, John; 21, 1st Lieut., 28 August 1771; 21, Capt.- Lieut., 1 September 1780;

Herbert, George; 59, Lieutenant, 14 October 1758; 59, Capt.- Lieut., 29 March 1775

Herbert, Thomas; 10, Captain, 28 June 1771; Retired 12 July 1777

Heron, Henry; 40, Ensign, 27 October 1777; 80, Lieutenant, 16 January 1778; From volunteer

Herring, Thomas; 6, Lieutenant, 26 November 1773

Hertzog, Andrew; 17, Ensign, 1 September 1779; Foreign born; Served 17 years prior to his commission; It is unclear whether this service was with the British army or perhaps the Hanoverian Army; His will showed substantial funds

Hertzog, James; 17, Quartermaster, 17 July 1776; Also Herkock

Hervey, Alexander; 30, Lieutenant, 31 January 1780

Hesketh, Robert; 14, Ensign, 27 February 1775; DOW Bunker Hill, 25 September 1775; It is possible he served with the 18th Foot at Bunker Hill

Hesketh, Thomas; 7, Captain, 27 October 1772;

Hesselburg, Isaac; 3/60, Ensign, 9 February 1776; 3/60, Lieutenant, 1 May 1779; Acting artillery and engineer officer at St. Augustine

Hessernan, Henry; 9, Ensign, 26 April 1780

Hessey, James; 43, Quartermaster, 17 October 1773

Hewetson, Brinsley; 26, Lieutenant, 15 August 1775; 2/71, Lieutenant, 16 October 1779; Captain; 12 April 1779, Town Major for New York, 1781-1783 Captaincy in Garrison Bn.; Died early August, 1783

Hewetson, William; 27, Lieutenant, 1 September 1771; 46, Capt.- Lieut., 22 December 1778; 46, Captain, 22 December 1778

Hewett, George; 70, Captain, 2 June 1775; 43, Major, 31 December 1781

Hewett, Thomas; 22, Lieutenant, 16 March 1775; 10, Captain, 12 July 1777; English, born 1752

Hewlett, William; 21, 2nd Lieut., 9 June 1781; From ensign, 2nd Bn. New Jersey Volunteers

Hewlett, William; 3/60, Ensign, 23 September 1780

Hickman, Robert; 19, Lieutenant, 25 May 1778; KIA Eutaw Springs, 8 September 1781

89

Hicks, Edward; 70, Major, 9 February 1775; Lt. Colonel, 17 November 1780

Hicks, Edward; 70, Ensign, 16 May 1778; 70, Lieutenant, 24 May 1779

Hicks, John; Hosp., Mate, Prior to 1783; Stationed at New York, 1783

Hickson, Robert; 5, Ensign, 8 November 1777; 5, Lieutenant, 26 August 1780; From volunteer

Higgins, Jn. Sackville; 47, Ensign, 25 May 1778

Higgins, John; 38, Lieutenant, 1 September 1771; Retired 25 May 1777

Higgins, Robert Harpur; 52, Lieutenant, 3 March 1772; DOW Bunker Hill, 24 June 1775

Highington, John; 10, Capt.- Lieut., 6 October 1778

Highmore, William; 8, Lieutenant, 12 October 1771; English, born 1748; First commissioned at age 18

Hill, -; 23, 2nd Lieut., 5 October 1781; Given name probably John

Hill, -; 47, Ensign, 11 July 1778

Hill, Benjamin; 5, Adjutant, 11 November 1775; 5, Lieutenant, 12 July 1775; 5, Captain, 21 January 1779

Hill, George; 5, Adjutant, 25 October 1780; From quartermaster sergeant

Hill, James; 64, Lieutenant, 25 December 1770, 15 September 1760

Hill, John; 9, Lt. Colonel, 10 November 1775, 11 September 1775

Hill, John; 38, Ensign, 6 July 1778

Hill, John; 7, Lieutenant, 5 December 1774

Hill, John; FG, Adjutant, December 1776; 2Bn., From sergeant; POW

Hill, John Forster; 64, Ensign, 12 July 1770; 64, Lieutenant, 7 October 1775; Retired 26 February 1778

Hill, Lloyd; 43, Adjutant, 10 October 1778; 43, Lieutenant, 10 October 1778

Hill, Robert; 5, Ensign, 6 February 1779; Died 9 April 1783

Hill, Rowley; 54, Lieutenant, 25 December 1765, 2 April 1762; 54, Capt.-Lieut., 16 November 1777; Died c.October 1779 shortly after resigning his commission

Hill, Thomas; 29, Lieutenant, 25 November 1774

Hill, Thomas; 52, Ensign, 10 March 1777

Hill, Trotter; 59, Surgeon, 30 April 1770

Hill, West; 33, Surgeon, 19 February 1774; Hosp., Surgeon, 5 November 1778; English, born 1751; From mate; Warranted mate,1772; To half pay 25 December 1783; M.D. St. Andrew, 1784; Died Chippenham, Wilts, 16 December 1834, aged 92

Hill, William; 45, Ensign, 13 May 1776; 45, Lieutenant, 27 October 1779

Hilliard, Christopher; 47, Lieutenant, 10 February 1770; KIA Bunker Hill, 17 June 1775

Hillman, Rawlins; 22, Captain, 9 May 1764; 22, Major, 3 November 1777, 23 July 1772; Lt. Colonel, 29 August 1777; English, born 1728; Resigned 5 December 1778

Hills, John; RE, Draftsman, date unknown; In America from 1776-1782; WIA Springfield, NJ, prior to 22 June 1780; Probably the I. Hills listed at MG Phillips's acting chief engineer at Petersburg, VA, 1781; Possibly also a RA officer

Hirst, Charles; 57, Lieutenant, 24 February 1775; WIA Iron Hill, DE, 3 September 1777

Hirst, George; 70, Lieutenant, 12 March 1778

Hoar, Charles; 18, Ensign, 10 June 1774; Also Hoare; English, born 1745; First commissioned at age 19

Hobart, Minchin; 24, Ensign, 28 January 1775; 21, 1st Lieut., 10 August 1777

Hobart, Robert; 7, Lieutenant, 1 May 1776

Hobson, Thomas; 34, Captain, 2 March 1776

Hockings, Richard; RE, Pract. eng. & 2nd Lt., 17 January 1776; In America in 1778; Served at Newfoundland

Hockley, Thomas; 35, Lieutenant, 16 June 1779

Hodgson, John; 4, Ensign, 20 May 1779

Hodgson, Studholme; 4, Colonel, 7 November 1768; Lieutenant General; 19 January 1761; General; 2 April 1778

Hodnet, John; 30, Lieutenant, 11 January 1779

Hoey, William; 9, Lieutenant, 3 March 1776; 9, Captain, 9 April 1782

Hogg, -; 28, Ensign, 27 January 1777

Hogg, George; 57, Lieutenant, 19 October 1778

Holdsworthy, Samuel; 23, 2nd Lieut., 30 August 1779

Holland, Henry; 70, Ensign, 24 May 1779

Holland, Samuel; Major, 1781; Director of Guides

Holland, Thomas; 52, Lieutenant, 30 August 1771; Died 25 or 26 April 1775

Hollandt, Sam. Jan.; Am., Major, 4 March 1776

Holliday, Robert; 33, Ensign, 23 May 1779

Hollier, Thomas; 29, Ensign, 28 March 1776; 29, Lieutenant, 23 May 1781, 15 January 1763

Holmes, Galbraith; 54, Ensign, 27 November 1775

Holmes, John; 20, Quartermaster, 1 June 1776

Holmes, Philip; 19, Lieutenant, 17 November 1780

Holmes, Robert; 69, Chaplain, 20 May 1778

Holmes, William; 4, Captain, 14 November 1771

Holyoke, Fra. Edw.; 17, Ensign, 18 September 1780

Home, Alexander; 1/42, Ensign, 26 August 1778; From 71st Foot; possibly as volunteer

Home, Luke; 16, Lieutenant, 12 April 1773; 16, Capt.- Lieut., 5 March 1782

Home, Walter; 7, Capt.- Lieut., 25 December 1770; 7, Captain, 22 November 1775, 25 May 1772; 1/42, Major, 28 April 1782; Also Hume

Honywood, William; 3, Lieutenant, 1 June 1778

Hood, John George; 40, Ensign, 9 September 1781

Hooke, Geo. Philip; 17, Captain, 15 August 1775, 25 May 1772

Hope, Erskine; 31, Ensign, 8 March 1776; Lieutenant, 16 April 1780

Hope, Falkiner; 63, Lieutenant, 21 November 1780

Hope, Falkiner; 80, Lieutenant, 22 March 1779

Hope, Henry; 44, Major, 3 May 1775; 44, Lt. Colonel, 5 October 1777; WIA Danbury, CT, April 1777; Cmd Gren. Bn.

Hope, Richard; 52, Surgeon, 21 June 1756; Hosp., Surgeon, 1 January 1776; Retired to half pay, 25 December 1783

Hopkins, Joseph; FG, Mate, 23 March 1776; POW Yorktown; To 1st Foot Guards, 16 June 1783

Hordon, William H.; RA, 2nd Lieut., 11 March 1778; RA, 1st Lieut., 14 June 1780; Also Horndon; Surrendered his men at Stony Point, 16 July 1779

Horler, Edward; Hosp., Surgeon, Prior to 1781; Listed twice in 1781 Army List

Horne, James; 53, Ensign, 24 May 1775; 53, Lieutenant, 25 February 1778

Horne, John; 17, Surgeon, 31 January 1777; From mate; By purchase; Died Long Island, August 1782

Horneck, Charles; 3FG, Lieut. & Capt., 7 June 1773; 3FG, Capt. & Lt. Col., 25 March 1782; POW Yorktown; Paroled August 1782; Retired 1789

Horsfall, Christopher; 23, Captain, 15 July 1768; 23, Major, 30 May 1778; To 72nd Foot as major, then returned to 23rd Foot

Hoskins, -; 28, Ensign, 21 January 1778

Howard, Abraham; 64, Surgeon, 31 August 1779; From mate; Exchanged to half pay, 89th Foot, 13 July 1785; Died c. 1805

Howard, John; 1FG, Capt. & Lt. Col., 22 February 1773; Colonel; 17 November 1780; Am., Brigadier General, 2 November 1780; WIA Guilford CH, 15 March 1781; Later Earl; Col. 97th in 1782

Howard, Thomas; 1FG, Capt. & Lt. Col., 10 July 1765; KIA aboard packet *Eagle* on passage to England, 21 September 1778

Howarth, Edward; RA, 2nd Lieut., 17 June 1772; WIA & POW, Bemis Heights, 7 October 1777

Howe, Hon. William K.B.; 23, Colonel, 11 May 1775; Major General; 25 May 1772; Lieutenant General; 29 August 1777; Am., General, 1 January 1776; 1729-1814; MP Northingham, 1758-1780; Commander in Chief, North America

Howe, William; 53, Captain, 29 March 1776

Howel, David; 16 LD, Cornet, 11 March 1774;16 LD, Lieutenant, 13 December 1777

Howell, John Fr.; 24, Chaplain, 14 March 1780

Howison; -; Captain, 1781; Acting Barracksmaster Long Island

Howse, John; 38, Lieutenant, 12 December 1770; 52, Captain, 6 July 1778; WIA Bunker Hill, 17 June 1775

Hoyes, Robert; 34, Captain, 9 May 1768, 1 October 1761; 34, Major, 1 November 1780, 29 August 1777

Hoysted, Fred. Wm.; 64, Ensign, 12 September 1777; 84, Lieutenant, 22 August 1780

Hubbard, Edward; 45, Captain, 23 March 1775; Died New York, December 1777

Huddlestone, Richard; 7, Surgeon, 6 December 1770; Hosp., Apothecary, 29 April 1780; Also Huddlestone; From mate; To half pay, 12 April 1782; Died November 1806

Huddleston, William Orch.; RA, Capt.- Lieut., 12 April 1768; RA, Captain, 7 July 1779, 25 May 1772, WIA Bunker Hill, 17 June 1775

Hudson, James; 45, Lieutenant, 20 February 1773

Hudson, John; 33, Ensign, 1 September 1779; 33, Lieutenant, 11 October 1781

Hudson, William; 65, Captain, 30 April 1768; KIA Bunker Hill, 17 June 1775

Hughes, Thomas; 33, Ensign, 24 May 1775; 33, Lieutenant, 8 October 1777; From volunteer; May have been WIA Guilford CH, 15 March 1781;Listed as John Hughes in Inman

Hughes, William; 53, Captain, 2 October 1765; 53, Major, 8 October 1777; Died of a "violent fever," 4 October 1778

Hughes, Wm. Carlyon; 7, Lieutenant, 14 March 1771; 3/60, Captain, 12 January 1779; 7, Captain, 19 October 1780, 12 January 1779

Hull, Edward; 43, Lieutenant, 26 December 1770; POW & DOW Concord, 2 May 1775

Hultaine, Theodore; 37, Captain, 2 October 1766, 5 April 1762

Humphreys, Fr. Richm.; 52, Captain, 25 December 1770, 17 October 1761; 52, Major, 18 June 1775; WIA Woodbridge, NJ, 1777; Exact date unknown

Humphreys, John Richmond W.; 44, Lieutenant, 15 August 1775, 21 October 1761

Humphreys, Thomas; 28, Adjutant, 16 February 1770; 28, Ensign, 29 October 1776; 28, Ensign, 13 January 1779

Hunt, James; 4, Adjutant, 25 June 1777; From Sgt. Major; WIA Germantown, 4 October 1777

Hunt, Thomas; 3, Lieutenant, 29 June 1780; Stayed in Ireland according to WO 8/6, 273-279

Hunter, John; Hosp., Physician, Prior to 1781

Hunter, Martin; 52, Ensign, 30 August 1771; 52, Lieutenant, 18 June 1775; 52, Captain, 21 November 1777; WIA Admiral Warren Tavern, 21 September 1777

Hunter, Peter; 80, Lieutenant, 2 February 1778

Hurdman, Benjamin; 55, Ensign, 5 November 1777; 46, Lieutenant, 31 January 1779; KIA off of Grenada serving as marine, 6 July 1779

Huson, Narcissus; 59, Lieutenant, 27 August 1760; 59, Captain, 5 December 1774

Hussey, James; 17 LD, Cornet, 16 February 1767, 10 November 1762; 17 LD, Lieutenant, 25 March 1776

Hutcheson, Francis; 2/60, Captain, 17 March 1769; Major; 17 November 1780, Major of Bde., 1774; Asst. Depty. Quartermaster General at New York, 1 June 1775; Ast. Secretary to Sir William Howe, 1778; Ast. Secretary to Sir Henry Clinton, 1779; Died 22 September 1780 prior to learning of promotion

Hutcheson, George; Captain, 1778; Extra Depty. Adjutant General, 1778

Hutchinson, Emanuel; 46, Ensign, 14 August 177664, Ensign, 12 August 1778

Hutchinson, Francis; Captain, 1777; Asst. Depty. QMG

Hutchinson, George; 23, Captain, 24 November 1775; ADC to Lt. Gen. Percy, 1777

Hutchinson, J. Francis; 69, Lieutenant, 31 October 1780

Hutchinson, Joseph; Hosp., Surgeon, 8 November 1780; To the Garrison at Bermuda, 8 November 1780 or 13 February 1781; Listed as Surgeon's Mate at Bermuda, 1782

Hutchinson, Richard; 44, Ensign, 15 May 1772; 44, Lieutenant, 23 November 1775; Drowned at sea, probably 28 October 1779

Hutchinson, Robert; 2/71, Lieutenant, 24 November 1775, 23 July 1772; 1/71, Capt.- Lieut., 3 August 1778; 2/71, Captain, 3 August 1778

Hutchinson, Thomas; 2/60, Capt.- Lieut., 24 September 1775; 4/60, Captain, 13 November 1776, 24 September 1775, Also Hutchins; Born an orphan in New Jersey; Charged with treason in 1779; Acquitted 11 February 1780; Made his way to Paris and offered his services to Benjamin Franklin; Served as surveyor for Continental Forces; Later US Surveyor General

Hutchinson, William; 46, Ensign, 1 June 1781

Hutchinson, William; 70, Quartermaster, 23 July 1775

Hyde, Thomas; 4, Ensign, 13 November 1776; 4, Lieutenant, 24 December 1779

Hyde, Thomas; 40, Ensign, 1 October 1778; KIA Groton, CT, 6 September 1777

Hyde, West; 1FG, Capt. & Lt. Col., 25 February 1767; 1FG, 2nd Major; 23 April 1779; Colonel 29 August 1777

Impett, John; 63, Ensign, 10 August 1778; 63, Lieutenant, 25 December 1780

Imrie, James; 82, Lieutenant, 14 January 1778

Inglis, William; 57, Ensign, 11 October 1779

Ingram, James; 33, Lieutenant, 10 June 1771; 70, Capt.- Lieut., 25 December 1779; 33, Capt.- Lieut., 17 August 1780; 33, Captain, 17 August 1780; English, born 1752; First commissioned at age 16; WIA South Carolina, June 1780

Inman, George; 17, Ensign, 28 August 1776; 26, Lieutenant, 29 June 1778; Native of MA; Attended Harvard; From private, Loyal American Associators, 1775; WIA Princeton, 3 January 1777

Innes, Alexander; 1/42, Ensign, 21 September 1776; 1/42, Lieutenant, 3 August 1778

Innes, Alexander; Am., Lt. Colonel, 20 January 1780; Scottish, born 1758; First commissioned at age 15

Innes, George; 82, Surgeon, 3 January 1778; To half pay, June 1784; M.D. Kings Coll. Abd., 1786; Died c.1828

Innes, Charles; 45, Ensign, 30 May 1778; 45, Lieutenant, 13 September 1780

Innes, George; 83, Quartermaster, 8 December 1780

Innes, James; 1/71, Captain, 1 December 1781

Innes, James; 2/71, Captain, 28 August 1776

Innes, James; 16, Lieutenant, 9 June 1781

Innes, James; 5, Lieutenant, 15 August 1775, 16 May 1759

Innes, James; 23, 2nd Lieut., 9 August 1780

Innes, Robert; 21, 1st Lieut., 22 February 1776

Innes, Thomas; 43, Lieutenant, 22 February 1765; 43, Capt.- Lieut., 22 November 1775; 43, Captain, 22 November 1775

Innes, Thomas; 33, Ensign, 30 October 1777; 33, Lieutenant, 23 May 1779

Innes, Thomas; 49, Lieutenant, 3 July 1772; Retired 27 April 1777

Innes, William; 64, Ensign, 1 June 1780; Scottish, born 1761; First commissioned at age 19

Ireland, James; 34, Ensign, 29 March 1776

Irvine, Charles; 57, Ensign, 5 September 1779; 57, Lieutenant, 12 November 1781; Also Irwin

Irvine, Gerrard; 47, Lieutenant, 30 April 1771; 47, Captain, 3 August 1781

Irving, Paulus AEmilius; 47, Captain, 29 October 1768; 47, Major, 31 March 1775; 47, Lt. Colonel, 3 August 1781, 17 November 1780

Irving, Robert; 70, Captain, 27 July 1775

Irwin, James; 4/60, Ensign, 11 February 1776

Irwine, Charles; 4, Ensign, 15 October 1778

Irwine, Christopher; 30, Lieutenant, 29 June 1780

Irwine, Sir John K.B.; 57, Colonel, 4 November 1767; Lieutenant General; 30 May 1772, Did not serve in America

Ivers, John Augustus; 30, Captain, 1 June 1763; Major; 29 August 1777

Ives, John Clement; 16 LD, Chaplain, 22 April 1774

Jackson, -; 45, Ensign, 23 November 1775;

Jackson, John; 5, Captain, 28 November 1771; WIA Bunker Hill, 17 June 1775; Retired 24 May 1776

Jackson, John; 5, Lieutenant, 14 March 1772; Died 1 April 1775

Jackson, John; 17, Ensign, 19 December 1781

Jackson, John; 64, Ensign, 24 September 1771; Died 16 December 1774

Jackson, Michael; 23, 2nd Lieut., 16 October 1776; 15, Lieutenant, 8 December 1777; Died 25 June 1781

Jackson, Robert; 57, Ensign, 28 November 1775; 57, Lieutenant, 29 June 1778

Jackson, Robert; 17, Ensign, 10 September 1780; Alternate date of commission, 8 September 1780; Listed in Army lists as retired, but transferred to the 4th Horse by 1783

Jacob, Michael; 64, Lieutenant, 2 March 1768; 64, Capt.- Lieut., 12 September 1777; 64, Captain, 18 August 1778; Also Jacobs; English, born 1743; First commissioned at age 22; WIA Brandywine, 11 September 1777

Jamaison, Andrew; 24, Captain, 26 September 1772

James, Richard; 62, Ensign, 21 December 1775; 62, Lieutenant, 20 September 1777

James, Thomas; RA, Lt. Colonel, 1 January 1771; Served at Boston; Died Blackheath, England, 6 March 1782 as colonel commandant

James, William; 46, Ensign, 7 June 1777; 46, Lieutenant, 25 January 1781

Jameson, John; Hosp., Apothecary, 19 October 1775; Also James as given name; From surgeon 28th Foot; Died 6 September 1776

Jamieson, Henry; 80, Lieutenant, 29 January 1778

Jaques, William; 29, Ensign, 20 November 1780

Jecelyn, George Robert; 49, Quartermaster, 20 November 1772; 49, Ensign, 16 July 1774; 49, Lieutenant, 7 June 1776; Also Jocelyn; KIA White Plains, 28 October 1776

Jefferies, John; Hosp., Apothecary, 14 December 1778; Hosp., Surgeon, 7 July 1779; Also Jeffries; Stationed at Halifax as apothecary; Trans. to NYC as surgeon; Retired 6 September 1780

Jefferson, Joshua; 63, Surgeon, 16 April 1779; From mate; To Royal Horse Guards, 5 October 1785; Retired 10 March 1788

Jemmitt, Thomas; 23, 2nd Lieut., 18 January 1777

Jenkins, Henry; 35, Captain, 22 August 1770; Retired 25 July 1775

Jenkins, Edward; 65, Lieutenant, 20 May 1771, 22 October 1758

Jenkins, Edward; 46, Ensign, 13 April 1778

Jenkins, Thomas; 22, Ensign, 29 July 1779; English, born 1763

Jenkyn, Meredith; 49, Surgeon, 31 January 1774; Retired 7 September 1776

Jephson, William; 28, Lieutenant, 8 September 1775; 28, Captain, 8 January 1778

Jephson, William; 17 LD, Cornet, 25 August 1780

Johnson, Benjamin; 18, Captain, 8 October 1767, 28 October 1760, Does not appear to have served in America, but was listed as KIA at Boston in late 1775

Johnson, Charles; 24, Lieutenant, 2 March 1776

Johnson, George; 4, Adjutant, 28 September 1778; 4, Ensign, 5 July 1777; 4, Lieutenant, 24 February 1780

Johnson, Hon. Henry; 28, Major, 23 August 1775; 17, Lt. Colonel, 4 October 1778; Cmd. 3rd L.I. Bn, 1776; POW Stony Point; CM and acquitted for negligence at Stony Point

Johnson, Mathew; 46, Captain, 12 December 1770; 46, Major, 12 October 1780, 17 November 1780

Johnson, Roger; Ast. Commissary, 1781

Johnson, Thomas; RA, Captain, 25 May 1772; Died New York, 30 November 1781

Johnson, William; 29, Ensign, 29 March 1776; 47, Lieutenant, 10 March 1780; WIA & POW, Bennington 16 August 1777; Served in Fraser's Marksmen; Also listed as a POW at Stillwater, 7 October 1777

Johnston, Christopher; 17 LD, Surgeon, 8 December 1767; Also Johnstone; To half pay 25 June 1796; Died c. 1812

Johnston, George; 29, Ensign, 1 November 1780

Johnston, James; 38, Ensign, 23 November 1775; 38, Lieutenant, 27 June 1780

Johnston, John; 37, Surgeon, 14 August 1772; Hosp., Apothecary, 27 June 1781; Also Johnstone; Served at Minorca, 1763; Stationed at New York, 1783; To half pay, 6 February 1784; Died at Gawsworth, 31 October 1793

Johnston, Joseph; 10, Quartermaster, 6 August 1767; DOW, 27 June 1775

Johnston, P.; 26, Ensign, 24 February 1776; Shot himself and died 13 November 1777 aboard a transport in the Delaware River

Johnston, Richard; 7, Lieutenant, 26 February 1772

Johnston, Robert; 19, Lieutenant, 29 June 1780

Johnston, Robert; 37, Captain, 3 March 1772

Johnston, William; RA, Captain, 1 January 1771; At Pensacola, 1780

Johnston, William; 70, Lieutenant, 9 April 1777

Johnston, William; 35, Ensign, 28 October 1778

Johnstone, Boulter; 70, Captain, 9 February 1775

Johnstone, Francis; 38, Lieutenant, 25 July 1771; Also Johnston; KIA Brandywine 11 September 1777

Johnstone, Mathew R.; 63, Ensign, 23 December 1780; Resident of Newport, RI

Johnstone, Robert; 3FG, Ensign, 5 April 1773; 3FG, Lieut. & Capt., 19 January 1777

Johnstone, Robert; 31, Ensign, 13 September 1776

Johnstone, William; 31, Lieutenant, 1 May 1772; 31, Capt.- Lieut., 13 September 1777

Jones, -; 20, Ensign, 20 September 1777; 44, Ensign, 29 June 1778; From volunteer 1st. L.I. Bn

Jones, Charles; 46, Quartermaster, 18 January 1770

Jones, Daniel; Am., Colonel, 1 January 1776; Am., Major General, 1 January 1776;

Jones, Dering; 33, Lieutenant, 21 October 1778; Also Daring; KIA 6 miles west of Williamsburg, VA, approximately 26 June 1781

Jones, Dering; RA, 2nd Lieut., 1 June 1778; From gentlemen cadet

Jones, Francis; 63, Lieutenant, 25 September 1761; 63, Capt.- Lieut., 22 November 1775; 63, Captain, 27 July 1776; WIA Ft. Clinton 6 October 1777; possibly DOW

Jones, G.Q. Dyall; 7, Lieutenant, 15 October 1778

Jones, George; 4, Ensign, 6 October 1780

Jones, Henry; 22, Chaplain, 11 March 1780; English, born 1737; Chaplain for Chatham Garrison; Never served in America

Jones, Humphrey; 3, Chaplain, 7 June 1776

Jones, James; 27, Ensign, 17 September 1778

Jones, John; 16, Quartermaster, 30 January 1768; 16, Lieutenant, 22 July 1769; 16, Captain, 20 November 1775

Jones, John; 24, Captain, 2 March 1776

Jones, John; 9, Capt.- Lieut., 1 September 1780; 9, Captain, 1 September 1781

Jones, John; 17 LD, Adjutant, 14 November 1777; 17 LD, Cornet, 14 June 1776; 17 LD, Lieutenant, 25 November 1780

Jones, John; 1FG, Ensign, 11 November 1775; 1FG, Lieut. & Capt., 29 October 1777; Major of Bde in South under Garth

Jones, John; 62, Ensign, 1 September 1771; WIA Hubbardton, 7 July 1777

Jones, John; Hosp., Chaplain, 3 February 1775

Jones, John; 70, Chaplain, 14 January 1782

Jones, Thomas; RA, Captain, 1 January 1771; DOW Freeman's Farm, 20 September 1777

Jones, Thomas; 57, Ensign, 16 January 1776; 57, Lieutenant, 16 February 1780

Jones, Townshend; 34, Lieutenant, 17 September 1733

Jones, Valentine; 52, Lt. Colonel, 4 March 1760; 62, Colonel, 15 January 1776, 25 May 1772; Am., Major General, 1 January 1776, 29 August 1777

Jones, Walter; 63, Lieutenant, 16 March 1775; 63, Captain, 26 October 1777; DOW Ft. Clinton, 13 October 1777

Jones, William; 46, Ensign, 7 June 1777

Jordan, -; Adjutant, 1781; Town Adjutant of New York

Julian, Richard; 23, 2nd Lieut., 21 November 1772; 23, 1st Lieut., 25 November 1775; 44, Captain, 12 May 1778

Kane, Nathaniel; 4, Ensign, 23 December 1776; 4, Lieutenant, 23 October 1778; Also Mathew

Kay, -; Hosp., Sprnmy. Mate, Prior to 1783; Stationed at Halifax, 1783

Kay, George; 3, Ensign, 24 December 1779

Kay, James; 70, Surgeon, 15 September 1780; From mate; Died prior to 6 August 1794

Kearsley, John; 4/60, Ensign, 18 September 1777; 4/60, Lieutenant, 3 September 1779

Keeling, William; 26, Ensign, 5 June 1777; Died 1 November 1777

Keily, John; 35, Ensign, 26 May 1780

Keir, James; FG, Mate, February 1777; POW, Yorktown, 1781

Keith, Robert; 3FG, Lieut. & Capt., 12 June 1765; 3FG, Capt. & Lt. Col., 16 May 1778; Left 3rd Foot Guards 1780

Kellock, Alexander; Hosp., Mate, 1776; Also Keoch; Born 25 July 1755; To surgeon, Queen's Rangers, 25 December 1782; To half pay, 1783; M.D. St. Andrew, 1784; Died 23 October 1844

Kelly, Dennis; 64, Ensign, 28 May 1774; Lieutenant, 3 May 1776; 64, Captain, 13 April 1778; Probably DOW Singleton's Mill, SC, 27 December 1780

Kelly, Francis John; 18, Ensign, 28 February 1772; 18, Lieutenant, 9 October 1775; English, born 1751; First commissioned at age 12

Kelly, George; 44, Ensign, 3 July 1772; 44, Lieutenant, 10 February 1776; 64, Captain, 5 October 1778; WIA Monmouth 28 June 1778

Kelly, John; 33, Ensign, 31 March 1779; 33, Lieutenant, 10 October 1781; WIA Guilford CH, 15 March 1781

Kelly, Waldron; 10, Lieutenant, 25 October 1771; WIA Concord & Bunker Hill; Promoted captain in RGB 20 September 1778

Kelly, William; 2/60, Captain, 28 April 1775; On duty at New York prior to southern campaign; Bde Major of Prevost's Force, 1779-1780

Kelso, Robert; 69, Ensign, 10 May 1780

Kemble, Peter; 4, Ensign, 23 June 1775; 4, Lieutenant, 29 May 1776; 46, Captain, 23 October 1778; WIA Germantown, 4 October 1777

Kemble, Peter; 35, Ensign, 17 July 1775

Kemble, Stephen; 1/60, Major, 20 September 1775, 27 January 1762, Deputy Adj. General; Army Rank also listed as 7 August 1772

Kemble, William; 34, Lieutenant, 1 September 1771; 34, Captain, 1 June 1777; Died 7 May 1778; Also listed incorrectly in the 37th Foot

Kemp, George; 3/60, Mate, date unknown

Kennedy, Archibald; 44, Lieutenant, 23 May 1776; KIA Monmouth, 28 June 1778

Kennedy, Archibald; 43, Ensign, 7 August 1775

Kennedy, George; 34, Ensign, 2 September 1779

Kennedy, Hugh Alexander; Hosp., Physician, 1 January 1776, 7 January 1762; Hosp., Insptr. of Regt. Hosps., July 1777; From half-pay; M.D. Edin, 1754; Physician Middlesex Hosp., 1 Feb. 1759; To half pay, 1783; Later served under the Duke of York, 1793

Kennedy, John; 43, Quartermaster, 8 July 1780

Kennedy, Primrose; 44, Captain, 15 May 1772; Scottish, born 1744; First commissioned at age 20; WIA Brooklyn, 27 August 1776

Kennevie, Robert; 82, Lieutenant, 22 January 1778

Kent, -; 38, Ensign, 10 October 1778

Keough, William; 44, Adjutant, 9 July 1760; 44, Lieutenant, 28 November 1771; 44, Capt.- Lieut., 1 November 1779

Keppel, Hon. William; 14, Colonel, 31 May 1765; Lieutenant General; 25 May 1772, 1727- March 1782; MP Chichester, 1767-1782

Keppell, William; 4/60, Lieutenant, 7 February 1777; 23, Capt.- Lieut., 30 July 1778; 23, Captain, 30 July 1778, 30 May 1778; 82, Major, 19 April 1782; Also Cable; ADC to Sir Henry Clinton 1781

Ker, Charles; 43, Ensign, 17 August 1773; 43, Lieutenant, 22 November 1775

Ker, Charles; 57, Ensign, 5 June 1771; 57, Lieutenant, 26 November 1775

Ker, John; 69, Captain, 14 July 1780

Ker, Mark; 17 LD, Lieutenant, 20 October 1773

Kerr, -; 40, Ensign, 8 March 1780

Kerr, Charles; Hosp., Mate, 1 January 1776; 37, Surgeon, 27 June 1781; Also Kerr; M.D. Edin, 1787; Retired 28 December 1815; Knight Bachelor, 1822; Died prior to November 1837

Kerr, Francis; 74, Lieutenant, 14 October 1781

Kerr, John; 33, Capt.- Lieut., 28 August 1775; 33, Captain, 26 November 1775; Scottish, born 1744; First commissioned at age 16; KIA Yorktown, 10 October 1781

Kerr, Mark; 1/71, Ensign, 19 October 1778

Kerr, Mathew; 57, Ensign, 12 August 1778; 57, Lieutenant, 17 February 1781

Kersteman, William; RE, Pract. eng. & 2nd Lt., 17 January 1776; In America from 1776-1781; Served at Rhode Island and New Yorl

Keymis, James; 9, Ensign, 7 July 1775; 9, Lieutenant, 3 June 1777

King, -; 14, Ensign, 29 October 1777

King, Fitz William; 40, Ensign, 27 February 1778; 40, Lieutenant, 6 March 1780

King, Henry; 5, Ensign, 4 April 1774; 5, Lieutenant, 15 April 1776

King, James; 57, Ensign, 24 December 1774

King, John; 40, Ensign, 17 June 1777; 40, Lieutenant, 24 October 1778

King, Robert; RA, 1st Lieut., 19 January 1782

King, Robert; 28, Lieutenant, 12 December 1774; Retired 14 March 1776

Kingscote, Nigell; 31, Ensign, 12 August 1777

Kingscote, Robert; 31, Lieutenant, 22 February 1776

Kingston, Robert; 28, Lt. Colonel, 13 October 1780, 29 August 1777

Kinlock, David; 1/71, Lieutenant, 5 December 1775; 80, Captain, 22 January 1778; Also Kinlock

Kinneer, Francis Wm.; 7, Captain, 14 March 1764; 63, Major, 7 October 1777; Also Kineer; His promotion to a majority caused resignations in disgust. He had never been in battle; Died Philadelphia, 12 June 1778

Kinnersley, R. Leighton; 8, Ensign, 27 March 1770; 8, Lieutenant, 23 November 1775

Kirkman, James; 29, Adjutant, 31 January 1776; 29, Lieutenant, 28 March 1776

Kirkman, Michael; 21, Adjutant, 23 February 1776; 21, 1st Lieut., 22 February 1768

Kirkman, Michael; 21, Capt.- Lieut., 8 June 1777; 21, Captain, 8 June 1777

Kirkman, Nathaniel; 38, Ensign, 11 August 1778

Kitson, George Richard; 40, Surgeon, 17 December 1779; Also Kittson; From mate 28th Foot; Died prior to 27 February 1794

Knight, Henry; 43, Captain, 2 September 1772; 35, Major, 21 May 1778; 45, Major, 20 September 1778; ADC to Sir Wm. Howe, 1776; WIA New Jersey, 17 June 1777

Knight, Joseph; 4, Lieutenant, 14 August 1767, 23 July 1762, DOW Concord, 20 April 1775; Brother of Henry

Knott, Thomas; 43, Ensign, 30 May 1780

Knowles, Richard; 4, Surgeon, 23 January 1769; Hosp., Surgeon, 5 July 1777; Commission also 4 July; Drowned at sea, 11 October 1780

Knox, Gilbert; 53, Ensign, 28 March 1777; Drowned 14 April 1778

Knox, Robert; Hosp., Physician, 1 January 1776; Hosp., Inspector, 14 January 1777; From half-pay; Inspector to the hospitals under the command of Gen. Carleton

Kortright, John; 16, Ensign, 18 September 1781

Kynnersley, Anthony; 8, Ensign, 15 February 1779; From Shropshire; Brother of Richard; To lieutenant 91st Foot; by raising men; Purchased captaincy, 91st Foot, 25 January 1780

Kynnersley, Richard Leight; 8, Ensign, 27 March 1770; 8, Lieutenant, 23 November 1775; From Shropshire, born 1755; Brother of Anthony; To captain, 91st Foot, 3 December 1779

Kyrwood, John; 24, Ensign, 1 March 1776; 24, Lieutenant, 1 March 1780

Lacey, St. John Pierce; 54, Captain, 25 November 1775, 11 January 1761

Laing, James; RA, 2nd Lieut., 23 March 1781

Lake, Gerard; 1FG, Capt. & Lt. Col., 11 January 1776; POW; Parole to 1783; Later Lord & 3rd Major in England

Laler, Mathew; 63, Ensign, 14 October 1777; 63, Lieutenant, 10 August 1778

Lamb, James; 35, Adjutant, 27 December 1775; 35, Lieutenant, 18 June 1775; 35, Captain, 18 October 1778; Depty. Judge Advocate General, 1777: Married 1778; POW with French 1781

Lambe, John; 6, Captain, 7 January 1771

Lambert, Oliver; 3, Captain, 11 November 1772

Lambton, John; 6, Captain, 15 August 1775, 18 March 1762

Lamond, Dugal; 82, Ensign, 18 September 1780

Lamont, Archibald; 3/60, Lieutenant, 2 September 1775, 15 May 1757

Lamont, Colin; 76, Lieutenant, 6 January 1778

Lamont, Hugh; 2/71, Lieutenant, 30 November 1775

Lamont, Normand; 15, Captain, 27 May 1768; 55, Major, 16 November 1777

Lamont, Normand; 2/71, Major, 24 November 1775, 25 May 1772; Lt. Colonel, 29 August 1777

Lancaster, John; 17, Ensign, 14 August 1780

Landeg, David; Hosp., Sprnmy. Mate, Prior to 1783; At Lancaster, PA as POW, 1783

Landreth, William; 33, Ensign, 20 October 1779

Lane, George; 54, Ensign, 29 September 1772; 54, Lieutenant, 26 November 1775; 54, Captain, 28 April 1779

Lane, John; FG, Quartermaster, 11 April 1779; Possibly William; From volunteer; Replaced 16 June 1779

Lane, Robert; 22, Lieutenant, 12 March 1774; English, born 1753; To additional company, 28 November 1775; Retired 28 November 1776

Lane, William; 7, Lieutenant, 11 October 1779

Larive, Richard; 27, Ensign, 28 September 1775; KIA or died of heat exhaustion, Monmouth, 28 June 1778

Latham, James; 8, Surgeon, 15 July 1767; Irish, born 1736; First commissioned at age 20 as a mate; Resigned 19 August 1775

Latham, Phanuel; 53, Ensign, 6 January 1776; 53, Lieutenant, 19 April 1779

Laton, Charles; 22, Adjutant, 21 February 1772; 22, Lieutenant, 21 April 1768; 64, Captain, 22 January 1776; English, born 1747; Captaincy also given as 24 January 1776

Laton, George; 64, Ensign, 2 March 1778; POW & WIA Eutaw Springs, 8 September 1781; Retired 3 April 1782; Also listed as DOW at Eutaw Springs

Lauder, George; 21, Quartermaster, 7 March 1766

Laurie, Andrew; 14, Lieutenant, 22 December 1772; 2/71, Captain, 30 November 1775; Died 28 February 1782

Laurie, Walter Sloane; 43, Captain, 21 December 1770; Buried Gen. Warren; Retired 19 December 1775

Law, Arthur; 4, Ensign, 3 November 1777

Law, Arthur; 1/71, Ensign, 6 February 1777

Law, Thomas; 18, Ensign, 12 March 1776

Lawe, -; 47, Ensign, 23 November 1775; Also Lanie; Retired 18 March 1776

Lawe, Arthur; 40, Lieutenant, 15 October 1778

Lawe, Robert; 3/60, Ensign, 3 September 1775; 3/60, Lieutenant, 19 August 1778, 20 June 1778, Also Law; Captain of King's Carolina Rangers, 1 May 1780

Lawler, -; Hosp., Sprnmy. Mate, Prior to 1783; Stationed at Halifax, 1783

Lawrence, Gerrard; 57, Captain, 21 May 1774

Lawrence, Thomas; 4, Ensign, 29 May 1776; 4, Lieutenant, 20 May 1779

Laws, George; 1/84, Captain, 21 June 1777; Also Law or Lawe; Died in late 1782

Laws, John Tunnandore; 1/84, Ensign, 20 October 1782; Also Law or Lawe; Son of George Laws

Lawson, Robert; RA, Captain, 11 March 1782; Bridge Master to the Army, 24 May 1779

Lawton, Abraham; 33, Ensign, 28 November 1775

Layard, Ant. Lewis; 7, Lieutenant, 4 April 1772; 7, Captain, 9 June 1778

Layard, John Thomas; 54, Lieutenant, 26 October 1775

Laye, Francis; RA, 2nd Lieut., 15 March 1771; Also Lea; WIA Hobkirk's Hill, SC, 25 April 1781

Le Conte, Peter; 8, Lieutenant, 25 December 1770, 1 January 1762, American; Also held a provincial commission; CM for raping an underage girl, punishment was to walk the parade ground with a placard announcing his crime

Le Maistre, Francis; 7, Adjutant, 8 October 1767; 7, Lieutenant, 18 July 1768, 28 October 1760; 7, Capt.- Lieut., 4 March 1777; 7, Captain, 6 May 1776; 8, Captain, 5 November 1777, 4 March 1777, Served as Cpt.-Lt. in 1/84th in 1775; Army Rank listed incorrectly in Army List

Learmonth, Colvil; 80, Lieutenant, 5 February 1778

Leche, Edward; 54, Ensign, 14 May 1774; 10, Lieutenant, 6 October 1776; Also Luck; Transferred to 7th Foot in 1777

Leche, James; 54, Lieutenant, 20 October 1774

Leche, John; 16 LD, Captain, 4 March 1775

Lechinwitz, William; 4/60, Lieutenant, 4 October 1775

Lechmore, Thomas; 27, Ensign, 5 January 1780

Lee, George; 70, Captain, 26 December 1773

Lees, James; 1/42, Ensign, 14 January 1775; Scottish, born 1758; First commissioned at age 16

Leeson, Patrick; 62, Ensign, 21 August 1781

Legard, George; 69, Lieutenant, 27 July 1779

LeGrange, James Brazier; 60, Ensign, 3 April 1782; Native of New Brunswick, NJ: From ensign and adjutant, 2nd Bn. New Jersey Volunteers

Leigh, -; 37, Ensign, 6 June 1776; 37, Lieutenant, 4 December 1778

Leigh, Charles; 3FG, Lieut. & Capt., 19 April 1770; 3FG, Capt. & Lt. Col., 12 April 1777

Leigh, Charles; 49, Captain, 14 October 1778

Leigh, Charles; 15, Ensign, 7 July 1775; 15, Lieutenant, 18 November 1775; WIA Harlem Heights, 16 September 1776 & Brandywine, 11 September 1777

Leigh, Thomas; 16 LD, Lieutenant, 2 August 1775; 17 LD, Captain, 13 December 1777

Leigh, Thomas; 6, Ensign, 5 March 1774; 6, Lieutenant, 22 July 1776

Leighton, Baldwin; 46, Captain, 12 March 1772; WIA Monmouth, 28 June 1778

Leith, -; 1/71, Ensign, 28 August 1775; 1/71, Lieutenant, 11 November 1778

Leith, Arthur; 69, Lieutenant, 22 July 1778; 69, Capt.- Lieut., 28 January 1782

Leith, James; 21, 2nd Lieut., 13 March 1779

Leith, John; Hosp., Mate, Prior to 1783; With Grenadiers, 1783

Leland, John; 1FG, Capt. & Lt. Col., 13 June 1774; 80, Colonel, 16 May 1782, 17 November 1780; Am., Brigadier General, 20 September 1779; From Captain in 98th Foot

Leland, Samuel; 44, Ensign, 6 April 1775; 44, Lieutenant, 4 October 1776; Probably died Burlington, Yorkshire, 4 October 1778

Lemoine, H.; 3/60, Ensign, 3 October 1781

Lemoine, John; 4/RA, Capt.- Lieut., 21 May 1769; 4/RA, Captain, 7 July 1779, 25 May 1772, WIA Bunker Hill, 17 June 1775

Lemoine, John; RA, 2nd Lieut., 30 June 1780

Lenthall, John; 23, 1st Lieut., 15 April 1774; WIA Bunker Hill, 17 June 1775; Retired 22 November 1775

Leonard, John; 10, Ensign, 28 December 1775

Lernoult, Richard Bern; 8, Captain, 15 July 1767; Major; 10 November 1780, English, born 1732; First commissioned at age 20

Leslie, Alexander; 82, Ensign, 4 January 1778; 82, Lieutenant, 10 September 1779

Leslie, David; 59, Ensign, 1 August 1775

Leslie, George; 9, Ensign, 8 October 1777; 9, Lieutenant, 9 April 1782

Leslie, George; 55, Quartermaster, 6 January 1779

Leslie, Hon. Alexander; 64, Lt. Colonel, 28 August 1768, 30 January 1762; 63, Colonel, 2 January 1782, 19 October 1775; Major General; 19 February 1779, Scottish, born 1731; First commissioned at age 16; ADC to the King, 1775

Leslie, Hon. John; 3, Captain, 29 May 1767; Major; 29 August 1777, Acting Major of Bde; WIA & POW Eutaw Springs, 8 September 1781

Leslie, Hon. William; 17, Lieutenant, 12 July 1773; 17, Captain, 26 February 1776; Born, 1751; Son of the Earl of Leven; Attended a public school; Extra Maj. of Bde 1777; KIA Princeton, 3 January 1777; Also listed as DOW

Leslie, James; 15, Captain, 25 May 1772; Retired 20 June 1777

Leslie, John Lord Lindores; 26, Ensign, 7 September 1768; 26, Lieutenant, 21 February 1776; 26, Capt.- Lieut., 25 September 1781

Leslie, Peter Henry; 14, Ensign, 12 August 1771; 14, Lieutenant, 16 December 1773; KIA Great Bridge, VA, 9 December 1775

Leslie, Robert; 2/42, Adjutant, 21 March 1780

Leslie, Samuel; 14, Captain, 8 February 1762

Leslie, William; 46, Captain, 11 May 1776; Retired 8 November 1778

Leslie, William; 44, Lieutenant, 27 May 1764, 30 March 1759; Scottish, born 1744; First commissioned at age 14; Captain, Royal Fencible Americans, 14 April 1776

Lethbridge, Robert; 4/60, Ensign, 12 February 1776

Leversuch, Arthur; 10, Quartermaster, 28 June 1775

Lewis, Benjamin; 21, 2nd Lieut., 10 September 1776; 21, 1st Lieut., 25 November 1779

Lewis, Benjamin; 65, Ensign, 24 November 1775

Lewis, John; 64, Lieutenant, 16 May 1766; 64, Capt.- Lieut., 3 May 1776; 64, Captain, 28 August 1776; English, born 1745; First commissioned at age 18; LI Major of Bde, 16 May 1776; Extra Major of Bde. 1777

Leybourne, William; 29, Lieutenant, 25 December 1775, 24 February 1762

Lightburne, Stafford; 37, Ensign, 15 August 1775; 37, Lieutenant, 10 February 1778; WIA Yorktown, October 1781

Lighthuzer, -; 70, Surgeon, 13 November 1775; From mate 30th Foot

Ligonier, Edward, Earl; 9, Colonel, 8 August 1771; Major General; 20 September 1775; Lieutenant General; 29 August 1777

Lind, John; 20, Lt. Colonel, 6 January 1776; Also Lynd; WIA Freeman's Farm, 19 September 1777

Lindegrin, Nath'l; 16, Ensign, 12 April 1773; 16, Lieutenant, 27 January 1778; ?/60, Lieutenant, 29 January 1778; Commission revoked after 1780

Lindsay, Alex. Perkins; 22, Ensign, 25 January 1779; 22, Lieutenant, 4 December 1782; Irish; Son of Robert Lindsay; Served with additional company until arrived in America in late 1782

Lindsay, Hon. Charles; 21, 2nd Lieut., 18 June 1778; 55, Lieutenant, 23 January 1773; 55, Capt.- Lieut., 26 April 1777; 55, Captain, 26 April 1777; Scottish, born 1755; First commissioned at age 16

Lindsay, David; 2/42, Captain, 26 March 1780; From 69th Foot

Lindsay, Hon. Rt. Ham.; 72, Captain, 31 December 1779; 21, Captain, 19 May 1780

Lindsay, Hon. James; 14, Ensign, 27 April 1774; 14, Lieutenant, 11 December 1775

Lindsay, James; 65, Lieutenant, 16 May 1766

Lindsay, John; 83, Lieutenant, 27 January 1778

Lindsay, Robert; 22, Lieutenant, 31 October 1762; 22, Capt.- Lieut., 30 October 1776; 22, Captain, 30 October 1776; Also Lindsey; Irish, born 1740; Asst. Barracks Master, Halifax, 29 May 1776; Died 15 July 1793

Lindsay, Marquis of; 7, Lieutenant, 9 May 1776; Also Robert, Duke of Ancaster

Lindsay, Sir David, Bt.; 59, Colonel, 12 January 1776, 7 August 1771

Lindsay, Waterhouse; 9, Captain, 15 May 1772; Died 31 August 1779

Lindsey, Bute; 14, Ensign, 28 August 1777

Lindsey, John; 55, Ensign, 12 February 1780

Lindsey, Wat Crymble; 24, Ensign, 14 July 1777

Lisle, Warren; 52, Ensign, 4 July 1775; From volunteer

Lisle, Wm. Pitt; 52, Lieutenant, 12 September 1777

Lister, Jeremy; 10, Ensign, 26 December 1770; 10, Lieutenant, 15 August 1775; WIA Lexington and Concord, 19 April 1775; Date of lieutenancy also given as 22 November 1775

Lister, Wm. Cavendish; 3FG, Lieut. & Capt., 12 March 1768; 3FG, Capt. & Lt. Col., 16 January 1777; Also quartermaster; Also Fred. Cavendish

Little, Walter; 26, Ensign, 1 August 1779

Litton, Edward; 37, Ensign, 15 August 1775; 37, Lieutenant, 23 March 1778

Livingstone, John; 26, Captain, 27 January 1772, 22 October 1761, Also Levingston; Retired 19 February 1777

Lloyd, Henry Hardress; 8, Ensign, 9 February 1780; Ensigncy not purchased; Neighbor of Bigoe Armstrong; Died 22 February 1781

Lloyd, Hugh; 15, Quartermaster, 22 February 1771; 15, Lieutenant, 9 October 1775

Lloyd, Humprhey; 14, Lieutenant, 11 May 1781

Lloyd, John; 19, Major, 4 October 1781

Lloyd, John; 3/60, Major, 22 October 1779; In Wales by September 1780

Lloyd, John; 46, Captain, 23 August 1775; "WIA Woodbridge, NJ, 19 April or June, 1777 & Monmouth, 28 June 1778; ADC to Sir Henry Clinton, 20 June 1778

Lloyd, John; 20, Lieutenant, 2 August 1775

Lloyd, Owen; 63, Ensign, 13 April 1778; 63, Lieutenant, 18 September 1780; Listed as KIA South Carolina, 25 August 1780, but not possible; WIA Eutaw Springs, 8 September 1781

Lloyd, Richard; 14, Ensign, 7 June 1779; Committed suicide in London, 1779

Lloyd, Richard; 17, Chaplain, 16 June 1780; From Clerk

Lloyd, Thomas; 10, Captain, 31 January 1778

Lloyd, Thomas; 46, Lieutenant, 16 March 1775; WIA prior to 14 November 1777; Killed in a duel with Surgeon Jobson in 1787 but included in Inman's Losses

Lloyd, Thomas; 46, Lieutenant, 1 June 1781

Lloyd, Thomas; 7, Lieutenant, 22 November 1775; 7, Adjutant, 5 September 1779; Also given as 5 September 1776

Locke, Robert; RA, 2nd Lieut., 1 June 1778; Also Lock

Lockell, N. F. C.; 3/60, Lieutenant, 21 November 1776; 3/60, Capt.-Lieut., 1 October 1781; Also Lockell, N.T.C.; With Prevost

Lockhart, John; 15, Capt.-Lieut., 30 September 1775; 15, Captain, 13 May 1776; Died September 1777

Lockhart, William; 33, Ensign, 30 May 1781; 33, Lieutenant, 29 March 1783; WIA Charleston, SC, 1782 or 1783

Loftus, William; 44, Captain, 28 November 1776

Loftus, William; 17 LD, Cornet, 29 September 1770, 2 June 1770, WIA Chatterton's Hill, NY, 28 October 1776

Logan, William; 80, Lieutenant, 25 January 1778; 57, Capt.-Lieut., 28 August 1775

Long, William; 57, Captain, 26 November 1775

Longfield, Robert; 53, Captain, 3 February 1776

Longmore, George; Hosp., Mate, Prior to 1783; Stationed at New York, 1783

Loraine, Alex.; 1/42, Ensign, 8 November 1778; 1/42, Lieutenant, 25 July 1781

Lord, Hugh; 18, Captain, 5 February 1770, 25 December 1762; English, born 1742; First commissioned at age 14; Promoted major in 75th Foot, 30 May 1778

Lord, Simeon; 53, Lieutenant, 25 April 1766, 14 July 1762; 53, Captain, 8 October 1777; POW Ft. Ticonderoga, 18 September 1777

Lorimer, John; Hosp., Surgeon, 14 March 1765; Hosp., Insptr. of Regt. Hosps., 14 October 1782; M.D. St. Andrew, 1764; Fellow of the Royal College of Physicians, Edinburgh; Surgeon to the garrison of West Florida from 1765; Stationed at New York, 1783; To half pay, 6 February 1784; Died London, 13 July 1795

Loring, Joshua; Commissary General, Prior to 1783; Commissary of Prisoners, 1781

Lorning, Benjamin; Hosp., Mate, Prior to 1776; Hosp., Surgeon, 6 September 1780; Stationed at New York, 1783; Died 5 February 1787

Losack, Henry; 29, Ensign, 27 September 1775

Losack, James; 43, Lieutenant, 17 August 1773; 43, Capt.-Lieut., 24 October 1781; Extra Major of Bde, 1782

Loudoun, James; 83, Lieutenant, 22 January 1778

Loup, George Fred.; 4/60, Lieutenant, 11 September 1777

Lovelace, Robert; 2FG, Lieut. & Capt., 6 May 1775; 2FG, Capt. & Lt. Col., 5 May 1780; Posted March 1781 but retired February 1781

Lovell, James; 21, Captain, 21 February 1772

Lovell, William King; RA, 2nd Lieut., 10 February 1776; From sergeant-major; KIA Bedford, NY, 27 August 1776

Lowe, Addison; 16, Quartermaster, 28 December 1776

Lucas, Charles; 16, Ensign, 13 April 1778

Lucas, Robert; 55, Lieutenant, 28 November 1771; 55, Capt.- Lieut., 11 May 1776; 55, Captain, 11 May 1776; Irish, born 1747; First commissioned at age 22; Retired 12 May 1778

Lucas, Thomas; 10, Ensign, 9 February 1778; 20, Lieutenant, 1 March 1776; KIA Freeman's Farm, 19 September 1777

Ludlow, Christopher; Hosp., Mate, Prior to 1783; Stationed at New York, 1783

Ludlow, George; 1FG, Lieut. & Capt., 16 March 1781; POW with troops after Yorktown

Ludlow, Robert; 17, Ensign, 7 August 1776

Luke, John; 55, Captain, 5 December 1764; English, born 1736; First commissioned at age 20; Retired 26 April 1777

Lumley, Thomas; 57, Chaplain, 25 February 1767

Lumm, Charles; 38, Captain, 7 March 1772; 44, Major, 14 April 1779; Lexington night rider; ADC to Maj. Gen. Pigot, 1777

Lumsden, Henry; 14, Ensign, 12 April 1776;

Lumsden, James; 55, Ensign, 18 August 1778; 55, Lieutenant, 24 July 1779

Lumsden, William; 55, Ensign, 6 February 1782

Lundin, James; 2/84, Lieutenant, 14 June 1775; 2/84, Capt.- Lieut., 11 December 1779; Also Lundy or Lundin; From half pay 35th Foot; Possibly served in 1/84th as well

Lunn, Samuel Geo.; 15, Ensign, 29 July 1778; 15, Lieutenant, 20 March 1781

Lupton, B. Schuyler; 54, Ensign, 6 November 1780; 54, Lieutenant, 14 October 1781

Luttrell, Wm. Hungerford; 49, Ensign, 26 October 1777; Announced 1 June 1778; 49, Lieutenant, 4 December 1779

Lyman, Gam. Dwight; 64, Ensign, 25 May 1772; 64, Lieutenant, 22 November 1775

Lyman, Wm. Charles; 30, Lieutenant, 29 June 1780

Lynch, Thomas Gruesbeck; 45, Ensign, 11 February 1777; 45, Lieutenant, 23 March 1780

Lyon, James; 35, Captain, 31 October 1770; Grenadier company cmd.; DOW Bunker Hill, 27 June 1775

Lyon, William; 45, Adjutant, 23 March 1775; 45, Ensign, 12 July 1773; 45, Lieutenant, 23 November 1775; 45, Captain, 11 August 1778

Lyons, Charles; 17, Captain, 6 August 1770; Town major at Halifax, July 1776; Involved in a duel; Resigned 20 February 1776

Lysaght, Henry; 63, Captain, 11 July 1775; WIA Hillborough NJ, 14 June 1777

Lysaght, Henry; 22, Major, 30 April 1781; Irish, born 1750

Lyster, Christopher; 63, Ensign, 28 April 1774; 63, Lieutenant, 15 May 1776; DOW Yorktown, 18 October 1781

Lyttleton, Thomas; 1/42, Lieutenant, 7 September 1775; English, born 1757; First commissioned at age 13

Lyttleton, Thomas; 5, Lieutenant, 7 October 1777; At Little Egg Harbor, 14 Oct. 1778

M'Alister, Archibald; 35, Captain, 25 July 1775; From Argyllshire

M'Allpin, Neil; 74, Ensign, 13 October 1781

M'Arthur, Archibald; 54, Captain, 1 September 1771, 18 October 1761; 2/71, Major, 16 November 1776, 29 August 1777

M'Cuming, Price; 31, Quartermaster, 21 February 1772

M'Donald, Angus; 1/71, Lieutenant, 18 September 1779

M'Donald, Colin; 26, Lieutenant, 16 November 1762, 18 July 1762, WIA Ft. Clinton 6 October 1777

M'Donald, Donald; 1/84, Major, 12 June 1775; Lt. Colonel; 29 August 1777, Also MacDonald; Former provincial officer; POW Carolina, 1776

M'Donell, Alexander; 2/84, Lieutenant, 14 June 1775; POW Mohawk River, 1776; Escaped

M'Donell, Colin; 82, Ensign, 11 April 1779

M'Donell, Donald; 2/71, Captain, 2 November 1778

M'Donell, Ronald; 74, Captain, 26 December 1777; From Keppoch; Served in F&I War 78th Foot; From 66th Foot; Married Sarah Cargill in Jamaica; Died at Keppoch, 1788

M'Donnell, -; 2/84, Ensign, 9 March 1781

M'Donnell, Alexander; 74, Lieutenant, 26 December 1777

M'Donnell, Angus; 1/71, Ensign, 6 December 1775

M'Donnell, Archibald; 1/84, Ensign, 27 February 1776

M'Donnell, John; 15, Lieutenant, 14 November 1763, 23 July 1757

M'Kinnon, John; 47, Lieutenant, 15 June 1764

M'Leod, Alexander; 1/42, Ensign, 25 August 1775; 1/42, Lieutenant, 25 April 1777; KIA Charleston, 15 May 1780 in powder magazine explosion

Mac Lean, Neil; 9, Capt.- Lieut., 10 August 1777; 9, Captain, 11 July 1778; Captaincy announced 30 September 1778

Macaiskell, William; 1/71, Ensign, 25 August 1776; 1/71, Lieutenant, 19 October 1778

MacBean, Alexander; 2/71, Lieutenant, 28 August 1776

MacBean, William; 6, Ensign, 30 May 1777

MacColme, Rob. H.; 76, Ensign, 30 December 1777

Macculloch, David; 17 LD, Cornet, 7 August 1780

Macculloch, David; 9, Lieutenant, 26 September 1772

MacDonald, -; 82, Lieutenant, 21 January 1778

MacDonald, -; 1/71, Ensign, 18 September 1780

MacDonald, Alexander; 2/84, Captain, 14 June 1775; Major; 19 May 1783, From half pay 77th Foot; POW Carolina, 1776

MacDonald, Allen; 76, Lieutenant, 28 December 1777

MacDonald, Angus; 1/71, Ensign, 7 October 1777; 1/71, Lieutenant, 14 October 1778; From volunteer

MacDonald, Angus; 76, Lieutenant, 5 January 1778

MacDonald, Angus; 2/84, Quartermaster, 14 June 1775; 2/84, Ensign, 3 January 1782; From sergeant, 26th Foot

MacDonald, Angus; 2/84, Ensign, 11 February 1783

MacDonald, Archibald; 1/84, Lieutenant, 20 October 1781

MacDonald, Donald; 3/60, Captain, 27 September 1775; Died February

MacDonald, Donald; 76, Lieutenant, 7 December 1778; Also McDonald; WIA Green Springs VA, 6 July 1781

MacDonald, Donald; 1/84, Lieutenant, 1 January 1781; May had served with 2/84th Foot

MacDonald, Dugald; 1/71, Ensign, 5 November 1780

MacDonald, Duncan; 76, Ensign, 9 April 1779

MacDonald, Forbes Ross; 59, Ensign, 1 November 1774

MacDonald, James; 76, Ensign, 29 December 1777; 76, Lieutenant, 9 September 1780

MacDonald, James; 2/84, Lieutenant, 14 June 1775

MacDonald, James; 76, Chaplain, 25 December 1777

MacDonald, John; 26, Captain, 21 February 1776

MacDonald, John; 2/84, Captain, 14 June 1775; Recruited 200 men; POW Mohawk River, 1776

MacDonald, John; 76, Captain, 26 December 1777

MacDonald, John; 76, Captain, 29 December 1777

MacDonald, John; 1/42, Lieutenant, 3 September 1775, 22 Oct. 1762, Retired 11 November 1777

MacDonald, John; 1/71, Lieutenant, 16 December 1775; Transferred & promoted 19 October 1778

MacDonald, John; 80, Lieutenant, 16 January 1778

MacDonald, John; 2/42, Ensign, 24 March 1780

111

MacDonald, John; 2/71, Ensign, 27 August 1776; Promoted & transferred, 22 October 1778

MacDonald, John; 2/84, Ensign, 7 October 1776; 2/84, Lieutenant, 20 September 1779; From volunteer; Lieutenancy also listed as 1780

MacDonald, Kenneth; 2/84, Ensign, 14 June 1775; POW Carolina, 1776

MacDonald, Lewis; 2/71, Ensign, 20 January 1781; KIA 2 March 1782

MacDonald, Ranald; 1/84, Adjutant, 25 June 1775; 1/84, Lieutenant, 25 December 1776; WIA Bunker Hill, 17 June 1775 with 52nd Foot

MacDonald, Ranald; 1/84, Lieutenant, 25 December 1776; Also M'Donnell; Died 19 January 1782

MacDonald, Ranald; 1/84, Ensign, 14 June 1776

MacDonald, Robert; 1/71, Lieutenant, 25 December 1775

MacDonald, Ronald; 76, Ensign, 10 November 1780

MacDonald, Simon; 76, Ensign, 28 December 1777; 76, Lieutenant, 20 September 1779

MacDonald, William; 1/42, Ensign, 5 October1777; 1/42, Lieutenant, 25 August 1778; Scottish, born 1761; First commissioned at age 15

MacDonnel, John; 76, Lt. Col. Comdt., 25 December 1777, 29 August 1777

MacDonnell, Aeneas; 76, Lieutenant, 3 January 1778

MacDonnell, James; 2/84, Ensign, 9 March 1781

MacDonnell, James; 2/84, Lieutenant, 14 June 1775; May be a duplicate of MacDonald

MacDowall, Hay; 2/71, Lieutenant, 1 September 1776; 1/42, Captain, 20 September 1779; Also McDoval

Mace, Benjamin; 22, Surgeon, 1 June 1762;Hosp., Surgeon, 22 February 1776; Hosp., Apothecary, 21 February 1778; English, born 1735; Transferred to the general hospital 22 February 1776; Stationed at New York, 1783; To half pay, 6 February 1784; Died Lynn Regis, Norfolk, 5 May 1793

MacFarlane, Robert; 74, Lieutenant, 22 December 1777; In Europe in 1781; Upset in being bypassed for promotion

MacHahon, John; 44, Ensign, 24 November 1775; 44, Lieutenant, 31 January 1778

MacHahon, John; Captain, 1781; Barrackmaster at Charleston

Machell, Christopher; 15, Captain, 9 October 1775; WIA Harlem Heights, 16 September 1776

Machrill, William; 43, Lieutenant, 24 October 1781

MacKarell, William; 64, Ensign, 4 October 1777; From volunteer

MacKay, Aeneas; 52, Adjutant, 6 March 1771; 52, Ensign, 18 June 1775; From volunteer; Received his ensigncy for "remarkably good and spirited behaviour" at Bunker Hill; Retired 18 April 1777

MacKay, Alexander; 69, Captain, 15 March 1776
MacKay, George; 3/60, Lieutenant, 3 September 1775, 20 March 1761,
Died 10 October 1778
MacKay, George; 52, Quartermaster, 28 May 1776; From lieutenant Nova
Scotia Volunteers
MacKay, Hon. Alexander; 21, Colonel, 10 November 1770; Major
General; 30 April 1770; Lieutenant General; 29 August 1777
MacKay, John; 65, Captain, 26 August 1767
MacKay, Robert; 21, 2nd Lieut., 13 June 1781
MacKay, William; 76, Adjutant, 25 December 1777; 76, Ensign, 15
October 1778; 76, Lieutenant, 9 November 1779
MacKennon, John; Captain, 1781; Deputy Quartermaster General;
Probably John McKinnon, 63rd Foot
MacKenzie, Alexander; 31, Lt. Colonel, 28 April 1773; Died 12
September 1777, probably in Canada
MacKenzie, Alexander; 76, Lieutenant, 27 December 1777
MacKenzie, Alexander; 1/42, Ensign, 12 July 1773; Scottish, born 1746;
First commissioned at age 14; KIA or DOW Harlem Heights, 16
September 1776
MacKenzie, Alexander; 2/84, Chaplain, 12 July 1777
MacKenzie, Alexander; 40, Surgeon, 14 March 1772; Died prior to 18
December 1779
MacKenzie, Charles Barring; 2/71, Lieutenant, 4 December 1775; 80,
Capt.- Lieut., 7 September 1781; POW Princeton
MacKenzie, Colin; 1/71, Lieutenant, 18 December 1775; KIA Ft.
Montgomery, October 1776
MacKenzie, Colin; 1/71, Captain, 27 November 1775; 92, Major, 27
December 1779; POW Boston, 19 June 1776
MacKenzie, Frederick; 23, Adjutant, 11 May 1763; 23, 1st Lieut., 3
October 1757; 23, Capt.- Lieut., 22 November 1775; 23, Captain, 6
October 1776; 23, Major, 9 August 1780; Asst. Adjutant General, 1781
MacKenzie, George; 1/42, Captain, 12 December 1770; Scottish, born
1744; First commissioned at age 16; To major 73rd Foot, 20 December
1777
MacKenzie, George; 1/42, Lieutenant, 25 August 1775, 26 October 1759,
From half-pay 87th Foot; WIA Harlem Heights, 16 September 1776;
Promoted to captain, 73rd Foot, 20 December 1777
MacKenzie, George; 27, Ensign, 21 September 1777; 15, Lieutenant, 20
March 1779; From volunteer; WIA Brandywine as volunteer
MacKenzie, George; 4/60, Ensign, 3 September 1775
MacKenzie, James; 23, 2nd Lieut., 10 August 1780
MacKenzie, John; 2/71, Lieutenant, 17 December 1775

MacKenzie, Kenneth; 37, Captain, 26 October 1775
MacKenzie, Kenneth; 21, 1st Lieut., 7 May 1776; KIA Freeman's Farm, 19 September 77
MacKenzie, Kenneth; 33, Lieutenant, 27 February 1771; English, born 1745; First commissioned at age 22
MacKenzie, Kenneth; 2/42, Quartermaster, 27 March 1781
MacKenzie, Lewis; 21, 2nd Lieut., 14 January 1782
MacKenzie, Robert; 43, Captain, 8 February 1775; WIA Bunker Hill, 17 June 1775; Sec. to Sir Wm. Howe, 1776; Resigned 20 March 1778
MacKenzie, Roderick; 1/71, Ensign, 21 September 1779; 2/71, Lieutenant, 18 October 1781
MacKewen, John; 38, Adjutant, 19 February 1777
MacKewen, John; 14, Ensign, 22 February 1775;; 38, Lieutenant, 1 June 1776
Mackham, Thomas; 83, Lieutenant, 30 September 1782
MacKilwaine, Andrew; 52, Lieutenant, 27 March 1770, 22 February 1763; 52, Capt.- Lieut., 18 June 1775; Retired 3 April 1776
MacKinnon, John; 76, Lieutenant, 11 January 1778
Mackintosh, Aeneas; 2/71, Captain, 3 December 1775
Mackintosh, Angus; 2/71, Captain, 24 November 1775; Also paymaster; Brother to John in 42nd Foot; Died Georgia, 23 August 1779
MacLagan, James; 1/42, Chaplain, 15 June 1764; Also McLaggan; Scottish, 1728-1805; Born Logierait, Perthshire; First commissioned at age 34; Resigned 1781; Minister, Church of Scotland, Blair Atholl and Strowan, 1781-1805
MacLaine, Allan; 1/84, Ensign, 1783
MacLean, Neil; 2/84, Captain, 14 June 1775; From half pay 21st Foot
MacLean, Neil; 1/84, Captain, 14 June 1775; POW Canada; CM for repeated neglect of duty, suspended for 6 mos., August 1780
MacLean, Neil; 1/84, Lieutenant, 14 June 1775; 1/84, Capt.- Lieut., 21 June 1777
MacLean, Neil; 1/84, Ensign, 25 December 1776; 1/84, Lieutenant, 26 September 1782; CM for using improper language and reprimanded, August 1781
MacLean, Neil; 21, 1st Lieut., 19 January 1771, 14 February 1762
MacLeod, John; 2/42, Lieutenant, 31 March 1780
MacLeod, Norman; 1/71, Captain, 7 December 1775; 2/42, Lt. Colonel, 21 March 1780; Scottish, from Isle of Skye; Entertained Johnson & Boswell, 1773; POW Boston, 19 June 1776; To 73rd Foot as Major after being exchanged
MacLeod, Norman; 1/71, Captain, 25 August 1779; Also McLeod; WIA Charleston, prior to 12 May 1780

MacLeod, Norman; 1/71, Capt.- Lieut., 25 August 1779
MacLeod, Norman; 1/42, Lieutenant, 31 August 1775, 4 November 1761
MacLeod, Norman; 1/84, Captain, 14 June 1775; Died December 1777;
May be the same as lieut. in 1/42d Foot
Maclure, Hamilton; 76, Surgeon, 25 December 1777
MacQueen, Donald; 76, Lieutenant, 9 January 1778
Macrea, Charles Alex.; 76, Lieutenant, 1 January 1778
Macrea, John; 2/42, Ensign, 26 December 1781
Madan, Charles; 33, Ensign, 24 April 1781
Madan, Frederick; 1FG, Lieut. & Capt., 21 August 1765; 1FG, Capt. &
Lt. Col., 9 November 1778; Bde. Paymaster, 18 Dec. 1778; Died in New
York, 25 December 1779
Madden, Edward; 15, Lieutenant, 18 July 1762; 15, Capt.- Lieut., 14 May
1776; 15, Captain, 20 July 1778; Acting Town Major Philadelphia 28
September 1777
Madden, John; 35, Ensign, 29 April 1775; Also Sladden; From volunteer
in 35th L.I. Coy.; DOW Bunker Hill, 16 October 1775
Maddison, George; 4, Lt. Colonel, 20 April 1763; English, born
Lincolnshire, -d 1807; Son of John of Stainton le Vale; Married Mary
Baugh, 1757; Retired 24 December 1775
Maddison, John Tho.; 4, Ensign, 26 February 1773; 4, Lieutenant, 16
December 1775
Maginnis, Hugh; 38, Captain, 31 December 1769; 38, Major, 17
November 1780
Magrath, Perkins; 17, Captain, 24 December 1775
Magrath, Andrew; 53, Ensign, 6 April 1778; Also McGrath; From
volunteer; Died 8 June 1781
Magrath, John; 28, Ensign, 2 August 1775; 28, Lieutenant, 26 December
1776; 28, Capt.- Lieut., 28 January 1782; Also MacGrath
Magrath, John; 1/84, Ensign, date unknown; CM for resisting arrest and
improper conduct; Dismissed from service, July 1782
Magrath, Terence; 45, Lieutenant, 30 May 1775; Also McGrath;
Reprimanded for conduct unbecoming a gentleman, 20 December 1775;
Retired 30 October 1777 for the value of his ensigncy
Mair, Alexander; 43, Ensign, 23 November 1773; 43, Lieutenant, 23
November 1775; 40, Captain, 10 August 1778; Also May or Murr; WIA
Brooklyn, 27 August 1776; ADC to Clinton 20 June 1778
Mair, Arthur; 63, Ensign, 4 March 1780
Mair, Charles; 2/71, Ensign, 24 November 1775; 1/71, Lieutenant, 10
March 1777; 23, 1st Lieut., 8 November 1778; KIA Gloucester Point, VA,
3 October 1781

Mair, Henry; 47, Lieutenant, 20 March 1758; 47, Capt.- Lieut., 12 February 1776; 47, Captain, 12 February 1776; Also Marr; ADC to Gen. Howe, 19 June 1775

Mair, Peter; 40, Ensign, 18 October 1778; 40, Lieutenant, 8 March 1780

Maitland, Alexander; 49, Ensign, 22 November 1775; 49, Lieutenant, 25 January 1777; 49, Captain, 6 August 1778

Maitland, Alexander; 2/42, Lieutenant, 29 March 1780

Maitland, Alexander; 55, Lieutenant, 4 October 1776

Maitland, Alexander; 9, Ensign, 25 July 1781

Maitland, Hon. Alexander; 49, Colonel, 25 May 1768; Major General; 25 May 1772; Lieutenant General; 29 August 1777

Maitland, Augustus; 1FG, Ensign, 26 April 1776; 1FG, Lieut. & Capt., 12 October 1779; WIA Guilford CH; POW on parole until May 1783

Maitland, Hon. John; 1/71, Lt. Colonel, 14 October 1777; 1732-1779; MP Haddington burghs, 1774-1779; ADC for Gen. Clinton, 4 November 1778; Cmd. 2nd L.I. Bn. 1776-1777; Died of fever, Savannah, 12 October 1779; Prior service as a marine officer

Maitland, Thomas; 55, Ensign, 7 July 1777

Majoribank, John; 19, Major, 17 November 1780, 29 August 1777; DOW Eutaw Springs, 3 October 1781

Malcolm, Allen; 1/71, Ensign, 30 November 1775; 43, Lieutenant, 6 February 1777; 33, Captain, 30 May 1780; KIA Camden, 16 August 1780

Mall, Alexander; 29, Lieutenant, 7 January 1771

Mallett, Jonathan; 45, Surgeon, 20 September 1775; Hosp., Purvyr. & Chief Surg., 11 February 1775; Hosp., Chief Surgeon, 24 January 1776; Hosp. Insptr. of Regt. Hosps., 6 September 1780; From mate in F&I; At Boston, 1775; Stationed at New York, 1783; Retired to half pay 25 December 1783; Died Marylebone, 21 November 1806

Mallom, John; 57, Lieutenant, 3 June 1767; 63, Capt.- Lieut., 12 September 1777; 63, Captain, 12 September 1777; Died 28 February 1782

Mallory, John; 29, Lieutenant, 27 December 1775

Mandeville, Daniel; Hosp., Apothecary, 1 January 1776; Hosp., Deputy Purveyor, 22 May 1777; Hosp., Purveyor, 4 January 1780; Staff surgeon at Quebec from 1767; At Boston, 1776; Also Purveyor of Stores and Medicines for the Jamaica Hospital, 1780

Mankham, Enoch; 46, Lt. Colonel, 11 May 1775, 25 May 1772; Colonel, 17 November 1780

Manley, Edward; 64, Ensign, 15 August 1775; Also Sir Edward Manley Pryce, Bt.

Manley, John; 33, Lieutenant, 28 August 1775; 33, Captain, 14 October 1778; English, born 1751; First commissioned at age 18

Manley, Robert Kenrick; 33, Ensign, 10 September 1779

Mann, Gother; RE, Eng. extra. & Cpt.-Lt., 2 March 1777; In America from 1778-?; Served at West Indies

Manning, George; 46, Capt.- Lieut., 11 July 1781; Captain; 12 October 1779

Manning, John; 4/60, Ensign, 24 April 1779; Died 24 June 1781

Manuel, William; 38, Lieutenant, 1 May 1773, 1 September 1771

Maquois, William; RA, 2nd Lieut., 29 March 1776; DOW Charleston, 15 October 1780

Markham, William; 83, Captain, 20 January 1778; Retired 28 June 1783

Markham, William; 15, Ensign, 29 June 1781

Markland, Ralph; 23, 2nd Lieut., 12 May 1778; 23, 1st Lieut., 2 August 1780

Marland, John; 40, Ensign, 14 October 1778

Marland, Peter; 55, Ensign, 14 May 1774; 55, Lieutenant, 11 May 1776; Retired 17 July 1777

Marley, George; 62, Captain, 16 August 1770; Major, 17 November 1780

Marr, John; RE, Sub-eng. & Lt., 23 February 1763; In America from 1761-1776 at Halifax, Quebec and the Great Lakes

Marsden, Francis; 5, Captain, 1 April 1773; WIA Bunker Hill, 17 June 1775; Retired 4 July 1777

Marsh, Francis; 65, Captain, 24 March 1762; 46, Major, 20 February 1773, 23 July 1772; 43, Lt. Colonel, 28 August 1776; Am., Brigadier General, 2 July 1781; Brig. Gen. commission date may not be correct

Marshall, Andrew; 83, Surgeon, 17 January 1778

Marshall, John; 30, Quartermaster, 15 January 1773; 30, Lieutenant, 8 February 1775

Marshall, John; Hosp., Surgeon, 9 April 1778, 13 June 1765, From 2nd Foot; Assigned to Halifax Hospital as surgeon, 1778 - 1783; To half pay, 25 December 1783; Died 20 April 1822

Marshall, Mathew; 37, Ensign, 27 August 1776; 7, Lieutenant, 7 November 1778; KIA 28 July 1781

Marshall, William; 63, Lieutenant, 15 August 1775, 17 December 1762; 63, Capt.- Lieut., 18 September 1780

Martelle, Norton Cha.; 69, Lieutenant, 17 October 1781

Martin, Alexander; 27, Ensign, 14 January 1777; 27, Lieutenant, 7 February 1778

Martin, Angus; 76, Lieutenant, 31 December 1777

Martin, Arthur George; 2FG, Capt. & Lt. Col., 11 January 1769; Colonel; 19 February 1779; Am., Brigadier General, 17 June 1779; Also Anthony; Cmd. 1 Bn. Of Guards, 1779

Martin, Charles; 26, Captain, 14 September 1779

Martin, Charles; 37, Ensign, 20 December 1776

Martin, Henry; 69, Lieutenant, 10 May 1780

Martin, William; RA, Captain, 2 April 1757; RA, Major; 23 July 1772; RA, Lt. Colonel, 16 May 1781, 29 August 1777; Am., Brigadier General, date unknown; Brig. gen. date not listed in NAAL, 1783

Martin, William; 35, Lieutenant, 16 September 1778; 35, Adjutant, 11 April 1780;

Martin, William; 37, Ensign, 7 October 1777; Probably the same as above

Martin, William; 4/60, Ensign, 7 September 1779

Martin, Willis; 33, Lieutenant, 25 November 1775, 28 January 1763, Also Willis; Army date also given as 18 January

Martyr, John; 55, Ensign, 3 December 1777

Mason, Edmond; 14, Captain, 19 October 1763, 8 December 1762; 27, Colonel, 19 February 1773, 25 May 1772; Am., Major General, 1 January 1776, 29 August 1777

Massey, Eyre; 27, Ensign, 1 September 1775; 27, Lieutenant, 12 September 1777

Massey, George; 49, Ensign, 7 June 1776; 15, Lieutenant, 14 October 1778

Massey, Hugh; 35, Lieutenant, 25 December 1762; 35, Capt.- Lieut., 22 November 1775; 35, Captain, 22 November 1775; Irish; Son of treasurer of Limerick; WIA Bunker Hill, 17 June 1775 & White Plains, 28 October 1776; Gren. captain at La Vigie, December 1778; Attended drinking parties with Maj. Drewe

Massey, John; Hosp., Surgeon, Prior to 1778; To Rhode Island Garrison; Died 23 September 1779

Massey, N. Williams; 27, Ensign, 5 December 1780

Massey, Robert; 21, 2nd Lieut., 29 September 1777

Master, Richard; 24, Captain, 14 March 1771

Masterson, Charles; 19, Lieutenant, 1 June 1778

Mathew, Edward; 2FG, Capt. & Lt. Col., 29 March 1762; 62, Colonel, 17 November 1779; Am., Brigadier General, 15 February 1776; Major General; 19 February 1779, Commanded Brigade of Guards in America, 1776

Mathew, George; 2FG, Ensign, 4 February 1776; 2FG, Lieut. & Capt., 20 November 1779; Retired June 1781

Mathews, George; 37, Lieutenant, 30 September 1775; 46, Captain, 13 April 1778

Mathews, Lowther; 62, Ensign, 28 April 1774; 62, Lieutenant, 21 November 1776

Mathews, Richard Greenal; 62, Capt.- Lieut., 2 March 1776; Died Canada, 27 March 1777

Mathews, Robert; 8, Adjutant, 10 April 1775; 8, Lieutenant, 27 March 1770; 8, Captain, 7 May 1777; Scottish, born, 1745; First commissioned at age 16

Mathias, Jas. Vincent; 6, Ensign, 16 April 1777

Mattay, Lewis; 3/60, Ensign, 1 September 1775; 3/60, Lieutenant, 29 May 1777; POW 1777; Held two years in Maryland; Resigned 13 December 1779

Matthews, Thomas; 33, Mate, 1775; English, born 1752; First commissioned at age 23

Mattier, Daniel; 14, Lieutenant, 27 March 1765

Maunsell, Sewell; 29, Lieutenant, 30 June 1774; 29, Captain, 23 May 1781; At Burgoyne's surrender

Mawby, George; 18, Ensign, 15 November 1776; English, born 1761; Son of Cpt.-Lt. Mawby; First commissioned at age 15

Mawby, John; 18, Adjutant, 4 February 1769; 18, Capt.- Lieut., 19 July 1771; Captain; 25 May 1772, English, born 1731; First commissioned at age 25

Mawby, John; 18, Lieutenant, 19 July 1771; English, born 1753; Son of Cpt.-Lt. Mawby; First commissioned at age 15

Mawhood, Charles; 17, Lt. Colonel, 26 October 1775, 17 June 1767; Colonel, 29 August 1777; Member of a landed Yorkshire family

Mawhood, Wm. John; 17, Ensign, 7 October 1777;, 17, Lieutenant, 21 November 1778; Son of a clothing merchant; related to Charles Mawhood; Arrested for marauding in 1778, released after a lengthy pre-trial confinement

Maxwell, Christopher; 30, Major, 7 June 1766

Maxwell, David; 83, Lieutenant, 13 February 1783

Maxwell, Edw. Phin.; 22, Quartermaster, 22 February 1773; 22, Lieutenant, 13 September 1769; 49, Captain, 29 May 1776; English, born 1744

Maxwell, Hamilton; 31, Lieutenant, 12 November 1773 At Burgoyne's surrender

Maxwell, Hamilton; 1/71, Captain, 1 December 1775; POW on transport Ann, 10 June 1776

Maxwell, James; 76, Captain, 1 May 1781

Maxwell, James; 80, Captain, 19 January 1778; Died 17 September 1780

Maxwell, James; 82, Lieutenant, 10 January 1778; POW since March 1779

Maxwell, John; 15, Lt. Colonel, 5 October 1777, 19 September 1775

Maxwell, John; 27, Lt. Colonel, 26 October 1775

Maxwell, Patrick; 54, Surgeon, 13 September 1781; From mate; By purchase; Retired 21 August 1793

Maxwell, William; 6, Major, 30 September 1772

Maxwell, William; 80, Major, 23 May 1778

Maxwell, William; 20, Captain, 2 August 1775

Maxwell, Wm. George; 38, Ensign, 2 August 1780

May, Charles; 43, Lieutenant, 31 December 1777; Died Yorktown, 23 October 1781

May, Charles; 57, Ensign, 27 November 1775

May, Henry; 20, Ensign, 20 September 1777; 1/84, Ensign, 21 June 1777; Held a dual commission

May, Humphrey; 17, Lieutenant, 24 December 1774; 46, Captain, 2 July 1777

Mayal, Miles; 57, Quartermaster, 15 August 1778

Maynard, William; 2FG, Ensign, 15 December 1773; 2FG, Lieut. & Capt., 25 June 1777; DOW Guilford CH, 17 April 1781

Mayne, John; 6, Ensign, 22 November 1775

Mayne, Richard; 3, Lieutenant, 31 January 1780; Stayed in Ireland according to WO 8/6, 273-279

McAlpin, Daniel; 2/60, Captain, 7 August 1771; Arrested as loyalist in 1775; Escaped to Canada, 1777; Raised Royal American Volunteers, 10 July 1777

McArthur, Archibald; 3/60, Lt. Colonel, 24 August 1781; On duty St. Augustine, 1782

McBean, Donald; 10, Captain, 15 August 1775, 25 May 1772

McBean, Donald; 2/71, Ensign, 1 November 1778; 1/71, Lieutenant, 4 November 1780; Also McBain; From volunteer; POW Boston, 17 June 1776

McBoyd, David K.; 38, Ensign, 2 February 1780

McCausland, Robert; 8, Surgeon, 18 August 1775; Scottish, born 1749; Entered service as mate at 19 in 1768; Died on half pay, Wigton, Cumberland, 26 October 1797

McClintock, John; 5, Lieutenant, 20 February 1773; WIA Bunker Hill, 17 June 1775

McCormick, James; Hosp., Sprnmy. Mate, Prior to 1783; Stationed at New York, 1783

McCummings, James; 29, Ensign, 1 November 1780

McDermot, Terence; 35, Ensign, 18 April 1777; 35, Lieutenant, 6 July 1779; POW with Maj. French 1775-1777; Gambled away his money; Died 19 February 1780 of yellow fever and drink, St. Lucia

McDermott, William; 47, Ensign, 15 May 1772; 16, Lieutenant, 16 May 1774

McDonald, Aeneas; 33, Ensign, 25 January 1776; 33, Lieutenant, 25 October 1779

McDonald, Alexander; 22, Captain, 26 May 1769, 25 March 1762; 2/71, Major, 10 March 1777; 1/71, Lt. Colonel, 25 October 1779; Scottish, born 1737; POW Cowpens

McDonald, Alexander; 76, Lieutenant, 26 December 1777; 76, Captain, 9 November 1779; Retired 5 September 1780

McDonald, Alexander; 2/84, Captain, 14 June 1775, 25 May 1772, From half pay, 77th Foot; Died late 1779

McDonald, Alexander; 1/84, Captain, 14 June 1775; Major; 19 May 1783

McDonald, Alexander; 4/60, Ensign, 2 September 1775; 4/60, Lieutenant, 18 September 1777

McDonald, Alexander; 76, Lieutenant, 30 December 1777

McDonald, Alexander; 2/84, Lieutenant, 14 June 1775

McDonald, Alexander; 34, Ensign, 2 August 1780

McDonald, Alexander; 2/42, Ensign, 22 March 1780; From ensign in Dutch service

McDonald, Allan; 59, Captain, 30 December 1755; Major; 23 July 1772; Retired 29 March 1775

McDonald, Allan; 2/84, Captain, 14 June 1775; Also served in 1/84th; POW Carolina, 1776

McDonald, Charles; 2/84, Lieutenant, 15 June 1775; Also MacDonald; POW Carolina, 1776

McDonald, Charles; 19, Ensign, 8 March 1780

McDonald, Charles; 2/84, Lieutenant, 18 May 1776; From volunteer with Lord Percy

McDonald, Colin; 76, Ensign, 26 December 1777; WIA Green Springs VA, 6 July 1781

McDonald, Donald; 22, Ensign, 14 October 1778; Commissioned in additional company

McDonald, Donald; 55, Lieutenant, 8 September 1775; 55, Captain, 24 July 1779; English, born 1756; First commissioned at age 19

McDonell, John; 2/84, Lieutenant, 9 April 1777; WIA & POW Canada

McDonnell, Archibald; 1/84, Ensign, 27 February 1776

McDonnell, Duncan; 1/84, Ensign, 20 October 1781

McDonnell, John; 1/71, Captain, 27 August 1776

McDonnell, John; 1/71, Major, 23 November 1775, 23 July 1772; Lt. Colonel; 29 August 1777

McDonnell, Ranald; 1/84, Lieutenant, 25 December 1777

McDoual, Hay; 2/71, Lieutenant, 1 September 1776; Also McDowall; Portrait in Strachan, plate 56

McDougal, Duncan; 1/84, Ensign, 25 December 1776; 1/84, Lieutenant, 25 June 1782; Ensigncy also listed as 9 April 1776; WIA Carolina, 1776

McDougal, John; 2/71, Adjutant, 5 June 1781

McDougal, Patrick; 2/71, Ensign, 14 October 1778; 1/71, Lieutenant, 18 September 1780; From volunteer; POW Boston 19 June 1776

McDougal, Robert; 8, Ensign, 6 May 1777; 8, Lieutenant, 12 December 1781; Native of America; Family involved in land speculation in the Northwest Territory

McDougall, George; 1/84, Captain, 14 June 1775; From half pay 60th Foot

McDougall, James; 1/84, Ensign, 25 June 1782; From volunteer

McDougall, John; 1/84, Captain, 14 June 1775; POW Canada

McDowall, William; 27, Lieutenant, 15 August 1775, 13 February 1762

McEvers, John; 23, 2nd Lieut., 13 October 1781

McFarlane, William; 53, Ensign, 24 May 1775; 53, Lieutenant, 10 July 1776

McGill, John; 19, Captain, 19 July 1769; Major; 17 November 1780

McGrath, John; 1/84, Ensign, 10 May 1777; From volunteer

McGray, Eugene; 55, Ensign, 31 January 1778; Died 23 October 1781

McGregor, Alexander; 1/42, Ensign, 8 May 1777; 1/42, Lieutenant, 5 June 1778

McGregor, Alexander; 2/42, Lieutenant, 5 June 1778; Recruiting in New York for 2/42 Foot

McGregor, Duncan; 1/71, Ensign, 19 September 1779; KIA Charleston, 25 April 1780

McGregor, John; 1/42, Lieutenant, 17 August 1775, 28 July 1760; 2/42, Captain, 22 March 1780

McGregor, John; 83, Lieutenant, 29 January 1783

McInnis, Ranald; 1/84, Adjutant, 25 June 1775

McIntosh, Alexander; 10, Captain, 25 December 1770, 24 July 1762; DOW White Plains, date given as 28 October or 17 November 1776

McIntosh, Allan; 1/71, Ensign, 14 October 1778; 1/71, Lieutenant, 16 October 1780; From volunteer

McIntosh, George; 3/60, Captain, 25 September 1775; Retired 27 April 1778

McIntosh, John; 1/42, Adjutant, 13 March 1772; Capt.- Lieut., 16 August 1775; 1/42, Captain, 5 October 1777; Scottish, born 1743; First commissioned at age 14; WIA Harlem Heights 16 September 1776; Retired by 18 February 1780

McIntosh, William; 1/71, Ensign, 3 November 1777; From volunteer; KIA Stono Ferry, SC, 20 June 1779

McIntyre, Donald; 43, Surgeon, 13 March 1772; Hosp., Surgeon, 1 March 1781; Also McIntire; Stationed at New York, 1783; To half pay, 1783; Died 28 October 1815

McKay, Alexander; Hosp., Mate, Prior to 1783; Stationed at New York, 1783

McKay, George; 40, Adjutant, 6 March 1780; 40, Ensign, 8 September 1781

McKenzie, George; 4/60, Adjutant, 18 September 1777; 4/60, Ensign, 2 September 1775; 4/60, Lieutenant, 1 May 1779; Also listed with lt. commission date of 25 Dec. 1778

McKenzie, James; 3/60, Ensign, 21 September 1779

McKenzie, Kenneth; 83, Lieutenant, 18 December 1782

McKinnon, Donald; 1/84, Lieutenant, 16 July 1776; Lieutenancy also listed as 16 April 1776

McKinnon, Donald; 2/84, Ensign, 10 March 1781; From volunteer

McKinnon, John; 63, Capt.- Lieut., 27 July 1776; 63, Captain, 12 September 1777; From captain in Royal Highland Emigrants, 14 June 1775

McKinnon, John; 74, Chaplain, 19 December 1777

McKinnon, Ranald; 2/84, Captain, 14 June 1775; From half pay 77th Foot

McLachlan, John; 55, Captain, 15 August 1775, 25 May 1772

McLachlan, Patrick; 76, Lieutenant, 13 January 1778

McLachlan, Peter; 74, Quartermaster, 20 Jan 1779

McLaren, Alexander; 2/71, Ensign, 13 Oct 1780, 30 December 1778

McLarin, William; 19, Quartermaster, 10 July 1776

McLarty, Colin; 24, Ensign, 1 March 1780

McLauchlin, P.; Ensign, 1781; Barrack Master at Penobscot

McLean, Alexander; 2/84, Ensign, 25 Dec 1776

McLean, Alexander; 80, Lieutenant, 9 March 1781; From volunteer 71st Foot; Died 31 January 1782

McLean, Allan; 1/42, Ensign, 23 May 1776; 1/42, Lieutenant, 3 August 1778; Drowned New York, 30 or 31 December 1780

McLean, Allan; 29, Ensign, 27 March 1781

McLean, Allen; 1/84, Lt. Col. Comdt., 12 June 1775, 25 May 1772; Colonel; 17 November 1780, From half pay 114th Foot

McLean, Allen; 1/84, Ensign, 5 September 1783

McLean, Angus; 76, Lieutenant, 9 April 1779

McLean, Archibald; 2/71, Lieutenant, 31 December 1775; POW Boston, 19 June 1776; WIA & POW Stony Point. NY, 16 July 1779

McLean, Archibald; 74, Lieutenant, 8 January 1778

McLean, Archibald; 1/84, Lieutenant, 14 June 1775; CM for perjury, suspended for 6 mos.; King dismissed him from service; Killed while attempting murder

McLean, Archibald; 9, Ensign, 6 September 1781;

McLean, Charles; 43, Capt.- Lieut., 10 July 1775; 43, Captain, 22 November 1775

McLean, Charles; 2/42, Ensign, 26 March 1780

McLean, Donald; 74, Ensign, 25 December 1777;

McLean, Francis; 82, Colonel, 16 December 1777, 29 August 1777, Died Halifax, winter 1780

McLean, Hector; 1/84, Lieutenant, 14 June 1775; POW Carolina 1776; Escaped

McLean, Hector; 1/84, Ensign, 12 June 1775; POW Carolina 1776; Escaped; Possibly confused with above

McLean, Hector; 2/84, Ensign, 14 June 1775;2/84, Lieutenant, 19 May 1778; McLean, Hector, 2/84, Adjutant, 25 April 1777; From volunteer in 45th Foot

McLean, Hector; 1/42, Quartermaster, 21 December 1779; Scottish, born 1750; Entered service at age 22; Probably from sergeant

McLean, John; 1/84, Lieutenant, 14 June 1775; 2/84, Capt.- Lieut., 9 April 1777; From half pay 114th Foot; Served in Portugal c.1771; Drowned 10 December 1779

McLean, Lauchlan; 1/84, Quartermaster, 14 June 1775; 1/84, Lieutenant, 14 June 1775; 1/84, Captain, 17 October 1782; POW Carolina, 1776; Escaped

McLean, Lauchlan; 2/84, Lieutenant, 14 June 1775; 1/84, Captain, 17 October 1782; Also MacLaine

McLean, Murdoch; 2/84, Captain, 14 June 1775; From from pay 114th Foot

McLean, Murdoch; 74, Lieutenant, 5 January 1778

McLean, William; 40, Captain, 1 April 1773

McLeod, Aeneas; 1/71, Ensign, 17 October 1779; Died 1 March 1782

McLeod, Donald; 47, Lieutenant, 16 December 1771; WIA Lexington and Concord, 19 April 1775; Promoted captain and adjutant general of the Highland Regulating Army; KIA Moore's Creek Bridge, NC, 26 or 28 February 1776

McLeod, Rory; 1/71, Lieutenant, 26 December 1775; POW Boston, 19 June 1776; Died 17 July 1780

McLeod, William; 20, Ensign, 25 June 1781

McLeod, William; 59, Ensign, 29 March 1775

McLeod, William; 2/71, Ensign, 18 October 1779

McLeroth, -; 64, Ensign, 22 August 1780; 63, Lieutenant, 22 October 1781

McLeroth, Robert; 64, Captain, 1 January 1766; 64, Major, 28 August 1776; 57, Lt. Colonel, 18 November 1780; Irish, born 1738; First commissioned at age 22; WIA Brandywine, 11 September 1777; Sold out 3 May 1782

McLeroth, Thomas; 64, Ensign, 18 August 1778; 63, Lieutenant, 1 June 1780; WIA Hobkirk's Hill, 25 April 1781; From volunteer

McLeroth, William; 16, Ensign, 5 March 1782

McMullen, Donald; 1/71, Ensign, 19 January 1781

McMurdo, Charles; 3, Capt.- Lieut., 9 December 1780

McMurdo, G. Lewis; 80, Captain, 20 January 1778

McNeal, -; 16 LD, Mate, date unknown; Transferred from 16th Light Dragoons to provincial cavalry

McNeill, John; 9, Lieutenant, 9 October 1775

McNeill, Roderick; 82, Lieutenant, 9 January 1778; DOW, 7 August 1779

McNivan, Donald; 1/42, Ensign, 4 May 1782; Scottish, born 1761; First commissioned at age 20

McPhail, Thomas; 2/71, Ensign, 20 October 1781; KIA 3 March 1782

McPherson, A.; 2/71, Ensign, 3 November 1780; Probably KIA Guilford CH, 15 March 1781

McPherson, Donald; 2/71, Ensign, 3 August 1778; KIA Guilford CH, 15 March 1781

McPherson, Donald; 1/71, Lieutenant, 19 October 1779; KIA Savannah, 24 November 1779

McPherson, Duncan; 1/71, Major, 25 November 1775; Lt. Colonel, 29 August 1777; Also Daniel

McPherson, Duncan; 1/42, Captain, 15 August 1775; WIA Piscataway, NJ, 10 May 1777

McPherson, Duncan; 2/71, Major, 31 December 1780, 23 July 1772

McPherson, Duncan; 63, Captain, 1 September 1771, 22 October 1761

McPherson, Evan; 82, Lieutenant, 20 January 1778

McPherson, Henry; 1/71, Ensign, 26 November 1775; 2/71, Lieutenant, 3 August 1778; KIA Savannah, 24 September 1779, with 1/71st when killed

McPherson, James; 17, Capt.- Lieut., 8 September 1775; 17, Captain, 28 August 1776; WIA & POW Princeton, 3 January 1777; Retired 16 June 1780

McPherson, James; 1/42, Captain, - September 1771, 18 October 1761, Scottish, born 1725; First commissioned at age 32; Retired 5 June 1778

McPherson, John; 82, Lieutenant, 4 January 1778; 82, Capt.- Lieut., 18 September 1780; 82, Captain, 3 January 1778

McPherson, John; 80, Lieutenant, 17 January 1778

McPherson, John; 2/42, Ensign, 27 March 1780

McPherson, John; 6, Ensign, 3 May 1776

McPherson, John; 82, Ensign, 7 January 1778

McPherson, William; 16, Adjutant, 26 July 1773; 16, Lieutenant, 26 July 1773

McQuary, Donald; 2/84, Ensign, 19 May 1778

McQuary, Lauchlan; 2/84, Ensign, 9 April 1777;
2/71, Lieutenant, 18 January 1781; From volunteer

McQuary, Lauchlan; 74, Lieutenant, 23 December 1777; From Ulva, born between 1715 & 1722; Last chief of his clan; Entertained Johnson and Boswell on October 16/17, 1773; Died 14 January 1818

McTavish, Alexander; 1/71, Ensign, 11 November 1778; 1/71, Lieutenant, 18 January 1778; From volunteer 2/71; POW Boston, 19 June 1776

McVean, Colin; 2/71, Ensign, 29 December 1778; From ensign 4th Bn.New Jersey Volunteers, 17 April 1777

Meacham, William; 28, Quartermaster, 8 September 1770; 28, Ensign, 22 February 1779

Meadows, Daniel; 44, Ensign, 12 April 1777; Died 7 September 1779

Meadows, William; 55, Lt. Colonel, 22 September 1775, 31 December 1769; 5, Lt. Colonel, 16 November 1777; Colonel, 25 November 1778; WIA Iron Hill, 3 September 1777 & Brandywine while commanding the 1st Gren. Bn.; ADC to the King, 1778; WIA La Vigie, 18 December 1778

Mecan, Thomas; 23, Capt.- Lieut., 28 August 1771;
23, Captain, 23 November 1775, 25 May 1772; 23, Major, 24 April 1779; Also McCan; Asst. Engineer at Boston, 1775; WIA Brandywine, 11 September 1777; Died of violent fever, 8 August 1780

Mecan, William; 54, Ensign, 28 November 1775; 44, Lieutenant, 26 January 1779; Drowned at sea, probably 28 October 1779

Meggs, George; 14, Ensign, 5 January 1776; 3/60, Lieutenant, 22 May 1778; 4/60, Capt.- Lieut., 1 February 1782; 4/60, Captain, 4 May 1782

Menzies, William; 1/84, Surgeon, 25 December 1780; Also Menzie; From mate; To half pay 1784; Died c. 1808

Menzies, Archibald; 10, Mate, date unknown; 10, Surgeon, 8 October 1778; Died prior to 7 August 1794

Menzies, Charles; 35, Lieutenant, 15 August 1775, 8 October 1761

Menzies, Charles; 1/71, Capt.- Lieut., 24 May 1780; Also 8 September 1780 for capt.- lieut.

Menzies, Robert; 2/71, Major, 26 November 1775; KIA on transport Annabelle, Boston, 16 June 1776

Mercer, Alexander; RE, Eng. ord. & Capt., 25 May 1772; In America from 1776-1780; Served at New York

Mercer, Daniel; 8, Ensign, 29 November 1771; 8, Lieutenant, 29 March 1776

Mercer, James; 64, Adjutant, 2 March 1778; 64, Ensign, 24 November 1775; 64, Lieutenant, 18 August 1778; Scottish, born 1758; First commissioned at age 18; WIA Danbury, CT, 27 April 1777

Meredith, John; 70, Lieutenant, 4 October 1770; 70, Captain, 24 April 1779; Married in 1780

Merida, Edward; 24, Ensign, 27 November 1776 Merwin, Joseph; Hosp., Sprnmy. Mate, Prior to 1783; Stationed at New York, 1783

Methan, Geo. Montgomery; 10, Ensign, 17 July 1771; 64, Lieutenant, 8 October 1775; 65, Captain, 24 May 1776; 21, Captain, 10 September 1776

Metzner, Fredrick; 17 LD, Cornet, 8 July 1767; 16 LD, Lieutenant, 3 June 1778; Also Mitzner; Sprnmy. ADC to Gen. Knyuphausen, 17 July 1777; Extra Major of Bde, 1781

Mewburn, Thomas; 16, Ensign, 26 July 1773; Retired 7 September 1776

Meyrick, Thomas; 28, Captain, 6 February 1781

Middleton, John B.; Hosp., Sprnmy. Mate, Prior to 1783; Stationed at New York, 1783

Middleton, Mid. Cornyn; 44, Chaplain, 28 July 1768; Replaced 24 December 1775

Miles, Lawford; 17, Lieutenant, 8 September 1775; 17, Captain, 18 September 1780;

Millar, William; 26, Surgeon, 21 May 1777; Retired on half pay, 15 August 1798; Died Stirling, 27 May 1805

Miller, -; 37, Ensign, 26 March 1776

Miller, Henry; 65, Adjutant, 24 May 1776; 65, Ensign, 16 April 1771; 65, Lieutenant, 16 August 1775

Miller, James; 59, Chaplain, 15 January 1756

Miller, William; 43, Adjutant, 17 August 1773; 43, Lieutenant, 13 February 1773; 43, Captain, 19 December 1775

Miller, William; 83, Lieutenant, 25 January 1778

Millett, Mathew; 64, Lieutenant, 24 February 1773; 38, Captain, 12 July 1777; Irish, born 1750; First commissioned at age 17; At Groton, 1781

Milligen, George; Hosp., Surgeon, 1775; Surgeon to the garrison at Mobile; From the garrison in South Carolina

Millington, George; 43, Ensign, 6 November 1779

Milward, Robert; 59, Major, 21 March 1765

Minchin, Charles; 27, Lieutenant, 28 August 1775; KIA Brandywine 11 September 1777

Minchin, Falkiner; 27, Ensign, 23 December 1775; 27, Lieutenant, 2 December 1777

Minchin, George; 27, Lieutenant, 8 September 1775

Minchin, John; 27, Ensign, 24 May 1775; 27, Lieutenant, 5 July 1777; Also Mencklin; WIA Danbury, CT, April 1777

Minchin, Joshua Paul; 5, Ensign, 14 March 1772; 5, Lieutenant, 23 June 1775; Also 2 March 1778

Minchin, Paul; 29, Captain, 17 March 1774

Mitchell, Andrew; 38, Quartermaster, 18 January 1770; 38, Ensign, 21 July 1775; DOW Bunker Hill, 8 September 1775; Resigned 20 July 1775

Mitchell, Andrew; 38, Surgeon, 25 August 1780; From mate; M.D. Edin., 1789; Died 31 October 1800

Mitchell, Edward; 5, Major, 31 January 1774; 27, Lt. Colonel, 3 November 1777, 7 October 1777; Lexington night rider; Captured Paul Revere; WIA Bunker Hill, 17 June 1775; Drowned while onboard the HMS Beaver during a hurricane, 11 October 1780

Mitchell, James; 1/42, Mate, 13 September 1777

Mitchell, James; 37, Ensign, 10 November 1780

Mitchell, John; 45, Captain, 8 September 1768; Died 29 May 1775

Mitchell, Thomas; 45, Ensign, 23 February 1781

Mitchelson, Walter; RA, Quartermaster, 8 March 1776; RA, Capt.- Lieut., 1 January 1771; Also Michelson; Died North America, 7 September 1777

Mitford, Wm. Hen.; 6, Ensign, 23 November 1775

Moland, Joseph; 26, Ensign, 11 May 1774; 26, Lieutenant, 7 October 1777; POW escaped 27 December 1776

Molesworth, Richard; Deputy Paymaster General, 1778

Molesworth, Wm. John; 46, Ensign, 22 March 1780

Molleson, -; Major, Wagon-master General

Mompesson, John; 8, Lieutenant, 9 December 1766; 8, Capt.- Lieut., 16 March 1776; 8, Captain, 11 May 1778; English, born 1748; Son of former lieutenant colonel of 8th Foot; First commissioned at age 12

Monck, Charles; 45, Lieutenant, 10 October 1776

Monck, Henry Stanley; 29, Ensign, 26 December 1775; 8, Lieutenant, 1 November 1780

Monckton, Hon. Henry; 45, Lt. Colonel, 25 July 1771; Cmd. 2nd Gren. Bn.; WIA Brooklyn, 27 August 1776, KIA Monmouth, 28 June 1778

Monckton, Hon. Robert; 17, Colonel, 25 October 1759; Lieutenant General; 30 April 1770, 1726-1782; MP Portsmouth, 1778-1782

Moncrief, James; RE, Eng. extra. & Cpt.-Lt., 10 January 1776; Major; 25 December 1779; Lt. Colonel; 27 September 1780, In America from 1776-1782; Served at St. Augustine, Charleston, Savannah; POW, on board Delaware

Moncrieffe, Ed. Cornw.; 38, Ensign, 18 June 1775; 38, Lieutenant, 12 September 1777; From volunteer

Moncrieffe, George; 10, Ensign, 23 November 1775; 10, Lieutenant, 2 June 1777; Promoted to captain in 81st Foot, 23 December 1777

Moncrieffe, George; 16, Ensign, 2 May 1775; Possibly transferred to 10th Foot

Moncrieffe, Patrick; 26, Lieutenant, 2 March 1770

Moncrieffe, Thomas; 59, Captain, 2 March 1768, 14 February 1760, Major of Bde, Gren. Bn., 22 May 1776

Moncrisse, Edward C.; 4/60, Lieutenant, 5 November 1780, 12 September 1777

Money, John; 9, Captain, 10 February 1770; 9, Major, 28 September 1781,17 November 1780, ADC to Cornwallis, 1781

Money, John; 63, Adjutant, 11 July 1775; 63, Ensign, 12 July 1773; 63, Lieutenant, 23 November 1775; Possibly a Major of Bde; DOW Blackstocks, 20 November 1780

Monin, Anthony; 8, Ensign, 22 October 1778

Monington, Richard; 69, Surgeon, 19 October 1763; Hosp., Apothecary, 1 January 1776; M.D. St. Andrews, 1787; Died c. 24 December 1805

Monins, David; 4/60, Lieutenant, 6 September 1775, 13 January 1763

Monoux, George; 57, Lieutenant, 28 November 1771; Also Meneaux; Retired 31 March 1777

Monro, Harry; 1/42, Lieutenant, 26 August 1775; 1/71, Captain, 2 February 1779; POW Boston, 19 June 1776

Monro, Harry; 28, Lieutenant, 8 September 1775; Retired 17 October 1778

Monsell, William; 29, Captain, 13 September 1769; 29, Major, 17 November 1780

Montague, George; 15, Lieutenant, 8 January 1773; 15, Captain, 1 December 1775

Monteith, Douglas; 49, Ensign, 4 June 1779

Montgomery, Isaac; 30, Lieutenant, 31 January 1780

Montgomery, James; 10, Chaplain, 30 July 1762

Montgomery, Rob. Alexr.; 54, Ensign, 26 November 1775; 54, Lieutenant, 2 September 1778

Montgomery, William; 40, Major, 6 March 1780; 64, Major, 18 February 1781

Montgomery, William; 37, Captain, 9 August 1771; 37, Major, 29 April 1781; KIA Groton, CT, 6 September 1781

Montgomery, William; 40, Quartermaster, 18 January 1770; 40, Capt.-Lieut., 14 January 1775; 40, Captain, 22 November 1775

Montgomery, Wm. Stone; 44, Lieutenant, 20 March 1775; 9, Captain, 6 January 1776; 17 LD, Captain, 25 February 1776; POW & DOW, Ft. Ann, 10 July 1777; LD commission was cancelled

Montresor, Henry T.; 23, 2nd Lieut., 13 September 1779

Montresor, John; RE, Eng. ord. & Capt., 25 May 1772; In America from 1757-1778; Served at Canada, West Indies, middle colonies: ADC to Sir Wm. Howe

Montresor, John; 80, Ensign, 20 September 1780

Montresor, Robert; 74, Major, 7 February 1781, 28 November 1779, Exchanged from 100th Foot

Moodie, Alexander; 62, Surgeon, 21 February 1776; Died prior to 8 November 1792

Moore, Benjamin; Hosp., Deputy Chaplain, Prior to 1783; Stationed at New York, 1783

Moore, Charles; 59, Captain, 28 May 1770; Requested Gage to allow him to retire 1775

Moore, Gustavus; 47, Ensign, 5 September 1779

Moore, Henry; 27, Ensign, 16 March 1775; 27, Lieutenant, 1 September 1775; 27, Captain, 18 January 1778

Moore, James; 3, Lieutenant, 29 November 1780; Stayed in Ireland according to WO 8/6, 273-279

Moore, John; 54, Ensign, 20 October 1774; 54, Lieutenant, 17 August 1777; 54, Captain, 2 September 1778

Moore, John; 82, Capt.- Lieut., 10 January 1778; 82, Captain, 10 January 1778; At Siege of Penobscott, 1779

Moore, John; 40, Lieutenant, 20 October 1774; 40, Capt.- Lieut., 8 September 1781

Moore, Joseph; 9, Ensign, 16 December 1775; 20, Lieutenant, 8 October 1777

Moore, N.; 22, Ensign, 22 November 1775; Resigned 21 November 1776; Never served in America

Moore, Oliver; 10, Ensign, 30 January 1776

Moore, Thomas; 27, Lieutenant, 16 March 1775; 27, Captain, 1 September 1775

Moore, Thomas W.; Captain, 1781; Barrack Master at Georgia

Moore, William; 45, Captain, 14 May 1774; Retired 7 February 1776

Morden, Charles Wm.; 14, Ensign, 13 April 1776; 7, Lieutenant, 19 February 1777; 46, Captain, 9 November 1778; Also held an ensigncy in the 2/84th Foot; Deputy BM Gen. at Halifax, 1779

Morden, Geo. Burgess; 70, Ensign, 13 October 1778; 70, Lieutenant, 2 September 1779

Morgan, Anthony; 7, Captain, 15 August 1775, 21 June 1762, Retired on half pay 4 March 1777

Morgan, Charles; 3/60, Chaplain, 11 June 1783; Also Mongan; From chaplain, 3rd Bn. New Jersey Volunteers

Morgan, George; 2FG, Capt. & Lt. Col., 26 May 1775; POW; Not on parole

Morgan, Lewis; Hosp., Mate, Prior to 1783; Stationed at New York, 1783

Morgan, Marcus Antony; 17, Lieutenant, 23 August 1775; Irish; Attended Kilkenny School; WIA Long Island, NY, 27 August 1776; DOW Germantown, 5 October 1777

Morris, Charles; 70, Ensign, 2 September 1779

Morris, Charles; Hosp., Deputy Purveyor, 14 April 1783; Stationed at New York, 1783; To half pay 11 February 1784; Died 14 March 1829

Morris, Edward; 24, Ensign, 1 October 1780

Morris, Michael; Hosp., Physician, 3 February 1775; Hosp., Inspector of Hosp., 10 or 14 January 1777; M.D. Rheims, 1754; Originally inspector of hospitals under Gen. Howe; Retired on half pay 17 January 1781; Fellow of the Royal Society; Physician to Westminster Hosp. For 30 years; Died 29 May 1791

Morris, Richard; RA, Mate, 12 August 1780

Morris, William; 43, Lieutenant, 2 September 1772; 43, Capt.- Lieut., 30 May 1780; 43, Captain, 30 May 1780

Morrison, George; 57, Lieutenant, 31 August 1770

Morrison, George; RE, Eng. ord. & Capt., 4 January 1758

Morrison, George; 17, Colonel, 29 May 1782, 22 December 1772, Entered the artillery as a gunner in the 1720s; Sent to Woolwich as cadet gunner after distinguished service in the Jacobite Rebellion; Originally commissioned an engineer; Then served as Quartermaster General from 1772

Morrison, James; 3, Ensign, 31 January 1780

Morrison, John; Deputy Commissary, 1778

Morrison, Theodore; 40, Lieutenant, 5 March 1775; 45, Captain, 30 October 1770

Morrison, Thomas; 28, Surgeon, 19 October 1770; From mate; Also surgeon of 2/84th Foot, 14 June 1775; To apoth. Leeward Isles, 6 November 1779; Retired half pay 1783

Morse, Robert; RE, Eng. extra. & Cpt.-Lt., 25 May 1772; In America from 1782-1783; Served at New York

Mortimer, Wm. Stone; 17, Lieutenant, 23 August 1775; Retired 23 May 1776

Morton, William; 3, Surgeon, 16 December 1773; Died 8 or 9 October 1781

Moseley, Charles Roper; 17, Ensign, 15 August 1775; Possibly KIA Stony Point, 16 July 1779; Army List lists him as resigning 16 June 1780

Moss, William; 27, Quartermaster, 27 August 1779

Mosse, John; 14, Ensign, 28 June 1777

Mostyn, Robert; 40, Captain, 6 May 1776; Possibly WIA Princeton, 3 January 1777; Retired 1 October 1778

Mostyn, Roger; 65, Ensign, 30 June 1768; 65, Lieutenant, 7 November 1774; Also Robert

Mostyn, Samuel; 49, Ensign, 29 March 1776; 49, Lieutenant, 31 May 1778; Also Moiston

Moultrle, Thomas A.; 52, Ensign, 12 September 1777; 52, Lieutenant, 15 August 1778; Also James A.; From volunteer; With 1st L.I. Bn., 8 August 1778

Mountain, George; 47, Ensign, 22 October 1779; Also possibly Mountaine

Mountaine, George; 47, Lieutenant, 9 December 1756; 47, Capt.- Lieut., 22 November 1775; 7, Captain, 12 February 1776

Mowatt, James; 1/84, Ensign, 9 April 1776

Mowatt, James Rider; 28, Lieutenant, 14 March 1772; CM and reprimanded; Retired 28 October 1778

Moxham, Joseph; 17 LD, Captain, 15 May 1772

Moyle, Th. Coppinger; 28, Captain, 21 July 1770; Major; 17 November 1780, KIA West Indies, 2 September 1781

Mudge, William; RA, 1st Lieut., 16 May 1781

Muir, George; 53, Lieutenant, 24 May 1775; 53, Captain, 25 February 1778

Muir, James; 3, Surgeon, 9 October 1781; From mate; Retired as ensign, 16 May 1787; Died Glasgow, 1 August 1809

Muir, William; 53, Lieutenant, 24 May 1775; 53, Captain, 19 April 1779

Muir, William; 82, Captain, 11 June 1779; Major of Bde for Guards, 26 April 1781; Later ADC to Gen. O'Hara, 2 October 1781; Retired 30 April 1784

Muirhead, John; 83, Lieutenant, 17 January 1778

Mulcaster, Fredrick George; RE, Eng. extra. & Cpt.-Lt., 25 May 1772; In America from 1768-1778; ADC to Sir Wm. Howe

Muller, -; 4/60, Ensign, 5 January 1780

Muller, Jacob; 3/60, Captain, 3 September 1775, 11 April 1763; Major; 29 August 1777; Died St. Augustine, 19 June 1778 or August 1778

Muller, John K.; 2/60, Capt.- Lieut., 13 November 1776; 2/60, Captain, 10 August 1777; Also John F. K.; KIA Ogaucheee River, GA, 2 February 1779

Mullins, W. Townsend; 63, Ensign, 23 February 1780

Munchausen, Fredrick Ernst von; Captain, 20 November 1776; ADC to Sir William Howe, 20 November 1776; Extant diary; German officer

Munro, Alexander; 1/42, Lieutenant, 2 September 1775, 28 Sept. 1762; 83, Captain, 23 January 1778

Munro, George; 2/71, Captain, 4 December 1775; Died 1 or 2 February 1780

Munr, Henry; 1/42, Lieutenant, 26 August 1775, 12 Dec. 1759; Also Monro; POW, 29 May 1776

Murcheson, Magnus; 2/71, Ensign, 3 August 1778; 2/71, Lieutenant, 18 October 1779; WIA Stono Ferry, SC, 20 June 1779; Died 20 January 1782

Murcheson, Roderick; 1/71, Lieutenant, 3 August 1778

Murchieson, Donald; 8, Ensign, 25 June 1781

Murchieson, John; 1/71, Ensign, 3 December 1775

Murdoch, Peter; 64, Ensign, 24 May 1776; 64, Lieutenant, 2 March 1778; 74, Captain, 23 November 1778

Murray, -; 63, Ensign, 22 November 1780; From volunteer; WIA Eutaw Springs, 8 September 1781

Murray, Adam; 28, Surgeon, 15 January 1781, c. 1780, From 89th Foot

Murray, Hon. Alexander; 2/84, Lieutenant, 24 November 1779; 2/84, Captain, 1 January 1781; Also Levenson as given name

Murray, Sir Alexander Bt.; 17, Captain, 23 August 1775; Attended a public school with Hon. WM. Leslie; KIA Long Island, NY, 27 August 1776

Murray, Duncan; 1/84, Quartermaster, 22 October 1779; From sergeant

Murray, Edward; 57, Adjutant, 23 November 1761; 57, Ensign, 21 May 1774; 57, Lieutenant, 31 March 1777

Murray, Henry; 15, Captain, 8 January 1773; Retired 25 November 1776

Murray, James; 3FG, Capt. & Lt. Col., 3-Nov-69; Retired 1777; Governor of Upnor Castle, September 1775

Murray, James; 2/42, Captain, 21 March 1780; Scottish; From half pay, 78th Foot

Murray, Sir James; 57, Adjutant, date unknown; 57, Captain, 30 April 1771; 4, Major, 31 January 1778; WIA Brandywine 11 September 1777 & Whitemarsh, 4 December 1777; Cmd. 1st L.I. Bn., 6 March 1778

Murray, James; 9, Quartermaster, 18 January 1770; 9, Lieutenant, 2 March 1776; WIA Ft. Ann, 9 July 1777

Murray, John; 80, Captain, 21 January 1778; At Yorktown

Murray, John; 46, Ensign, 25 January 1781

Murray, John; 1/84, Quartermaster, 29 April 1783

Murray, Lord John; 1/42, Colonel, 25 April 1745; General; 30 April 1770, Scottish, born 1708; First commissioned at age 30; General date also given as 1780

Murray, Mervyn; 17, Ensign, 23 August 1775; 17, Lieutenant, 2 July 1777; Retired 28 November 1778

Murray, Patrick; 4/60, Captain, 28 September 1775; WIA Roupel's Ferry, SC., 3 February 1779

Murray, Somerville; 43, Ensign, 25 February 1774; 43, Lieutenant, 10 March 1777; Retired 17 October 1778

Murray, Thomas; 16, Captain, 26 February 1780, 20 October 1773; 2/84, Major, 17 February 1781; ADC to Gen. Clinton, 10 June 1778; ADC to Lt. Gen. Robertson, 1782

Murray, Thomas; 10, Ensign, 23 October 1771; 10, Lieutenant, 13 May 1776

Murray, Thomas; 35, Lieutenant, 28 December 1775; Resigned 16 September 1778; Transferred to Garrison Battalion, 10 November 1778

Murray, William; 1/42, Major, 7 September 1771; 27, Lt. Colonel, 5 October 1777; Scottish, born 1738; First commissioned at age 17; WIA Harlem Heights, 16 September 1776; Died 2 November 1777, probably in Britain

Murray, Lord William; 1/42, Ensign, 27 August 1775; 1/42, Lieutenant, 27 October 1777; 1/42, Captain, 3 August 1778, 30 December 1777; Scottish, born 1729; Son of Lord George Murrary; Commission date also 27 September 1777; Promoted to captain in 77th Foot

Musgrave, Thomas; 64, Captain, 20 August 1759; 64, Major, 17 August 1774, 23 July 1772; 40, Lt. Colonel, 28 August 1776; Am., Brigadier General, Unknown; English, born 1733; First commissioned at age 21;WIA Pells Point, 18 October 1776; Cmd. 1st L.I. Bn. 1776; Brig. gen. date not listed in NAAL, 1783

Mussle, Ebenezer George; 69, Ensign, 16 June 1780

Myers, William; 38, Adjutant, 25 July 1771; 38, Lieutenant, 3 July 1772; 26, Captain, 19 February 1777; 26, Major, 25 September 1781; WIA Bunker Hill, 17 June 1775; With 2nd Gren. Bn., 2 June 1778; Married 1 September 1779

Nailor, John; 46, Quartermaster, 3 December 1779; 64, Captain, 12 July 1770; English, born 1735; First commissioned at age 21; KIA Brandywine, 11 September 1777; His servant was captured as well

Nairne, John; 1/84, Captain, 14 June 1775; 53, Major, 4 October 1780, 29 August 1777; Served in Dutch Scots Brigade; F&I War 78th Foot; Died 14 July 1802

Nairne, John; 1/71, Lieutenant, 27 November 1775; 1/71, Capt.- Lieut., 18 September 1780

Nairne, William; 1/71, Lieutenant, 28 November 1775; 1/71, Capt.- Lieut., 20 June 1781

Naish, John; 44, Ensign, 11 August 1781

Napier, Francis Lord; 31, Lieutenant, 21 March 1776; 31, Captain, 17 November 1779

Napier, Hon. George; 80, Captain, 18 January 1778; Wife died c. 5 January 1780

Napier, Robert John; 45, Ensign, 17 December 1779

Napier, Sir James; Hosp., Superintendent-General, 25 June 1777; Born, 1701; Served as surgeon since 1744; Knt. Bachelor, 1778; Fellow of the Royal Society; Retired on half pay, 1781; Died London, 21 December 1799

Napier, William; 14, Lieutenant, 16 September 1771; DOW Great Bridge, VA, 10 or 11 December 1775

Nares, Geo. Strange; 70, Ensign, 9 June 1778; 70, Lieutenant, 24 May 1779

Nash, -; 63, Ensign, 20 October 1779

Nash, John; 62, Captain, 28 April 1774

Nash, Thomas; 16 LD, Captain, 3 January 1775

Nash, Thomas; 52, Ensign, 10 March 1777; Died 29 May 1778

Nassau, W. Hen.; 1FG, Ensign, 3 May 1773; 1FG, Lieut. & Capt., 4 June 1776; Retired June 1777

Naylor, Wm. Pendred; 62, Ensign, 12 March 1774; 62, Lieutenant, 21 November 1776; POW near Stillwater, 12 October 1777

Neal, N. Hill; 46, Ensign, 3 September 1781

Needham, Hon. Francis; 17 LD, Captain, 21 May 1774; 76, Major, 10 August 1790; At New York City, 17 February 1781

Needham, John; 27, Lieutenant, 28 November 1771; 28, Capt.- Lieut., 13 October 1780; 28, Captain, 13 October 1780; Assigned to the Engineer Dept. Halifax, 3 June 1776

Needham, St. John; 5, Surgeon, 22 November 1780;

Neilson, Andrew; 52, Capt.- Lieut., 27 April 1768; 52, Captain, 18 June 1775, 25 May 1772, Also Nelson; Date of captaincy is not certain; WIA Bunker Hill, 17 June 1775; KIA Brooklyn, 27 August 1776

Nesbitt, Albert; 17, Ensign, 23 August 1775; 17, Lieutenant, 4 January 1777; POW prior to Monmouth; Resigned 23 September 1778

Nesbitt, Alexander; 31, Major, 4 March 1776

Nesbitt, Colebrooke; 82, Captain, 5 January 1778; Also Colebrook; ADC to Gen. Mathew; WIA Wilmington, NC, 29 January 1781

Nesbitt, Richard; 63, Captain, 28 July 1768; WIA Ft. Clinton, 6 October 1777; Retired 11 August 1778

Nesbitt, William; 47, Lt. Colonel, 21 March 1765, 24 November 1762; At Concord; Died Quebec, 4 November 1776

Nesmyth, John; 69, Lieutenant, 14 May 1781

Nettles, Harry; 17 LD, Lieutenant, 1 January 1764; 17 LD, Capt.- Lieut., 7 March 1782; WIA Cowpens, 17 January 1781

Nevin, Hugh; 45, Captain, 28 September 1759; Died 10 January 1777

Newburgh, Robert; 18, Chaplain, 18 November 1772; 15, Chaplain, 4 May 1776; CM for six counts including conduct unbecoming a gentleman and unnatural acts with a solider, 1774; acquitted

Newburgh, Thomas; 15, Ensign, 16 December 1775

Newland, John; 16, Ensign, 23 December 1775; 16, Lieutenant, 19 October 1780

Newman, Michael; 35, Ensign, 4 January 1776; From volunteer; CM for forging bills of exchange, 17 February 1777; Dismissed from service

Newmarsh, Timothy; 7, Captain, 18 July 1766; 4/60, Major, 10 November 1780; WIA Cowpens, 17 January 1781; Although he had been promoted into the majority of the 4/60, he was serving with the 7th at Cowpens; Retired 15 September 1783

Newport, William; 28, Ensign, 15 May 1782

Newton, Charles; 52, Adjutant, 8 April 1777; 52, Ensign, 19 August 1773; 52, Lieutenant, 4 July 1775; 52, Captain, 15 August 1778

Newton, Hibbert; 33, Ensign, 6 January 1776; 53, Lieutenant, 11 January 1782

Newton, Hibbert; 62, Ensign, 1 March 1776; 62, Lieutenant, 19 April 1780

Newton, Phillips; 45, Captain, 16 March 1775; Retired 2 March 1776

Newton, William; Asst. Paymaster General, 1778

Nichola, John; 83, Captain, 18 January 1778

Nicholas, Nicholas Harris; 44, Lieutenant, 11 May 1776; WIA Christiana Bridge/Iron Hill, DE, 3 September 1777; From marines

Nichols, Northend; 54, Lieutenant, 1 September 1771; 37, Capt.- Lieut., 18 February 1781

Nichols, Thomas; 33, Lieutenant, 28 August 1775; 70, Capt.- Lieut., 17 August 1780; Also Nicholl; English, born 1754; First commissioned at age 16; WIA Brandywine, 11 September 1777

Nicholson, Malcom; 2/71, Chaplain, 24 November 1775

Nicholson, William; 80, Adjutant, 15 February 1779; 80, Lieutenant, 21 January 1778

Nicoll, Philip; 83, Lieutenant, 12 March 1782

Nisbet, Thomas; 5, Ensign, 27 December 1778

Nivien, William; 83, Lieutenant, 20 January 1778

Nixon, John; 49, Captain, 14 January 1775

Noble, Mungo; 21, 1st Lieut., 20 September 1777; 3/60, Capt.- Lieut., 9 June 1781; 7, Captain, 28 April 1782; Also first name Munrow; ADC to Major Gen. Wm. Phillips, 1781; ADC to Gen. Paterson 1782

Nodder, Bright; 34, Lieutenant, 7 September 1771; Also served as captain 1/84th Foot, 1781

Nodes, John; 17, Lieutenant, 15 August 1775, 3 December 1760; 17, Captain, 16 June 1780; Also Nodder

Nooth, Edward Trafford; 9, Ensign, 5 April 1781

Nooth, John Mervin; Hosp., Purveyor and Phys. Extra., 19 October 1775; Hosp., Superintendent-General, 10 April 1779; M.D. Edin. 1766; Listed as "Dr." in 1776 Army List; Listed as Chief Surgeon in 1776 Army List; Stationed at New York, 1783; To half pay 6 February 1784; Returned to full pay 1788; Retired 1807; Died Bath, 3 May 1828

Norford, William; 33, Ensign, 28 August 1776; 33, Lieutenant, 31 March 1779

Norman, Charles; 38, Captain, 30 April 1771; DOW Elizabethtown, NJ, 26 June 1780

Norman, Charles; 49, Ensign, 21 July 1775; 49, Lieutenant, 26 October 1777; Died 8 or 9 October 1778

Norman, Richard; 20, Lieutenant, 24 February 1775

Norris, Ja. Valentine; 10, Ensign, 30 October 1777

Norris, Richard; 17, Quartermaster, 12 March 1774; 17, Lieutenant, 2 August 1775; 27, Captain, 10 September 1778

North, Hon. Francis; 49, Captain, 9 April 1781, 14 April 1780; 83, Major, 17 April 1783

North, Richard; 15, Ensign, 9 October 1775; 15, Lieutenant, 12 September 1777

Northeast, Moses; 49, Ensign, 1 October 1779

Northey, Edmund; 54, Ensign, 16 January 1776

Norton, Hon. Chapel; 2FG, Capt. & Lt. Col., 1 June 1774; From 1st Foot; WIA Young's House, NY, 3 February 1780; 2nd Major in England in 1786

Norton, William; 44, Lieutenant, 3 July 1772; 44, Captain, 7 December 1775; English, born 1749; First commissioned at age 22

Norwood, Charles; 70, Ensign, 29 September 1781

Notter, William; 2/60, Surgeon, 28 June 1775; From mate; Died prior to 26 April 1779

Nugent, George; 7, Lieutenant, 23 November 1775; 57, Captain, 28 April 1778

Nugent, Robert; 28, Lieutenant, 1 September 177-, 22 April 1762; 28, Capt.- Lieut., 19 August 1778; 28, Captain, 19 August 1778; Also printed as George Nugent

Nunn, -; 57, Adjutant, 6 September 1780

Nunwick, William; 5, Ensign, 16 March 1774; 5, Lieutenant, 23 November 1775

Nutt, George Anson; 33, Ensign, 28 August 1771; 33, Lieutenant, 26 October 1775; 33, Capt.- Lieut., 1 October 1780; 33, Captain, 1 October 1780; English, born 1751; First commissioned at age 17

Nye, James; 45, Ensign, 23 March 1780

O'Brien, Edward; 19, Lieutenant, 2 June 1778

O'Brien, James; 17, Ensign, 24 March 1775; 17, Lieutenant, 3 May 1776; WIA Princeton, 3 January 1777; KIA Stony Point, 16 July 1779

O'Byrn, Matthais; 15, Ensign, 30 March 1774; 15, Lieutenant, 14 November 1775; Retired 10 October 1778

O'Connor, -; 16, Ensign, 15 August 1775; 37, Lieutenant, 24 April 1779

O'Connor, James; 19, Ensign, 6 June 1778

O'Hara, Augustus; RA, 1st Lieut., 7 July 1779; KIA Guilford CH, 15 March 1781

O'Hara, Charles; 2FG, Capt. & Lt. Col., 3 November 1769; 22, Colonel, 18 April 1782, 30 April 1780; Am., Brigadier General, 25 October 1778; WIA Guilford CH, 15 March 1781; Not on parole after Yorktown; Commanded Brigade of Guards in America, 1776

O'Hara, Henry; 55, Lieutenant, 16 March 1775; Irish, born 1757; First commissioned at age 16; Assigned to 2nd Gren. Bn., 1 June 1778

O'Meara, Charles; 49, Lieutenant, 26 October 1777

O'Meara, Daniel; 20, Ensign, 3 March 1776; 20, Lieutenant, 20 September 1777

O'Meara, Richard; 49, Lieutenant, 16 July 1774; 49, Capt.- Lieut., 26 October 1777; 49, Captain, 26 October 1777

O'Reilly, -; Captain, date unknown; Town Major at New York, 1779

O'Sullivan, Thomas; 44, Ensign, 4 November 1779

Oakes, Hildebrand; 33, Lieutenant, 16 April 1771; 33, Captain, 8 August 1776; English, born 1753; First commissioned at age 14

Obias, Michael; 20, Lieutenant, 9 March 1776; Also Obin; KIA Bemis Heights, 7 October 1777

Obins, Hamlet; 70, Ensign, 5 July 1780

Obins, Hamlet; 17 LD, Lieutenant, 18 February 1769

Ochiltree, Duncan; 2/71, Quartermaster, 18 April 1780; Possibly the same man as Ortiltry below

Ochiltree, Robert; 1/71, Surgeon, 10 February 1782; From mate; To half pay, 1784; Died c. 1805

Offral, John; 29, Surgeon, 28 February 1776; Also Offrell; Retired half pay 1802

Ogden, Jonathan; Hosp., Mate, Prior to 1783; Stationed at New York, 1783

Ogilvie, David; 17 LD, Cornet, 26 December 1775; Retired 31 July 1780

Ogilvie, George; 3FG, Capt. & Lt. Col., 14 January 1763; Cmd. 2nd Bn Guards

Ogilvie, James; 4, Major, 22 April 1774; 4, Lt. Colonel, 4 June 1777

Ogilvie, James; 53, Ensign, 5 October 1778

Ogilvie, William; 2/71, Quartermaster, 24 November 1775; 1/71, Ensign, 3 August 1778; 2/71, Lieutenant, 19 September 1779; WIA & POW Boston, 6 June 1776; Died 12 April 1780

Ogilvy, William; 4, Ensign, 23 November 1775

Ogle, Charles; 14, Ensign, 25 March 1774; 14, Lieutenant, 10 December 1775

Ogle, John; 6, Chaplain, 19 April 1774

Ogle, William; 6, Ensign, 3 April 1776; 53, Lieutenant, 13 September 1781

Oldham, William; 62, Ensign, 19 April 1780; 62, Lieutenant, 11 January 1782

Oliver, John; 44, Ensign, 3 November 1779

Oliver, John; 65, Ensign, 22 November 1775

Orchard, Thomas; 9, Ensign, 3 June 1777; 9, Lieutenant, 19 September 1781

Ord, Daniel; 38, Ensign, 4 May 1776; 38, Lieutenant, 25 May 1777; Sent home 4 July 1777 with invalids

Ord, Thomas; RA, Col. Comdt., 1 January 1774

Ord, Thomas; 7, Lieutenant, 27 October 1777; 9 June 1778; Died New York, 17 or 18 August 1778

Ore, Alexander; 35, Surgeon, 17 January 1774; Also Ord; Died 11 October 1780

Ormsby, Jos. Mas.; 3, Lieutenant, 25 July 1778; Stayed in Ireland according to WO 8/6, 273-279

Ortiltry, Alexander; 1/71, Quartermaster, 18 April 1780

Osborn, John; 29, Ensign, 10 May 1781

Osborn, Sir George, Bt.; 3FG, Capt. & Lt. Col., 19 November 1765; 1742-1818; Cousin to Lord North; MP Penryn, 1774-1780 & Horsham, 1780-1784; Guards, Muster Master

Oswald, John; 1/42, Ensign, 25 August 1778; 2/42, Lieutenant, 22 March 1780

Otter, John; 28, Lieutenant, 25 December 1780

Ottley, George; 15, Ensign, 12 November 1779; 46, Lieutenant, 24 May 1781, 22 November 1780

Ottley, Robert Wm.; 53, Ensign, 4 October 1780

Oughton, Sir J. Adolphus, K.B.; 31, Colonel, 20 August 1762; Lieutenant General; 30 April 1770

Ourry, Lewis; 15, Captain, 15 July 1772, 12 December 1760

Overend, John Collins; 45, Ensign, 25 November 1775; 45, Lieutenant, 9 August 1778

Overing, Henry; 54, Ensign, 1 July 1779; 54, Lieutenant, 7 September 1781; Native of Newport, RI

Owen, Charles; 59, Quartermaster, 23 April 1765; 59, Lieutenant, 13 September 1769; Probably DOW Bunker Hill, 28 June 1775

Owen, Humphrey; 7, Captain, 20 May 1772

Owen, John; 59, Colonel, 27 November 1760; Lieutenant General; 25 May 1772

Owen, John; 28, Ensign, 8 January 1778

Owens, Onesiphorus Elliott; 57, Ensign, 5 December 1777; 57, Lieutenant, 11 October 1779; 57, Captain, 12 November 1781

Pack, Samuel; 62, Ensign, 25 March 1777; 62, Lieutenant, 1 June 1780

Packenham, Hon. Robert; 64, Lieutenant, 13 December 1770; Irish, born, 1747; First commissioned at age 19

Page, Thomas Hyde; RE, Sub-eng. & Lt., 8 June 1774; In America in 1775; Served at Boston; WIA Bunker Hill, 17 June 1775

Paine, William; Hosp., Apothecary, 19 October 1775; Hosp., Physician, 23 October 1782; Also Payne; Born Worcester, MA; B.A. Harvard, 1768; M.D. Maris. Coll. Abd., 1775; Stationed at Halifax, 1783; Died Worcester, 19 April 1833

Pakenham, Richard; 27, Lieutenant, 1 September 1775; 27, Captain, 5 July 1777; Died St. Lucia,   March 1779

Pallay, Edward; 37, Ensign, 21 March 1776; 7, Lieutenant, 26 October 1777

Palmer, -; 45, Ensign, 24 November 1775

Palmer, Charles; 40, Ensign, 30 October 1777; Retired 15 October 1778

Palmer, Francis; 52, Lieutenant, 25 December 1770, 29 June 1760

Palmer, Hugh; 14, Chaplain, 17 December 1756

Palmer, Jeremiah; 30, Lieutenant, 1 June 1778;

Palmer, Robert; 1/60, Lieutenant, 12 November 1776; Retired 15 April 1781 while in Ireland

Palmer, Thomas; 54, Ensign, 16 November 1777; 54, Lieutenant, 28 November 1779; Married 28 August 1782

Pape, Joseph; Depty. barracksmaster general at New York, 1778

Parke, Andrew; 8, Lieutenant, 13 April 1766, 21 November 1761; 8, Capt.- Lieut., 22 November 1775; 8, Captain, 4 March 1776; From Sligo, born 1747; First commissioned at age 12; Later major, Retired 1793

Parke, Charles; 27, Ensign, 2 December 1777

Parke, Thomas; 45, Ensign, 31 January 1774; 14, Lieutenant, 30 September 1776

Parker, Edward; 31, Captain, 10 September 1776, 27 September 1775

Parker, Edward; 65, Captain, 5 July 1776

Parker, George; 1FG, Ensign, 24 June 1774; 1FG, Lieut. & Capt., 2 September 1777; WIA New Haven, 5 July 1779; Retired April 1780

Parker, Hon. Geo. Lane; 20, Colonel, 11 May 1773; Major General; 30 April 1760; Lieutenant General; 29 August 1777, 1724-1791; MP Tregony, 1774-1780

Parker, Jones; 62, Ensign, 20 September 1777; 62, Lieutenant, 18 March 1782; From volunteer

Parker, Nicholas; 27, Captain, 1 September 1775; ADC to Gen. Massey 22 May 1776, revoked 7 June 1776

Parker, William; 27, Captain, 28 November 1771

Parker, William; RE, Sub-eng. & Lt., 24 January 1774; In America from 1771-1783; Served at New York

Parkhurst, Charles; 16 LD, Cornet, 13 November 1777

Parr, John; 20, Ensign, 26 September 1775; 20, Lieutenant, 1 June 1778

Parr, Peter; 53, Captain, 1 March 1776, 25 May 1772

Parry, Powell; 65, Ensign, 14 November 1771; 65, Lieutenant, 23 November 1775

Parry, Spencer C.; RA, 2nd Lieut., 3 November 1780

Parry, Thomas; 35, Captain, 18 April 1770; Retired 20 October 1777

Parslow, John; 30, Colonel, 30 April 1779; Lieutenant General; 30 April 1770

Parslow, Thomas; 70, Chaplain, 24 May 1758

Parsons, Lawrence; 10, Captain, 4 December 1769; WIA Concord and Bunker Hill; Resigned by 1776

Partridge, Robert; 54, Ensign, 6 March 1782

Partridge, Walter; 23, 2nd Lieut., 9 June 1779; 23, 1st Lieut., 5 October 1779

Paschall, -; 52, Ensign, 5 May 1778; Also Perchall or Pascal; From volunteer

Pasquada, Anthony; 3/60, Lieutenant, 25 January 1781

Passingham, Jonathan; 37, Ensign, 28 April 1778; 37, 2nd Lieut., 2 October 1781

Passingham, Robert; 37, Ensign, 17 May 1779

Paterson, Daniel; 30, Lieutenant, 8 May 1772

Paterson, James; 63, Lt. Colonel, 15 June 1763; Colonel, 29 August 1777; Adjutant General, 9 June 1776

Paterson, Josias; 37, Lieutenant, 14 December 1776, 18 August 1762

Paterson, Stephen; 46, Surgeon, 23 May 1780; From mate; Promoted apoth. Leeward Isles, 12 October 1780; Died prior to 22 September 1782

Paterson, Wm. Love; 54, Ensign, 7 July 1775; Died 5 or 6 October 1776

Pateshall, Matthew; 17 LD, Lieutenant, 2 April 1768; WIA Camden, 16 August, 1780; Died of heatstroke, c. 2 July 1783

Patrick, Robert; 5, Ensign, 3 July 1772; 5, Lieutenant, 22 November 1775; Also listed as lieutenant in the 10th Foot with same date

Patterson, Stephen; Hosp., Apothecary, 12 October 1780; From 46th Foot: Died 20 September 1781

Patterson, Thomas; 17 LD, Cornet, 31 December 1777; Also Paterson, KIA Cowpens, 17 January 1781

Pattison, James; RA, Col. Comdt., 25 April 1777; Major General; 19 February 1779

Pattison, Mark; RA, 2nd Lieut., 20 January 1780

Pattison, Thomas; 17 LD, Cornet, 26 March 1776; Also Pattinson

Patton, James Susanna; 6, Lieutenant, 7 January 1771; 6, Captain, 18 June 1776

Pauli, Christopher; 3/60, Captain, 29 September 1775; From half-pay; Died 13 July 1776 at St. Vincent

Paumier, Mungo; 46, Lieutenant, 21 June 1772; 15, Capt.- Lieut., 31 January 1779; 15, Captain, 31 January 1779; WIA Monmouth, 28 June 1778, with 2nd Gren. Bn.

Paumier, Peter; Deputy Commissary, 1778

Pawlett, William; 59, Captain, 28 June 1771, 28 October 1760, WIA Boston, lost a leg, 23 September 1775; Transferred to Invalid Coy. on Isle of Jersey

Pawlett, William; 8, Ensign, 23 February 1781; Son of Wm. Pawlett of the 59th Foot

Paxton, William; 47, Quartermaster, 19 November 1775; 47, Ensign, 1 January 1780

Payne, Benjamin Charnock; 18, Captain, 8 August 1771, 27 January 1764, Irish, born 1736; First commissioned at age 21; Act. DQMG, later Depty. BMG at Philadelphia, 1778

Peacocke, George; 6, Lieutenant, 4 October 1770; 6, Capt.- Lieut., 2 May 1776; 6, Captain, 2 May 1776

Peacocke, George; 7, Lieutenant, 7 January 1767, 2 March 1763, 7, Captain, 18 January 1777; POW 1775; Died 18 October 1780

Pearce, -; 37, Ensign, 15 August 1775

Pearce, Richard; 15, Ensign, 16 September 1778

Pearse, Richard; 70, Adjutant, 13 August 1776; 70, Lieutenant, 10 April 1777; Retired 14 October 1778

Peddie, James; 21, 2nd Lieut., 20 September 1777; 21, 1st Lieut., 14 January 1782

Peebles, John; 1/42, Lieutenant, 31 March 1770; 1/42, Capt.- Lieut., 5 October 1777; 1/42, Captain, 18 August 1778; Scottish, born 1741; First commissioned at age 22; WIA Bonumtown, NJ, 8 March 1777; Extant diary; Resigned 1782

Peers, William; 63, Ensign, 23 November 1776; 63, Lieutenant, 2 December 1777

142

Peirse, James; 15, Lieutenant, 15 August 1775; 15, Captain, 20 June 1777; Died while AWOL, May 1781

Pemberton, William; 21, Surgeon, 3 June 1771; From mate; Died prior to 5 May 1789

Pemble, William; RA, Mate, 1 April 1760; RA, 2nd Lieut., 1 December 1775; 26, Lieutenant, 2 November 1778; WIA Rhode Island, August or September 1778

Penefather, Kingsmill; 15, Ensign, 15 August 1775; 15, Lieutenant, 19 January 1776; KIA near Philadelphia, 7 December 1777

Pennington, John; 37, Lt. Colonel, 15 February 1773; 1737-1813; MP Milbourne Port, 1781-1796

Pennington, Lowther; 2FG, Lieut. & Capt., 20 October 1772; 2FG, Capt. & Lt. Col., 14 December 1778; Seriously wounded in duel with Captain John Tollemach of the HMS Zebra, 25 September 1777 in New York; Not at Yorktown

Pennington, Robert; 24, Adjutant, 1 May 1775; 24, Lieutenant, 10 February 1770, 13 February 1762, Died near Quebec, 26 November 1776

Pepyat, Thomas; 8, Ensign, 15 August 1775; 8, Lieutenant, 11 May 1778; Ensigncy not purchased; Related to Bigoe Armstrong

Peraro, Joseph; 22, Ensign, 12 July 1777; 9, Lieutenant, 29 July 1778

Percy, Hugh, Earl; 5, Colonel, 7 November 1768, 26 October 1764; Am., Major General, 11 July 1775, 29 September 1775; Am., Lieutenant General, 1 January 1776, 29 August 1776, 1742-1817; MP Westminster, 1763-1776

Percy, John; 18, Ensign, 21 August 1775, 4 August 1774

Percy, John; 47, Ensign, 12 March 1776

Perks, Edward; 45, Ensign, 5 January 1780

Perry, John; Hosp., Sprnmy. Mate, Prior to 1783; Stationed at New York, 1783

Perryn, J. Barrington; 19, Ensign, 29 June 1780

Perryn, James; 1FG, Lieut. & Capt., 22 February 1781; POW Yorktown

Persse, Henry; 46, Capt.- Lieut., 8 September 1775

Peters, Thomas; 22, Ensign, 16 March 1775; 64, Lieutenant, 6 June 1776; 23, Captain, 21 March 1778; WIA Brandywine, 11 September 1777; With 2nd Gren. Bn.; WIA Guilford CH, 15 March 1781; Paymaster, 16 April 1781

Petersham, Chas. Viscount Stanhope; 29, Captain, 26 July 1773; 1753-1829; MP Westminster, 1776-1779; ADC to Lt. Gen. Burgoyne

Petrie, George; 21, Captain, 23 February 1776

Pettener, George; 6, Lieutenant, 28 March 1774, 13 September 1760

Pettigrew, James; 10, Lieutenant, 28 June 1771; WIA Bunker Hill, 17 June 1775

Pexton, John; 65, Lieutenant, 3 May 1771; Also Paxton; WIA Bunker Hill, 17 June 1775,

Peyton, Edw. Ireson; 49, Ensign, 26 November 1777

Philip, Henry Brockholst; 23, 2nd Lieut., 18 August 1778; 7, Lieutenant, 5 November 1778; Died 12 November 1780

Philips, Cha. Fred.; 22, Ensign, 13 January 1777; 70, Lieutenant, 14 October 1778; . Also Phillips; Born, Tarrytown, NY (Philipsburg Manor), brother of Nathaniel

Philips, Edward; 63, Chaplain, 1June 1769

Philips, Erasmus John; 35, Captain, 25 March 1775; Shot by one of his own sentinels, Boston, 2 August 1775; KIA Princeton, 2 January 1777 with flank company recruits

Phillips, -; Ind.Dept., Lieutenant, 1780; From sergeant, 8th Foot

Phillips, Levinge Cosby; 62, Ensign, 20 December 1776; DOW Freeman's Farm, 21 September 1777

Phillips, Nathaniel; 38, Lieutenant, 6 December 1763, 11 September 1760; 38, Capt.- Lieut., 22 November 1775; 38, Captain, 22 November 1780; Sec. to Gen. Jones, 4 May 1778; Asst. Sec. to Clinton, 1781; Major of Bde., 1782

Phillips, Nathaniel; 17, Ensign, date unknown; WIA Princeton, 3 January 1777; KIA Germantown, 4 October 1777; Also Philip; American, brother of Charles Fredrick Philip.

Phillips, Noblet; 49, Lieutenant, 9 August 1775; Died 24 January 1777

Phillips, Phil; RA, 2nd Lieut., 8 November 1780

Phillips, Thomas Wood; 70, Adjutant, 15 October 1781; 70, Ensign, 5 March 1779; Also Charles; Promoted to captain-lieutenant in King's American Regt. 20 August 1783; Drowned in late 1783 or 1784

Phillips, William; RA, Captain, 12 May 1756; RA, Major, 25 April 1777; RA, Lt. Colonel, 6 July 1780; Colonel, 25 May 1772; Am., Major General, 1 January 1776, 29 August 1777, 1730-1781; First commission at age 15; MP Boroughbridge, 1775-1780; POW 1777-1781; Died Virginia, 13 May 1781

Philpott, John; 47, Quartermaster, 18 January 1770

Phipps, Henry; 1FG, Ensign, 8 August 1775; 1FG, Lieut. & Capt., 2 April 1778; Also Lord Mulgrave; Never posted to America

Phipps, Hon. Henry; 45, Quartermaster, 9 January 1770; 45, Lieutenant, 9 January 1782, 4 October 1780

Pidcock, Thomas; 16 LD, Lieutenant, 6 November 1772

Piercy, Thomas; 9, Lieutenant, 11 July 1778

Pigott, John; 59, Lieutenant, 25 December 1770, 19 June 1755

Pigott, Sir Robert Bt.; 55, Colonel, 7 September 1775; 38, Colonel, 11 December 1775; 25 May 1772; Am., Major General; 1 January 1776, 29 August 1777; Lt. General, 20 November 1782; 1720-1796

Pilkington, William; 35, Ensign, 23 April 1774; Irish; Attended Ballitore School; Retired 25 May 1778

Pilmer, Henry; 24, Captain, 28 March 1775; Napier, p. 312

Pilot, Henry; 31, Captain, 23 September 1772

Piper, John; 6, Lieutenant, 25 December 1770, 12 September 1762, Asst. DQMG at RI, 1777 to early 1778

Pitcairn, Thomas; 14, Lieutenant, 13 January 1776; 82, Captain, 7 January 1778; POW

Pitcher, James; Commissary of Musters, 1777

Pitt, John, Viscount; 47, Ensign, 14 March 1774; ADC to Major Gen. Carleton, 1775; Son of the Earl of Chatham

Pitts, Mathew; RE, Eng. extra. & Cpt.-Lt., 7 May 1779; In America from 1776-1779; Served in America and West Indies

Pitts, Thomas; RA, Capt.- Lieut., 1 January 1771; Captain, 25 May 1772

Place, Edward; 23, 2nd Lieut., 2 October 1779; Died 13 October 1781

Place, Wm. de la; 26, Captain, 18 April 1766

Playfair, John; 83, Ensign, 13 December 1782

Pleydell, Samuel; 80, Ensign, 8 March 1781

Plowman, Donald; 2/42, Quartermaster, 21 March 1780

Plumber, Enoch; 3/60, Lieutenant, 22 September 1779; WIA Roupel's Ferry, SC., 3 February 1779

Plunkett, Oliver; 62, Ensign, 21 August 1781

Poe, James; 47, Adjutant, 12 July 1775; 47, Ensign, 10 February 1770; 47, Lieutenant, 18 June 1775

Poe, John Nathaniel; 15, Mate, date unknown; Died 17 February 1777

Pole, Edward; 6, Adjutant, 18 May 1774; 6, Ensign, 24 June 1771; 6, Lieutenant, 23 November 1775

Pole, Munday; 10, Captain, 13 February 1762; Major; 29 August 1777; At Lexington and Concord and Bunker Hill

Pollard, Edward; 23, 2nd Lieut., 14 September 1779

Pollard, Rob.; 8, Ensign, 8 May 1777

Pomeroy, John; 64, Colonel, 1 October 1766; Major General; 25 May 1772; Lieutenant General; 29 August 1777, Irish, born 1725; First commissioned at age 20

Pope, Thomas; 37, Ensign, 15 August 1775; 37, Lieutenant, 20 October 1777

Porbeck, William; 4/60, Ensign, 4 September 1775; 4/60, Lieutenant, 1 May 1779; Also Probick or Van Borbeck; Lieutenancy also listed as 26 Dec. 1778 in 4/60

Porteous, James; Asst. Commissary, 1778

Porter, Richard; 22, Ensign, 24 June 1775; 22, Lieutenant, 2 February 1777; From volunteer; English, born 1755; Deputy Judge Advocate, 1782

Porter, William; 40, Lieutenant, 6 January 1781; Depty. Commissary of Musters, 1777; Commissary of Musters, 1783

Porterfield, Boyd; 17, Lieutenant, 28 September 1775

Porterfield, Boyd; 22, Lieutenant, 23 November 1775; 2/71, Captain, 5 December 1775; Scottish, born 1753; To additional company, 21 November 1775; To 71st Foot, 7 August 1776; Captaincy date also 7 August 1776; Died 10 November 1778

Potter, Leonard; 28, Ensign, 23 August 1775; 28, Lieutenant, 3 January 1778

Pottinger, Henry; 38, Captain, 18 September 1780

Pottinger, Henry; 37, Ensign, 20 October 1777; 37, Lieutenant, 10 August 1778

Potts, Alexander; 1/42, Surgeon, 10 April 1764, 8 November 1762; Hosp., Surgeon, 11 September 1777; Scottish, born 1741; First commissioned at age 22; From half pay 60th Foot to 42nd; Died near Hawick, NB, 3 May 1796

Potts, Henry; 54, Ensign, 28 November 1779

Potts, Robert; 1/42, Lieutenant, 12 July 1773; 1/42, Capt.- Lieut., 31 December 1780; 1/42, Captain, 27 July 1783; Scottish, born 1749; First commissioned at age 22

Potts, William; 8, Quartermaster, 13 April 1768; 8, Capt.- Lieut., 12 October 1771; 8, Captain, 22 November 1775, 25 May 1772, English, born 1738; Son of a Carlisle grocer; First commissioned at age 18

Poulett, Hon. Vere; 29, Captain, 24 October 1781, 13 December 1780

Powell, Giles; 63, Chaplain, 7 January 1779

Powell, Henry; 8, Captain, 22 November 1775; Irish; May not have purchased his captaincy; Neighbor of Bigoe Armstrong

Powell, Henry Watson; 53, Lt. Colonel, 25 July 1771; Colonel, 19 February 1779; English

Powell, Hugh; 15, Captain, 15 August 1777, 30 December 1755; Major; 23 July 1772; Lt. Colonel; 29 August 1777

Powell, John; 52, Capt.- Lieut., 28 August 1776; 52, Captain, 28 August 1776; WIA Bunker Hill, 17 June 1775; DOW Monmouth, 5 July 1778; Arm shattered

Powell, John; 49, Lieutenant, 16 August 1770, 21 July 1770, WIA Long Island, 27 August 1776

Powell, Kenny; 8, Captain, 15 August 1775, 25 May 1775, Died 10 May 1778

Powell, Richard; 54, Quartermaster, 18 January 1770; 54, Lieutenant, 14 March 1772; 54, Captain, 27 April 1779; WIA Groton, CT, 6 September 1781

Power, Bolton; 20, Captain, 2 March 1776

Power, Francis; 49, Ensign, 30 April 1781

Power, James; 24, Ensign, 28 March 1775

Power, William; 55, Ensign, 16 March 1775; Irish, born 1754; First commissioned at age 21; Also Powell; Killed Cpt. Trevor in a duel, November 1777; CM and acquitted for the duel; Resigned 3 December 1777

Powlett, Hor. Arm.; 45, Captain, 15 August 1775, 19 October 1761; Major; 29 August 1777

Poynton, Brereton; 21, Captain, 25 February 1777, 13 April 1772

Poyntz, Wm. Deane; Deputy Paymaster Gen. at New York, 1782; Also W.D. Poyat

Pratt, Robert; 5, Lieutenant, 16 March 1774; WIA La Vigie, 18 December 1778

Pratt, William; 5, Adjutant, 20 May 1779; Resigned 24 October 1780

Prentice, Samuel Walter; 1/84, Ensign, 25 December 1776; CM for promoting a shipboard riot; Cashiered and pardoned by Cmd. in Chief

Prescott, Richard; 7, Lt. Colonel, 19 November 1761; 7, Colonel, 12 November 1776, 22 June 1772 Am., Major General, 1 January 1776, 29 August 1777, POW 14 July 1777

Prescott, Richard; 7, Lieutenant, 18 September 1780

Prescott, Robert; 28, Lt. Colonel, 8 September 1775, 10 December 1762; Colonel, 29 August 1777

Prescott, William; 15, Captain, 2 May 1762; 15, Major, 26 October 1775; Retired 12 July 1777

Preston, Charles; 26, Major, 7 September 1768

Preston, George; 17 LD, Colonel, 9 November 1770; Major General; 25 May 1772; Lieutenant General; 29 August 1777

Preston, John; 26, Chaplain, 23 February 1742

Prevost, Augustine; 4/60, Col. Comdt., 18 September 1775; Joined regt. in 1756

Prevost, Augustine; 3/60, Captain, 12 November 1776, 23 September 1775, From Cpt.-Lt. & Adj. 2/60th

Prevost, Augustine Fredrick; 1/60, Ensign, 7 September 1780; Act. Dept. Adj. Gen. for Prevost in Ga.; Depty. Inspector General at New York, February 1783

Prevost, Geo. W. Aug., 3/60, Ensign, 15 March 1779

Prevost, George; 4/60, Ensign, 3 September 1779

Prevost, James Mark; 2/60, Major, 21 September 1775; Am., Lt. Colonel, 29 August 1777; DOR as major in America 23 July 1772; Died Jamaica, 19 October 1781

Price, David; 53, Quartermaster, 29 March 1776

Price, David; 1/84, Lieutenant, 21 June 1777

Price, John; 43, Ensign, 15 August 1775

Price, John; Hosp., Sprnmy. Mate, Prior to 1783; With QM General Dept. at New York, 1783

Price, Joseph; 2/60, Surgeon, 8 December 1774; Died possibly in St. Augustine, 27 June 1775

Prideaux, Edmund; 18, Ensign, 12 January 1770; 18, Lieutenant, 21 August 1775; English, born 1744; First commissioned at age 15

Prideaux, Edmund; 7, Lieutenant, 6 November 1778; From 2nd Bn. New Jersey Volunteers; Died 19 September 1780

Priedenbach, James; 4/60, Lieutenant, 21 November 1777; Also Breitenbach

Prince, William; 9, Lieutenant, 7 July 1775; 9, Capt.- Lieut., 5 April 1781; WIA Freeman's Farm, 19 September 1777

Pringle, Henry; 24, Ensign, 4 March 1776

Pringle, James; 1/84, Ensign, 16 July 1776; Ensigncy also given as 14 June 1776; CM for conduct unbecoming, reprimanded, August 1781

Pringle, John; 35, Lieutenant, 13 April 1767, 23 October 1762, Died Boston, 28 April 1775 apparently of natural causes; Clarke erroneously lists him as KIA at Bunker Hill

Pringle, Robert; RE, Eng. extra. & Cpt.-Lt., 6 March 1775; Am., Lt. Colonel, 21 September 1780; In America from 1772-?

Pringle, William; 54, Ensign, 18 September 1781; From lieutenant Nova Scotia Volunteers; Transferred to 64th Foot

Prior, John Murray; 63, Lieutenant, 25 July 1771

Pritchard, John; RA, 2nd Lieut., 9 July 1779; Died near Wilmington, NC, 25 April 1781; Death also given as 1782

Probyn, Thomas; 70, Ensign, 11 October 1779

Proctor, George; 46, Ensign, 13 April 1778; 46, Lieutenant, 7 July 1779

Proctor, Henry; 43, Ensign, 5 April 1781; 43, Lieutenant, 30 December 1781

Proctor, Richard; 5, Surgeon, 15 May 1761; Hosp., Apothecary, 7 September 1776; Hosp., Physician, 12 February 1781; M.D. St. Andrews, 1774; Surgeon to Sir Henry Clinton?; Stationed at New York, 1783; To half pay, 6 February 1784; Died c24 June 1804

Proctor, Richard, junior; Hosp., Sprnmy. Mate, Prior to 1783; Stationed at New York, 1783

Proctor, William; 22, Ensign, 7 August 1776; From volunteer; WIA Boston, 1775; From 2nd lieutenant, Royal Fencible Americans; DOW Rhode Island, 9 September 1778

Prowse, Henry; 4, Quartermaster, 7 August 1776

Pryce, David; 1/84, Lieutenant, 21 June 1777

Pryce, Edward; 23, 2nd Lieut., 28 August 1776; 23, 1st Lieut., 18 August 1778; WIA Danbury Raid, April 1777

Purdon, Peter; 38, Lieutenant, 21 July 1775; Also Pardon; Asst. Depty. Quartermaster General, 1781; Retired 4 March 1782

Pye, Robert Hampden; 1FG, Lieut. & Capt., 29 April 1771; 1FG, Capt. & Lt. Col., 23 April 1779; Retired February 1781

Pynchon, Thomas R.; Hosp., Quartermaster, Prior to 1783; Stationed at New York, 1783

Pyne, William; 19, Lieutenant, 30 June 1780

Quarme, George; 37, Ensign, 7 November 1778

Quin, George; 49, Ensign, 10 March 1777; 35, Lieutenant, 4 June 1779; CM and acquitted for ungentlemanly conduct, September 1782; The trial partially dealt with his relationship with the wife of a sergeant in the 87th Foot; Retired as a major in 1801

Quin, William; 55, Ensign, 22 December 1780

Radford, Ebenezer; 63, Ensign, 6 November 1772; 63, Lieutenant, 23 November 1775

Rafters, -; 45, Ensign?; Died 29 May 1778; Not listed possibly confused promotion of Wm. Ruxton?

Rainey, Robert; 54, Adjutant, 6 December 1763; 54, Capt.- Lieut., 21 June 1772; 54, Captain, 26 November 1775; Died 17 August 1777

Rainsford, Andrus; Captain, 1781; Barracksmaster at Pensacola

Rainsford, Charles; 44, Colonel, 4 May 1771; Major General; 29 August 1771

Rainsford, William; 54, Ensign, 18 February 1781; WIA Groton, CT, 6 September 1781

Ramsay, George; 30, Captain, 17 March 1780, 6 March 1780

Ramsay, Hon. Malcolm; 21, Captain, 25 December 1770; 83, Major, 21 December 1777; Lt. Colonel; 24 August 1781, WIA Freeman's Farm, 19 September 1777

Ramsay, Martin; 16, Ensign, 5 July 1776

Ramsay, William; 14, Capt.- Lieut., 10 December 1775; 14, Captain, 10 December 1775

Randall, Thomas; 52, Ensign, 3 June 1771; 52, Lieutenant, 26 April 1775

Rankine, William; 45, Ensign, 30 October 1777; 16, Lieutenant, 20 August 1778; Also Rankin; From volunteer; Extra deputy asst. QMG, 1779

Ravenhill, Henry; 31, Lieutenant, 8 March 1776

Rawdon, Francis, Lord; 5, Lieutenant, 20 October 1773; 63, Captain, 12 July 1775; Lt. Colonel, 15 June 1778; ADC to Lt. Gen. Clinton 1777; Also AG America, same date; To colonel, Volunteers of Ireland, 25 May 1778

Rawdon, Hon. George; 9, Ensign, 1 May 17759, Lieutenant, 20 December 1776; 63, Captain, 2 November 1778; From half pay, 63rd Foot

Rawdon, Hon. John; 4, Captain, 4 June 1777; WIA Brandywine, 11 September 1777

Rawdon, Hon. Thomas; 15, Ensign, 13 November 1773; 15, Lieutenant, 26 October 1775; First name also John Theophilus; WIA White Plains, 28 October 1776

Rawerton, -; 37, Ensign, 20 May 1778

Rawerton, James; 7, Lieutenant, 17 May 1779

Ray, Lewis; 35, Captain, 15 August 1775; To half pay list, 16 August 1776; Had not purchased any of his commissions

Raymond, James; 5, Ensign, 28 November 1771; 5, Lieutenant, 4 April 1774; Resigned 15 April 1776

Raymond, William; 22, Captain, 23 May 1779; English, born 1760; POW Yorktown

Raynor, James; 70, Ensign, 13 September 1780;

Reed, John; 22, Ensign, 28 November 1776; 22, Lieutenant, 26 June 1780; Also Read or Rud; English, born 1758; To additional company, 12 July 1777; Returned to America, June 1779

Read, Robert; 1/42, Lieutenant, 7 September 1771; Also Reid; Scottish, born 1751; First commissioned at age 16

Read, Thomas; 55, Adjutant, 24 November 1777; 55, Ensign, 5 October 1777; 5, Lieutenant, 27 December 1778; Also listed as adjutant in West Indies; Died 25 May 1779

Read, William; 10, Lieutenant, 2 June 1777; Also Reed; Retired 3 March 1778

Read, William; 10, Ensign, 15 August 1775

Reed, John; RA, Adjutant, 1 January 1771

Reed, Thomas; 24, Lieutenant, 3 March 1776

Reeves, John; 82, Lieutenant, 6 January 1778

Reeves, Thomas; 46, Ensign, 6 January 1776

Reid, George; RA, 1st Lieut., 7 July 1779; Probably John

Reid, John; RA, 2nd Lieut., 1 January 1771; RA, Capt.- Lieut., 12 July 1780

Remmington, -; 43, Lt. Colonel, date unknown; Retired on his pay 10 December 1780; No such officer, possibly Lt. Chas. Fra. Repington of the 6th Dragoons

Remmington, Samuel; RA, 1st Lieut., 7 July 1779

Revett, Nicholas; 5, Ensign, 15 March 1776

Reynell, Thomas; 62, Lieutenant, 3 May 1770; KIA Freeman's Farm, 19 September 1777; Married, his wife accompanied Burgoyne's army

Reynett, -; 64, Ensign, 2 November 1778; From volunteer

Reynett, Henry James; 7, Lieutenant, 29 November 1779

Reynolds, -; 9, Ensign, 9 April 1782

Reynolds, Decimus; 55, Capt.- Lieut., 8 September 1775; 55, Captain, 11 May 1776; English, born 1745; First commissioned at age 16; Retired 12 July 1777

Reynolds, George; 49, Captain, 15 August 1775, 18 October 1761; Major; 29 August 1777

Reynolds, John; 19, Ensign, 30 April 1781

Rhind, John; 53, Ensign, 8 October 1777; Also Rynd; From volunteer; Ensigncy also given as 25 September 1778

Rich, Dan. D'Anvers; 3FG, Lieut. & Capt., 31 October 1770; 3FG, Capt. & Lt. Col., 1 September 1777; Retired 1782

Richardson, Abraham; 37, Ensign, 2 July 1777; Died 9 November 1780

Richardson, Alexander; 9, Ensign, 9 October 1775; 9, Lieutenant, 17 August 1777;

Richardson, Francis; 1FG, Lieut. & Capt., 23 April 1779; Major of Bde; ADC to Gen. Mathew; POW with convalescents in New York

Richardson, John; 45, Quartermaster, 11 January 1777; From sergeant and quartermaster 2nd Gren. Bn., 17 May 1776

Richardson, W. Mad.; 3, Captain, 22 October 1766; Major; 29 August 1777

Richardson, William; 18, Lieutenant, 16 February 1770; 18, Captain, 20 April 1775; Irish, born 1757; First commissioned at age 19; WIA Bunker Hill, 17 June 1775 while still serving as a lieutenant

Richardson, William; 43, Capt.- Lieut., 24 April 1779; WIA near Elizabethtown, NJ, 6 June 1780

Richardson, William; 26, Lieutenant, 31 October 1770

Richardson, William; 34, Lieutenant, 2 March 1776; WIA Hubbardton, 7 July 1777 & Bemis Heights 7 October 1777

Richardson, William; 45, Lieutenant, 1 March 1773; Retired 2 March 1776

Riches, Isaac; 29, Lieutenant, 14 March 1775

Ricketts, James; 2/60, Ensign, 6 January 1773; 2/60, Lieutenant, 1 October 1775; 2/60, Capt.- Lieut., 27 December 1778; 2/60, Captain, 19 October 1780; From Elizabeth, NJ; On duty in New York; Retired 14 December 1782

Ridley, John; 23, 1st Lieut., 2 April 1772; 28, Captain, 16 December 1775; Died Philadelphia, 22 December 1777

Ridout, John Christ.; 46, Lieutenant, 8 September 1775

Ridsdate, Twisdale Griff.; 44, Lieutenant, 14 May 1774; 44, Captain, 23 May 1776; Drowned at sea, probably 28 October 1779

Ried, John; RA, Adjutant, 1 January 1771; RA, 2nd Lieut., 19 February 1782; Also Reed

Rio, Alexander; 44, Sergeant Major, 29 September 1777; Acting Town Adjutant at Philadelphia, 1778

Ritchie, John; 44, Ensign, 5 October 1778; 1/42, Lieutenant, 6 September 1780; 37, Captain, 28 April 1781

Rivers, James; 43, Ensign, 29 June 1775; 43, Lieutenant, 29 February 1776; It is unclear why there are two distinct dates for James River's lieutenancy in the Army lists, unless they are two separate men

Rivers, James; 43, Lieutenant, 13 September 1776; 3/60, Captain, 10 October 1778; It is unclear why there are two distinct dates for James River's lieutenancy in the Army lists, unless they are two separate men

Rivers, James; 80, Lieutenant, 10 October 1778;

Riverton, -; 37, Ensign, 20 May 1778; From Queen's Rangers

Rivington, James; 1/42, Ensign, 28 February 1782; English, born 1764; First commissioned at age 17

Robb, Robert; 80, Captain, 8 September 1781

Roberts, Charles; 40, Ensign, 23 November 1775; 57, Lieutenant, 18 August 1778

Roberts, David; 43, Lieutenant, 11 August 1778; 57, Captain, 31 December 1781

Roberts, Edward; 30, Ensign, 2 September 1781

Roberts, John; 65, Capt.- Lieut., 3 May 1771; Died Boston, 8 September 1775; Date of death also given as 15 August 1775

Roberts, John; RA, 1st Lieut., 7 July 1779; Also served in 2/84th Foot

Roberts, John; 63, Lieutenant, 18 June 1775; 63, Capt.- Lieut., 13 June 1778; 63, Captain, 13 June 1778; Also Jonathan

Roberts, Wm. Robert; Hosp., Apothecary, 11 February 1776; Hosp., Surgeon, 25 June 1775; Hosp., Physician, 1 April 1779; Surgeon date also given as 13 July 1775; To half pay, 25 December 1783; Died Beverly, 20 February 1801

Roberts, Sam.; 44, Ensign, 19 February 1776; Resigned 12 April 1777

Roberts, Sam. Wildey; 28, Major, 13 October 1780

Roberts, William; 49, Lieutenant, 21 July 1775; WIA White Plains, 28 October 1776

Roberts, William S.; RA, 2nd Lieut., 14 February 1782

Robertson, Alexander; 82, Major, 1 January 1778

Robertson, Alexander; 15, Captain, 3 March 1779

Robertson, Alexander; 35, Capt.- Lieut., 6 February 1777; 35, Captain, 6 February 1777; From 48th Foot; Asst. Dept. QMG, 1777

Robertson, Alexander; 43, Lieutenant, 25 December 1770, 1 November 1761; WIA Bunker Hill, 17 June 1775; Asst. Depty. Quartermaster General, 23 May 1776

Robertson, Alexander; 21, 2nd Lieut., 9 May 1776; DOW Freeman's Farm, 28 September 1777

Robertson, Archibald; RE, Eng. extra. & Cpt.-Lt., 2 February 1775; In America from 1775-1782; Served at West Florida and New York

Robertson, Charles; 76, Lieutenant, 8 January 1778

Robertson, Archibald; 47, Captain, 15 August 1775, 6 May 1762, Extra Depty. QMG, 1778; DOW Yorktown, 30 November 1781

Robertson, Daniel; 1/84, Captain, 14 June 1775; From half pay, 42nd Foot; POW Canada, 1776

Robertson, Daniel; 53, Ensign, 6 April 1778; 53, Lieutenant, 13 September 1781; From volunteer

Robertson, David; 2/71, Captain, 18 September 1780

Robertson, David; 63, Ensign, 12 September 1777; 63, Lieutenant, 20 April 1778; From volunteer

Robertson, Donald; 69, Lieutenant, 14 July 1780

Robertson, Duncan; 49, Lieutenant, 15 August 1775, 26 April 1762

Robertson, James; 2/60, Col. Comdt., 25 May 1772; Am., Major General, 1 January 1776, 29 August 1777, Barracksmaster General, 1775

Robertson, James; 16, Lt. Colonel, 17 August 1768; 16, Colonel, 14 May 1778;

Robertson, James; 3/60, Lieutenant, 5 December 1776; 3/60, Capt.-Lieut., 12 January 1779; 4/60, Captain, 25 August 1779, 12 January 1779, On staff at New York, 1778; To half-pay, 25 April 1784

Robertson, James; 2/84, Ensign, 30 October 1776; 2/84, Lieutenant, 6 November 1780; From volunteer, 42nd Foot

Robertson, James; 1/84, Ensign, 1 July 1782; To 44th Foot,

Robertson, John; 1/71, Lieutenant, 8 November 1778

Robertson, John; 2/71, Captain, 24 August 1779

Robertson, John; 1/42, Lieutenant, 29 August 1775, 18 October 1761

Robertson, John; 44, Ensign, 1 August 1782; Not listed in 1783 NAAL

Robertson, John; 1/71, Ensign, 21 October 1781

Robertson, John; 1/42, Ensign, 19 October 1778; From volunteer

Robertson, John Murray; 2/42, Ensign, 21 March 1780; 2/42, Lieutenant, 25 December 1781

Robertson, Robert; 2/42, Ensign, 23 March 1780

Robertson, Robert; 2/84, Ensign, 20 September 1779

Robertson, Samuel; 3/60, Lieutenant, 5 February 1776

Robertson, William; 63, Ensign, 24 November 1775; 55, Lieutenant, 18 December 1777

Robertson, William; 1/42, Mate, 1 May 1774; 1/42, Surgeon, 11 September 1777; Also Robison; Scottish, born 1753; Entered the service at age 20

Robertson, William; 23, Surgeon, 9 November 1772; From mate 37th Foot; Died prior to 4 October 1786

Robinson, -; 23, Quartermaster, 31 October 1776; Died 22 September 1781

Robinson, Allan; 2/42, Lieutenant, 30 March 1780

Robinson, Andrew; Lieutenant, 26 October 1775

Robinson, Andrew; 35, Lieutenant, 27 August 1772, 2 August 1769

Robinson, Andrew; 20, Ensign, 4 March 1777

Robinson, Fredrick Philipse; 17, Ensign, 11 September 1778; 4/60, Lieutenant, 1 September 1779; 38, Lieutenant, 4 November 1780, 1 September 1779, From ensign, Loyal American Regiment

Robinson, James; 19, Lieutenant, 10 June 1771

Robinson, John; 44, Captain, 14 January 1775

Robinson, Robert; 44, Ensign, 13 January 1779; 44, Lieutenant, 4 November 1779

Robinson, Thomas; 52, Lieutenant, 21 February 1783, 11 October 1779, From 87th Foot; KIA Cannanore, India, 14 December 1783

Robinson, William; 23, 2nd Lieut., 30 December 1778; KIA Guilford CH, 15 March 1781

Roche, George; 35, Surgeon, 12 October 1780, 25 November 1779, From 90th Foot; Retired 14 November 1782

Roche, James; 34, Lieutenant, 3 March 1776

Roche, Joshua; 49, Ensign, 24 November 1775; 49, Lieutenant, 26 November 1777

Roche, Richard; 28, Lieutenant, 2 August 1775

Roche, Winthrophe; 43, Ensign, 23 November 1773; 43, Lieutenant, 17 October 1778; Also Roach; Ensigncy date also 17 October 1775; WIA Rhode Island, 28 August 1778

Roche, Winthrophe; 46, Ensign, 27 October 1775

Rochford, Henry; 28, Ensign, 8 September 1775; Resigned 3 November 1777

Rochford, William; 4, Ensign, 22 November 1775; 64, Lieutenant, 12 September 1777; 30, Captain, 29 June 1780; Irish

Rock, Andrew; 30, Lieutenant, 3 June 1778

Rogers, Benjamin; 53, Ensign, 29 March 1776; 53, Lieutenant, 2 August 1780

Rogers, E.H. Rogers; RA, 2nd Lieut., 14 February 1782

Rogers, Henry; RA, 1st Lieut., 7 July 1779

Rogers, John; 49, Captain, 28 January 1775; Retired 29 May 1776

Rogers, Jonathan; 30, Lieutenant, 8 March 1780

Rogers, Luke; 3/60, Ensign, 20 May 1780; Date as 1782 in NAAL, 1783

Rolland, George; Hosp., Mate, Prior to 1783; Stationed at New York, 1783

Rollinson, James; 20, Captain, 3 March 1772

Rollo, Robert; 57, Captain, 1 September 1771, 19 October 1761

Rollo, Robert; 1/42, Ensign, 26 August 1775; 1/42, Lieutenant, 8 May 1777; Retired 5 September 1780

Romain, Thomas; 17 LD, Cornet, 11 February 1777, 2 March 1770

Romeine, Thomas; 45, Ensign, 2 March 1776

Romer, John. Wm.; 31, Capt.- Lieut., 6 March 1776; 31, Captain, 6 March 1776; 31, Captain, 13 September 1779

Ronaldson, James; 34, Surgeon, 12 October 1779; From mate; Died prior to 9 February 1785

Rooke, Charles; 3FG, Lieut. & Capt., 8 September 1775; ADC to Gen. Jones

Rooke, Harry; 52, Captain, 18 June 1775; ADC to Gen. Gage, 1775

Rorison, Robert; 37, Lieutenant, 22 January 1773

Rose, Alexander; 2/42, Ensign, 25 December 1781; 2/42, Lieutenant, 1 April 1780

Rose, James; 2/42, Adjutant, date unknown; 1/42, Ensign, 1 January 1781; Scottish, born 1746; First commissioned at age 34; From sergeant major; May have not actually joined 2/42; Eventually major 1/42nd

Rose, Hugh; 76, Lieutenant, 14 January 1778

Rose, Joseph; 5, Mate, 25 March 1770; To surgeon, 68th Foot by purchase, 5 December 1775; M.D. St. Andrew, 1800; Died prior to March 1834

Rose, William; 1/42, Lieutenant, 23 January 1776, 4 August 1762, Died 16 September 1777

Rose, William; 37, Ensign, 10 August 1778; Died 22 February 1780

Rose, William; 9, Ensign, 20 April 1780

Rosehagen, Philip; 8, Chaplain, 18 November 1767; English, born 1740; First commissioned at age 28

Ross, Alexander; 14, Lieutenant, 18 September 1765; 14, Captain, 22 February 1775; Major; 25 October 1780

Ross, Alexander; 45, Capt.- Lieut., 30 May 1775; 45, Captain, 22 November 1775; Major; 29 August 1777, ADC to Lt. Gen. Cornwallis, 9 June 1778

Ross, Alexander; 2/71, Captain, 26 August 1776

Ross, Andrew; 31, Captain, 9 March 1776

Ross, Arthur; 35, Lieutenant, 29 April 1775; Served in Queen's Rangers; Maj. of Bde, 1778; WIA La Vigie, 18 December 1778

Ross, Arthur; 69, Capt.- Lieut., 1 February 1781; KIA St. Kitts, 28 January 1782

Ross, David; 21, 2nd Lieut., 22 February 1776; 21, 1st Lieut., 20 September 1777

Ross, David; 2/71, Lieutenant, 1 January 1776; Probably WIA Stony Point, NY, 16 July 1779; Promoted to 2/73rd as captain 30 September 1778; Served Ferguson's Rifles as captain in 1778

Ross, John; 34, Captain, 14 March 1772; WIA Hubbardton, 7 July 1777

Ross, John; 1/71, Lieutenant, 27 December 1775

Ross, Thomas; RA, 2nd Lieut., 1 January 1771

Rotton, John; 47, Ensign, 28 January 1775; 47, Lieutenant, 10 July 1776; 4/60, Captain, 1 July 1782; Also Rotten; POW with Maj. French, 1775 Exchanged, 1776; ADC, 2 May 1782; To half pay, 25 April 1784

Rousselet, John; 7, Lieutenant, 28 July 1781

Row, John; 9, Lieutenant, 19 October 1772; Also Rowe; WIA Hubbardton, VT, 7 July 1777

Rowe, Pierce; 30, Ensign, 31 January 1780

Rowland, John; 4, Lieutenant, 15 August 1775, 7 September 1756; 22, Capt.- Lieut., 3 November 1777; 7, Captain, 15 October 1780

Royse, Sothwell; 34, Lieutenant, 26 September 1772; Died 31 October 1780

Rudd, Thomas; 17, Chaplain, 6 April 1770; Retired 16 June 1780

Rudow, -; 3/60, Ensign, 19 August 1778

Rudyard, Henry; RE, Sub-eng. & Lt., 13 July 1774; In America from 1776-1781; Served in Canada

Rumbold, Wm. Richard; 6, Ensign, 5 May 1777; 1760-1786; MP Weymouth & Melcombe, 1781-1784; Father was Gov. of India. In India 1778-1781

Rush, John; Hosp., Apothecary, 4 May 1782; FG, Surgeon, 29 April 1777; POW Yorktown; Paroled

Rushworth, William; 33, Quartermaster, 23 February 1776

Russ, John; 5, Chaplain, 20 July 1762

Russel, Joseph; Hosp., Mate, Prior to 1783; Stationed at New York, 1783

Russell, Ambrose; 5, Ensign, 7 August 1776; 52, Lieutenant, 4 January 1777

Russell, John; 74, Adjutant, 19 December 1777; WIA Fort Clinton, 6 October 1777

Russell, Peter; 64, Lieutenant, 15 August 1775, 9 January 1760; 64, Capt.- Lieut., 18 August 1778; 64, Captain, 18 August 1778; Sec. to Sir Henry Clinton, 1781

Russell, Thomas; 4, Ensign, 2 October 1771; 4, Lieutenant, 22 November 1775; 38, Captain, 20 September 1778

Russell, William; 5, Ensign, 28 April 1774; 23, 1st Lieut., 6 October 1776; Retired 24 April 1778

Rutherford, And.; 82, Lieutenant, 8 January 1778; POW in March 1779

Rutherford, Arch.; 22, Lieutenant, 15 March 1773; WIA Pell's Point, 18 October 1776

Rutherford, Archibald; 27, Captain, 13 January 1777; WIA Danbury, CT, April 1777

Rutherford, John; 1/42, Lieutenant, 31 March 1770; 1/42, Capt.- Lieut., 18 August 1778; 1/42, Captain, 18 August 1778; Scottish, born 1747; First commissioned at age 17

Rutherford, Richard; 21, 2nd Lieut., 10 February 1776; 21, 1st Lieut., 3 October 1776; Nickname "Little Dick;" WIA Freeman's Farm, 19 September 1777

Ruvijines, Fran. Gabriel de; Am., Major, 23 July 1772, 9 August 1769

Ruxton, Charles; 30, Ensign, 14 February 1779; Died South Carolina, 2 September 1781

Ruxton, Samuel; 45, Lieutenant, 14 March 1772; 45, Capt.- Lieut., 22 December 1777; WIA Brandywine, 11 September 1777

Ruxton, William; 45, Ensign, 21 August 1775; 38, Lieutenant, 30 May 1778

Ryan, -; 54, Ensign, 6 October 1776

Rynd, David; RA, 2nd Lieut., 3 November 1780; DOW Pallet's Mill, VA, 26 January 1781

Saint George, Richard; 1FG, Ensign, 1 April 1776; 1FG, Lieut. & Capt., 16 September 1779; ADC to Clinton; Depty. Adj. General; Transferred to 2nd Foot, September 1782

Salans, Alexander Baron; 9, Ensign, 2 September 1776; Also de Salans or Sallans; Served with Fraser's Marksmen; WIA & POW Bennington, 16 August 1777

Saltonstall, Leverett; 23, 2nd Lieut., 30 May 1778; 23, 1st Lieut., 9 August 1780; Also Saltar; From volunteer; Died 20 December 1782

Salvin, Anthony; 33, Ensign, 15 February 1776; 33, Lieutenant, 1 October 1777; 33, Capt.- Lieut., 24 April 1781; 33, Captain, 11 October 1781; WIA Guilford CH, 15 March 1781

Sandford, Edward; 10, Colonel, 14 January 1763; Lieutenant General; 30 April 1770

Sandford, Thomas; FG, Quartermaster, 1777; Served with 2nd Bn.

Sandford, William; 31, Captain, 29 March 1774

Sandon, Thomas; 69, Surgeon, 8 November 1780; From mate; Resigned 20 October 1792

Sandys, Richard; 45, Ensign, 17 September 1773; 10, Lieutenant, 13 May 1776

Sanxay, James; 57, Ensign, 31 March 1777; Prepared to sell out 12 August 1778

Sanxay, James; 6, Ensign, 23 December 1775

Sargent, Henry; 49, Ensign, 26 May 1781

Sargent, John; 38, Lieutenant, 18 June 1775; 38, Capt.- Lieut., 27 June 1780; Won lottery in Rivington Gazette, 11 April 1778; WIA Bunker Hill, 17 June 1775

Saumarez, Durell; 8, Ensign, 6 April 1776; 8, Lieutenant, 5 January 1780

Saumarez, Thomas; 23, 2nd Lieut., 25 January 1776; 23, 1st Lieut., 22 November 1777; 23, Captain, 13 September 1779; Sgt. Roger Lamb's company commander from 1781-1782

Saunders, Alexander; 29, Quartermaster, 27 September 1775; 29, Ensign, 27 February 1776; 29, Lieutenant, 10 May 1781; From sergeant major

Saunders, Jo. Stratford; 64, Ensign, 26 May 1779

Saunderson, Alexander; 37, Ensign, 30 September 1775; 37, Lieutenant, 20 May 1778; 17, Captain, 29 April 1781

Saunderson, Rob. Cha.; 47, Ensign, 11 March 1781

Saurin, Marcus Anthony; 46, Ensign, 12 December 1774; 46, Lieutenant, 29 February 1776; WIA White Plains, 28 October 1776

Savage, Charles; 6, Ensign, 9 September 1775

Savage, George; 69, Ensign, 25 April 1782

Savage, Henry; 37, Captain, 15 April 1774; 16, Major, 28 April 1781; Extra Dept. QMG 23 November 1776 through 1779 went to RI with Clinton

Savage, William; 34, Ensign, 13 October 1777

Savory, Sam.; 20, Ensign, 28 March 1777, 1 January 1777

Sawkins, Joseph; 34, Ensign, 10 May 1776

Saxton, John; 45, Major, 20 October 1774; Died Britain, 19 September 1778

Scalch, Jacob; RA, 1st Lieut., 1 January 1771

Schaak, John; 57, Lieutenant, 1 September 1771; 57, Capt.- Lieut., 17 February 1781

Schaceldon, Charles; 53, Ensign, 9 June 1781

Schlacter, Michael; 3/60, Chaplain, 1 September 1775

Schlagel, Geo. Edw.; 21, Adjutant, 27 June 1781; 21, 1st Lieut., 26 February 1773

Schoedde, Chas. Louis Theo. Alex.; 4/60, Ensign, 18 May 1776; 2/60, Lieutenant, 25 December 1778

Schoen, Hen. Gascogne; 3, Ensign, 9 September 1781; From volunteer

Schoen, Hen. Gascoyne; 4, Ensign, 16 April 1776; 4, Lieutenant, 18 August 1778; WIA Germantown, 4 October 1777; In 1779, printed as John Henry Schoen

Schutz, Rd. Spencer; 29, Ensign, 19 April 1778; 29, Lieutenant, 7 August 1781

Schutz, William; 2FG, Ensign, 20 November 1775; 2FG, Lieut. & Capt., 28 October 1779; DOW Guilford CH, 21 March 1781; 2FG, Capt. & Lt. Col., 15 December 1773; Captaincy also listed as 15 December 1772

Scot, George; RA, 2nd Lieut., 11 March 1778; From Provincial establishment as "gentleman cadet:; Date also given as 1 June 1778

Scotland, Thomas; 40, Ensign, 16 September 1780; 43, Lieutenant, 31 December 1781

Scott, -; 62, Ensign, 1 January 1781

Scott, Alexander; 53, Captain, 24 May 1775; Drowned, 5 April 1778

Scott, Alexander John; RA, Capt.- Lieut., 22 January 1768; Cmd. RA on Martha's Vineyard Raid, September 1778; Died Newfoundland, 24 September 1779

Scott, David; RA, Captain, 7 July 1779, 25 May 1772

Scott, Edward; 3, Lieutenant, 10 June 1774

Scott, Fra. James; 7, Captain, 4 October 1770

Scott, George; 83, Colonel, 16 December 1777; Major General; 19 October 1781

Scott, George; 83, Lieutenant, 29 November 1778

Scott, Hugh; 26, Ensign, 30 July 1779

Scott, John; 26, Colonel, 14 January 1763; Major General; 30 April 1770, Scottish, 1725-1775; MP Fifeshire, 1768-1775; Died 26 December 1775

Scott, Matthew; 19, Lieutenant, 1 June 1778

Scott, Thomas; 24, Lieutenant, 7 June 1765; 24, Capt.- Lieut., 14 July 1777; 24, Captain, 14 July 1777; Possibly served as a spy and courier

Scott, Thomas; 53, Captain, 8 October 1777; Possibly served as a spy and courier

Scott, Thomas; 3, Lieutenant, 1 May 1779; Stayed in Ireland according to WO 8/6, 273-279

Scott, Thomas; 35, Mate, date unknown; To surgeon, 89th Foot, 18 October 1779; Retired 15 January 1781

Scott, William; 17, Captain, 23 August 1775; Extra Major of Bde., 1781

Scott, William; 6, Quartermaster, 16 December 1776; 6, Lieutenant, 30 July 1771, 27 September 1762

Scrimpshire, Tho. Pellet; 14, Ensign, 12 May 1773

Scroggs, William; 22, Lieutenant, 7 December 1772; English, born 1752; Resigned 25 July 1775

Sealy, William; 3, Ensign, 27 October 1779; 3, Lieutenant, 8 November 1781

Sealy, William; 3/60, Lieutenant, 7 December 1782

Searle, Charles; 17 LD, Cornet, 15 March 1778

Seaton, Christopher; 54, Ensign, 17 August 1777; Also Setton; From volunteer

Seaton, John; 2/84, Ensign, 9 April 1777

Sebright, Sir John, Bt.; 18, Colonel, 1 April 1762; Lieutenant General; 30 April 1770, English, 1725-1794; First commission at age 16; MP Bath, 1763-1774 & 1775-1780

Sedgwick, Hunter; 34, Captain, 31 March 1770

Seeley, Henry; 9, Surgeon, 21 February 1776; Also Seelly or Shelley; To half pay, 7 February 1783

Seix, Michael; 64, Lieutenant, 11 February 1775, 13 January 1762; 22, Capt.- Lieut., 10 March 1777; 22, Captain, 3 November 1777; POW 9 January 1776; Barracks Master, New York, 1777; To additional company, 1778

Selwyn, Henry Charles; 7, Quartermaster, 12 May 1773;; 7, Lieutenant, 25 December 1770; 7, Capt.- Lieut., 7 October 1777; 7, Captain, 7 October 1777

Serle, Thomas; 18, Ensign, 20 April 1775; English, born 1754; First commissioned at age 20

Seton, Christopher; 54, Lieutenant, 28 July 1779

Seton, James; 80, Ensign, 15 February 1779

Seton, James; 26, Lieutenant, 16 October 1779, 20 September 1779

Seymour, Francis C.; RA, 2nd Lieut., 17 June 1772; Resigned 9 May 1776; Also reported as dead in 1775 at Halifax

Seymour, George; 17, Lieutenant, 12 December 1774; 17, Capt.- Lieut., 4 January 1777; 17, Captain, 4 January 1777

Shadwell, Hen. Thurlor; 52, Ensign, 15 August 1775

Shand, Alexander; RA, 1st Lieut., 1 January 1771; WIA Bunker Hill, 17 June 1775 & Brandywine, 11 September 1777

Sharman, Joseph; 30, Lieutenant, 1 June 1778

Sharpe, Gideon; 17, Lieutenant, 23 August 1775; 70, Captain, 10 April 1777; ADC to Gen. Leslie, 1782

Sharpe, Walter; 6, Ensign, 25 November 1775

Shaw, Alexander; 4/60, Adjutant, 1 September 1775; 4/60, Lieutenant, 1 September 1775, 12 December 1756; 4/60, Capt.- Lieut., 14 November 1776; 4/60, Captain, 14 November 1776; Date taken from promotion to captain-lieutenancy

Shaw, Daniel; 35, Ensign, 18 June 1775; 35, Lieutenant, 4 January 1777; From volunteer; Ensigncy also given as 25 June 1775

Shaw, John; 76, Adjutant, 1 April 1781; 76, Lieutenant, 29 December 1777; 76, Captain, 31 December 1781

Shaw, Robert; 64, Lieutenant, 2 February 1770; 40, Capt.- Lieut., 21 September 1777; 40, Captain, 21 September 1777; Irish, born 1748; First commissioned at age 15

Shaw, William; 47, Lieutenant, 20 February 1773, 17 October 1762

Shaw, William; 43, Ensign, 9 November 1778

Shawe, Charles; 64, Ensign, 7 September 1774; 22, Lieutenant, 30 October 1776; English, born 1756

Shawe, Henry; 6, Captain, 13 February 1775; Major; 23 July 1772

Shawe, Meryick; 10, Lieutenant, 26 December 1770

Sheaffe, Roger Hall; 5, Ensign, 1 May 1778

Shee, John; 18, Captain, 1 January 1766; 18, Major, 25 July 1775; Also Shea; Irish, born 1741; First commissioned at age 15; To lieutenant colonel 75th Foot, 13 October 1779

Sheldon, James; 15, Lieutenant, 2 August 1775; 9, Captain, 14 October 1775

Sheppard, Hon. Philip; 69, Colonel, 8 September 1775; Lieutenant General; 29 August 1777

Sheppard, John; 28, Capt.- Lieut., 8 September 1775; 28, Captain, 29 October 1776; Retired 9 April 1777

Sheridan, Henry Fortick; 31, Lieutenant, 25 May 1772; Major, New York Volunteers, 20 August 1778

Sheriffe, Charles; 1781; Barrackmaster at St. Augustine, Florida

Sheriffe, William; 47, Captain, 25 December 1765, 28 September 1762; Major; 25 July 1768; Lt. Colonel; 20 January 1776; Depty. Quartermaster General in America, 22 December 1776

Sherlock, William; 43, Ensign, 10 March 1777; 43, Lieutenant, 15 September 1779; Also Shurlock

Shewbridge, William; 16, Lieutenant, 15 August 1775, 20 October 1761

Shield, Thomas; 46, Surgeon, 12 October 1780, 4 October 1779, Also Shields; From 87th Foot; Died prior to 26 June 1784

Showrd, Daniel; 8, Ensign, 27 May 1771; 8, Lieutenant, 6 May 1777; Also Shourd; Shot by accident with his own gun and DOW, 27 October 1778 on Vincennes Expedition

Shrapnel, Zach. Scrope; 5, Ensign, 21 January 1779

Shrimpton, John; 62, Captain, 17 September 1773; WIA Hubbardton, 7 July 1777

Shuckburg, Stewkley; 37, Ensign, 16 September 1778

Shuldham, Thomas; 55, Ensign, 11 May 1776; 7, Lieutenant, 5 November 1777; Retired 13 October 1778

Shuttleworth, Ashton; RA, 2nd Lieut., 17 June 1772; RA, 1st Lieut., 7 July 1779; Also Shutworth; WIA Bunker Hill, 17 June 1775

Shuttleworth, Edmund; 7, Lieutenant, 9 April 1777; 7, Lieutenant, 21 July 1779

Shuttleworth, John Ashton; 7, Lieutenant, 20 May 1772; 7, Captain, 10 June 1778

Silk, Stephen; 80, Lieutenant, 15 February 1779; Died 9 March 1781

Sill, Francis Bushill; 63, Major, 20 October 1773; Also Sile; KIA Ft. Clinton, 6 October 1777

Silvaugh, Michael; 38, Adjutant, 9 February 1779; 38, Ensign, 27 June 1780

Silvester, Edward; 3, Lieutenant, 13 January 1777; Also Sylvester; WIA & POW Eutaw Springs, 8 September 1781

Simcoe, John Graves; 35, Adjutant, 27 March 1772; 35, Lieutenant, 12 March 1774; 40, Captain, 27 December 1775; Major; 4 August 1780; Lt. Colonel; 19 December 1781, Studied at Eton and Oxford; Studied law at Lincoln's Inn; WIA Brandywine, 11 September 1777 & Monmouth, 28 June 1778; Major Queen's American Rangers,15 October 1777; Lieutenant colonel of Queen's Rangers; Lieutenant colonelcy to date from 1 July 1776

Simondson, Warren; 33, Lieutenant, 26 September 1771, 1 August 1760; 64, Capt.- Lieut., 28 August 1776; 64, Captain, 12 September 1777; Also Symardson; English, born 1740; First commissioned at age 17; Retired 2 May 1782

Simpson, Ambrose; 59, Adjutant, 5 July 1775; 59, Ensign, 6 October 1769; 59, Lieutenant, 29 March 1775

Simpson, George; 40, Ensign, 10 August 1778

Simpson, Noah; 31, Captain, 21 February 1776; Helped Ackland at Stillwater, 1777

Simpson, William; 17, Lieutenant, 24 September 1778; WIA Stony Point, 16 July 1779; Assistant Engineer, 1781

Sims, -; 43, Mate, date unknown ; Scout at Lexington and Concord; Assigned to L.I. Bn., 9 June 1775

Sinclair, -; 57, Lieutenant, 6 September 1780;

Sinclair, George; 65, Captain, 28 February 1766, 2 June 1762, WIA Bunker Hill, 17 June 1775

Sinclair, James; 4/60, Ensign, 24 April 1779

Sinclair, James; 2/71, Lieutenant, 20 October 1781

Sinclair, Patrick; 1/84, Captain, 1 April 1780, 13 April 1772, Born Lybster, Caithness, 1736-1819; First commission at age 22; Lt. Governor at Mackinac

Sinclair, Wol. B.; 17, Ensign, 29 June 1778; 17, Lieutenant, 19 September 1780; From volunteer; Father killed at Havana, 1762

Skelley, Francis; 1/71, Captain, 28 November 1775; Major of Bde for Gen. Vaughn, 28 May 1778; ADC to Gen. Leslie, 1781; nephew to Lord Adam Gordon

Skene, Andrew Philip; 43, Lieutenant, 15 April 1774, 30 October 1762, Major of Bde, 1775; With Fraser's marksmen after 10 September 1777; Strach, p. 173-174

Skene, David; 28, Captain, 6 October 1762, 19 October 1761, Retired 11 December 1775

Skene, Philip; 69, Lt. Colonel, 20 April 1771; Colonel; 19 February 1779

Skene, Robert; 59, Captain, 14 April 1756; Colonel; 25 May 1772, Inspector of Roads in Highlands, 1767-1780; Colonel 99th Foot, 1781; 48th Foot, 1783; MP Fifeshire, 1779-1780

Skerrett, John; 19, Captain, 27 May 1776

Skinner, Cortlandt; 70, Ensign, 11 November 1780

Skinner, John; 70, Captain, 10 June 1768; Major; 10 November 1780

Skinner, John; 16, Ensign, 4 September 1772; 16, Lieutenant, 23 November 1775; Attached to Tarelton's Legion at Black Stocks, SC

Skinner, Joseph; Hosp., Mate, date unknown; At Lancaster, PA as POW, 1783

Skinner, Philip Kearny; 23, 2nd Lieut., 12 December 1782; Native of Perth Amboy, NJ; From ensign, 1st Bn. New Jersey Volunteers

Skinner, William Campbell; RE, Sub-eng. & Lt., 2 February 1775; In America from 1775-1778; Served at Boston and West Indies

Slack, Benjamin; RE, Pract. eng. & 2nd Lt., 4 March 1776; In America from 1782-1783; Served at New York and Bermuda; Drowned 1783 aboard HMS Mentor

Sladden, George; 67, Captain, 1 February 1775; ADC to Gen. Howe; WIA Bunker Hill, 17 June 1775

Sladden, John; 35, Ensign, 29 April 1775

Slater, Henry; 18, Ensign, 17 May 1774; English, born 1754; First commissioned at age 20

Slater, Thomas; 6, Ensign, 22 July 1771; 6, Lieutenant, 24 November 1775

Sleigh, Jeremiah; 4, Captain, 15 August 1775, 29 January 1760, Died 16 December 1775

Sleigh, William; 19, Captain, 17 November 1780

Sloper, John; 17 LD, Cornet, 28 December 1775

Small, John; 21, Captain, 30 April 1765, 6 August 1762; 2/84, Major, 13 June 1775, 29 August 1777; 2/84, Lt. Colonel, 17 November 1780; Major of Bde, 1777

Small, Robert; 83, Chaplain, date unknown; Retired in 1782 or early 1783

Smeallie, Thomas; 31, Ensign, 10 December 1779; Died 22 April 1783

Smelt, Cornelius; 14, Adjutant, 18 June 1775; 14, Lieutenant, 21 February 1772; 35, Captain, 13 January 1777

Smelt, Thomas; 47, Captain, 20 March 1758; 65, Major, 16 August 1775, 23 July 1772, WIA Bunker Hill, 17 June 1775; Retired 20 January 1776

Smibert, William; 26, Ensign, 12 January 1770; 26, Lieutenant, 22 February 1776; Died 31 October 1776

Smith, Carew; 16, Lieutenant, 13 April 1772; 16, Captain, 13 April 1778

Smith, Charles; 28, Captain, 28 November 1771; WIA St. Kitts, 28 January 1782

Smith, Colin; 1/42, Quartermaster, 20 March 1776; Died 20 December 1779

Smith, David; 1/84, Lieutenant, 25 December 1776; Dismissed for long history of misconduct; Allowed to sell out

Smith, David; 2/84, Ensign, 24 November 1779

Smith, David; 5, Ensign, 8 September 1780;

Smith, Francis; 10, Lt. Colonel, 13 February 1762, 16 January 1762; WIA Lexington and Concord, 19 April 1775

Smith, George Amos; 52, Captain, 3 March 1772; KIA Bunker Hill, 17 June 1775

Smith, Hen. Wm.; 40, Ensign, 22 November 1775; 40, Lieutenant, 30 October 1777; DOW Groton, CT, 7 September 1781

Smith, J. Hayward; 31, Chaplain, 4 January 1777

Smith, James; 64, Ensign, 29 December 1781

Smith, John; RACC, 1st Lieut., 22 January 1768; Captain; 13 October 1774, Served in RA since enlisting in 1742; Died Halifax, 10 December 1783

Smith, John; 19, Captain, 28 August 1775;

Smith, John; 37, Captain, 25 May 1772; Sec. to Gen. Clinton, 24 May 1778; Retired 10 August 1778

Smith, John; 1/42, Capt.- Lieut., 14 January 1775; Captain, 16 August 1775; Scottish, born 1732; First commissioned at age 25; POW on Oxford, Boston, 19 June 76; Died Powles Hook, NJ, July 1783

Smith, John; 5, Capt.- Lieut., 13 April 1768; 5, Captain, 25 May 1772; DOW Bunker Hill, 2 August 1775

Smith, John; 9, Lieutenant, 16 December 1768; 9, Capt.- Lieut., 11 July 1778; 9, Captain, 11 July 1778

Smith, John; 22, Ensign, 13 April 1779; 22, Lieutenant, 1 February 1782; English, born 1758; Arrived in America, June 1781

Smith, John; 65, Ensign, 16 May 1766; 65, Lieutenant, 16 May 1766; DOW Bunker Hill, 2 August 1775

Smith, John; RA, 2nd Lieut., 15 March 1771; WIA Stillwater, 7 October 1777; POW with French

Smith, John; 1/84, Ensign, 12 June 1775; Served in F&I War

Smith, Robert; 83, Captain, 21 January 1778

Smith, Robert; 63, Surgeon, 2 October 1765; Hosp., Surgeon, 1 April 1779; To half pay, 25 December 1783; Later served under Duke of York; Died 12 March 1807

Smith, Thomas; 70, Ensign, 25 June 1781; Retired as lieutenant 13 October 1778

Smith, William; 64, Ensign, 22 October 1781; Native of New York

Smith, William D.; Hosp., Mate, Prior to 1783; Stationed at New York, 1783

Smith, William Peter; RA, 2nd Lieut., 15 March 1771; WIA & POW Bemis Heights, 7 October 1777

Smithies, William; FG, Surgeon, 23 February 1776; Returned to England, 28 April 1777

Smithson, Walter; 4, Ensign, 2 December 1777; 4, Lieutenant, 29 September 1780; From volunteer; WIA Germantown

Smyth, Charles; 18, Ensign, 26 February 1776; Also Smith; English, born 1755; First commissioned at age 23; Did not serve in America

Smyth, Dalton; 64, Ensign, 6 May 1777

Smyth, James; 31, Ensign, 19 September 1776; 31, Lieutenant, 2 September 1781

Smyth, James; 79, Lieutenant, 9 March 1779; At New York City, 20 August 1782

Smyth, Robert; Hosp., Surgeon, 1 April 1779; From 63rd Foot; Noted as "MD" in 1782 Army List; Served as surgeon general at Portsmouth, 1781

Smyth, Thomas; 69, Lieutenant, 31 July 1781

Smythe, Hon. Lionel; 49, Lieutenant, 7 September 1771; 49, Capt.-Lieut., 29 October 1776; 23, Captain, 26 October 1777; Also Smith; 29 October 1779; ADC to Lt. Gen. Percy, 1777; Married 8 September 1779

Snieder, George; 3/60, Lieutenant, 5 September 1775, 27 September 1762; 3/60, Captain, 26 December 1778; Also Sneyder or Schnieder

Snodgrass, John; 82, Lieutenant, 18 January 1778; Drowned Egg Harbor, NJ, 21 March 1779 in wreck of transport, *Mermaid*

Snowe, William; 45, Lieutenant, 1 September 1771; 45, Capt.- Lieut., 11 January 1777; 45, Captain, 11 January 1777

Snowe, William; 64, Adjutant, 26 January 1770; 64, Ensign, 16 August 1768; 64, Lieutenant, 28 May 1774; 64, Captain, 2 March 1778; Irish, born 1751; First commissioned at age 17; Resigned as adjutant, 2 March 1778

Soden, Ambrose; 4, Ensign, 18 December 1777; From volunteer

Sommers, John; 3/60, Surgeon, 10 November 1775; Also Sumoners; Exchanged to QM 60th Foot, 28 April 1784; To half pay, 30 April 1784; Returned to full pay, 1787; To ensign independent coy. At Sheerness, 9 July 1788; Died prior to 8 November 1792

Sone, Samuel; 24, Surgeon, 30 April 1771

Sotheron, William; 62, Captain, 29 February 1776

Southouse, Charles; 29, Lieutenant, 23 May 1781

Southouse, Edward; 29, Ensign, 10 March 1780

Spaight, William; 65, Lieutenant, 12 January 1770; Asst. Dpty. QMG, July 1776

Span, Geo. Fred. Aug.; 28, Lieutenant, 23 August 1775

Sparrow, Boduchan; 35, Lieutenant, 20 July 1780

Speake, Edward; 37, Lieutenant, 6 May 1773, 21 May 1763

Speake, Edward; 37, Captain, 18 November 1775; Ford lists him in 35th Foot, POW Germantown; Exchanged 1778

Spearlman, Alex. Young; 35, Ensign, 7 April 1779; 35, Lieutenant, 1 February 1781; Also Spearman

Spence, John; 1/42, Ensign, 24 February 1776; 1/42, Lieutenant, 11 November 1777; Transferred to 95th Foot as captain-lieutenant, 9 April 1780

Spencer, Boyle; 24, Lieutenant, 1 March 1776, 21 March 1759

Spencer, Brent; 15, Ensign, 18 January 1778; 15, Lieutenant, 12 November 1779

Spencer, John Simpson; RA, Capt.- Lieut., 28 May 1766; Captain; 25 May 1772; Died Jamaica, June 1776

Spencer, Walter; 9, Ensign, 19 December 1776; 9, Lieutenant, 1 June 1780

Spendlove, Roger; 43, Major, 8 February 1775, 23 July 1772, DOW Bunker Hill, 9 July 1775

Spens, George; 16, Ensign, 17 January 1780; 16, Lieutenant, 18 April 1782

Spens, James; 1/42, Ensign, 5 June 1778; 2/42, Lieutenant, 21 March 1780

Spiessmacher, Fredrick Christian; 2/60, Captain, 4 October 1770; 1/60, Major, 14 May 1778; To 2/60, 6 June 1778; POW Boston; At Bath December 1780; Retired 30 September 1782

Spooner, Thomas; 47, Ensign, 22 July 1776

Spread, William; 64, Ensign, 21 November 1778; 93, Lieutenant, 26 May 1780

Sproule, George; 59, Ensign, 13 February 1765, 30 July 1762; 16, Lieutenant, 1 August 1775; 16, Capt.- Lieut., 9 June 1781; 16, Captain, 9 June 1781

Spry, William; RE, Eng. ord. & Capt., 25 May 1772; In America from 1758-1783; Served at Quebec and Halifax

Squire, Thomas; 47, Ensign, 11 March 1780

St. Clair, David; 29, Captain, 22 April 1774

St. Clair, John; 7, Captain, 13 December 1765; Major; 23 July 1772

St. Clair, John; 17 LD, Adjutant, 2 September 1767; 17 LD, Cornet, 15 May 1772; 17 LD, Lieutenant, 1 June 1777

St. Clair, John; 17 LD, Cornet, 13 September 1779; Secretary to Brig. Gen. Birch, 14 September 1780

St. Clair, John; 17 LD, Cornet, 23 April 1778; Cornetcy also given as 15 March 1778

St. Clair, William; 1/71, Lieutenant, 8 December 1775; Also Sinclair; Died New York or New Jersey, 9 March 1777

St. Elroy, Edward; 24, Lieutenant, 3 February 1776

St. George, Henry; 62, Chaplain, 18 December 1766

St. George, Richard; 1FG, Lieut. & Capt., 16 September 1779; Depty. Adjutant General for America, 1 December 1780; ADC to Henry Clinton, 1780-1781

St. George, Rd. St. George Mansergh; 4, Ensign, 15 April 1776; 52, Lieutenant, 23 December 1776; 44, Captain, 31 January 1778; Lieutenancy also given as 11 December 1776; WIA Brandywine 11 September 1777 & Germantown 4 October 1777; From volunteer in 4th Foot

St. Germain, Henry; 8, Ensign, 12 December 1781; Son of the tutor of the Earl of Uxbridge

St. John, Hon. George; 33, Ensign, 17 August 1780

St. Lawrence, Hon. Hen.; 3, Lieutenant, 1 June 1778; Stayed in Ireland according to WO 8/6, 273-279

St. Ledger, John; 17 LD, Captain, 25 December 1775

St. Leger, Barry; 34, Lt. Colonel, 20 May 1775, 25 May 1772; Colonel; 17 November 1780

St. Leger, Hayes; 63, Lieutenant, 5 March 1775; 63, Captain, 12 June 1777; CM for mutinous and disrespectful behavior, guilty of latter, May 1780; DOW Eutaw Springs, 11 October 1781; Possibly POW

St. Leger, John; 55, Captain, 24 September 1778; Portrait, Strachan plate 57; Promoted major 90th Foot, 26 November 1779

St. Leger, William; 17 LD, Cornet, 25 December 1775; 17 LD, Lieutenant, 13 April 1779

St. Leger, William; 45, Ensign, 30 May 1775; 33, Lieutenant, 30 May 1780

St. Our, Charles; 1/84, Capt.- Lieut., 29 May 1783; Dismissed from service; Killed in duel shortly afterward

Standish, David; RA, Captain, 1 January 1771; POW captured aboard the Delaware

Stanley, Edwin Thomas; 28, Capt.- Lieut., 3 December 1781;, 11

Stanley, Edwin Thomas; 55, Ensign, 20 October 1773; 55, Lieutenant, 11 May 1776; Irish, born 1755; First commissioned at age 17

Stanley, James; 49, Ensign, 13 May 1776; 49, Lieutenant, 6 August 1778

Stanley, John; 20, Captain, 9 March 1776; WIA Freeman's Farm, 19 September 1777

Stanley, Samuel; 83, Captain, 25 December 1782; First name may be incorrect; Retired 12 February 1783

Stanley, Thomas; 16 LD, Cornet, 31 March 1775

Stanley, Thomas; 83, Ensign, 13 February 1783

Stanley, Hon. Thomas; 17 LD, Captain, 25 February 1776; 1753-1779; MP Lancashire, 1776-1779; To major, 79th Foot, 11 February 1778; Died in Jamaica

Stannus, Ephriam; 64, Captain, 12 November 1768; Irish, born 1742; First commissioned at age 16; Retired 2 March 1778

Stanton, John; 14, Captain, 25 May 1772; Major, Nova Scotia Volunteers, 25 December 1775

Stanton, Robert; 83, Ensign, 30 September 1782

Staples, Lawrence; 16 LD, Cornet, 30 December 1775

Stapleton, Fran. Sam.; 9, Captain, 31 May 1773; DOW Hubbardton, VT, 9 July 1777

Stapleton, John; 17 LD, Cornet, 10 December 1777; 17 LD, Capt.- Lieut., 31 December 1780; Asst. Depty. Quartermaster General, 1781

Stapleton, William; 22, Mate, 22 March 1775; To General Hospital, 10 October 1776

Stark, David; 44, Ensign, 4 October 1776; 44, Lieutenant, 5 October 1778

Stark, William; 44, Surgeon, 3 July 1772

Starkey, Nicholas; 57, Lieutenant, 28 August 1775

Starkie, Nicholas; 21, Captain, 18 October 1778; WIA Freeman's Farm, 19 September 1777

Stawell, Eustace; 44, Captain, 20 December 1769; Irish, born 174; First commissioned at age 20

Stead, William; 3FG, Lieut. & Capt., 12 April 1777; Returned to England, June 1779

Stedman, John; 33, Ensign, 25 December 1776; 64, Lieutenant, 13 April 1778; Died in horse accident, Long Island, NY, reported 5 January 1782

Steel, Thomas; 63, Ensign, 18 December 1777

Steel, Thomas; Hosp., Mate, Prior to 1783; Stationed at New York, 1783

Steele, George; 63, Ensign, 22 November 1775; 63, Lieutenant, 13 April 1778; Not joined by May 1777

Steele, Lawrence; 3, Lieutenant, 3 June 1778

Steele, Samuel; 34, Capt.- Lieut., 2 March 1776; 34, Captain, 2 March 1777

Steele, Thomas; 29, Lieutenant, 3 November 1773; KIA Hubbardtown, 7 July 1777

Stelfox, Thomas; 55, Lieutenant, 15 August 1775, 10 November 1762

Stephans, George; 47, Ensign, 10 July 1776; 47, Lieutenant, 17 May 1782

Stephens, Humphry; 3FG, Capt. & Lt. Col., 9 May 1768; Colonel, 29 August 1777; Retired in 1791 as major general

Stephenson, Charles; 5, Capt.- Lieut., 28 October 1778; ADC to Gen. Clinton, 1782

Steplin, Thomas; RA, 2nd Lieut., Not listed in WO 65; Died Boston, 26 December 1775

Sterling, James; 1/42, Ensign, 22 April 1777; 1/42, Lieutenant, 3 August 1778; Scottish, born 1749; First commissioned at age 15

Sterling, Thomas; 1/42, Lt. Colonel, 7 September 1771; Colonel; 19 February 1779, Scottish, born 1735; First commissioned at age 12; WIA Elizabethtown, NJ, 6 June 1780

Stevelly, Joseph; 9, Ensign, 1 January 1774; 9, Lieutenant, 19 December 1776; Also Stavely; WIA Ft. Ann, 9 July 1777; Died 31 May 1780

Stevens, Alexander; 2/84, Ensign, 8 July 1783;

Stevens, Edmond; 2FG, Lieut. & Capt., 2 December 1768; 1FG, Capt. & Lt. Col., 15 May 1778; From cornet 1st Dragoons; Extra Major of Bde, 1777

Stevens, Samuel; 37, Ensign, 23 February 1781

Stevenson, Charles; 10, Ensign, 30 March 1775; 35, Lieutenant, 31 May 1776

Stevenson, Henry; Hosp., Mate, Prior to 1783; Stationed on Long Island with Legion, 1783

Stevenson, James; 4/60, Captain, 25 December 1778; Major; 10 November 1780

Stevenson, John; 82, Ensign, 18 September 1780

Stevenson, William; 15, Ensign, 22 November 1780

Stevenson, William; FG, Mate, 22 March 1776; Assigned to 2nd Bn. Bde of Guards; Died February 1777

Stewart, Alexander; 3, Lt. Colonel, 7 July 1775; Am., Brigadier General; 1781, From Afton,1739-1794; MP Afton, 1786-1794; Given 3rd Foot to improve them, previously had done same with 37th Foot in Germany; WIA Eutaw Springs, 8 September 1781

Stewart, Alexander; 1/42, Ensign, 28 August 1775; 1/42, Lieutenant, 17 December 1777; Scottish, born 1757; First commissioned at age 17

Stewart, Alexander; 1/42, Mate, 25 August 1775; Scottish, born 1762; Entered service at age 20

Stewart, Alexander Gordon; 3, Ensign, 12 August 1779, 9 October 1778

Stewart, Charles; 63, Captain, 15 August 1775, 20 October 1761; Major; 29 August 1777, Also Stuart

Stewart, Charles; 74, Lieutenant, 29 December 1777

Stewart, Donald; 74, Ensign, 19 December 1777; 74, Lieutenant, 20 January 1779;

Stewart, Duncan; 74, Ensign, 21 December 1777; 74, Lieutenant, 7 July 1780

Stewart, Francis; 26, Captain, 25 December 1770, 13 February 1762, Also Stuart; KIA Ft. Clinton, 6 October 1777

Stewart, George; 4/60, Capt.- Lieut., 6 May 1782; Captain-lieutenancy also listed as 4 May 1782; Returned to 33rd Foot, 11 October 1782

Stewart, George; 2/71, Lieutenant, 3 December 1775

Stewart, George; 80, Lieutenant, 6 February 1778; Died Newport News, VA, 7 March 1781

Stewart, George Walker; 82, Lieutenant, 18 September 1780

Stewart, Hon. James; 1FG, Capt. & Lt. Col., 4 April 1775; KIA Guilford CH, 15 March 1781

Stewart, James; 64, Captain, 12 January 1770; Scottish, born 1742; First commissioned at age 22

Stewart, James; 33, Ensign, 16 January 1776

Stewart, James; 5, Ensign, 15 August 1775; WIA Germantown, 4 October 1777

Stewart, John; 37, Captain, 25 December 1770, 16 July 1762, Retired 2 July 1777

Stewart, John; RA, Captain, 25 April 1777, 25 May 1772

Stewart, John; 1/71, Surgeon, 5 April 1778; From mate; To Royal Horse Guards, 29 January 1782; Retired 5 October 1785

Stewart, W.; 17 LD, Lt. Colonel; Advertised for deserters 21 June 1780; Not listed in WO 65

Stewart, William; 28, Ensign, 24 February 1775; 28, Lieutenant, 14 March 1776; 28, Captain, 14 July 1777

Stewart, William; 1/42, Lieutenant, 4 September 1775, December 1773, WIA Piscataway, NJ, 10 May 1777; Removed to Cpt. Coote's Ind. Co. of invalids at Landguard Fort, 18 March 1778

Stiel, Robert; 24, Lieutenant, 14 November 1775

Stiell, William; 3/60, Lt. Colonel, 21 September 1775; At Pensacola, 1779; Retired 1780; Died 1810,

Stirke, Henry; 10, Ensign, 3 July 1775; 10, Lieutenant, 18 November 1776; From volunteer

Stirke, Henry Bethune; 63, Adjutant, 30 May 1780; 63, Ensign, 29 September 1775; 63, Lieutenant, 14 October 1777; To captain 88th Foot, 3 March 1780

Stirke, Julius; 10, Capt.- Lieut., 28 June 1771; 10, Captain, 22 November 1775, 25 May 1772, Resigned 31 January 1778

Stirling, Thomas; 1/71, Colonel, 13 February 1782, 19 February 1779; Major General; 20 November 1782, Scottish, 1733 - 1808; Son of Sir Henry Stirling of Ardoch; Married Anne Gordon; Served in Dutch Brigade

Stoddart, John; 80, Ensign, 22 July 1778; 80, Lieutenant, 24 September 1779

Stopford, Hon. Joseph; 7, Major, 27 October 1772; 15, Lt. Colonel, 31 January 1778, 29 August 1777; Colonel; 20 November 1782; POW Ft. Chambly, October 1775

Stopford, William; 63, Captain, 30 December 1768; WIA Bunker Hill, 17 June 1775; Retired 10 July 1775

Stordy, Robert; 31, Lieutenant, 28 April 1773

Storey, John; 27, Ensign, 3 May 1775; 27, Lieutenant, 14 January 1777

Storey, John; 1/71, Lieutenant, 27 August 1776, 25 October 1761

Storey, Thomas; 47, Lieutenant, 6 June 1770, 29 April 1763; 47, Capt.- Lieut., 6 April 1778; 20, Captain, 1 April 1780

Stotesbury, Robert; 55, Lieutenant, 16 July 1774; Irish, born 1749; First commissioned at age 23; Died of fever, prior to 17 January 1779

Stothard, Adam; 3, Lieutenant, 1 June 1778; Died 8 October 1782

Stovin, Richard; 17, Ensign, 16 June 1780; 17, Lieutenant, 16 May 1782; Also Storin; Listed as with additional company 1780

Stowe, Richard; 24, Ensign, 2 March 1776; 24, Lieutenant, 1 October 1780

Stracey, John Charles; 28, Ensign, 14 July 1777; 28, Lieutenant, 17 October 1778

Strangways, Hon. Ste. Digby; 24, Captain, 17 April 1769; 20, Major, 1 December 1778; KIA Bemis Heights, 7 October 1777

Stratford, Hon. Ben. Neale; 55, Captain, 31 August 1770; Irish, born 1751; First commissioned at age 12

Stratton, Alexander; 1/84, Lieutenant, 14 June 1775; POW Carolina, 1776

Stratton, James; RE, Pract. eng. & 2nd Lt., 2 February 1775; In America from 1775-1780; Served at Boston and New York

Stratton, Robert Gervais; 55, Ensign, 31 August 1774; Irish, born 1754; First commissioned at age 16; Resigned 10 May 1776

Straubenzee, Turner von; 17 LD, Captain, 10 February 1770; 17, Major, 7 February 1776; 52, Lt. Colonel, 5 October 1778; Also Straubensie; Cmd. L.I. Bn. in Boston, 1776; WIA Harlem Heights, 16 September 1776; Also wounded in Jerseys in 1776; Accused of atrocities in 1778; Involved in an adultery trial in London in 1782

Stribling, Thomas; 52, Ensign, 18 April 1777

Strickland, William; 5, Ensign, 23 November 1775

Strong, John; 26, Captain, 31 October 1770

Strong, John Kennedy; 64, Ensign, 28 August 1772; 64, Lieutenant, 23 November 1775; 64, Captain, 12 August 1778; CM for neglect of duty & acquitted, August 1780; WIA and POW, Eutaw Springs 8 September 1781

Stuart, -; 76, Quartermaster, 6 September 1780

Stuart, Archibald; 62, Lieutenant, 1 March 1776, 10 October 1759, Also Stewart; KIA Bemis Heights, 7 October 1777

Stuart, Dugald; 1/71, Ensign, 21 January 1781

Stuart, George; 1/42, Lieutenant, 1 September 1781

Stuart, George; 82, Ensign, 5 January 1778; 82, Lieutenant, 18 September 1780; Asst. Depty. Quartermaster General, 1781

Stuart, Hon. Charles; 43, Major, 8 October 1775; 26, Lt. Colonel, 26 October 1777; Son of Lord Bute, From Branser, Bute, 1753-1801; MP Bossiney, 1776-1790; Portrait in Strachan, plate 8

Stuart, James; 1/42, Lieutenant, 7 October 1777; Also Stewart; Scottish; Portrait in Mollo/McGregor; WIA Piscataway, 10 May 1777

Stuart, John; 49, Captain, 14 January 1775; WIA Brandywine, 11 September 1777

Stuart, John; 2/71, Ensign, 3 August 1778; 1/71, Lieutenant, 18 September 1780

Stuart, John; 74, Lieutenant, 20 December 1777

Stuart, John; 76, Lieutenant, 4 January 1778

Stuart, John; 3FG, Ensign, 7 August 1778; WIA Guilford CH, 15 March 1781 and sent home; Later Knight of Bath

Stuart, John; 2/42, Ensign, Unknown; Also Stewart; Escaped from a Philadelphia jail with 6 others, 20 January 1781

Stuart, John; 1/42, Chaplain, 21 March 1780

Stuart, John; 46, Surgeon, 31 August 1762; Hosp., Surgeon, 25 December 1776; Hosp., Purveyor, 2 February 1782; Also Stewart; Was purveyor for the Leeward Islands; To half pay, 25 December 1783; Died Perth, 23 November 1808

Stuart, Patrick; 26, Ensign, 2 November 1777

Stuart, Patrick; 26, Lieutenant, 1 August 1779

Studholme, Gilfred; 40, Adjutant, Unknown; Captain, Nova Scotia Volunteers, 27 December 1775; Captain, Royal Fencible Americans, 15 July 1776; Extra Major of Bde, 1777; Colonel, Sunbury County, Nova Scotia Militia, 6 December 1777

Sturdy, John; 54, Ensign, 8 March 1782

Style, William; 3, Colonel, 21 April 1779; Major General; 29 August 1777

Surman, Thomas; 9, Ensign, 5 January 1780; Died 24 July 1781

Surtcliffe, John; 54, Surgeon, 15 May 1772; Also Sutcliffe; Retired 30 July 1779

Sutherland, Alex.; 83, Ensign, 31 March 1783

Sutherland, Alexander; 2/71, Lieutenant, 26 November 1775; 2/71, Captain, 29 December 1778

Sutherland, Alexander; RE, Sub-eng. & Lt., 30 October 1775; In America from 1775-1780; Served at New York and with Cornwallis

Sutherland, Charles; 2/42, Ensign, 21 March 1780; 2/42, Lieutenant, 25 July 1781

Sutherland, David; 1/42, Ensign, 2 February 1779

Sutherland, David; 1/84, Ensign, 1782; Also served with Bulter's Rangers

Sutherland, Hugh; 5, Ensign, 6 October 1776; 5, Lieutenant, 6 February 1779

Sutherland, James; 53, Ensign, 1 March 1776

Sutherland, John; 7, Lieutenant, 5 October 1777; Died 26 September 1783

Sutherland, John; 40, Ensign, 12 September 1777

Sutherland, Nicholas; 21, Major, 21 February 1772; 47, Lt. Colonel, 5 November 1776; POW; Paroled, returned to England and died 18 July 1781

Sutherland, William; 38, Lieutenant, 18 June 1766, 17 October 1761; 55, Captain, 14 April 1776; At Lexington and Concord as a supernumerary officer; WIA Concord Bridge, 19 April 1775, by the militia's first volley, making him the first officer casualty of the war; Sprnmy. ADC to Gen. Clinton, 10 July 1777; ADC to Gen. Clinton, 25 May 1778; Cmd. Garrison Bn. 26 September 1778 at NYC; Returned to 55th 29 August 1780

Sutherland, William; 1/71, Ensign, 21 March 1779; 2/71, Lieutenant, 19 January 1781

Sutherland, William; 53, Ensign, 20 March 1777

Sutton, -; 47, Ensign, 14 July 1777; From volunteer; WIA Skenesboro, 6 July 1777

Sutton, Robert; 14, Captain, 15 August 1775, 22 May 1761, Died 23 October 1776

Swan, Rowland; 26, Lieutenant, 7 September 1768; 26, Captain, 11 May 1774

Swanton, Thomas; 3FG, Lieut. & Capt., 6 July 1773; 3FG, Capt. & Lt. Col., 20 June 1782; WIA Guilford CH, 15 March 1781; At Charleston; Left Guards. 1794

Swayne, Charles; 33, Ensign, 3 May 1779; Drowned 17 August 1780

Sweetenham, George; 9, Captain, 2 March 1776; WIA Freeman Farm, 19 September 1777

Sweetland, Thomas; 7, Lieutenant, 13 November 1781; 3/60, Captain, 28 April 1782

Swindell, John Cosby; 55, Ensign, 23 August 1775; 55, Lieutenant, 7 July 1777

Swiney, John; 27, Lieutenant, 24 May 1775; Retired 17 September 1778

Swiney, Shapland; 38, Ensign, 29 September 177238, Lieutenant, 4 May 1776; WIA Bunker Hill, 17 June 1775

Swymmer, Thomas; 70, Lieutenant, 16 May 1778

Sylvester, Edward; 3, Lieutenant, 18 January 1777; WIA Eutaw Springs, 8 September 1781

Symes, Cha. Jeff.; 45, Ensign, 7 September 1778; 7, Lieutenant, 9 November 1778

Symes, Charles; 40, Ensign, 11 September 1781

Symes, James; 5, Lieutenant, 25 December 1776; Sent home with invalids 4 July 1777

Symes, Richard; 2/84, Lieutenant, 14 June 1775

Symes, Richard; 52, Captain, 6 July 1772; Extra Major of Bde, 1777; POW in James Allen's diary, probably March to June 1776

Taggart, George; 19, Lieutenant, 1 June 1778

Talbot, -; 33, Ensign, 1 October 1780; KIA Guilford CH, 15 March 1781

Talbot, Wm. Henry; 16 LD, Lieutenant, 11 March 1774; 17 LD, Captain, 3 June 1778; Died 6 March 1782

Tarleton, Banister; 1DG, Cornet, 20 April 1775; 79, Captain, 8 January 1778; Also Lt. Colonel Commanding, British Legion, 1 August 1778; Born Liverpool, 1754-1833; Educated at the University of Liverpool and Oxford; First commissioned at age 21; WIA New Garden, NC, 15 March 1781 & Yorktown, 3 October 1781; To half pay, 24 October 1783

Tawse, Thomas; 1/71, Lieutenant, 6 December 1775; Also Tawes; KIA Savannah, 9 October 1779; May have been assigned to light dragoons or mounted infantry

Tayler, George; 62, Ensign, 2 March 1776

Tayler, William; 3/60, Col. Comdt., 17 September 1775, 17 September 1762; 24, Colonel, 15 January 1776; Major General; 29 September 1775; Lieutenant General; 29 August 1777; Also Taylor

Tayler, Wm. Tho.; 21, Captain, 26 February 1773; Retired 18 May 1780

Taylor, Alex. Fr.; 28, Ensign, 8 March 1782

Taylor, Charles; 43, Ensign, 4 April 1781; 43, Chaplain, 2 October 1775

Taylor, George; 62, Ensign, 2 March 1776; KIA Freeman's Farm, 19 September 1777

Taylor, I. Bladen; 31, Ensign, 6 June 1778; 45, Lieutenant, 23 March 1775; Also adjutant from 10 August 1778 until 11 September 1778

Taylor, Nathenial; 7, Quartermaster, 22 September 1781; From sergeant major

Taylor, Policarpus Wm.; 57, Ensign, 8 April 1777; 57, Lieutenant, 11 October 1779

Taylor, Thomas; 63, Ensign, 12 July 1777

Taylor, Thomas; 7, Quartermaster, 29 November 1777; Died 21 September 1780

Taylor, William; 28, Lieutenant, 14 May 1768; 28, Capt.- Lieut., 29 October 1776; 28, Captain, 29 October 1776; WIA White Plains, 28 October 1776

Taylor, William; 3, Quartermaster, 7 January 1778

Temple, Richard; 23, Captain, 15 August 1775, 23 May 1762; Major; 29 August 1777, Served with grenadiers, 20 September 1781

Templer, Dudley; 26, Lt. Colonel, 7 September 1768; Retired 26 October 1777

Terrott, Elias; 52, Ensign, 26 April 1775; 52, Lieutenant, 10 March 1777; Given name also Alexander

Tew, Francis; 17, Captain, 14 November 1771; Irish; Supported several spinster sisters; KIA Stony Point, 16 July 1779

Thomas, David; Dep. Paymaster General, Prior to 1783

Thomas, Edwin; 16, Surgeon, 14 May 1768; Also Edwyn; From mate; Resigned 18 August 1782

Thomas, Frederick; 1FG, Lieut. & Capt., 3 May 1773; 1FG, Capt. & Lt. Col., 26 December 1779; Not at Yorktown; Killed in duel 1783 near London by Col. Cosmo Gordon

Thomas, George; 15, Ensign, 28 August 1775; 15, Lieutenant, 13 May 1776; WIA Germantown, 4 October 1777; Retired 29 July 1778

Thomas, John; RA, 1st Lieut., 1 January 1771; Died at the Toricas on the Mississippi River, 17 June 1776

Thomas, John; 28, Ensign, 15 August 1775; 28, Lieutenant, 11 June 1778; Probably Deputy Paymaster General, 1781

Thomas, John; 28, Ensign, 9 June 1778

Thomas, Lewis; 52, Ensign, 8 May 1777; WIA Fort Clinton, 6 October 1777; Died 7 May 1778

Thomas, Robert; 26, Ensign, 2 March 1770; 26, Lieutenant, 31 October 1776;

Thomas, William; 5, Ensign, 31 March 1777; 5, Lieutenant, 19 February 1779; WIA Germantown, 4 October 1777

Thomasson, Thomas; 18, Surgeon, 18 February 1767; 18, Ensign, 14 June 1771; 18, Lieutenant, 25 July 1775; English, born 1743; First commissioned at age 23; Held commission as surgeon while a line officer; Resigned as surgeon 8 October 1779; Promoted to 96th Foot as captain, 1780

Thomlinson, Thomas; 4, Captain, 25 December 1770; 4, Major, 29 September 1779

Thompson, -; Adjutant, 1777; Town Adjutant of New York City

Thompson, Alexander; 21, 2nd Lieut., 26 February 1773; Died 15 August 1775

Thompson, Alexander; 31, Ensign, 10 November 1779

Thompson, Andrew; 80, Ensign, 23 January 1778; 80, Lieutenant, 13 September 1780

Thompson, Anthony; 15, Ensign, 21 May 1779

Thompson, Berkeley; 34, Lieutenant, 10 May 1776

Thompson, Edward; 26, Adjutant, 22 February 1769; 26, Lieutenant, 1 March 1770; 26, Capt.- Lieut., 2 December 1777; 26, Captain, 8 January 1778

Thompson, George; 43, Captain, 25 December 1770; 3/60, Major, 24 October 1781, 29 August 1777; Lt. Colonel; 19 February 1783, On leave for health reasons until 25 July 1783

Thompson, George; 40, Chaplain, date unknown; Commission date not published in Army Lists; Retired by December 178-

Thompson, Henry J.; RA, 1st Lieut., 7 July 1779

Thompson, John; 52, Lieutenant, 27 April 1768, 24 October 1761; 52, Captain, 18 June 1775; WIA Bunker Hill, 17 June 1775; Died 12 April 1778

Thompson, John; 69, Captain, 9 October 1775; Extra Ast. DQMG, 1779

Thompson, Joseph; 46, Ensign, 12 August 1778; 40, Lieutenant, 8 April 1781

Thompson, Richard; 37, Adjutant, 18 October 1778; 37, Ensign, 4 December 1778; 37, Lieutenant, 17 September 1780

Thompson, Thomas; 57, Adjutant, 28 December 1776; 57, Lieutenant, 21 May 1774; 57, Captain, 16 May 1779; Replaced "Murray" via purchase as adjutant

Thompson, Wm. Aug.; 57, Ensign, 28 November 1771; 57, Lieutenant, 26 November 1775

Thorne, Francis Peregrine; 4, Adjutant, 6 October 1775; 4, Lieutenant, 10 June 1771; 4, Capt.- Lieut., 10 March 1777; 4, Captain, 4 May 1777; Lexington night rider; Resigned as adjutant, 25 June 1777; WIA Danbury, CT, 27 April 1777 & Germantown, 4 October 1777

Thorne, William; 43, Lieutenant, 14 November 1770; 43, Capt.- Lieut., 10 March 1777; 43, Captain, 26 April 1779, 10 March 1777, Possibly WIA Yorktown, October 1781

Thornhill, Edward; 57, Ensign, 1 September 1771, 13 February 1762; 57, Lieutenant, 27 November 1775

Thoroton, Thomas; 2FG, Ensign, 20 October 1772; 2FG, Lieut. & Capt., 13 June 1776

Thwaites, George; 10, Adjutant, 14 December 1770; 10, Lieutenant, 27 March 1767; 10, Capt.- Lieut., 30 October 1777; 10, Captain, 29 June 1778; Resigned as captain and adjutant, 7 October 1778

Tickell, J.; Chaplain, 1778; Chaplain to the garrison at St. John's, Newfoundland

Tidswell, William; 54, Captain, 26 October 1775; Retired 2 September 1778

Tidy, John; 26, Ensign, 13 October 1780

Tidy, Thomas Holmes; 26, Chaplain, 8 March 1781

Timms, Richard; 9, Ensign, 28 May 1781

Timpson, Robert; 22, Captain, 20 May 1773; Irish, born 1737; Retired 1 May 1782

Tingling, George; 57, Ensign, 14 July 1780

Tingling, Isaac; 20, Ensign, 1 June 1778

Tinker, Jeremiah; 33, Captain, 23 November 1768; English, born 1736; First commissioned at age 19; Listed as retired 25 December 1776; ADC to Gen. Cornwallis 28 January 1777

Tinling, William; 29, Ensign, 31 August 1780

Titford, Isaac; 1/60, Surgeon, 2 December 1782; Also Telford or Tetford; From Hosp. mate; To half pay 1783; Died 3 April 1834

Titler, Patrick; 57, Ensign, 24 February 1775; 57, Lieutenant, 8 May 1777; Also Tytler

Todd, William; 43, Lieutenant, 3 September 1775; 43, Captain, 20 March 1778

Tone, Jonathan; 22, Ensign, 6 December 1778; 22, Lieutenant, 6 September 1781; Irish, born 1754; Ensigncy date also given as 20 September 1778

Tonge, John Wickenworth; 22, Ensign, 20 July 1783; From Royal Fencible Americans

Toosey, Finch; 37, Lieutenant, 14 January 1775; 37, Capt.- Lieut., 20 October 1777; Lost at sea, 12 August 1778

Toosey, Philip; 37, Chaplain, 9 May 1766

Torpichen, James, Lord; 21, 2nd Lieut., 16 August 1776; 62, Lieutenant, 6 January 1779; 24, Captain, 20 June 1781

Torre, Henry; 29, Ensign, 2 March 1780

Torriano, Charles; 20, Quartermaster, 1 December 1779; 20, Lieutenant, 14 November 1775

Torriano, George; 64, Ensign, 14 March 1775; 64, Lieutenant, 28 November 1776; 64, Capt.- Lieut., 12 February 1783; Scottish, born 1759; First commissioned at age 16; WIA Brandywine, 11 September 1777; Possibly WIA Charleston, April 1780

Tovey, John; 70, Adjutant, 10 March 1778; 70, Lieutenant, 13 October 1778

Towell, John; 27, Lieutenant, 16 July 1774; 27, Captain, 14 January 1777

Townshend, Gregory; Assistant Commissary, 1778

Townshend, Hon. Charles; 4, Ensign, 24 January 1777; 43, Lieutenant, 20 March 1778; 45, Captain, 11 August 1778

Tozer, Aaran; 26, Ensign, 18 May 1780

Trail, John; 76, Lieutenant, 12 January 1778

Traille, Peter; RA, Captain, 1 January 1771; Major; 7 June 1782

Trapaud, Cyrus; 52, Colonel, 14 May 1778

Travers, Jonas; 55, Ensign, 10 March 1781

Treby, John; 43, Captain, 15 August 1775, 15 September 1758; Major; 23 July 1772, Died possibly in Rhode Island, 9 March 1777

Trelawney, Charles; 2FG, Ensign, 4 March 1773; 2FG, Lieut. & Capt., 17 January 1777; Adjutant of the 2nd Bn. of the Brigade of Guards

Trelawney, Henry; 2FG, Capt. & Lt. Col., 21 August 1762; 2FG, 1st Major, 5 May 1780; Colonel, 29 August 1777; Cmd. 1st Bn. Guards;WIA & POW Monmouth, 28 June 1778

Trench, Nich. Power; 37, Lieutenant, 15 August 1775

Trevor, James Taylor; 55, Captain, 16 July 1774, 25 May 1772, Irish, born 1755; First commissioned at age 12; Killed in duel 4 November 1777 with Ens. Power of same regiment; Mother was Lady Sarah Trevor

Trewren, Thomas; 16 LD, Captain, 2 August 1775

Treydal, -; 10, Ensign, 18 November 1776

Trist, Nicholas; 18, Ensign, 26 December 1770; 18, Lieutenant, 20 April 1775; Resigned 1775; Possibly remained in America

Trotter, Thomas; RA, 2nd Lieut., 1 January 1771

Troughton, William; 82, Ensign, 24 January 1782

Trumbull, -; 57, Surgeon, 1 March 1781

Tryon, William; 1FG, Capt. & Lt. Col., 30 September 1758; Tryon, William; 1FG, Major, 8 August 1775; 70, Colonel, 14 May 1778; Am., Major General, 1 January 1776, 29 August 1777, Governor of New York

Tucker, Mart. Bladen; 38, Ensign, 11 September 1779
Tucker, Thomas; 17 LD, Cornet, 10 April 1779;
Tuckey, Timothy; 23, 2nd Lieut., 8 December 1777; 23, 1st Lieut., 30 December 1778; Died 4 June 1783
Tuffie, John; 44, Quartermaster, 4 October 1776
Tulliken, James; 14, Ensign, 15 August 1775; 14, Lieutenant, 7 August 1777
Turnbull, Adam; 57, Surgeon, 1 March 1781; From mate; Retired 25 June 1798; Died Midcalder, 6 February 1821
Turnbull, Alexander; 53, Chaplain, 8 December 1780
Turnbull, George; 21, 2nd Lieut., 3 May 1776; KIA Freeman's Farm, 19 September 1777
Turner, George; 29, Chaplain, 17 March 1774
Turner, Thomas; 47, Adjutant, 28 May 1768; 47, Ensign, 17 December 1772; 47, Lieutenant, 22 November 1775
Twentyman, Samuel; 18, Ensign, 25 July 1775; English, born 1755; First commissioned at age 20
Twisleton, Thomas; 3FG, Capt. & Lt. Col, 18 March 1767; Colonel, 29 August 1777
Twiss, William; RE, Eng. extra. & Cpt.-Lt., 18 December 1778; In America from 1777-1783; Served with Burgoyne in Canada
Twistleton, Sir. W. Bt.; 7, Lieutenant, 14 October 1778
Tydd, Thomas; 40, Ensign, 24 November 1775
Tyler, Patrick; 80, Capt.- Lieut., 24 January 1778; 80, Captain, 24 January 1778
Underwood, Caleb; 10, Ensign, 2 June 1777; 7, Lieutenant, 22 May 1778
Uniake, Norman; 40, Lieutenant, 12 December 1774; Retired 16 January 1777
Unwin, Samuel; Hosp., Mate, Prior to 1783; Stationed at Halifax, 1783
Upton, Henry; 6, Ensign, 29 May 1777
Urmston, Edward; 65, Colonel, 10 November 1770; Lieutenant General; 25 May 1772
Urquhart, -; 40, Quartermaster, 2 February 1782
Urquhart, James; 14, Capt.- Lieut., 22 December 1772; 14, Captain, 22 November 1775
Usher, Thomas; 16, Lieutenant, 20 November 1765; 16, Capt.- Lieut., 22 November 1775;
Vallancy, Charles; 16, Ensign, 24 November 1775; Promoted to lieutenant in 33rd Foot, 18 October 1778
Vallancy, Geo. Prest.; 62, Adjutant, 12 October 1777; 62, Lieutenant, 1 September 1771; 62, Capt.- Lieut., 18 August 1778; 62, Captain, 18 August 1778; Asst. Depty. Quartermaster General, 1781

Vallancy, Rupert Preston; 55, Quartermaster, 18 January 1770; 55, Lieutenant, 31 August 1774; Irish, born 1757; First commissioned at age 16; Died of fever, prior to 17 January 1779

Van Braam, Jacob; 3/60, Captain, 31 August 1775, 19 September 1761; 3/60, Major, 14 June 1777; In cmd. at St. Augustine, 1777 to 1778

Vaniper, Marin; 4/60, Ensign, 4 October 1775; 1/60, Lieutenant, 11 December 1780; Also Vanipur

Vans, David; 52, Ensign, 18 June 1775; From Royal Artillery volunteer; Died 24 November 1775

Vatass, John; 10, Captain, 5 May 1760; 10, Major, 13 January 1776; Resigned 30 October 1777

Vaudeleur, Walter; 16, Ensign, 18 March 1782

Vaughan, Gawen; 29, Lieutenant, 26 December 1775

Vaughan, Gwynne; 10, Ensign, 31 January 1778

Vaughan, Hon. John; 46, Colonel, 11 May 1775, 25 May 1772; Am., Major General, 1 January 1776, 29 August 1777, WIA Kip's Bay, 15 September 1776

Vaughan, John; 40, Ensign, 7 March 1780; 46, Lieutenant, 1 January 1781, 30 July 1780

Vaughan, William; 63, Ensign, 21 January 1778

Vaughn, Thomas Leonard; RA, 1st Lieut., 8 March 1776; Captured aboard the "Delaware;" KIA Monmouth, 28 June 1778

Vaumorel, Philip de; 57, Ensign, 16 February 1780

Vavasour, Ebenezer; 49, Lieutenant, 17 September 1773

Veale, Richard; Hosp., Physician, 28 September 1775; Also Veal; Previously surgeon 45th Foot; Retired to half pay, c1787; Died 11 January 1788

Veal, Richard; 26, Ensign, 13 June 1778; From volunteer in 23d Foot at Danbury

Veitch, John; 80, Lieutenant, 28 January 1778

Vennel, Henry; 22, Quartermaster, 1 February 1782; English, born 1749; Enlisted 1769 as private; Promoted corporal, 1778; Sergeant 1779

Venters, Charles; 37, Quartermaster, 2 June 1777; 37, Ensign, 23 March 1778; 37, Lieutenant, 29 July 1780

Verchild, James; 24, Captain, 14 November 1775

Verner, Thomas; 10, Lieutenant, 6 May 1772; DOW Bunker Hill, 29 June 1775

Vigers, Nich. Aylward; 29, Captain, 27 February 1776

Vignoles, Charles; 43, Ensign, 24 November 1775; 43, Lieutenant, 30 May 1780

Vincent, Dormer; 33, Ensign, 18 September 1780; 22, Lieutenant, 2 February 1782; English, born 1761

Vincent, George; 9, Lieutenant, 31 May 1773; 9, Capt.- Lieut., 28 September 1781

Vincent, Richard; 16, Captain, 14 August 1765

Vincent, William; 19, Lieutenant, 12 November 1778

Von Braam, Jacob; 3/60, Major, 14 June 1777; Retired 21 October 1779

Waddell, James; 9, Ensign, 4 March 1776

Waddle, Robert; 57, Lieutenant, 9 October 1775

Wade, George; 9, Ensign, 3 March 1776

Wade, George; 16 LD, Cornet, 6 November 1777

Wade, John; RE, Eng. extra. & Cpt.-Lt., 26 March 1779; In America from 1776-1777; Possibly WIA Iron Hill, DE, 3 September 1777

Wade, John; RA, 2nd Lieut., 3 November 1780

Wade, Nicholas; 49, Captain, 23 January 1773, 6 May 1769

Wade, Nicholas; 27, Major, 13 October 1778; ADC to Gen. Massey, 7 June 1776; WIA Brandywine, 11 September 1777; Died 3 December 1779

Wade, William; 38, Lieutenant, 30 April 1771

Vavasour, Ebenezer; 27, Capt.- Lieut., 15 August 1779

Wade, William; 38, Captain, 3 May 1776; Retired 10 October

Wadman, Arthur; 26, Lieutenant, 29 November 1760; 26, Capt.- Lieut., 21 February 1776; 26, Captain, 7 October 1777

Walcott, William; 5, Lt. Colonel, 31 January 1774; WIA White Plains 28 October 1776; DOW Germantown 6 October 1777

Waldron, Arthur; 57, Ensign, 16 May 1779; Also Weldron

Waldron, Francis; 57, Captain, 25 November 1775, 25 May 1772

Walker, Alexander; 26, Ensign, 14 August 1775; 26, Lieutenant, 2 December 1777

Walker, Charles; RA, 2nd Lieut., 4 March 1776; Died St. Kitts or St. Lucia, August 1779; Had served at Germantown, Whitemarsh and Monmouth in Downman's Coy.

Walker, John; 7, Chaplain, 5 May 1769

Walker, John; 64, Ensign, 24 October 1781; English, born 1763; First commissioned at age 19

Walker, Robert; 15, Ensign, 13 May 1776; 7, Lieutenant, 20 April 1778

Walker, Thomas; Hosp., Mate, Prior to 1783; Stationed at New York, 1783

Walker, William; 74, Ensign, 24 December 1777

Walker, William H.; RA, 1st Lieut., 27 January 1781

Walkingshaw, James; 49, Captain, 14 March 1772; Retired 11 August 1778

Walkinshaw, William; 2/71, Lieutenant, 26 August 1776, 20 October 1761

Wall, John; 45, Ensign, 1 March 1773; 45, Lieutenant, 22 November 1775; Married 30 November 1777

Wallace, Hill; 14, Ensign, 9 April 1771, 20 March 1771; 14, Lieutenant, 15 December 1773; 14, Capt.- Lieut., 24 October 1776; WIA Dumfries, VA, 23 July 1776

Wallace, Hugh; 22, Ensign, 29 May 1776; 22, Lieutenant, 11 February 1779; Also Wallas; Resigned 4 December 1782

Wallace, John; 64, Ensign, 28 November 1776; 22, Lieutenant, 28 July 1779, 2 November 1778, Irish, born 1760

Wallace, Sir Thomas Bt.; 82, Lieutenant, 8 January 1778; 44, Captain, 9 September 1779

Wallace, William; 83, Captain, 13 February 1783

Wallace, William Oxford; RA, 2nd Lieut., 1 January 1771; KIA or DOW Georgia, 15 May 1780

Wallis, Robert; 40, Lieutenant, 12 May 1779, 7 May 1762

Wallis, Wm. Ogle; 23, 2nd Lieut., 9 April 1776; 23, 1st Lieut., 24 April 1778; Also Wallace

Walpole, -; 23, 2nd Lieut., 12 August 1780

Walsh, Anthony; 45, Ensign, 24 September 1777; 45, Lieutenant, 16 June 1780

Walsh, Joseph; 9, Lieutenant, 1 March 1776, 17 February 1763

Walsh, Luke; 3/60, Ensign, 21 April 1779; 3/60, Lieutenant, 2 October 1781

Walsh, Peter; 1/60, Surgeon, 29 April 1767; Also Welch; From mate; Apothecary under Gen. Dalling, 1 December 1782; To half pay 25 December 1783; Died 24 May 1784

Walsh, Stephen; Chaplain, date unknown; Chaplain to the garrison at St. John's; Died prior to December 1775

Walton, James; 57, Ensign, 8 May 1777; 57, Lieutenant, 16 May 1779

Warburton, William; 31, Ensign, 6 March 1776; 31, Lieutenant, 10 December 1779

Ward, Bernard Geo.; 47, Lieutenant, 15 August 1775

Ward, Charles; 3/60, Adjutant, 8 January 1781; 3/60, Lieutenant, 16 March 1779; WIA and left behind at Pensacola, 8 May 1781

Warde, George; 33, Quartermaster, 22 October 1778; 33, Adjutant, 14 March 1774; 33, Ensign, 28 August 1775; 33, Lieutenant, 28 August 1776; Irish, born 1738; First commissioned at age 35

Wardlow, -; 63, Ensign, 18 September 1780

Wardrop, Andrew; 17, Surgeon, 15 July 1772; Purchased commission; Retired 31 January 1777

Wareham, Joseph; 16 LD, Cornet, 29 December 1775

Waring, Samuel; 27, Captain, 3 May 1775

Warner, John; 64, Ensign, 26 February 1778; 64, Lieutenant, 19 February 1781

Warner, Thomas; 27, Ensign, 20 March 1779

Warr, David de; 1/71, Lieutenant, 5 November 1780

Warren, John; 55, Ensign, 17 September 1773; 55, Lieutenant, 28 September 1775; 55, Capt.- Lieut., 25 September 1780; Also Waring; Irish, born 1758; First commissioned at age 15; WIA & POW La Vigie, 18 December 1778

Warsfeld, William; 43, Ensign, 25 December 1775; Ensigncy also given as 12 December 1775

Watkins, George; 3FG, Ensign, 7 June 1773; 3FG, Lieut. & Capt., 1 September 1777; Left the Guards in 1781

Watkins, George; 53, Chaplain, 31 January 1756

Watson, Andrew; 27, Captain, 15 August 1775, 13 October 1762

Watson, Andrew; 57, Ensign, 22 March 1780

Watson, George; 23, Adjutant, 25 October 1778; 23, 2nd Lieut., 16 March 1781; From sergeant major

Watson, James; 52, Lieutenant, 15 August 1775, 26 October 1760; 9

Watson, James; Hosp., Sprnmy. Mate, Prior to 1783; Stationed at New York, 1783

Watson, John; 65, Quartermaster, 27 March 1770; 65, Lieutenant, 16 August 1768; 65, Capt.- Lieut., 22 November 1775; 65, Captain, 22 November 1775

Watson, John; 28, Ensign, 3 January 1778; 28, Lieutenant, 2 August 1780; From volunteer; Commission revoked, 12 June 1778?

Watson, John; 63, Ensign, 13 April 1778

Watson, John; Hosp., Apothecary, 12 October 1780; From mate; Stationed at New York, 1783; Retired 1784; Died Edinburgh, 29 May 1795

Watson, John W. T.; 3FG, Lieut. & Capt., 28 April 1773; 3FG, Capt. & Lt. Col., 20 November 1778; Cmd. Gds. in New York; Not at Yorktown; Cmd. Prov. Lt. Inf.; ADC Clinton

Watson, Jonas; 65, Lieutenant, 28 February 1766; 65, Captain, 18 June 1775

Watson, Tho. Samwell; 15, Ensign, 30 July 1778

Watson, William; 63, Ensign, 30 October 1779

Watts, Samuel; 17 LD, Cornet, 10 May 1776; Resigned 14 March 1778, for value of cornetcy

Watts, Stephen; 1/84, Capt.- Lieut., 14 June 1775; 8, Captain, 8 March 1778; American; Lost leg in F&I War; Also held a provincial commission

Watts, Thomas; 2/71, Lieutenant, 2 August 1780

Waugh, David; 83, Ensign, 29 January 1783

Waugh, Gilbert; 57, Captain, 18 September 1779

Waugh, Gilbert; 2/71, Ensign, 4 December 1775; 2/71, Lieutenant, 3 August 1778

Waugh, Gilbert; 35, Ensign, 27 December 1775; Killed in a duel

Waugh, Robert; 57, Ensign, 31 December 1777

Waugh, Robert; 43, Surgeon, 1 March 1781; Resigned 28 February 1792; Recommissioned 93th Foot, 1793; Died Dover, 4 February 1819

Wayet, Tho. Heardson; 31, Chaplain, 27 May 1780

Webb, James; 8, Captain, 2 November 1755; Major; 23 July 1772, Irish, born 1731; Captaincy also given as 1753; Also Dpty. Commissary of Musters, May 1775; First commissioned at age 13

Webb, Richmond; 40, Lieutenant, 16 August 1770; Retired 14 March 1777

Webber, Rich. Brook; 16, Ensign, 13 April 1778

Webster, James; 33, Lt. Colonel, 9 April 1774; Colonel, 17 November 1780; Scottish, born 1741; First commissioned at age 17; WIA Camden, 16 August 1780; DOW Guilford CH, 23 March 1781

Webster, John; 4, Captain, 5 May 1769

Weir, Daniel; Commissary General of Stores & Provisions, 1776; Also Wier; Died November 1781; Aged 47

Weir, John; 43, Ensign, 21 March 1775; 43, Lieutenant, 19 September 1775; WIA Brooklyn, 27 August 1776 & Germantown, 4 October 1777

Weir, John; Hosp., Surgeon, 1 January 1776, 11 February 1775, From mate; From 3rd Drag. Grds.; Stationed at New York, 1783; To Jamaica, 9 October 1784; First director of the Army Medical Department; M.D. (hon.) Kings College, Abd., 1794; Died London, 9 April 1819

Weir, Launcelot; 62, Ensign, 20 September 1777; 62, Lieutenant, 21 August 1781

Welch, Thomas; 23, 1st Lieut., 18 November 1768, 3 September 1761, Also Walsh or Welsh

Welch, Thomas; 17, Capt.- Lieut., 28 August 1775; 17, Captain, 28 August 1775; ADC to Gen. Richard Prescott, 8 October 1776

Weld, Richard; 3, Lieutenant, 1 June 1778

Weldon, Thomas; 9, Ensign, 1 March 1776

Wells, John; 6, Captain, 26 November 1773

Wells, Jonathan; 80, Quartermaster, 17 January 1778

Wells, Mathew; 10, Ensign, 22 November 1775

Wells, Thomas; 46, Ensign, 22 June 1781

Wells, Thomas; 70, Ensign, 23 September 1780

Wellwood, Robert; 82, Adjutant, 3 January 1778; 82, Lieutenant, 7 January 1778

Welsh, Piers; 29, Lieutenant, 17 March 1774

Wemyss, Francis; 20, Captain, 1 March 1776, 25 May 1772, WIA Freeman's Farm, 19 September 1777

Wemyss, James; 40, Captain, 14 March 1771; 63, Major, 10 August 1778; ADC to Gen. Robertson, 20 April 1777; WIA Brandywine, 11 September 1777 & near Camden, 9 November 1780; Cmd. Queen's Rangers, Summer 1777

Wemyss, James; 31, Ensign, 10 September 1776

Wemyss, James; 65, Ensign, 16 March 1776

Wemyss, John; 47, Ensign, 8 September 1780

Wemyss, John; 2/42, Lieutenant, 24 March 1780

Wemyss, William; 76, Ensign, 27 December 1777; 76, Lieutenant, 6 September 1780; WIA Green Springs VA, 6 July 1781

Wesketh, Robert; 14, Ensign, 27 February 1775

West, Gregory; Hosp., Apothecary, 23 October 1782; Stationed at Halifax, 1783; To half pay 11 February 1784; M.D. Kings Coll, Abd.1786; Died 9 December 1821

West, James; 1/42, Lieutenant, 19 May 1780; To 79th Foot as captain-lieutenant

West, John; 4, Captain, 25 September 1771; WIA Bunker Hill; At Lexington and Concord

West, Tho. Milborne; 47, Ensign, 15 May 1772

West, Malbourne; 2/84, Ensign, 1 July 1783

West, William; 4, Ensign, 7 January 1776; 4, Lieutenant, 2 December 1777; WIA near Philadelphia, December 1777

West, William Augustus; 2FG, Ensign, 3 June 1774; 2FG, Lieut. & Capt., 21 November 1777; Viscount Cantilupe, later Earl of Delaware; Died 1783 in Lisbon

Westenra, Peter; 15, Ensign, 25 November 1776

Westenra, Thomas; 15, Lieutenant, 29 July 1778; KIA Brimstone Hill, St. Kitts, January or February 1782

Westropp, Richard; 9, Lieutenant, 1 January 1774; KIA Ft. Ann, 9 July 1777

Westroppe, John; 65, Adjutant, 13 October 1772; 65, Ensign, 26 January 1768; 65, Lieutenant, 3 June 1774; 5, Captain, 24 May 1776 Westroppe, John;, 4

Wetherall, Fred. Aug.; 17, Ensign, 23 August 1775; 17, Lieutenant, 27 August 1776

Wey, William; 27, Ensign, 5 July 1780

Wheat, Clifron; 20, Lieutenant, 9 December 1775; 44, Captain, 7 May 1782

Wheeler, Paliser; 35, Ensign, 31 January 1774; 35, Lieutenant, 22 November 1775; 35, Captain, 28 November 1778; Irish; Attended drinking parties with Maj. Drewe

Wheeler, Richard; 40, Ensign, 5 October 1777, 25 January 1777

Wheeler, Thomas; 55, Lieutenant, 15 January 1779

Wheeler, Thomas Lucas; 70, Ensign, 23 August 1779

Wheldale, Thomas; RE, Pract. eng. & 2nd Lt., 17 January 1776; In America from 1779-1781; Served in West Indies

Whiston, William; 6, Lieutenant, 25 May 1772

White, Benjamin; 22, Lieutenant, 4 June 1777; Irish, born 1755; From 27th Foot; WIA Charleston, May 1780

White, Fredrick C.; 64, Ensign, 19 February 1781; 16, Lieutenant, 30 December 1781

White, John; 18, Ensign, 25 April 1776; English, born 1760; First commissioned at age 15

White, Joseph; 17 LD, Cornet, 25 November 1780

White, William: 2/42, Ensign, 25 March 1780

Whitelocke, Bulstrode; 26, Ensign, 31 October 1776; 26, Lieutenant, 30 July 1779

Whiteman, James; 22, Mate, date unknown; 22, Surgeon, 21 February 1778; Also Wightman; Irish, born 1754; To 76th Foot, 25 December 1787; Died c. 1798

Whitty, Edward; 47, Chaplain, 20 May 1767

Whitty, Irvine; 47, Chaplain, 9 September 1775

Whitworth, Charles; 1FG, Lieut. & Capt., 1 April 1776; Transferred to the 104th Foot in 1783

Wickham, Benjamin; 2/60, Lieutenant, 3 June 1772, 26 September 1762; 2/60, Captain, 20 May 1778; At Savannah

Wigglesworth, John; 49, Adjutant, 13 May 1776; 49, Ensign, 9 August 1775; 49, Lieutenant, 9 October 1778; Ensigncy also given as 29 October 1776

Wight, John; 53, Captain, 13 April 1768; Also White or Wright; DOW Stillwater, 8 October 1777

Wilcocks, Andrew; 3/60, Ensign, 2 October 1781

Wilcocks, Joshua; 62, Lieutenant, 2 March 1776

Wild, Henry; 53, Ensign, 24 May 1775; 53, Lieutenant, 6 April 1778; Also Wills

Wilkie, Thomas; 30, Lieutenant, 26 December 1770; Died South Carolina, September or October 1781

Wilkington, John; 64, Ensign, 15 March 1783;

Wilkins, John; 18, Lt. Colonel, 13 June 1765; English, born 1726; First commissioned at age 20

Wilkinson, Aaron; 52, Quartermaster, 21 February 1772; Retired 28 May 1776

Wilkinson, Edward; RA, 2nd Lieut., 1 January 1771

Wilkinson, John; 64, Captain, 30 September 1781; Married 14 August 1782; Retired 23 June 1782

Wilkinson, John; 23, 2nd Lieut., 11 April 1775; 23, 1st Lieut., 21 August 1776

Wilkinson, John; 43, Lieutenant, 1 February 1781

Wilkinson, John; 54, Ensign, 7 February 1779

Wilkinson, Robert; 17, Ensign, 2 May 1782

Wilkinson, Thomas; 43, Ensign, 2 April 1772; 43, Lieutenant, 10 July 1775; Resigned 7 August 1775

Wilkinson, Wilfred; 30, Ensign, 26 January 1781; 30, Captain, 17 November 1780

Wilkinson, William; 62, Lieutenant, 1 May 1775; Acting asst. engineer for the Saratoga Campaign; Served with Fraser's Advanced Corps

Wilkinson, William; 23, 2nd Lieut., 22 April 1777

Willcock, Archibald; 40, Ensign, 27 April 1781; KIA Groton, CT, 6 September 1781

Willcox, John; 40, Ensign, 15 October 1780

Williams, Arthur; 52, Major, 20 April 1771; KIA or DOW Bunker Hill, 17 June 1775

Williams, Charles; 29, Lieutenant, 22 April 1774; 29, Captain, 18 January 1781; WIA Bemis Heights, 7 October 1777

Williams, Charles; 24, Lieutenant, 16 July 1774

Williams, Edward; RA, Capt.- Lieut., 1 August 1767; RA, Captain, 15 February 1778, 25 May 1772, Extra Maj. of Bde., 1777; WIA and POW Stillwater,12

Williams, Geo. Hanbury; 8, Ensign, 26 April 1776

Williams, George; 62, Ensign, 20 September 1777

Williams, Grifith; RA, Captain, 22 February 1760; Major; 17 February 1776; POW Bemis Heights, 7 October 1777

Williams, Henry; 6, Ensign, 15 August 1775; 6, Lieutenant, 16 April 1777

Williams, Henry; 46, Chaplain, 31 May 1774

Williams, Rice; FG, Quartermaster, date unknown; Died 6 August 1777

Williams, Richard; 23, 1st Lieut., 13 May 1773; Retired 20 May 1776

Williams, Seth; 89, Lieutenant, 19 October 1779; Native of Taunton, MA: From private, Loyal American Associators, 1775; Captain, Loyal Rhode Islanders, 1777

Williams, Thomas; 35, Lieutenant, 20 October 1774; 35, Capt.- Lieut., 4 June 1779; WIA LaVigie, December 1778

Williams, Wm. Fred. Hanbury; 17, Ensign, 12 July 1777; 17, Lieutenant, 10 September 1778

Williamson, -; Quartermaster, 17 May 1776; From sergeant; For 1st Gren. Bn.

Williamson, Adam; 18, Lt. Colonel, 9 December 1775; English, born 1735; First commissioned at age 17; Did not serve in America

Williamson, George; 70, Lieutenant, 8 February 1777

Williamson, Henry; 57, Ensign, 26 November 1775, 22 September 1775; 57, Lieutenant, 12 December 1777

Williamson, John; 29, Ensign, 28 December 1775

Williamson, Thomas; 52, Lieutenant, 21 February 1772; 52, Capt.- Lieut., 29 May 1776; 52, Captain, 28 August 1776; Also Williams; KIA Princeton, 3 January 1777, while on detached duty with flank company recruits

Willington, Charles; 44, Captain, 1 September 1771, 13 February 1762, Irish, born 1732; First commissioned at age 22; Retired 23 May 1776

Willington, Edward Pearce; 26, Ensign, 16 May 1766, 13 January 1763; 26, Lieutenant, 19 June 1775

Willington, Edward Pearce; 1/71, Lieutenant, 16 October 1779

Willington, James; 57, Lieutenant, 4 April 1765, 12 January 1760; 57, Capt.- Lieut., 26 November 1775; 58, Captain, 18 August 1778; Also John Wallington; ADC to Gen. Tryon, 1778

Willington, John; 3, Ensign, 9 December 1780

Willington, John; 37, Ensign, 14 January 1775

Willis, Cecil; 38, Chaplain, 20 December 1775

Willis, Samuel; 2/60, Ensign, 10 August 1777; From sergeant; With Gen. Robertson in New York in 1780

Willis, Thomas; 45, Lieutenant, 1 May 1773

Willoe, Samuel; 8, Lieutenant, 23 November 1768; 8, Captain, 6 May 1777; Irish, born 1743; First commissioned at age 18

Wills, Henry; 53, Ensign, 24 May 1775; 53, Lieutenant, 5 October 1779; Also Wild

Wills, Thomas; 23, Captain, 10 October 1776; DOW & POW Monmouth, 30 July 1778

Wills, William; 23, 2nd Lieut., 15 August 1775; 23, 1st Lieut., 28 August 1776

Wilmer, Richard; 53, Ensign, 5 October 1779

Wilmot, Simon; 16 LD, Lieutenant, 30 October 1775

Wilmot, Val. Henry; 26, Ensign, 5 June 1777

Wilmott, Joseph; 8, Ensign, 12 April 1776; 8, Lieutenant, 6 January 1780

Wilson, -; 14, Ensign, 24 November 1775

Wilson, Alexander; 5, Ensign, 24 November 1775; 5, Lieutenant, 6 May 1776

Wilson, David; 27, Quartermaster, 1 September 1775; Died 14 August 1779

Wilson, Edward; 9, Ensign, 21 September 1781

Wilson, George; RA, 2nd Lieut., 15 March 1771; RA, 1st Lieut., 7 July 1779; Court martialed and reprimanded for leaving post, 6 April 1778

Wilson, James; 49, Captain, 16 July 1774

Wilson, James; 55, Ensign, 15 August 1775; 55, Lieutenant, 26 April 1777; Retired 20 April 1778

Wilson, James; 23, 2nd Lieut., 10 February 1776; Retired 7 August 1778

Wilson, James; RA, 2nd Lieut., 26 March 1773

Wilson, John; 23, 2nd Lieut., 6 January 1773

Wilson, John; 28, Lieutenant, 18 February 1769; 28, Capt.- Lieut., 22 December 1776; 28, Captain, 19 August 1778

Wilson, John; 59, Captain, 17 December 1762, 12 January 1761

Wilson, John; 1/71, Ensign, 3 August 1778; Wilson, John, 1/71, Lieutenant, 20 September 1779; From volunteer; POW Boston, 19 June 1776; Appointed asst. engineer, 25 May 1778; WIA Charleston, prior to 12 May 1780

Wilson, John; 23, 1st Lieut., 9 February 1776

Wilson, John; 22, Chaplain, 1 May 1775; Resigned 10 February 1780

Wilson, Ralph; RA, 1st Lieut., 1 January 1771; RA, Capt.- Lieut., 1 July 1779; WIA Stono Ferry, SC 20 June 1779

Wilson, Robert; 49, Capt.- Lieut., 9 August 1775; 49, Captain, 22 November 1775; Retired 6 August 1778

Wilson, Robert; FG, Adjutant, 25 November 1776; From Bde of Guards sergeant major; Adj. 1st Bn. of Guards Bde; Recommended for a commission in the invalids on his return to England

Wilson, Sir Tho. Spencer Bt.; 50, Colonel, 30 April 1777; Am., Major General, 29 August 1777; English, 1727-1798; MP Sussex, 1774-1780; In America, 1777-1779

Wilson, Thomas; 59, Lieutenant, 13 February 1762

Wilson, Thomas John; 46, Ensign, 23 August 1775; 46, Lieutenant, 5 April 1777; Died at sea, probably 2 July 1782

Wilsone, Henry P.; 83, Lieutenant, 3 February 1778

Winchelsea, George, Earl of ; 87, Major, 4 October 1779; Lt. Colonel; 17 January 1780, Served with 1st Bn. Gren. 1780

Winchester, Robert Wm.; 20, Captain, 9 December 1775

Wingfield, Halton; 5, Ensign, 4 December 1778

Wingrove, Anthony; 34, Ensign, 16 December 1775; 34, Lieutenant, 1 June 1777

Winslow, John; Deputy Commissary of Prisoners, 1781

Winstanley, Robert; 27, Ensign, 7 February 1778

Winter, John; 30, Captain, 25 May 1772

Wiseman, James; 53, Captain, 2 August 1775

Winterton, John; 38, Ensign, 8 February 1779

Winthroppe, Stephen; 65, Lieutenant, 13 January 1768, 28 October 1760; 65, Capt.- Lieut., 16 August 1775; 65, Captain, 16 August 1775

Wintour, Edward; 49, Ensign, 29 October 1776

Wintringham, Thos.; 16, Ensign, 22 September 1773

Wogan, James; 45, Ensign, 30 September 1776

Wogan, Samuel; 22, Ensign, 7 September 1778; 44, Lieutenant, 25 January 1779; First name also listed inaccurately as James; Did not serve in America with the 22nd Foot

Wolfe, Charles B.; 27, Ensign, 28 September 1775; 64, Lieutenant, 21 September 1777; 52, Lieutenant, 2 December 1777

Wolfe, William; 40, Captain, 5 March 1775; KIA Paoli, 21 September 1777

Wolseley, Arthur St. George; 69, Ensign, 4 October 1780

Wood, Alexander; 31, Ensign, 22 February 1775; 31, Lieutenant, 4 or 13 September 1777

Wood, Charles; RA, Capt.- Lieut., 1 January 1771

Wood, George; 27, Lieutenant, 24 May 1775

Wood, James; 74, Surgeon, 19 December 1777; To half pay, 25 May 1784; To full pay as "Medical Practitioner in Edinburgh," 31 August 1804 to 1806; Died December 1826

Wood, James; 74, Ensign, 20 January 1779

Wood, Mathew; 64, Ensign, 23 November 1778; 64, Lieutenant, 29 December 1781; From volunteer; Asst. Judge Advocate, 1781

Wood, Richard; Hosp., Surgeon, 30 October 1779; To the Garrison at Providence, RI; Date also given as 24 September 1779

Wood, Robert; 23, 1st Lieut., 15 August 1775, 27 January 1761, Died at New York or Punk Hill, NJ, 9 or 16 March 1777

Wood, Thomas; 9, Chaplain, 12 April 1777

Wood, Vincent; Hosp., Apothecary, 1 January 1776; Hosp., Surgeon, 7 May 1782; From 15th Drag.; Retired 1798; Died 10 September 1814

Wood, William; 34, Quartermaster, 19 February 1778; 34, Lieutenant, 25 February 1767; 34, Captain, 22 October 1779

Wood, William; 23, 1st Lieut., 8 February 1773; 45, Captain, 23 February 1776

Wood, William; 15, Ensign, 24 May 1781

Wood, William; Hosp., Mate, date unknown; Hosp., Surgeon, 26 November 1779; At Providence, R.I., 1779; Died c. 1804

Woodford, John; 1 FG, Capt. & Lt. Col., 21 February 1776
Woodley, William; 17 LD, Cornet, 31 December 1781
Woods, Charles; RA, Captain, 7 July 1779, 25 May 1772
Woods, Thomas; 49, Ensign, 31 August 1774; 49, Lieutenant, 29 October 1776
Woods, William; 1/84, Ensign, 14 June 1776; Also Wood
Woodward, Den. Mil.; 59, Lieutenant, 28 May 1770
Wools, Tho. Appleford; 14, Adjutant, 6 December 1776; 14, Ensign, 18 June 1773; 14, Lieutenant, 22 November 1775
Woolseley, I. Rogerson; 20, Ensign, 28 June 1777
Woolseley, James; 9, Ensign, 3 July 1777
Worsfold, Wiliam; 43, Ensign, 23 May 1776; Also Warsfold or Westmacott; Died 25 June 1783
Worsley, James; 44, Ensign, 9 September 1779
Wray, William; 19, Lieutenant, 1 June 1778
Wright, Charles; 64, Ensign, 3 May 1776; 52, Lieutenant, 21 November 1777; 64, Lieutenant, 2 December 1778
Wright, James; 4/60, Quartermaster, 18 September 1777; 4/60, Lieutenant, - February 1780; Also Henry as given name
Wright, James; 9, Lieutenant, 1 September 1771; KIA Bennington, 16 August 1777
Wright, John; 45, Captain, 17 September 1773; Retired 9 August 1778
Wright, John; 14, Chaplain, 14 June 1777
Wright, Thomas; Hosp., Mate, Prior to 1783; Stationed at New York, 1783
Wright, William; 63, Ensign, 2 August 1780
Wrixon, Henry; 63, Ensign, 5 March 1775; 63, Lieutenant, 12 June 1777; KIA Ft. Clinton, 6 October 1777
Wrottesley, John; 1FG, Capt. & Lt. Col., 10 November 1770; 1744-1787; First commission at age, 17; MP Staffordshire, 1768-1787; From 85th Foot
Wulff, William; 4/60, Captain, 30 September 1775; Also Wolfe or Wulfe; KIA 24 August 1779, in an attack on a privateer. Also listed as KIA in South Carolina, Summer 1779
Wybranis, William; 62, Ensign, 1 May 1775; 62, Lieutenant, 25 March 1777; 62, Captain, 21 August 1781
Wynyard, George; 33, Ensign, 1 September 1777; 33, Lieutenant, 14 October 1778; From volunteer; WIA Camden, 16 August 1780 & Guilford CH, 15 March 1781
Wynyard, William; 20, Colonel, 25 March 1780; Major General; 19 February 1779
Wynyard, William; 74, Captain-Lieutenant, 3 March 1782; At Antigua in 31 July 1782

Wynyard, William; 64, Ensign, 23 November 1775; 64, Lieutenant, 12 June 1777; WIA Brandywine, 11 September 1777; Possibly WIA Charleston, April 1780 or Torriano; Extra Major of Bde., 1781

Wyvill, Rd. Aug.; 38, Ensign, 8 March 1780; 38, Lieutenant, 25 February 1782

Yonge, Henry; 8, Ensign, 16 September 1767; 8, Lieutenant, 18 November 1774; Also Young; English, born 1747; Son of Rector of Torrington in Devon; Family owned lands in Shropshire and Devon; First commissioned at age 21; Died 2 November 1779

Yorke, John; 33, Captain, 10 June 1768; 33, Major, 8 August 1776; 22, Lt. Colonel, 11 October 1778; 33, Lt. Colonel, 24 April 1781; English, born 1746; First commissioned at age 15; Cmd. 1st Gren. Bn., May 1780

Yorke, John H.; RA, 2nd Lieut., 15 March 1771; POW Bemis Heights, 7 October 1777

Yorke, William; 69, Major, 24 June 1777

Young, George; Hosp., Physician, Prior to 1780

Young, Henry; 62, Ensign, 21 November 1776; Son of William Young; DOW Freeman's Farm, 29 September 1777

Young, John; 1/42, Ensign, 3 August 1778; 1/42, Lieutenant, 15 May 1780; From ensign in the Pennsylvania Loyalists, 14 October 1777

Young, William; Hosp., Mate, Prior to 1783; Stationed at New York, 1783

Young, William; Asst. Depty. Quartermaster General, 1782

BIBLIOGRAPHY

Published Sources

Atkinson, C. T. (1937). "British Forces in North America, 1774-1781: their distribution and strength," *Journal of the Society of Army Historical Research.* 16: 3-23.

Atkinson, C.T. (1940). "British Forces in North America, 1774-1781: Part II," *Journal of the Society of Army Historical Research.* 19: 163-166.

Balderston, Marion & David Syrett. (1975). *The Lost War: Letters from British Officers during the American Revolution.* New York: Horizon Press.

Barker, John. (1924). *The British in Boston: The Diary of Lieut. John Barker.* Reprinted: New York: New York Times and Arno Press, 1969.

Boatner, Mark. (1966). *Encyclopedia of the American Revolution.* New York: David MacKay Inc.

Cannon, Richard. (1848). *Historical Record of the Eighteenth or the Royal Irish Regiment of Foot.* London: Parker, Furnivall, & Parker.

Carman. W. Y. (1957). *British Military Uniforms from Contemporary Pictures.* New York: Arco.

Cayton, Mary Kupiec, Elliot J. Gorn & Peter W. Williams. (1993). *Encyclopedia of Social History.* New York: Scribner.

Chichester, Henry & George Burges-Short. (1900). *The Records and Badges of Every Regiment and Corps in the British Army.* 2nd ed. London: Gale & Polden. London. Fredrick Muller, Ltd. Reprint 1970.

Clinton, Henry. (1954). *The American Rebellion; Sir Henry Clinton's Narrative of His Campaigns, 1775-1782, with an Appendix of Original Documents.* William Wilcox, ed. New Haven: Yale University Press.

Colley, Linda. (1992). *Britons: Forging the Nation 1707-1837.* New Haven, CN: Yale University Press.

Commager, Henry & Richard B. Morris. (1983). *The Spirit of 'Seventy-Six*. New York: Bonanza Books.

Curtis, Edward. (1926). *The Organization of the British Army in the American Revolution*. New Haven, CN: Yale University Press.

Dictionary of National Biography. (1917). Leslie Stephen and Sidney Lee, ed. Oxford University Press.

Downman, F. (1898). Diary of Captain Francis Downman, R.A., 22 August 1777 - 12 January 1779, *Proceedings of the Royal Artillery Institute*.

Elting, John. (1974). *Military Uniforms in America: The Era of the American Revolution*. San Rafael, CA: Presidio Press.

Evelyn, W.G. (1971). *Memoir and Letters of William Glanville Evelyn*. Scull, G.D., ed. Oxford, England: James Parker and Co., 1879; reprint ed. The New York Times and Arno Press, 1971.

Ford, Worthington Chauncey. (1897). *British Officers Serving in the American Revolution*. Brooklyn, NY: Historical Printing Company.

Houlding, J. A. (1981). *Fit for Service: The Training of the British Army, 1715-1795*. Oxford: Clarendon Press.

Howe, William. (1890). *Howe's Orderly Book at Charleston, Boston, and Halifax, June 17, 1775 to May 26, 1776 to which is added the Official Abridgement of General Howe's Correspondence*. Benjamin Stevenson, ed. Port Washington, NY: Reprinted by Kennikat Press, 1970.

Inman, George. (1903). Losses of the Military and Naval forces engaged in the War of the American Revolution. *Pennsylvania Magazine of History and Biography*. 27: 176-205.

Johnston, W. (1917). *Roll of Commissioned Officers in the Medical Service of the British Army: Who served on full pay within the period between the access of George II and the formation of the Royal Army Medical Corps*. Aberdeen: University of Aberdeen Press.

Kane, John. (1891). *List of Officers of the Royal Regiment of Artillery from the year 1716 to the Present Date*. Woolwich, n.p.

Kehoe, Vincent. (1993). *A Military Guide*. Somis, CA: Published for the author.

Kelby, W. (1972). *Orderly Book of the Three [1st, 2nd, 3rd] Battalions of Loyalists Commanded by Brigadier-General Oliver De Lancey, 4 February 1777 - 30 June 1778; and List of N.Y. City Loyalists*. Baltimore: Genealogical Publishing Company.

Kemble, S. (1972). *Journals of Lieut-Col. Stephen Kemble, 1773-1778, and British Army Orders: Gen. Sir William Howe, Gen. Sir Henry Clinton, 1778; and Gen. Daniel Jones, 1778*. New York: The New-York Historical Society, 1884; reprint ed. Boston: Gregg Press.

Kitzmiller, J. M. (1988). *In search of the "Forlorn Hope": A comprehensive guide to locating British regiments and their records (1640-WWII)*. Ogden, UT: Meridian Press.

Lamb, Roger. (1809). *An Original and Authentic Journal of Occurrences during the Late American War from its Commencement to the Year 1783*. Dublin: Wilkinson & Courtney. Reprinted Arno Press, 1968.

Leslie, N. B. (1974). *The Succession of Colonels of the British Army from 1660 to the Present Day*. London: Gale and Polden, Ltd.

Mileham, Partick. (1996). *The Scottish Regiments: 1633-1996*. Staplehurst, Kent [UK]: Spellmount Ltd.

Moore, Frank. (1860). *Diary of the American Revolution from Newspapers and Original Documents*. New York: Charles Scribner. Reprint ed., New York: The New York Times and Arno Press, 1969.

Namier, Lewis & John Brooke. (1964). *The House of Commons: 1754-1790*. London: History of Parliament Trust. 3 vol.

Neave-Hill, W.B.R. (1970). The rank titles of brigadier and brigadier-general. *Journal of the Society for Army Historical Research* 48(190): 96-116.

Newsome, A.R., (1932). British [Brigade of Guards] Orderly Book, 27 August 1780 - 20 March 1781. *The North Carolina Historical Review* 9: 57-78, 163-198, 273-298, & 366-379.

Peebles, J. (1998). *John Peebles' American War: the Diary of a Scottish Grenadier, 1776-1782*. Ira Gruber, ed. Mechanicsburg, PA: Stackpole Books.

Robertson, James. (1983). *The Twilight of British Rule in America: The New York Letter Book of General James Robertson, 1780-1783*. Milton Klein & Ronald Howard, ed. Cooperstown, NY: New York State Historical Association.

Robson, E. (1951). *Letters from America: 1773-1780: Being the Letters of a Scots Officer, Sir James Murray, to His Home During the American War of Independence*. Manchester, England: The University of Manchester Press.

Rogers, H.C.B. (1977). *The British Army of the Eighteenth Century*. New York: Hippocrene Books, Inc.

Scott, K. (1973). Rivington's New York Newspaper: Excerpts from a Loyalist Press, 1773-1783. *The New-York Historical Society Collections* 84. New York: The New-York Historical Society; reprint ed. 1973.

Simes, Thomas. (1776). *A Military Guide for Young Officers*. Philadelphia: Humphreys, Bell, and Aitken.

Stevens, B.F. (1890). *General Sir William Howe's Orderly Book, 17 June 1775 - 26 May 1776*. London: B.F. Stevens.

Strach, S. (1985). A Memoir of the Exploits of Captain Alexander Fraser and His Company of Marksmen, 1776-1777. *Journal of the Society of Army Historical Research*, 63: 91-98, 164-179.

Strachan, Hew. (1975). *British Military Uniforms 1768 – 96: The Dress of the British Army from Official Sources*. London: Arms and Armour Press.

Sumner, Percy, (1925). Army inspection returns 1753-1804. *Journal of the Society of Army Historical Research*. 4: 23-37; 91-116; & 168-176.

Valentine, Alan. (1970). *The British Establishment, 1760-1784: An Eighteenth-Century Biographical Dictionary*. Norman, OK: University of Oklahoma Press.

Webber, M. L. (1916). Death Notices from The South Carolina and American General Gazette, and its continuation The Royal Gazette (May 1766-June 1783). *South Carolina Historical & Genealogical Magazine* 17 (1916): 46-50, 87-93, 121-128, 147-166; 18 (1917): 37-41.

Manuscript Sources

1st Grenadier Battalion Orderly Book, 6 February - 17 March 1776. Peter Force MS, Library of Congress.

17th Foot Orderly Book, October 11 to 28 December 1776. Microfilm. Wisconsin State Historical Society. Madison.

28th Regiment Orderly Book, 23 February - 20 May 1778. Rutgers University Library MS.

43rd Regiment Orderly Book, 26 September 1776 - 2 June 1777." Early American Orderly Books, 1747-1817. Reel #4, Document No. 40.

49th Regiment Orderly Book, 25 June-10 September 1777. George Washington Papers Microfilm, Series 6B (Volume 2), Reel 117, P37436.

Clinton Papers, University of Michigan, Ann Arbor.

Colonial Office Series 5: Returns of the Killed, Wounded, Missing & ca. of the Troops in North America. Public Record Office, Kew, England.

Cox and Meir, Co. Account and ledger books of the Cox and Meir Co. Lloyds of London Archives. London.

Gage Papers, University of Michigan, Ann Arbor.

Haldimand Papers, microfilm. Newberry Library, Chicago.

National Archives Records Group 93: Orders, Returns, Morning Reports and Accounts of British Troops, 1776-1781. National Archives, Washington, DC.

War Office Series 12 papers: Regimental Muster or Pay Rolls. Public Record Office, Kew, England.

War Office Series 27 papers. Inspection returns of British and Irish Establishment Regiments, Public Record Office, Kew, England.

War Office Series 65 papers. Army Lists. Public Record Office, Kew, England.

War Office Series 71 papers. General Court Martial Returns, Public Record Office, Kew, England.

George Washington Papers. National Archives, Washington, DC.

CPSIA information can be obtained at www.ICGtesting.com
Printed in the USA
LVOW08s1051061014

407438LV00001B/163/P